TOURISM IN TURBULENT TIMES

TOWARDS SAFE EXPERIENCES FOR VISITORS

ADVANCES IN TOURISM RESEARCH

Series Editor: Professor Stephen J. Page
University of Stirling, U.K.
s.j.page@stir.ac.uk

Advances in Tourism Research series publishes monographs and edited volumes that comprise state-of-the-art research findings, written and edited by leading researchers working in the wider field of tourism studies. The series has been designed to provide a cutting edge focus for researchers interested in tourism, particularly the management issues now facing decision-makers, policy analysts and the public sector. The audience is much wider than just academics and each book seeks to make a significant contribution to the literature in the field of study by not only reviewing the state of knowledge relating to each topic but also questioning some of the prevailing assumptions and research paradigms which currently exist in tourism research. The series also aims to provide a platform for further studies in each area by highlighting key research agendas, which will stimulate further debate and interest in the expanding area of tourism research. The series is always willing to consider new ideas for innovative and scholarly books; inquiries should be made directly to the Series Editor.

Recent published titles in this series include:
Destination Marketing Organisations
Pike

Small Firms in Tourism: International Perspectives
Thomas

Tourism and Transport
Lumsdon & Page

Tourism Public Policy and the Strategic Management of Failure
Kerr

Managing Tourist Health and Safety in the New Millennium
Wilks & Page

Indigenous Tourism
Ryan & Aicken

Taking Tourism to the Limits
Ryan, Page & Aicken

An International Handbook of Tourism Education
Airey & Tribe

Forthcoming titles include:

Benchmarking National Tourism Organisations and Agencies
Lennon, Smith, Cockerel & Trew

Cold Water Tourism
Baldacchino

Tourism Local Systems and Networking
Lazzeretti & Petrillo

New Europe
Thomas & Augustyn

Tourism Micro-Clusters and Networks: The Growth of Tourism
Michael

Related Elsevier Journals — sample copies available on request:
Annals of Tourism Research
International Journal of Hospitality Management
Tourism Management
World Development

TOURISM IN TURBULENT TIMES

TOWARDS SAFE EXPERIENCES FOR VISITORS

EDITED BY

JEFF WILKS

The University of Queensland, Australia

DONNA PENDERGAST

The University of Queensland, Australia

PETER LEGGAT

James Cook University, Australia

ELSEVIER

Amsterdam – Boston – Heidelberg – London – New York – Oxford
Paris – San Diego – San Francisco – Singapore – Sydney – Tokyo

ELSEVIER B.V.
Radarweg 29
P.O. Box 211, 1000 AE
Amsterdam, The Netherlands

ELSEVIER Inc.
525 B Street, Suite 1900
San Diego, CA 92101-4495
USA

ELSEVIER Ltd
The Boulevard, Langford Lane
Kidlington, Oxford OX5 1GB
UK

ELSEVIER Ltd
84 Theobalds Road
London WC1X 8RR
UK

First edition 2006

British Library Cataloguing in Publication Data
A catalogue record is available from the British Library.

ISBN-10: 0-08-044666-3
ISBN-13: 978-0-08-044666-0

All chapters in this book were independently peer reviewed prior to acceptance.

♾ The paper used in this publication meets the requirements of ANSI/NISO Z39.48-1992 (Permanence of Paper).
Printed in The Netherlands.

Working together to grow
libraries in developing countries

www.elsevier.com | www.bookaid.org | www.sabre.org

ELSEVIER   BOOK AID
             International   Sabre Foundation

Contents

Part 2 Safety and Security

Part 3 Adventure

Part 4 Government and Industry Initiatives

Conclusions

List of Figures

List of Tables

Contributors

Peter Aitken
Peter Aitken, MBBS, FACEM, is Senior Consultant in Emergency Medicine at the Townsville Hospital, in north Queensland, Australia. He is also Adjunct Senior Lecturer at the Anton Breinl Centre, James Cook University. He has extensive experience in aeromedical retrieval.

David Beirman
David Beirman, PhD, is Director of the Israel Tourism Office in Sydney, Australia. He is a board member of the Association of National Tourist Office Representatives and represented ANTOR in negotiations with the Australian government that resulted in the "Charter for Safe Travel".

Tim A. Bentley
Tim Bentley, PhD, is a Senior Lecturer in the Department of Management and International Business, Massey University at Albany, Auckland, New Zealand. Tim is an injury prevention and ergonomics specialist, and has a special interest in adventure tourism safety.

Christopher Coxon
Chris Coxon is the Principal Workplace Health and Safety Inspector for diving with Workplace Health and Safety Queensland, Department of Industrial Relations. He is based in Cairns, Queensland and works primarily with the recreational diving and snorkelling industry.

Rob Davis
Rob Davis is Principal of Davis Legal & Strategic on the Gold Coast of Queensland, Australia. An experienced plaintiff lawyer, he also serves as an Adjunct Professor with the Centre for Tourism & Risk Management at The University of Queensland.

Kay Dimmock
Kay Dimmock is a Lecturer in the School of Tourism & Hospitality Management, Southern Cross University, Australia. She teaches and researches in a number of tourism-related areas, including managing tourism organisations, tourism education and dive tourism. Kay is currently studying for her PhD.

David Grant
David Grant is Professor of Law and Director of the Travel Law Centre, Northumbria University, UK. He is also an editor of the International Travel Law Journal. David has a special interest in package holiday law and the rights of travelling consumers. He has written extensively in this area.

Henryk Handszuh
Henryk Handszuh is an economist and heads the Quality and Trade in Tourism programme of the World Tourism Organization (Trade/Enterprise, Safety & Security, Standards). He has the background of tourism industry, government official, researcher and lecturer in Poland, his country of origin.

Travis W. Heggie
Travis Heggie, PhD, is the Tort Claims Officer and the Public Risk Management and Injury Control Specialist for the United States National Park Service in Washington, DC.

Mervyn Jackson
Mervyn Jackson, M.Beh.Sci., is a Senior Lecturer and programme leader in the Division of Psychology at RMIT University, Melbourne, Australia. He has had a long interest, extensive teaching experience and on-going publishing history in Tourism Psychology.

Ian Kemish
Ian Kemish AM was the head of Consular Branch at the Australian Department of Foreign Affairs and Trade (DFAT) at the time of the Bali 2001 terrorist attack. Ian currently runs the South and South East Asian Division of the department.

Malcolm Khan
Malcolm Khan is a Barrister at Law and Principal Lecturer in Law at Northumbria University, UK. His main teaching area is Medical Law and Ethics and his particular interest is the Law on Consent to Medical Treatment.

Peter Leggat
Peter Leggat, MD, PhD, DrPH, is Associate Professor in the Anton Breinl Centre for Public Health and Tropical Medicine, James Cook University, Australia. As a registered specialist in Public Health Medicine, Peter is actively involved in international travel medicine and occupational health programmes.

Stephen Mason
Stephen Mason is a solicitor with Stephen Mason Solicitors in Leeds, UK. He is an acknowledged expert in holiday law issues with extensive experience acting for travel companies, and is co-author — with David Grant — of the text *Holiday Law* (3rd ed, 2003).

Damian Morgan
Damian Morgan is a Lecturer in the Department of Management at Monash University, Australia. His research interest is in tourism and recreation risk management.

Faisal Al-Mubarak
Faisal Al-Mubarak, PhD, is the Assistant Deputy Secretary-General, Strategic Planning & Monitoring, with the Supreme Commission for Tourism in the Kingdom of Saudi Arabia.

Stephen J. Page
Stephen Page, PhD, is Scottish Enterprise Forth Valley Chair in Tourism and Professor of Tourism Management at the University of Stirling, Scotland. Prior to this appointment, he was Professor of Tourism Management at Massey University, New Zealand.

Nick Parfitt
Nick Parfitt, BA (Oxon) operates 2003 Research Works, a marketing research consultancy in Brisbane, Australia specialising in tourism, service industry and educational consultancies.

Donna Pendergast
Donna Pendergast, PhD, is a Senior Lecturer and Programme Director in the School of Education at The University of Queensland, Australia. Donna has extensive experience in the area of public health, especially injury prevention, and also in hospitality education and training.

Jeff Roach
Jeff Roach OAM was Director of the Consular Information and Crisis Management Section at DFAT at the time of the Bali 2001 terrorist attack. Jeff is currently posted with the Australian Embassy in Paris.

Claire Schmierer
Claire Schmierer, MBA, was the Director of Nursing of a multi-purpose service along the Great Ocean Road in South–West Victoria, Australia. She is now Director of Nursing at Hobsons Bay Nursing Centre. Claire has an interest in tourism and health, health promotion and injury prevention.

Alison Specht
Alison Specht, PhD, is an Associate Professor and environmental scientist at Southern Cross University, Australia. Her primary interest is in the long-term sustainable management of our natural environment, with a particular focus on Australia.

Peter E. Tarlow
Peter Tarlow, PhD, is president of Tourism & More and teaches at universities both in the United States and Latin America. He is a world specialist on tourism security and tourism event risk management.

Annelies Wilder-Smith
Annelies Wilder-Smith, MD, PhD, is an Associate Professor at the Department of Community, Occupational and Family Medicine, National University of Singapore and Head of the Travellers' Health & Vaccination Centre at Tan Tock Seng Hospital. Her research interests include travel health, SARS, dengue fever and meningococcal disease.

Jeff Wilks

Jeff Wilks, PhD, is Professor of Tourism and Director of the Centre for Tourism and Risk Management at The University of Queensland, Australia. A qualified psychologist and lawyer, he has a special interest in the health and safety of tourists.

Michael Yates

Michael Yates provides strategic marketing consultancy services to travel & tourism clients around Asia Pacific through his company Taramax Consultants. Michael managed Project Phoenix, the SARS recovery campaign, for the Pacific Asia Travel Association.

Dedication

This book is dedicated to our daughter Kyrra, 2 years old at the time of writing and already showing a love of travel and meeting new people. According to *The Oxford Dictionary of Proverbs* (Speake, 2003) Thursday's Child "has far to go". So travel is written in the stars for you Kyrra. We hope that resilient tourism, even with its turbulent times, will always be an enjoyable part of your life.

Jeff and Donna
Runaway Bay, Australia
January 2005

Speake, J. (Ed). (2003). Monday's child is fair of face. *The Oxford Dictionary of Proverbs*. Oxford: Oxford University Press.

Foreword

Back in the 1920s and 1930s there were smaller numbers of people moving around the world. Most of these travellers were adventurers, or at least intrepid types — curious people who, in many instances travelled to study cultures and geography, expand colonial outposts or establish business ventures in far-off lands. They were knowledge seekers rather than pleasure seekers per se, and restricted by the forms of transport available to them at the time. All of this changed with the technology explosion post World War II, which enabled men and women to travel for more hedonistic reasons.

This huge increase in the movement of people changed the nature of tourism from early 'fully independent' travellers aware of the dangers involved in travel (and to a greater or lesser extent, excited by the prospect of danger) to more larger group 'packaged' travel, sold and guided by intermediaries. Whereas the early travellers understood that safety was their own responsibility, the changing legal culture of the 1990s and 21st century has created a new environment where customers often look for someone to blame if the adventure package they purchased proves to be too dangerous.

With all of these changes going on, the people acting as intermediaries have taken on additional responsibilities. Not only do they now provide the key items of tourism: transport, accommodation and excursions; but they have both general and specific 'duties of care' to their customers as well. At the destination level it is increasingly apparent that customers also expect the holiday or business venues to be safe. Recent events such as terrorism attacks and outbreaks of infectious disease have reinforced the general public concern about safe travel.

This book is a timely contribution to our understanding of safe travel. It examines new and emerging risks for travellers and presents initiatives to ensure that the tourism industry system is equipped to deliver the 'duty of care' requirements that legislation and judicial precedent now impose. It goes further by bringing us back to the fundamentals. Safety is a key element of quality service. In delivering quality service, the modern tourism industry needs to take account of inexperienced travellers doing unexpected things in unfamiliar environments, as well as global threats that are beyond the industry's immediate control. While a range of recent shocks suggests that the tourism industry is experiencing turbulent times, it is pleasing to see that this book focuses on positive responses and stories of success in delivering quality service.

I congratulate the editors and contributors on a book that draws together a wide range of industry, government and academic perspectives on providing safe experiences for travellers. The high level of involvement by tourism industry members and government officials in a book like this is unusual, but also extremely encouraging for the collaborative partnerships needed to deliver quality services in tourism. From the thousands of travellers taking care of themselves in the 1920s and 1930s, we now have millions of travellers who are very much reliant on the tourism industry for safe experiences.

Sir Frank Moore, AO
Chair, Cooperative Research Centre for Sustainable Tourism, Australia

Acknowledgments

The editors would like to thank Ms Joy Reynolds for her administrative assistance in the initial stage of this project. Special thanks to the anonymous reviewers who assessed the submitted chapters. The support of the Cooperative Research Centre for Sustainable Tourism (CRC Tourism *www.crctourism.com.au*) is also gratefully acknowledged, as a partner in the Centre for Tourism & Risk Management at The University of Queensland and as a key funding agency for tourism research. Chapters 9 (Natural Disaster Management) and 20 (Shadows Across the Sun: Response to the Public Liability Crisis in Queensland) were developed from CRC pilot projects.

Preface

Life is not a rehearsal (Kyle Mills, 2002. *Sphere of Influence*)

In our previous book *Managing Tourist Health and Safety in the New Millennium* (Wilks & Page, 2003) we suggested that the terrorist attacks in the United States of America on 11 September 2001 had changed forever our views of traveller safety and security. Since then there have been other shocks to the global tourism industry, including the Bali Bombings (2002), Iraq war (2003), SARS (2003) and most recently the Asian Tsunami (2004).

While these events and the overall current climate for tourism operations can be viewed as one of turbulent times, this text is not about doom and gloom. Rather, it acknowledges the difficulties and challenges faced by the tourism industry, and it describes the positive steps taken by individuals, groups, governments and destinations to manage health, safety and security for visitors.

This positive and proactive stance taken by many tourism operators is in keeping with the relatively recent adoption of risk management policies and practices by businesses around the world. Risk management is all about understanding your business and the environment in which it operates. Safety and security, while traditionally elements of quality service that were either overlooked or at least given minimal attention, have become a key focus for the travelling public. Those destinations that are perceived to be dangerous, unhealthy or generally unsafe are now actively avoided by informed consumers, especially families. Current government travel advisories provide further weight to these decisions, with failure to heed warnings likely to result in a travel insurance policy being rendered void.

Partnerships between the tourism industry and other agencies that specialise in health, safety and security are clearly essential for protecting visitors. Sectors of the tourism industry still struggle with the idea of handing over the lead role to another agency or group where their customers are involved. To some extent this is because tourism is the business of selling dreams and it may be difficult to accept that things sometimes go wrong, even if the cause is an external event beyond one's control. Throughout this book we present some excellent examples of the positive partnerships available to the tourism industry in turbulent times.

Jeff Wilks
Managing Editor

References

Mills, K. (2002). *Sphere of influence.* New York: Signet.

Wilks, J., & Page, S.J. (Eds). (2003). *Managing tourist health and safety in the new millennium.* Oxford: Pergamon.

INTRODUCTION

Chapter 1

Current Issues in Tourist Health, Safety and Security

Jeff Wilks

Introduction

In his Foreword to the recent Asia Pacific Economic Cooperation (APEC) report 'Tourism Risk Management for the Asia Pacific Region' Sir Frank Moore (2004, p. iii) noted that:

> In times of crisis, for any tourist destination the first concern must be for visitors. Away from home, in unfamiliar surroundings, they are quickly disorientated and very reliant on their hosts and the host communities in general. Adequate planning for what has in the past been seen as the 'unexpected' can be the difference between a well-managed problem and a human and economic disaster.

The catalyst for the APEC report was the October 2002 terrorist bombings in Bali. However, these observations have sadly been proven equally correct by the December 2004 Asian Tsunami disaster, where thousands of foreign nationals were totally reliant on local people at various tourist destinations for their survival. While it might be argued that the Asian Tsunami was different from other shocks experienced by the tourism industry in recent years (for example, terrorist acts, Severe Acute Respiratory Syndrome) in that the devastation was so widespread that it encompassed tourists and locals equally, the fact remains that tourists are a particularly vulnerable group who are reliant on others in times of need. This book is about ensuring that visitors to the world's tourist destinations have safe and enjoyable experiences, taking into account the various direct and indirect threats that may impact on the tourism industry. Safety in this context is all about preventing injury or harm to individuals and/or groups (Wilks, 2003a). While the term 'safety' technically covers the main threats to tourists, it is common in the tourism and travel literature to distinguish between health, safety and security. This distinction mainly reflects the background and orientation of the different disciplines contributing to this area. The convention is loosely adopted here, with Part 1 of the book devoted to Health, while Part 2 presents Safety and Security chapters. However, there is also recognition that effective responses to the challenges facing tourism will only be possible through cross-disciplinary collaboration and partnerships between the industry and governments.

Delivering Quality Service

Before turning to specific issues, it is important to establish the position and importance of visitor health, safety and security within the realm of tourism. In their seminal work, Zeithaml, Parasuraman and Berry (1990) identified 10 dimensions of Service Quality (see Table 1.1).

Security, defined as freedom from danger, risk or doubt, was included in the original list, though until recently it has been a largely neglected area of service consideration in tourism (Wilks & Oldenburg, 1995). In fairness, tourism is about selling dreams and any public focus on visitor illness, injury or mishap is not conducive to selling holidays (Wilks, 2004a). However, particularly after the terrorist attacks in the United States on 11 September 2001 people wanted to be assured of their safety (Taylor, 2001). Destinations can now rise or fall on these perceptions (Beirman, 2003), so the second issue for tourist health, safety and security is that it must be seen as a critical and legitimate element of quality service, both by the tourism industry and by governments (the first issue was recognizing the vulnerability of visitors). Interestingly, within the World Tourism Organization (WTO) (www.world-tourism.org) the tourism safety and security programme has always been part of the quality department (see Chapter 16).

Table 1.1: Ten dimensions of service quality.

Tangibles	Appearance of physical facilities, equipment, personnel, and communication materials
Reliability	Ability to perform the promised service dependably and accurately
Responsiveness	Willingness to help customers and provide prompt service
Competence	Possession of the required skills and knowledge to perform the service
Courtesy	Politeness, respect, consideration, and friendliness of contact personnel
Credibility	Trustworthiness, believability, honesty of the service provider
Security	Freedom from danger, risk, or doubt
Access	Approachability and ease of contact
Communication	Keeping customers informed in language they can understand and listening to them
Understanding the customer	Making the effort to know customers and their needs

Source: From Zeithaml et al. (1990, pp. 21–22). Adapted with the permission of The Free Press, a Division of Simon & Schuster Adult Publishing Group, from DELIVERING QUALITY SERVICE: Balancing Customer Perceptions and Expectations by Valarie A. Zeithml, A. Parasuraman, Leonard L. Berry. Copyright © 1990 by The Free Press. All rights reserved.

One of the difficulties in establishing health, safety and security within tourism is that the roles of the required personnel are very different to that of mainstream tourism staff. A seat on a plane not sold on the day, or a hotel room vacant overnight is a lost opportunity for income that cannot be recovered. The tourism industry therefore tends to be focused on active selling and servicing of its products. The role of protecting these valuable, but somewhat intangible assets, involves planning, staff training and practice exercises, audits, monitoring and evaluation — all tasks that do not necessarily generate income or produce obvious benefits. This is why the Communications or Marketing Manager in many tourism organizations is the default crisis management person — it is an 'add-on' consideration, with assumptions that day-to-day operations will take care of safety and that external agencies like the police will always be available in a crisis. As theory and practice clearly show, quality crisis management does not automatically attach to a job description (Marriott, 2004), so tourism must accept the need for employed personnel whose primary responsibility is to protect the product. The days of relying solely on insurance for protection are largely over (Liability Insurance Taskforce, 2002). By analogy, construction sites employ security staff to ensure their building materials are not stolen or the premises vandalized. As a very current issue, tourism needs to adopt the same approach to protecting its assets and reputation.

Identifying Current Issues

There are a number of ways to identify other current issues in tourist health, safety and security. Perhaps the most useful barometer is what the tourism industry considers its most pressing matters. For example, the International Hotel and Restaurant Association (IH&RA) conducts regular 'think tank' discussions on key topics for its members. The 1998 Think Tank on Safety and Security in Orlando, Florida, for example, identified crime, terrorism and food safety as the three primary concerns by participants (IH&RA, 1998). Delegates also expressed major concerns about the lack of information and information structures to assist the industry in addressing challenges in these areas.

Around the same time, the Federation of Tour Operators (FTO) in the United Kingdom released their Health and Safety Handbook (FTO, 1999) emphasizing for members the topics of fire, swimming pool and gas safety. Also highlighted were children's clubs and illness (specifically legionellosis, meningitis, gastroenteritis and food poisoning). So, from an industry perspective there are clearly some readily identified and enduring health and safety issues that must be regularly addressed. The chapter topics for this book were intentionally chosen to respond to issues commonly identified by the tourism and hospitality industry.

A second important source of information on current issues comes from governments around the world and is most readily identifiable through their travel advisories. The role of travel advisories is covered by David Beirman in Chapter 21; however, for the purposes of identifying global health, safety and security issues facing tourism the Consular Information Sheets provided by the US Department of State (http://travel.state.gov/travel_warnings.html) are a very relevant and useful resource. Consular Information Sheets are issued for every country in the world, with information on such matters as the health conditions, crime, unusual currency or entry requirements, any areas of instability, and the location of the nearest US embassy or consulate in the subject country. General information on safety issues for travelling overseas is also provided by the Department under the headings presented in Table 1.2. A separate section of information is provided for health issues, including a list of Air Ambulance or Medi-Vac providers (see also Chapter 3).

The State Department also uses a two-tiered advisory system of Travel Warnings and Public Announcements. A Travel Warning is issued when the Department recommends that Americans avoid a certain country. As at 20 January 2005, there were Travel Warnings issued for 26 destinations; most of these were related to security issues.

The next level down are Public Announcements, which are a means to disseminate information about terrorist threats and other relatively short-term and/or trans-national conditions posing significant risks to the security of American travellers. These are made any time when there is a perceived threat and usually have Americans as a particular target group. In the past, Public Announcements have been issued to deal with short-term coups, bomb threats to airlines, violence by terrorists and anniversary dates of specific terrorist events. As at 20 January 2005, there were Public Announcements issued for 14 destinations. There was also a current World Wide Caution on terrorist activity. Among the 14 destinations, Thailand and Sri Lanka were listed because of the tsunami; others were listed for security reasons.

In terms of current issues in tourism health, safety and security, it is important to recognize both regional similarities and differences, especially in the use of travel advisories (Chapter 21). For example, a recent review of risk management for 21 tourist destinations in Oceania

Table 1.2: Topics presented under safety issues by the U.S. Department of State (http://travel.state.gov/travel/tips/safety/safety_1180.html).

The information below contains helpful precautions to minimize the chance of becoming a victim of terrorism and also provides other safety tips for Americans travelling overseas.

    A safe trip abroad
    Road safety overseas
    Death abroad
    Emergency information
    More help abroad
    Overseas security advisory council
    Diplomatic security releases
    Help for American victims of crime overseas
    Rail transport abroad

A safe trip abroad contains specific advice on:

    Safety on the street
    Safety in your hotel
    Public transport
    Handling money
    Photography
    Purchasing antiques
    Terrorism
    Travel to high-risk areas, and
    Hijacking/hostage situations

using Travel Information and Advisory Reports from the Canadian Department of Foreign Affairs and International Trade (http://voyage.dfait-maeci.gc.ca/destinations/menu_e.htm) revealed that many of the Pacific Island nations have a similar profile (Wilks, 2005). That is, no serious safety or security concerns, some petty crime, typhoons and seismic activity, and a range of possible infectious diseases (most notably dengue fever, hepatitis A and typhoid fever). Malaria was specifically noted for the Solomon Islands and Vanuatu, while Japanese B encephalitis was mentioned for the Northern Marianas. In late 2000, Micronesia had experienced an outbreak of cholera. The range of infectious diseases prevalent in this region highlighted the need for all travellers to carry appropriate travel health insurance, especially cover for emergency medical evacuation. In many smaller and remote destinations, it was noted that adequate medical care would not be available should a tourist require emergency treatment. The importance of travel insurance, especially for medical evacuations is expanded upon in Chapter 3.

So, in terms of current issues, the tourism industry (with a customer focus) and national governments (in the interests of their citizens) share some common concerns about terrorism, crime, food safety, infectious disease and personal injury. However, as we shall see, based on their resources, responsibilities and priorities, the groups respond to tourist health, safety and security issues in very different ways. Another point worth emphasizing is that current issues change, especially at tourist destinations, which is why travel advisories must be kept up-to-date.

The third source of information on current issues comes from international associations and groups like the United Nations. Some are expert in tourism matters (e.g. the WTO); others have expertise in specific areas of activity rather than an industry. A good example of the latter is the International Strategy for Disaster Reduction (ISDR) that provides global leadership on mitigating all types of natural and human-made disasters (http://www.unisdr.org/) (see Chapter 9). International groups are very important for providing a 'big picture' view of current issues, and as discussed below, frameworks for accommodating the many and varied issues that are not necessarily prioritized by industry groups or all national governments. A good example is child sex tourism, where countries that are party to the UN Convention on the Rights of the Child (1989) (http://www.unicef.org/crc/crc.htm) have undertaken to protect children from all forms of sexual exploitation and sexual abuse, including the exploitative use of children in prostitution or other unlawful sexual practices (Article 34).

Algeria, Australia, Austria, Belgium, Canada, China, Cyprus, Denmark, Ethiopia, Finland, France, Germany, Ireland, Iceland, Italy, Japan, Laos, Luxembourg, Mexico, Morocco, New Zealand, the Netherlands, Norway, Portugal, Slovenia, Spain, Sweden, Switzerland, Taiwan, Thailand, the United Kingdom and the USA have already changed their laws to prosecute at home their citizens who abuse children abroad.

Sources of Health, Safety and Security Risk in Tourism

According to the WTO (WTO, 1997; Wilks, 2002), risks to the safety and security of tourists, host communities and tourism employees originate from the following four sources:

- The human and institutional environment outside the tourism sector
- The tourism sector and related commercial sectors

- Individual travellers (personal risks)
- Physical or environmental risks (natural, climatic and epidemic).

While the focus of this book is on visitor safety — which includes protection of life, health, and the physical, psychological and economic integrity of travellers — the WTO framework for sources of risk is very valuable for making sense of the many current issues canvassed above. Indeed, the framework has been used successfully in several international projects (for example, Wilks & Moore, 2004), so it is presented here again in detail. Adoption of a robust framework is also a step towards addressing one of the continuing concerns in this area — that there are few mechanisms in place to gather and disseminate timely information to protect tourism interests (IH&RA, 1998; Wilks & Moore, 2004).

The Human and Institutional Environment

The risks from the human and institutional environment exist when visitors fall victim to:

- common delinquency (e.g. theft, pick-pocketing, assault, burglary, fraud, deception);
- indiscriminate and targeted violence (e.g. rape) and harassment;
- organized crime (e.g. extortion, slave trade, coercion);
- terrorism and unlawful interference (e.g. attacks against state institutions and the vital interests of the state), hijacking and hostage taking;
- wars, social conflicts and political and religious unrest; and
- a lack of public and institutional protection services.

Risks that occur in the broader community impact similarly on tourists and residents. Tourists are not always targeted, but they are often caught up in events by being in the wrong place at the wrong time (see Chapter 7). Protection of tourists at this level is the responsibility of national governments and contributes to whether a destination is perceived to be safe. As demonstrated with travel advisories, this is an area where national governments are very active in trying to assist their travelling citizens, while at the same time, visitors are particularly reliant on the security services of the host nation.

Tourism and Related Sectors

Through defective operation, tourism and sectors related to tourism such as transport, sports and retail trade can endanger visitors' personal security, physical integrity and economic interests through:

- poor safety standards in tourism establishments (e.g. fire, construction errors, lack of anti-seismic protection);
- poor sanitation and disrespect for the environment's sustainability;
- the absence of protection against unlawful interference, crime and delinquency at tourism facilities;
- fraud in commercial transactions;
- non-compliance with contracts; and
- strikes by staff.

The protection of tourists from problems occurring in areas directly related to tourism is a joint responsibility of individual operators, tourism authorities at each destination, tourism industry associations and relevant sectors of local government. Problems in this area are not necessarily the 'fault' of the tourism industry, but can have a dramatic and negative effect on a destination's image. As emphasized by FTO (1999, 2003), with appropriate standards in place, tourism can take ownership and responsibility for health, safety and security in relation to its operations. Again, reviews show that the same core issues continue to present challenges for key industry sectors like hotels (Surawski & Wilks, 2002). Legal obligations, especially 'duty of care' responsibilities, are now clearly articulated for many areas of travel and tourism (Atherton & Atherton, 2003); further reinforcing the need to provide safe experiences for visitors in areas that are directly related to tourism.

Individual Travellers

Travellers or visitors can endanger their own safety and security, and those of their hosts by:

- practicing dangerous sports and leisure activities, dangerous driving and consuming unsafe food and drink;
- travelling when in poor health, which may deteriorate during the trip;
- causing conflict and friction with local residents, through inappropriate behaviour towards local communities or by breaking local laws;
- carrying out illicit or criminal activities (e.g. trafficking in illicit drugs);
- visiting dangerous areas; and
- losing personal effects, documents and money through carelessness.

Most travel health and safety incidents occur at the level of individual travellers. Many problems are the result of visitors being in an unfamiliar environment and/or participating in unfamiliar activities. For example, motor vehicle crashes remain the leading cause of injury-related death for tourists worldwide (Wilks, 1999; Page, Bentley, Meyer, & Chalmer, 2001), followed by drowning (Wilks, 2002). In support of the unfamiliar environment thesis, detailed analyses of motor vehicle crashes involving tourists in Australia show that:

- international visitor crashes were *less likely* to involve high-risk driving behaviours such as alcohol use or speeding; and
- international visitor crashes were *more likely* to involve disorientation, particularly driver fatigue, failure to keep to the left (correct) side of the road, head-on crashes and overturning their vehicle (Wilks, 2004b).

Unfamiliar adventure activities, such as scuba diving, also account for a significant number of tourist hospital admissions each year (Wilks & Coory, 2000, 2002), while travelling with pre-existing illness continues to be the main cause of overseas visitor fatalities (Wilks, Pendergast, & Wood, 2002). Some very innovative and useful visitor safety programmes are discussed in the Adventure section of this book; however, as Tarlow points out in Chapter 7, tourists behave differently when away from home, often doing things in a state of disorientation or '*anomie*'. So the tourism response must go beyond the minimum duty of care responsibilities in many cases, to understand and prevent reasonably foreseeable incidents from occurring in the first place. This is not to suggest that tourists do not have to take personal responsibility for their actions, but rather that the relevant authorities need to assist them in making informed choices. For example, some countries have severe penalties for drug trafficking. This should be drawn to the attention of visitors so that there can be no misunderstanding of the consequences if local laws are disregarded. Many tourists are unaware that the drug laws of the host country are applicable, not those of the tourist's citizenship.

Malaysia, for example, strictly enforces its drug laws. Malaysian legislation provides for a mandatory death penalty for convicted drug traffickers. Individuals arrested in possession of 15 g (1/2 ounce) of heroin or 200 g (7 ounces) of marijuana are presumed by law to be trafficking in drugs (http://travel.state.gov/malaysia.html).

Physical and Environmental Risks

Finally, physical and environmental damage can occur if travellers:

- are unaware of the natural characteristics of the destination, in particular its flora and fauna;
- are not medically prepared for the trip (vaccinations, prophylaxis);
- do not take the necessary precautions when consuming food or drink or for their hygiene; and
- are exposed to dangerous situations arising from the physical environment (e.g. natural disasters and epidemics).

Physical and environmental risks are also largely personal risks, but are not caused deliberately. Rather, these result from the traveller's ignorance or their disregard for potential risks. In our earlier book on tourist health and safety (Wilks & Page, 2003), we mentioned that physical and environmental risks do not feature prominently in the tourist health and safety literature, but that a single environmental disaster has the potential to claim a large number of lives. As at 22 January 2005, the confirmed death toll around Asia from the tsunami stood at more than 219,000 and was still expected to rise (Anonymous, 2005). Nationals from more than 50 countries were killed.

In Chapter 9, Alison Specht provides coverage of natural disaster management in relation to tourism, which draws on both tourism and mainstream emergency and disaster management literature. As a current issue for tourism it is worth distinguishing between a risk, a crisis and a disaster (Wilks & Moore, 2004). To some extent the relationship between the three is one of escalation (Figure 1.1), but there are also basic differences in the literatures for each, and the people who specialize in the associated fields.

According to the Australian and New Zealand Standard (Standards Australia and Standards New Zealand, 1999, p. 3), a *Risk* is:

> The chance of something happening that will have an impact upon objectives. It is measured in terms of consequences and likelihood.

Risk --------------▶ --------Crisis----------▶ ------------Disaster

Figure 1.1: An escalation of events.

Risk Management is defined as:

> An iterative process consisting of well-defined steps which, taken in sequence, support better decision-making by contributing a greater insight into risks and their impacts. The risk management process can be applied to any situation where an undesired or unexpected outcome could be significant or where opportunities are identified (p. iii).

These terms are important because they draw our attention to proactive opportunities to take control of a situation through early identification and prevention of risk, as well as strategies to manage risks that emerge from time to time. There is always a chance of some undesirable event occurring, so effective risk management aims to prevent an event escalating 'out of control' and becoming a crisis. According to the Pacific Asia Travel Association (PATA, 2003, p. 2), a *Crisis* can be defined as:

> Any situation that has the potential to affect long-term confidence in an organization or a product, or which may interfere with its ability to continue operating normally.

When a Crisis, in turn, escalates we then have a *Disaster*, defined by Zamecka and Buchanan (2000, p. 8) as:

> A catastrophic event that severely disrupts the fabric of a community and requires the intervention of the various levels of government to return the community to normality.

The view presented in the APEC report was that a systematic approach to risk management by both the tourism industry and governments will in many cases prevent a crisis or disaster from occurring (Wilks & Moore, 2004). However, not all adverse events can be avoided, so risk management must be used to respond quickly and effectively to negative situations. Government leadership is critical for the success of this process, since in the final analysis it is the government at each tourist destination that has the resources and the responsibility to provide a safe experience for visitors.

The benefit of the WTO framework for identifying sources of risk is that it shows where tourism is exposed to threats. For the tourism-related areas and with individual travellers the industry can take an active and leading role in risk management. Where events external to tourism are the source of threats the industry must establish partnerships with other specialist agencies.

A Risk Management Approach

The recommendation that tourism adopts a risk management approach to protecting its assets, including customers, reflects the widespread use and acceptance of risk management processes by national (Emergency Management Australia, 2000) and international crisis and disaster response agencies (International Strategy for Disaster Reduction, 2002). Indeed, many of the traditional crisis and emergency classification frameworks are now being challenged and replaced by the risk management approach advocated here (see Crondstedt, 2002).

The Australian and New Zealand Standard for Risk Management (Standards Australia and Standards New Zealand, 1999) provides a step-by-step framework for taking control of risks and their impacts. The basic framework is presented in Figure 1.2, and is well suited to managing the risks associated with the tourism industry.

The important thing to note about effective risk management is that the five central steps need to be implemented in sequence and then continually evaluated through monitoring/review and communication/consultation. Having a documented plan that sits on the shelf is often more dangerous than not having a plan at all. For the purpose of this chapter, only the first two steps in the risk management process will be discussed. It is in starting the process that most current issues and challenges for tourism are to be found. A full description of the process, with tourism examples provided is available in Wilks and Moore (2004).

Risk Management Step 1 — Establish the Context

The first step in the risk management process is focused on the environment in which any tourism organization or destination operates. This is the point where basic parameters or boundaries are set within which risks must be managed. This step requires an understanding of crucial elements that will support or impair the risk management process. Among the crucial elements are internal and external stakeholders. In the case of tourism, without the support of senior government officials there is little point in continuing the process. This was the point made about government leadership previously. In addition to the national government, the following stakeholder groups should be involved in the risk management process at this early stage:

- Politicians (at all levels of government) who may have an electoral or portfolio interest
- Union groups

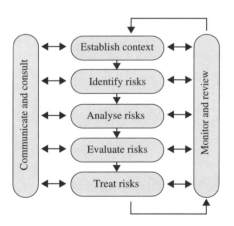

Figure 1.2: Risk management overview.
Source: Standards Australia and Standards New Zealand (1999). With permission.

- Financial institutions
- Insurance organizations
- Tourism businesses and related commercial interests at each destination
- Regulators and other government organizations that have authority over activities (e.g., police, emergency services)
- Non-government organizations such as environmental and public interest groups
- The media, who are potential stakeholders as well as conduits of information to other stakeholders.

A critical decision at this first stage is which group or agency should be given the lead role in risk management/crisis or disaster response. This is where an understanding of the risk, crisis and disaster definitions is important. Traditionally, risk planning and low-level problems are retained by tourism authorities (e.g. educational campaigns for tourists about sun protection). A crisis response is traditionally coordinated by police (e.g. a hotel fire), whereas a disaster (e.g. a major flood) is managed by emergency services, often with assistance from the military. In establishing the risk management context for any tourism destination, the roles and responsibilities of various stakeholders must be made clear at the outset. This should be documented as part of national policy, and linked to any wider government disaster management plan. Legislative authority and resources must be in place.

The view expressed in the APEC report (Wilks & Moore, 2004) was that, where possible and appropriate, the police should be given the lead coordinating role in all levels of risk response, since they have legal authority to act on behalf of the government in a range of situations. Tourism has a major responsibility to ensure that policy, plans and partnerships are in place across the tourism sector to support the active role of the police in the event of a crisis situation. One way of achieving these aims is through the formation of a National Tourism Safety and Security Committee (Wilks, 2003b).

There are two main issues for tourist health, safety and security at this first step. One is that tourism traditionally does not engage fully with health, law enforcement or emergency service agencies in prevention and planning activities, instead relying on these agencies only when problems arise. The general lack of coordination between tourism and health authorities in many destinations affected by SARS is testimony to this lack of existing collaborative relationships. The second issue is the need to convince governments at the highest level of the importance of protecting tourism. In the APEC report this formed the lead chapter titled 'Protecting Tourism', which documented the economic benefits of tourism to the 21 APEC member states through income, jobs and foreign investment and trade opportunities (Wilks & Moore, 2004). Only by having genuine commitments at the highest levels of government can the tourism industry cater for the safety of visitors in turbulent times.

Risk Management Step 2 — Risk Identification

The second step in the risk management process is identifying the risks to be managed. According to the Australian/New Zealand Standard, comprehensive identification using a well-structured systematic process is critical, because a potential risk not identified at this stage is excluded from further analysis. Identification should include all risks, whether or not they are under the control of the tourist destination or national government. Examination of the potential 'indirect' shocks to the tourism industry identified in the

Table 1.3: Examples of potential tourism shocks

Direct
Tourism-related industrial dispute/business collapse (e.g. Ansett Airlines)
Natural disasters in tourism areas (e.g. cyclones, flooding, bushfires)
Tourist deaths/injuries (e.g. murders, Irukandji, drownings, Childers Hostel fire)

Indirect
Terrorist/military activities (e.g. 11 September, Gulf War)
Public Liability Insurance (PLI)
Economic downturn (e.g. Asian financial crisis)
Currency fluctuations
Exotic animal diseases (e.g. Foot & Mouth Disease)

Source: Tourism Queensland (2003). With permission.

Queensland Tourism Crisis Management Plan (Table 1.3) shows that risks such as currency fluctuations and economic downturns are largely beyond the ability of any one government to control. However, a fairly comprehensive general list of possible risks can be developed based on the WTO framework and the various tourism industry and government sources discussed earlier.

It is also worth adding general business industry publications to the list of risk sources because for a destination they can be very influential, even if they are not specifically directed at tourism. A good example is the annual RiskMap published by Control Risks Group in London (www.crg.com). RiskMap is described as a guide to conducting business in an uncertain world. Countries are rated according to two types of risk — Political and Security — on a five level scale (insignificant, low, medium, high and extreme) with accompanying commentary. For potential investors and global companies involved in tourism-related activities these risk assessments can have far-reaching consequences. By way of illustration, the 2003 ratings for APEC economies are presented in Table 1.4.

Genuine Partnerships

One of the most common mistakes in risk management generally is starting with Step 2 (identifying risk) and then moving on towards finding and applying solutions (Step 5 — treating risks) without ever having secured the authority, cooperation or resources to complete the task properly (Step 1 — establish the context). This is why there are so many sources of valuable information about the risks or threats to the tourism industry, but very few best practice models of how governments and industry are working together in a systematic and effective way. While the WTO (1991) recommended that 'every country develop a national policy on tourism safety commensurate with the prevention of tourist risks', most countries still have no operational policies for the health, safety and security of their visitors. This again comes back to not having high-level political support in the

Table 1.4: RiskMap 2003 ratings for APEC Economies.

	Political risk	**Security risk**
Australia	Insignificant	Low
Brunei Darussalam	Low	Low
Canada	Low	Low
Chile	Low	Low
China	Medium	Low
Hong Kong	Low	Low
Indonesia	Medium	Medium (high in Aceh, Maluku, West Papua)
Japan	Insignificant	Insignificant
Korea (South)	Low	Low
Malaysia	Low	Low
Mexico	Medium	Medium
New Zealand	Insignificant	Insignificant
Papua New Guinea	Medium	Medium (high in Port Moresby, Lae, Mount Hagen)
Peru	Medium	Medium (high in Upper Huallaga Valley, Huánuco, San Martin departments, Ayacucho department)
Philippines	Medium	Medium (high in south-western Mindanao)
Russia	Medium	Medium (high in North, extreme in Chechnya, Caucasus)
Singapore	Insignificant	Low
Chinese Taipei	Low	Low
Thailand	Medium	Low
USA	Low	Low (medium in deprived urban areas)
Vietnam	Medium	Low

Source: From Control Risks Group (2003). With permission.

first place. Of all the current issues challenging the global tourism industry, this must rank as one of the highest priorities.

It is now well accepted that a whole-of-government approach is needed in this area. Tourism must engage the other areas of government that have specialized expertise in health, safety and especially security to form genuine partnerships. The emphasis here is on genuine, since there are many examples of lip service paid to tourism by other arms of government. Demonstrating the huge economic contribution tourism makes in many countries is a sound approach to gaining political support for protecting the tourism industry and its clients (Wilks & Moore, 2004).

The Structure of this Book

Tourism in Turbulent Times presents an international review of the challenges faced by the world's largest industry and governments around the world to provide safe and enjoyable experiences for visitors. The book draws on the background and expertise of contributors from 11 countries, representing scholars, government officers and industry practitioners. It addresses traditional concerns for tourism (such as crime) as well as emerging challenges posed by the global movement of infectious disease and terrorism. Recognizing that tourists are most likely to experience difficulties due to being in unfamiliar environments and participating in unfamiliar activities, an examination is made of popular adventure tourism pursuits. The chapter topics are examined by specialists who share a view that tourism can weather turbulent times through adopting appropriate risk management strategies and continuing to provide quality service for customers.

Chapter 1 has provided an overview of the current issues in tourist health, safety and security, emphasizing that tourists are a vulnerable group that must be assisted through genuine partnerships between the tourism industry and governments. Protection of visitors is an essential part of quality service and in many cases is legally required by statute or a common law duty of care. The tourism industry must accept that employment of appropriately skilled staff is required; risk and crisis management are not 'add-on' duties for personnel with other responsibilities. Key sources of information were then identified for the current issues in tourist health, safety and security — noting that risk identification was actually the second step in a formal risk management approach to visitor protection. The first step was Establishing the Context and in particular gaining the authority, cooperation and resources to complete the task properly.

The development of genuine partnerships across industry and government is a theme that runs throughout this book. The benefit of using the WTO framework for identifying sources of risk is that it shows where tourism is exposed to threats. For the tourism-related areas and with individual travellers the industry can take an active and leading role in risk management and visitor protection. Where events external to tourism are the source of threats the industry must establish partnerships with other specialist agencies, and to a large extent rely on the leadership of national governments. The government and industry initiatives presented in Part 4 show the benefits of genuine partnerships in ensuring visitor health, safety and security.

References

Anonymous. (2005). 219,000 and rising. *Courier Mail* (Brisbane, Australia), 22 January, p. 16.

Atherton, T., & Atherton, T. (2003). Current issues in travel and tourism law. In: J. Wilks, & S.J. Page (Eds), *Managing tourist health and safety in the new millennium* (pp. 101–115). Oxford: Pergamon.

Beirman, D. (2003). *Restoring tourism destinations in crisis: A strategic marketing approach.* Sydney: Allen & Unwin.

Control Risks Group. (2003). *RiskMap 2003*. London: Control Risks Group.

Crondstedt, M. (2002). Prevention, preparedness, response, recovery — an outdated concept? *Australian Journal of Emergency Management, 17*(2), 10–13.

Emergency Management Australia. (2000). *Emergency risk management applications guide.* Canberra: EMA.

Federation of Tour Operators (FTO). (1999). *Health and safety handbook.* Lewes, UK: Federation of Tour Operators.

Federation of Tour Operators (FTO). (2003). *Preferred code of practice.* Lewes, UK: Federation of Tour Operators.

International Hotel & Restaurant Association (IH&RA). (1998). *Think-tank findings on safety and security. Executive summary.* Unpublished Report. Orlando, FL, 18 & 19 August.

International Strategy for Disaster Reduction. (2002). *Living with risk. A global review of disaster reduction initiatives.* Geneva: ISDR (CD Rom, preliminary version July).

Liability Insurance Taskforce. (2002). Report to the Queensland Government. [Online] Available at www.premiers.qld.gov.au/about/pcd/economic/insurancetaskforce.pdf, accessed August 2003.

Marriott, D. (2004). Nobody's perfect — but a team can be! In: J. Wilks, & S. Moore, *Tourism risk management for the Asia Pacific region* (pp. 41–42). Southport: CRC for Sustainable Tourism.

Moore, F. (2004). Foreword. In: J. Wilks, & S. Moore, *Tourism risk management for the Asia Pacific region* (p. iii). Southport: CRC for Sustainable Tourism.

Pacific Asia Travel Association (PATA). (2003). *Crisis. It won't happen to us!* Bangkok: PATA.

Page, S.J., Bentley, T.A., Meyer, D., & Chalmer, D.J. (2001). Scoping the extent of tourist road safety: Motor vehicle transport accidents in New Zealand 1982–1996. *Current Issues in Tourism, 4*(6), 503–526.

Standards Australia and Standards New Zealand. (1999). *Risk management. Australian/New Zealand standard: AS/NZS 4360:1999.* Strathfield, New South Wales: Standards Association of Australia.

Surawski, M., & Wilks, J. (2002). Hotel safety in Australia: Current legal issues. *International Travel Law Journal, 3*, 164–179.

Taylor, H. (2001). Many people unprepared for terrorist attacks or other disasters. *The Harris Poll* # 60, 5 December.Available at www.harrisinteractive.com/harris_poll/searchpoll.asp

Tourism Queensland. (2003). *Tourism crisis management plan.* Brisbane: Tourism Queensland.

Wilks, J. (1999) International tourists, motor vehicles and road safety: A review of the literature leading up to the Sydney 2000 olympics. *Journal of Travel Medicine, 6*, 115–121.

Wilks, J. (2002). *Safety and security in tourism: Partnerships and practical guidelines for destinations.* Report prepared for the World Tourism Organization. Madrid: WTO.

Wilks, J. (2003a). Safety. In: J. Jenkins, & J. Pigram (Eds), *Encyclopaedia of leisure and outdoor recreation* (pp. 442–443). London: Routledge.

Wilks, J. (2003b). Safety and security for destinations: WTO case studies. In: J. Wilks, & S.J. Page (Eds), *Managing tourist health and safety in the new millennium* (pp. 127–139). Oxford: Pergamon.

Wilks, J. (2004a). Tourism recovery after a crisis. Paper presented at the Asia Pacific Homeland Security Summit and Exposition, Honolulu, HI, 16 November.

Wilks, J. (2004b). Injuries and injury prevention. In: J. Keystone, P. Kozarsky, H.D. Nothdurft, D.O. Freedman, & B. Connor (Eds), *Travel medicine* (pp. 453–459). London: Mosby.

Wilks, J. (2005). Destination risk management in Oceania. In: C. Cooper, & C.M. Hall (Eds), *Oceania: A tourism handbook* (pp. 335–352). London: Channel View.

Wilks, J., & Coory, M. (2000). Overseas visitors admitted to Queensland hospitals for water-related injuries. *Medical Journal of Australia, 173*, 244–246.

Wilks, J., & Coory, M. (2002). Overseas visitor injuries in Queensland hospitals: 1996–2000. *Journal of Tourism Studies, 13*, 2–8.

Wilks, J., & Moore, S. (2004). *Tourism risk management for the Asia Pacific region.* Southport, Australia: CRC for Sustainable Tourism.

Wilks, J., & Oldenburg, B. (1995). Tourist health: The silent factor in customer service. *Australian Journal of Hospitality Management, 2*, 13–23.

Wilks, J., & Page, S.J. (Eds). (2003). *Managing tourist health and safety in the new millennium.* Oxford: Pergamon.

Wilks, J., Pendergast, D.L., & Wood, M.T. (2002). Overseas visitor deaths in Australia: 1997–2000. *Current Issues in Tourism, 5,* 550–557.

World Tourism Organization (WTO). (1991). *Recommended measures for tourism safety.* Madrid: WTO.

World Tourism Organization (WTO). (1997). *Tourist safety and security: Practical measures for destinations* (2nd ed.). Madrid: WTO.

Zamecka, A., & Buchanan, G. (2000). *Disaster risk management.* Brisbane: Queensland Department of Emergency Services.

Zeithaml, V.A., Parasuraman, A., & Berry, L.L. (1990). *Delivering quality service: Balancing customer perceptions and expectations.* New York: The Free Press.

PART 1

HEALTH

Chapter 2

Travel Medicine and Tourist Health

Peter Leggat

Introduction

There has been an increasing trend for people to travel internationally (Behrens, 1990). Ease of air transportation has ensured that more than 700 million people currently travel internationally each year to every part of the globe (World Tourism Organisation, 2003). These people are potentially exposed to infectious diseases for which they have no immunity, as well as other serious threats to well-being, such as accidents and exacerbation of pre-existing medical and dental conditions. Conservatively, it is estimated that between 30 and 50% of travellers and tourists become ill or injured while traveling (Steffen, Rickenbarh, Wilhelm, Helminger, & Schar, 1987; Cossar et al., 1990). Relative estimated monthly incidence rates of various health problems have been compiled elsewhere (Steffen et al., 1987). The risk of severe injury is thought to be greater for people when travelling abroad (Behrens, 1990; Cossar et al., 1990; Steffen & DuPont, 1994).

This chapter briefly reviews current health and safety issues in travel medicine and tourist health, describes the discipline of travel medicine and how this may usefully impact on tourist health, highlights recent developments in the area, and discusses the various agencies working in this area.

Morbidity and Mortality of Travellers

In terms of morbidity, infectious diseases such as respiratory tract infection and travellers' diarrhoea, and injuries are important concerns for travellers (Behrens, 1990; Cossar et al., 1990; Bewes, 1993). The main health complaints of returned Australian travellers reported in a 1999 survey of travel insurance claims included respiratory (20%), musculoskeletal (17%), gastrointestinal (14%), ear, nose and throat (12%), and dental conditions (7%) (Leggat & Leggat, 2002). This compares with the major specified illnesses and accidents reported in a recent Swiss study, which included infectious diseases (43.5%), accidents involving the extremities (15.3%), psychiatric conditions (8.2%), pulmonary disorders (4.7%), and accidents involving the head (4.7%) (Somer Kniestedt & Steffen, 2003).

Fortunately, few travellers die abroad and those that do tend to die of pre-existing conditions, such as myocardial infarction in travellers with known ischaemic heart disease. However, accidents are also a major cause of travel-related mortality (Prociv, 1995). A study published by Baker, Hargarten, and Guptill (1992) analysed deaths of Americans while overseas (nearly 5000 per year) and concluded that most Americans who die overseas do so in developed countries of Western Europe and the causes of death are similar to the U.S.A. Moreover, deaths of Americans in less developed countries are not from infections and tropical diseases, but are mainly from chronic diseases, injuries, drownings, suicides, and homicides. Similarly, studies of deaths of Australian, Canadian, American, and Swiss travellers abroad found that cardiovascular disease, accidents, and injuries, were among the most common causes of death abroad (Baker et al., 1992; MacPherson et al., 2000; Prociv, 1995; Steffen, 1991).

Defining Travel Medicine

Travel medicine and tourist health is a new multidisciplinary specialty area, which is emerging in response to the needs of the travelling population worldwide.

> Travel medicine seeks to prevent illnesses and injuries occurring to travellers going abroad and manages problems arising in travelers coming back or coming from abroad. Tourist health is also concerned about the impact of tourism on health and advocates for improved health and safety services for tourists (Leggat, Ross, & Goldsmid, 2002, p. 3).

The latter aspect recognises the impact of travel on ecosystems around the world, particularly the introduction and spread of diseases and disease resistance. Specialists in travel medicine consider and advise on various aspects of travel-related health, including fitness to travel and the health risks of travelling in itself, as well as exposure to infectious diseases and diseases arising from travel. In this respect, travel medicine can be regarded as a continuum (see Figure 2.1), which provides for pre-, during-, and post-travel health advice for travellers. This may necessitate the provision of malaria and other chemoprophylaxis or treatment, and various vaccinations. In this respect, Steffen and DuPont (1994, p. 1) state that:

> ...the art of travel medicine is selecting the necessary prevention strategy without unnecessary adverse events, cost or inconvenience.

and that:

> Travel medicine prevention should be based on epidemiological data (Steffen, 1991, p. 156).

The Continuum of Travel Medicine

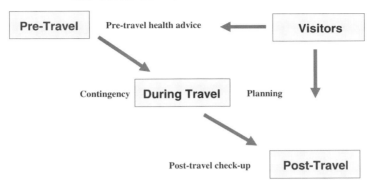

Figure 2.1: The continuum of travel medicine.
Source: Figure reproduced with permission from Leggat, Ross and Goldsmid (2005).

The areas that may be covered in the pre-travel health consultation with travellers are listed in Table 2.1.

International Developments in Travel Medicine and Tourist Health

Several key developments in the past decade have ensured the continuing emergence of travel medicine and tourist health as a specialty area. World Health Organization (WHO), International Health Regulations, and compulsory immunisation contributed significantly to the creation of travel medicine. Current travel health practice often relies on travellers' need for compulsory yellow fever immunisation based on the epidemiology of the disease. The development of WHO (2005) guidelines on travellers' health, *International Travel and Health*, was also an important advance as this recognised the need to develop a consensus strategy for combating commonly encountered infectious diseases and other problems encountered by travellers.

Professional Initiatives

The International Society of Travel Medicine (ISTM), established in 1991, has taken the lead in establishing a global professional base for travel medicine. Some of the important early initiatives of the ISTM were the provision of travel health alerts to subscribers, a journal, biennial conferences, a global listing of travel health practitioners, and a collaborative disease-reporting network (GeoSentinel) with the United States Centers for Disease Control and Prevention (Freedman, Kozarsky, Weld, & Cetron, 1999). Geosentinel has played a role regionally in examining health problems post travel (Freedman et al., 1999; Shaw, Leggat, Weld, Williams, & Cetron, 2003). More recently, the ISTM has developed an examination programme based on a detailed Body of Knowledge in travel medicine leading to a Certificate of Travel Health (Kozarsky & Keystone, 2002). GeoSentinel is an

Table 2.1: Areas that might be covered in pre-travel preparation of Australians going abroad. [Modified from Leggat et al. (2002) and Ingram and Ellis-Pegler (1996).]

Insects	Repellents, nets, permethrin
Advise/discuss	
Ingestions	Care with food and water
Infections	Skin; environment
Indiscretions	STIs, HIV
Injuries	Accident avoidance, safety
Immersion	Schistosomiasis
Insurance	Health and travel insurance
	Finding medical assistance abroad
	First aid advice
Vaccinate	
Always	National immunisation schedule vaccines
Often	Hepatitis A
Sometimes	Japanese encephalitis
	Meningococcal disease
	Polio
	Rabies
	Tetanus-diphtheria
	Typhoid
	Yellow fever
Older travellers	Pneumococcus
	Influenza
Prescribe	
Always	Regular medication
Sometimes	Antimalarial medication
	Diarrhoeal self-treatment
	Condoms
	Traveller's medical kit

excellent example of the contribution of travel medicine to the early detection and reporting of imported infections to which sites globally contribute (Freedman et al., 1999).

Regional societies of travel medicine have also flourished, such as the Asia Pacific Travel Health Association, which conducts biennial conferences in travel medicine and tourist health in the Asia-Pacific region, in alternate years to the ISTM's Annual Conference. The two major journals in the travel medicine area are presently the ISTM's *Journal of Travel Medicine*, published by BC Decker, and *Travel Medicine and Infectious Diseases*, published by Elsevier Science. The British Travel Health Association has also produced a journal, which is available online.

Comprehensive international guidelines in travel medicine and tourist health are published by the WHO (2005), as well as by many member countries, which provide guidelines and advice for travel medicine practice. In addition, there are a number of useful Internet and related resources, which provide valuable information on disease distribution and prevention (see Table 2.2), which have also been discussed elsewhere (Leggat, 2003). Access to current policy guidelines and up-to-date health intelligence, usually provided in travel medicine from Internet-based resources, is essential. Continuing research is also essential for a better understanding of the epidemiology of travel-related diseases and injuries, which in turn leads to the development of improved guidelines in travel medicine and more effective preventive measures to combat infectious diseases and prevent injuries associated with travel.

Postgraduate Education

Travel medicine and tourist health education is available both nationally and internationally through a range of postgraduate study options, including certificate, diploma, or masters' degree-level programmes. Several courses in travel, tropical, and migrant medicine are available throughout the world and many are listed at the ISTM website. As previously mentioned, the professional certificate of knowledge initiative from the ISTM includes recognition for successful examination candidates with a Certificate in Travel Medicine. Other international programmes in travel medicine and tourist health have been listed elsewhere (ISTM, 2004).

Travel Medicine Practice

Three main challenges initially confront the establishment of effective travel medicine practice. The first challenge is that travellers must recognise the need for travel health advice before travelling abroad, particularly given that a recent airport survey suggested that only 50% of Australian travellers abroad had sought pre-travel health advice (Wilder-Smith, Khairullah, Song, Chen, & Torresi, 2004). The second challenge is ensuring that travellers seek travel health advice in a timely manner, preferably at least 6–8 weeks before travel. The third challenge is for travellers to obtain travel health advice from a qualified source (Leggat, 2000). The airport survey previously discussed mentioned that only one-third

Table 2.2: Examples of major Internet and related resources available for travel medicine practice.

Name of resource	Internet address*
WHO, International Travel and Health	http://www.who.int/ith/index.html
WHO, Weekly Epidemiological Record	http://www.who.int/wer
CDC**, Health Information for International Travel	http://www.cdc.gov/travel/index.htm
CDC, Morbidity and Mortality Weekly Report	http://www.cdc.gov/mmwr
International Society of Travel Medicine	http://www.istm.org

*Internet sites accessed 01 December 2004.
**Centers for Disease Control and Prevention (USA).

of travellers had sought pre-travel health advice from a health professional (Wilder-Smith et al., 2004).

Many of these challenges can be at least partially addressed through industry and government co-operation, particularly at the level of the travel agent or airline, which will have initial contact with travellers. Although general practitioners (GPs) remain at the forefront of the provision of travel health advice, there has been an explosion in the establishment of dedicated specialist travel clinics, many operated commercially with others being developed within teaching hospitals and general practices (Hill & Behrens, 1996). From earlier studies, it has been found that only 44% of travellers were seeking pre-travel health advice, mostly from travel agents (Cossar et al., 1990), although other studies have shown preferences for seeing GPs as high as 65% (Cossar et al., 1990).

Travel Clinics

Travel clinics are usually designed to provide comprehensive pre- and post-travel health services, including the provision of advice and chemoprophylaxis as well as vaccination and other commercial items, such as travellers' medical kits, mosquito nets and repellents, and water purifiers. In travel clinics, typically, health advice would be provided by a physician in 40.7% of cases, the nurse and the physician in 41.9%, and the nurse only in 15.6% (Hill & Behrens, 1996). It has been suggested that about 5000 patients per year were needed to economically sustain a dedicated travel medicine clinic (Freedman, 1996), however, only 13% of the world's travel clinics see more than 5000 patients per year (Hill & Behrens, 1996). The average number seen by these clinics was 750 (range 6–50,000) patients per year (Hill & Behrens, 1996), with a median opening time of 35 h per week. Often these clinics would need to undertake other work, such as occupational health, aviation medicine, public health, or general practice in order to operate full time. Considerable variability in the accuracy and extent of advice provided by North American travel health advisers has been found previously (Keystone, Dismukes, Sawyer, & Kozarsky, 1994).

General Practice

A survey of GPs in Glasgow indicated that 87% believed that primary care was the best level to provide travel health advice, and only about 8% of GPs recommended a travel medicine clinic (Cossar & Reid, 1992). Several studies have shown that general practitioners usually provide advice on travel vaccinations, malaria chemoprophylaxis, insect bite avoidance, geographic diseases, and traveller's diarrhoea during travel health consultations (Seelan & Leggat, 2003; Leggat, Heydon, & Menon, 1999). However, the adequacy of advice given by GPs has also been the subject of some studies, and one study went as far as to suggest that general practice was not the best place to provide travel health advice (Jeffries, 1989). Considerable variability in the advice provided by GPs has been found in studies done elsewhere (Holden, 1989; Anonymous, 1994). A study by Carroll, Behrens, and Crichton (1998) of GPs and practice nurses in the UK indicated that more nurses (98%) gave pre-travel health advice and immunisations to travellers than GPs (87% and 48%, respectively) and nurses saw more travellers than GPs per month (28 compared with 10).

Travel Industry

Although there are still relatively few studies looking at the travel health advice provided by the travel industry, there have been deficiencies noted in brochures provided by travel agents. In one report (Reid, Cossar, Ako, & Dewar, 1986) health information was absent from one-third of brochures; only 11% gave specific health information, and around half of the brochures gave very general health advice. There have also been deficiencies noted in the knowledge of and advice given by travel agents to travellers concerning their health while travelling (Lobel, Campbell, Papaioanou, & Huong, 1987; Lobel et al., 1990; Malcolm, 1996). The airline industry serving Australia, for example, has been shown to have a paucity of destination-specific information in their in-flight magazines (Leggat, 1997).

Other Sources of Health Advice

It has been proposed that public health was "generally better equipped to offer comprehensive updated advice than are private practitioners" in the area of travel medicine (MacDonald & Buchan, 1995). Travel health advice may also be obtained from the Internet and the media. The information provided at travel medicine internet sites and in the media tends to be fairly general or "regional", which can be misleading unless the travellers or the travel health adviser has the knowledge and training to source and interpret the best information available.

Infectious Hazards of Travel

One of the most important factors in whether travellers seek health advice at all is the perceived risk and severity of tropical diseases (Behrens, 1990), despite their relatively low health and safety risk to travellers in comparison to accidents and less exotic conditions like travellers' diarrhoea. In addition to the prevention of potentially lethal diseases and injuries among travellers abroad, the importance of providing travel health services is also increasingly being recognised in relation to early detection and reporting of imported infections, such as through GeoSentinel (Freedman et al., 1999). Important infectious hazards of travel include vector-borne diseases, including malaria and arboviral diseases, and vaccine preventable diseases.

Vector-Borne Diseases

Vector-borne diseases remain among the great personal concerns for travellers abroad, especially those travelling to more remote tropical areas. Some vector-borne diseases also represent a potential public health problem when returning home. Malaria remains the single most important vector-borne disease problem of travellers; however, arboviral and rickettsial diseases are also becoming increasing important international travel-related health problems.

Malaria   Malaria is a serious disease caused by a protozoan parasite largely confined to the tropics. The WHO estimates that there are more than 300 million cases of malaria infection and 2.5 million deaths due to malaria worldwide (WHO, 2004). Most cases and deaths occur due to infection with *Plasmodium falciparum* species of malaria; however, infection due to *P. vivax* also remains important, especially as dormant liver stages of the life cycle can cause relapses, sometimes several, for months after returning home.

Standard malaria-preventive measures are considered as part of pre-travel health planning for travellers based on disease patterns and policy guidelines. Current disease prevention measures against malaria include the use of malarial chemoprophylaxis, personal protective measures against insect bites, environmental health measures against disease vectors, malaria eradication treatment for liver stages, including hypnozoites and gametocytes on return home, and early detection and treatment of malaria cases in order to avoid serious complications of the infection.

Guidelines for malaria chemoprophylaxis and treatment are described in various travel health guidelines. The growing incidence of chloroquine and multidrug resistance in *P. falciparum* and more recently, *P. vivax*, has limited the antimalarial drug options for malaria chemoprophylaxis. Current recommended malaria chemoprophylaxis options generally include doxycycline (one 100 mg tablet daily), mefloquine (one tablet weekly), and atovaquone plus proguanil or Malarone® (one tablet daily, which consists of 250 mg of atovaquone and 100 mg of proguanil) (Zuckerman, 2002). Chloroquine continues to be recommended as malaria chemoprophylaxis for malaria in the few areas where there is no chloroquine resistance. Current eradication treatment for malaria is primaquine (two 7.5 mg tablets twice daily for 2 weeks), although tafenoquine has recently been trialed as both an alternative eradication treatment (400 mg daily for three days) and as a weekly dose chemoprophylactic agent (Edstein, Nasveld, & Rieckmann, 2001).

Due to the incidence of neuropsychiatric side effects, such as anxiety and nightmares, it is advisable for travellers taking mefloquine for the first time to take several trial doses, possibly commencing as early as 3 weeks before departure (Looareesuwan, Chulay, Canfield, & Hutchinson, 1999). A protocol for determining eligibility for prescribing mefloquine has been described elsewhere. It is also advisable that travellers are given trial doses of other antimalarials, such as doxycycline and Malarone® that they might be taking for the first time well before departure. This is to ensure that there is time to consider alternative chemoprophylactic drugs (Zuckerman, 2002). If travel is commenced at short notice, modification to antimalarial regimens may have to be done abroad, which is less satisfactory. There are varying opinions on how long antimalarial drugs should be continued after leaving an antimalarial area. However, antimalarial drugs, which have no pre-erythrocytic effects on the liver stages of the malarial parasite, such as doxycycline and mefloquine, should be continued for up to 4 weeks afterwards. This relates to the time it takes for parasites to develop in the liver and infect the blood stream. Chemoprophylaxis with Malarone®, which also has some effects on the hepatic stages of *P. falciparum* parasites, may be given for shorter periods after return, e.g. 1 week after return (Looareesuwan et al., 1999).

For travellers to more remote areas, standby treatment, in the event of overt malaria infection while abroad, may also be useful. "Standby treatment consists of a course of antimalarial drugs that travelers to malaria endemic areas can use for self-treatment if they are unable to gain access to medical advice within 24 hours of becoming unwell" (Zuckerman, 2002, p. 262). In these situations, a travellers' medical kit may be supplied with a thermometer, possibly an immunochromatographic test (ICT) malaria diagnostic kit and written instructions, an appropriate malaria treatment course and written instructions, and travellers must seek medical advice as soon as possible. Newer antimalarials, which may be useful for standby treatment, include Malarone® and artemether containing compounds such as Riamet® (20 mg artemether and 120 mg lumefantrine) (Omari, Preston, & Garner, 2002).

Arboviral diseases   There are many arboviral diseases that may impact on travellers and about two-thirds of the world's population live in areas infested with yellow fever and dengue vectors, mainly *Aedes aegypti* mosquitoes. Two of the most important arboviral diseases for travellers are dengue fever and Japanese Encephalitis (JE), as people are travelling to more remote areas in recent years, where these diseases are endemic. These diseases are in addition to Yellow Fever, which has a widespread distribution in many parts of South American and African countries and is controlled by International Health Regulations (WHO, 2005).

Dengue fever is a major global public health problem. The WHO estimates that there are more than 50 million cases per year (WHO, 2002). Dengue is a viral illness transmitted by *Aedes* sp. of mosquito, classically *A. aegypti*. Infection may range from being subclinical to fever, arthralgia, and rash, or be complicated by haemorrhagic diatheses or shock syndromes. Treatment is supportive, while management of the problem is directed towards early detection of the disease and preventing transmission upon return to receptive countries (Malcolm, Hanna, & Phillips, 1999). Numerous outbreaks of Dengue have been attributed to travellers returning with the disease associated with delays in detecting the condition in recent work conducted in northern Australia (Malcolm et al., 1999). With travellers arriving or returning from abroad during the incubation period of the disease, it is vital that there is a collaborative effort made by various civilian public health authorities to contain and prevent the transmission of the disease among the local population (Kitchener, Leggat, Brennan, & McCall, 2002). Until a vaccination becomes available, the mainstays of dengue prevention are personal protective measures and environmental health measures against disease vectors (Malcolm et al., 1999).

JE is the leading cause of viral encephalitis in Asia. The WHO estimates that there are more than 70,000 cases annually in South East Asia (Kitchener, 2002). Up to one-third of clinical cases die and about one-half of clinical cases of JE have permanent residual neurological sequelae (Kitchener, 2002). Despite the availability of vaccines against JE, the immunogenicity or effectiveness of these vaccines has recently been questioned and concerns have been raised regarding adverse reactions reported with vaccination (Kurane and Takasaki, 2000). The current development of safer and more immunogenic second-generation JE vaccines will be important for travellers in this region in the future (Kitchener, 2002).

Prevention of Infectious Diseases through Vaccination

A number of infectious diseases of travellers can be prevented by immunisation. There are few mandatory vaccines, for which certification is necessary, and these include yellow fever and meningococcal meningitis. Yellow fever vaccination is required for all travellers entering or returning from a yellow fever endemic area, which is prescribed by the WHO (2005). Meningococcal vaccination is required for travellers to Mecca (WHO, 2005).

The travel medicine consultation is also an opportunity to update routine and national schedule vaccinations, which may afflict travellers anywhere. There are also a variety of vaccinations, which may be required for travellers to particular destinations. It would seem prudent to vaccinate travellers against diseases, which might be acquired through food and water, such as hepatitis A, typhoid, and polio (Zuckerman, 2002), as well as using other measures to combat these diseases. The most common vaccine preventable disease is hepatitis A (Steffen, 1991); however, typhoid vaccination should also be considered for travel to many developing countries. Polio vaccination is rarely required these days, with a concerted campaign for global eradication; however, it may be required in situations where polio outbreaks have been reported (Zuckerman, 2002).

There are a number of other infectious diseases, such as hepatitis B, JE, and rabies, which may afflict travellers to certain destinations or are a result of the nature of their travel, that are vaccine preventable (see Table 2.1). For older travellers, pneumococcal and influenza vaccinations should also be considered. The development of combination vaccines, such as hepatitis A plus typhoid and hepatitis A plus B, has greatly reduced the number of injections required (Zuckerman, 2002). The development of rapid schedules for travellers departing at short notice has been useful in providing protection within 4 weeks (Zuckerman, 2002). Many diseases have no vaccination. For example, some parasitic diseases, such as intestinal and filarial Helminths, can only be prevented through personal protective measures against the infective stages of the parasite and/or through periodic treatment or eradication treatment on return.

Non-Infectious Hazards of Travel

Despite the emphasis on infectious disease in travel medicine, the single most common preventable cause of death among travellers is accidental injury (Prociv, 1995; Baker et al., 1992; MacPherson et al., 2000; Steffen, 1991). About 35% of deaths of Australian travellers abroad were the result of ischemic heart disease, with natural causes overall accounting for some 50% of deaths (Prociv, 1995). Trauma accounted for 25% of deaths of Australians abroad (Prociv, 1995). Injuries were the reported cause of 18% of all deaths, with the major group being motor vehicle accidents, accounting for 7% of all deaths, which appeared to be over-represented in developing countries (Prociv, 1995). A similar pattern of mortality was observed in American (Baker et al., 1992), Canadian (MacPherson et al., 2000), and Swiss (Steffen, 1991) travellers abroad. Deaths of Australian tourists overseas have also resulted from air crashes, drowning, boating accidents, skiing accidents, bombs, and electrocution (Prociv, 1995). Homicides, suicides, and executions combined accounted for about 8% of all deaths (Prociv, 1995). Most fatal accidents in American and Swiss travellers were traffic or swimming accidents (Baker et al., 1992; Steffen, 1991). Deaths of tourists visiting Australia were similarly found to be due mainly to motor vehicle accidents and accidental drowning (Wilks, Pendergast, & Wood, 2003).

Infectious disease was reported as the cause of death in only 2.4% of Australians who died while travelling abroad (Prociv, 1995).

Issues in Aviation Medicine

Travel medicine and tourist health is also a key component of the activities of many health professionals working in aviation medicine. In addition to undertaking aviation medical examinations and advising their own staff who are travelling, airline medical departments review passengers' clearances to fly and provide advice to travel health advisers. Some travellers need special clearance to fly in cases of aeromedical evacuation (AME) on commercial aircraft and in certain prescribed circumstances of normal travel, such as with recent surgery or serious physical or mental incapacity (Graham, Putland, & Leggat, 2002), and liaison by travel health advisers with the airline medical departments is usually advisable. Health professionals working in aviation medicine also involve in developing policies and guidelines for dealing with in-flight emergencies involving travellers, as well as training for flight attendants in first aid. Physicians working in aviation medicine have their own national or regional professional organisations, such as the International Academy of Aviation and Space Medicine and the Aerospace Medicine Association in the United States of America.

While some medical practitioners undertake the work of Designated Aviation Medical Examiners (CASA, 2004), particularly in respect of pilots, air traffic controllers, and in some instances, flight attendants (Leggat & Putland, 2004), travel health advisers also need to be aware of the potential health effects of modern airline travel. These include the effects of reduced atmospheric pressure, low humidity, closed environment, inactivity, the effects of crossing several time zones on circadian rhythm, alcohol, and the general effects of aircraft motion and movement (Graham et al., 2002). These effects can produce conditions such as barotrauma, dehydration, jet lag, motion sickness, claustrophobia and panic attacks, air rage, spread of infectious disease, and contribute to the development of deep venous thrombosis (DVT) and venous thromboembolism (VTE) (Graham et al., 2002). There have also been concerns raised about the transmission of tuberculosis through close proximity to infected travellers on commercial aircraft (WHO, 2001). The provision of travel health advice and preventive measures for these conditions also largely falls to the travel medicine provider.

While considerable attention has been focussed on DVT and VTE, it remains uncertain what the contribution of air travel is to the development of this condition among travellers (see Chapter 8). What seems to be clear is that the development of DVT and VTE is multifactorial (Mendis, Yach, & Alwan, 2002). While the identification of travellers with predisposing risk factors would seem useful, it is only an option where the risks of side-effects of the screening procedure do not outweigh the risks of developing deep vein thrombosis after a long haul flight, which is estimated to be about 1 in 200,000 for travellers on a 12-h long haul journey (Gallus & Goghlan, 2002). In the meantime, conservative measures should be recommended, such as in-flight exercises, restriction of alcoholic and caffeinated beverages, and drinking lots of water. Other preventive measures for some at-risk cases, such as sub-cutaneous heparin, are worthy of investigation (Zuckerman, 2002). Current epidemiological research and pathophysiological studies are helping to establish which travellers are at greatest risk, which will in turn lead to appropriate intervention studies.

Travel Advisories

In recent times, travel advisories have assumed great importance in endeavouring to secure the safety and security of travellers (see Chapter 21). National governments regularly update their travel advisories, which are often included as part of information supplied by computerised databases used in travel medicine. Travellers and tourists have been confronted by recent acts of terrorism, resulting in numerous casualties, most recently during the 12 October, 2002 bombings in Kuta, Bali, Indonesia, which required a rapid multia-gency response to rescue foreign nationals trapped in Bali, where under-resourced local health facilities were quickly overwhelmed by both local and tourist casualties (Leggat & Leggat, 2004; Hampson, Cook, & Frederiksen, 2002).

Travel Insurance

Because of the potentially high costs of medical and dental treatment abroad, which may not be covered by private health insurance or local national health services, and the potential high costs associated with AME, all travellers should be advised of the need for comprehensive travel insurance. Travel insurance policies normally underwrite travel-related, medical and dental expenses incurred by travellers abroad under conditions specified by the travel insurance policy. In addition, travel insurance companies often provide a direct service, usually through their emergency assistance service contractors, to assist travellers abroad. This may include assisting with accessing or obtaining medical care while overseas, including AME (see Chapter 3). Claims for reimbursement of medical and dental expenses abroad made up more than two-thirds of all travel insurance claims in Australia (Leggat et al., 2002). In that study, almost one in five Australian travellers abroad have been found to use the travel insurer's emergency assistance service (Leggat et al., 2002).

Travel insurance is the most important safety net for travellers in the event of illness, injury or unforeseen events, and should be reinforced by travel health advisers. Recent studies have shown about 60% of GPs in New Zealand (Leggat, Heydon, & Menon, 1998), 39% of GPs in Australia (Seelan & Leggat, 2003), and 39% of travel clinics worldwide (Hill & Behrens, 1996) usually advise travellers concerning travel insurance. In addition, 54% of GPs in New Zealand also usually advised travellers about ways to find medical assistance abroad, but in the same study only 19% of GPs recommended travel insurance companies as a source of medical assistance while travelling (Leggat et al., 1998). However, it is not known what proportion of travel agents or airlines routinely give advice on travel insurance.

Summary

Travel medicine and tourist health is emerging as a new multidisciplinary specialty area catering for an increasing number of travellers worldwide. Travel health advisers, primarily associated with travel clinics and general practice, are engaged in the provision of pre-travel health advice, chemoprophylaxis against travel-related diseases, traveller's medical kits, and post-travel assessments and eradication treatment for various travel-related diseases. They are also in a key position to liaise with public health authorities on possible imported disease risks. In terms of risk assessment and provision of preventive measures, accidents, vector-borne diseases, in particular malaria and the arboviral diseases, stand out as major concerns for travellers. However, common problems such as travellers' diarrhoea and respiratory tract infection also need to be addressed. Travel medicine and tourist health and aviation medicine have many linkages, especially in terms of fitness to fly and dealing with problems that may arise in travellers due to physiological and psychological stresses of travel. In the face of recent terrorism and conflict, travel advisories have assumed great importance in travellers planning. Travel insurance remains an important safety net for travellers, which provides coverage for medical and dental treatment abroad as well as an emergency assistance service, which may include AME.

References

Anonymous. (1994). Don't miss malaria. *Medical Protection Society CaseBook*, No. 3, 4–5.

Baker, T.D., Hargarten, S.W., & Guptill K.S. (1992). The uncounted dead — American civilians dying overseas. *Public Health Report*, *107*, 155–159.

Behrens, R.H. (1990). Protecting the health of the international traveler. *Transactions of the Royal Society of Tropical Medicine and Hygiene*, *84*, 611–612, 629.

Bewes, P.C. (1993). Trauma and accidents: Practical aspects of the prevention and management of trauma associated with travel. *British Medical Bulletin*, *49*, 454–464.

Carroll, B., Behrens, R.H., & Crichton, D. (1998). Primary health care needs for travel medicine training in Britain. *Journal of Travel Medicine*, *5*, 3–6.

Civil Aviation Safety Authority (CASA). (2004). *Designated aviation medical examiner handbook* (Revised 2004). Available at: http://www.casa.gov.au/manuals/htm/dame/dame.htm (accessed 19 April 2004).

Cossar, J.H., & Reid, D. (1992). Health advice for travelers: The GP's role. *British Journal of General Practice*, *42*, 260.

Cossar, J.H., Reid, D., Fallon, R.J., Bell, E.J., Riding, M.H., Follett, E.A., Dow, B.C., Mitchell, S., & Grist, N.R. (1990). A cumulative review of studies on travelers, their experience of illness and the implications of these findings. *Journal of Infection*, *21*, 27–42.

Edstein, M.D., Nasveld, P.E., & Rieckmann, K.H. (2001). The challenge of effective chemoprophylaxis against malaria. *Australian Defence Force Health*, *2*, 12–16.

Freedman, D.O. (1996). Travel medicine: The future of an emerging specialty (Abstract). In: J. Koehler, R. Speare, & P.A. Leggat (Eds), *Proceedings of the fifth annual scientific meeting of the Australasian college of tropical medicine*, Bali, Indonesia, June 26.

Freedman, D.O., Kozarsky, P.E., Weld, L.H., & Cetron, M.S. (1999). GeoSentinel: The global emerging infections sentinel network of the International Society of Travel Medicine. *Journal of Travel Medicine*, *6*, 94–98.

Gallus, A.S., & Goghlan, D.C. (2002). Travel and venous thrombosis. *Current Opinion on Pulmonary Medicine, 8,* 372–378.

Graham, H., Putland, J., & Leggat, P.A. (2002). Air travel for people with special needs. In: P.A. Leggat, & J.M. Goldsmid (Eds), *Primer of travel medicine* (3rd ed., pp. 100–112). Brisbane: ACTM Publications (Chapter 8).

Hampson, G.V., Cook, S.P., & Frederiksen, S.R. (2002). The Australian Defence Force response to the Bali bombing, 12 October 2002. *Medical Journal of Australia, 177,* 620–623.

Hill, D.R., & Behrens, R.H. (1996). A survey of travel clinics throughout the world. *Journal of Travel Medicine, 3,* 46–51.

Holden, J.D. (1989). General practitioners and vaccination for foreign travel. *Journal of the Medical Defence Union,* (Spring), 6–7.

Ingram, R.J.H., & Ellis-Pegler, R.B. (1996). What's new in travel medicine? *New Zealand Public Health Report, 3,* 57–59.

International Society of Travel Medicine (ISTM). (2004). Educational opportunities. Available at: http://www.istm.org (accessed 19 April 2004).

Jeffries, M. (1989). Booster for GP travel vaccine clinics. *Monitor, 2,* 10–11.

Keystone, J.S., Dismukes, R., Sawyer, L., & Kozarsky, P.E. (1994). Inadequacies in health recommendations provided for international travelers by North American travel health advisors. *Journal of Travel Medicine, 1,* 72–78.

Kitchener, S. (2002). Most recent developments in Japanese encephalitis vaccines. *Australian Military Medicine, 11,* 88–92.

Kitchener, S., Leggat, P.A., Brennan, L., & McCall, B. (2002). The importation of Dengue by soldiers returning from East Timor to north Queensland, Australia. *Journal of Travel Medicine, 9,* 180–183.

Kozarsky, P.E., & Keystone, J.S. (2002). Body of knowledge for the practice of travel medicine. *Journal of Travel Medicine, 9,* 112–115.

Kurane, I., & Takasaki, T. (2000). Immunogenicity and protective efficacy of the current inactivated Japanese encephalitis vaccine against different Japanese encephalitis virus stains. *Vaccine, 18* (Suppl 2), 33–35.

Leggat, P.A. (1997). Travel health advice provided by in-flight magazines of international airlines in Australia. *Journal of Travel Medicine, 4,* 102–103.

Leggat, P.A. (2000). Sources of health advice for travelers. *Journal of Travel Medicine, 7,* 85–88.

Leggat, P.A. (2003). Travel medicine online: International sources of travel medicine information available on the Internet. *Travel Medicine and Infectious Disease, 1,* 235–241.

Leggat, P.A., Griffiths, R., & Leggat, F.W. (2005). Emergency assistance provided abroad to insured travelers from Australia. *Travel Medicine and Infectious Disease, 3,* 9–17.

Leggat, P.A., Heydon, J.L., & Menon, A. (1998). Safety advice for travelers from New Zealand. *Journal of Travel Medicine, 5,* 61–64.

Leggat, P.A., Heydon, J.L., & Menon, A. (1999). Health advice provided by general practitioners for travelers from New Zealand. *New Zealand Medical Journal, 112,* 158–161.

Leggat, P.A., & Leggat, F.W. (2002). Travel insurance claims made by travelers from Australia. *Journal of Travel Medicine, 9,* 59–65.

Leggat, P.A., & Leggat, F.W. (2004). Emergency assistance provided abroad to insured travelers from Australia following the Bali bombing. *Travel Medicine and Infectious Disease, 2,* 41–45.

Leggat, P.A., & Putland, J. (2004). Medical screening for flight attendants? *Journal of the Australasian Society of Aerospace Medicine, 1,* 11–14.

Leggat, P.A., Ross, M.H., & Goldsmid, J.M. (2002). Introduction to travel medicine. In: P.A. Leggat, & J.M. Goldsmid (Eds), *Primer of travel medicine* (3rd ed., pp. 3–21). Brisbane: ACTM Publications.

Leggat, P.A., Ross, M.H., & Goldsmid, J.M. (2005). Introduction to travel medicine. In: P.A. Leggat, & J.M. Goldsmid (Eds), *Primer of travel medicine* (3rd ed., pp. 3–21). Brisbane: ACTM Publication.

Lobel, H.O., Campbell, C.C., Papaioanou, M., & Huong, A.Y. (1987). Use of prophylaxis for malaria by American travelers to Africa and Haiti. *Journal of the American Medical Association, 257,* 2626–2627.

Lobel, H.O., Phillips-Howard, P.A., Brandling-Bennett, A.D., Steffen, R., Campbell, C.C., Huong, A.Y., Were, J.B., & Moser, R. (1990). Malaria incidence and prevention amongst European and North American travelers to Kenya. *Bulletin of the World Health Organization, 68,* 209–215.

Looareesuwan, S., Chulay, J.D., Canfield, C.J., & Hutchinson, D.B. (1999). Malarone (atovaquone and proguanil hydrochloride): A review of its clinical development for treatment of malaria. Malarone Clinical Trials Study Group. *American Journal of Tropical Medicine and Hygiene, 60,* 533–541.

MacDonald, A., & Buchan, S. (1995). Inadequacies in health recommendations. *Journal of Travel Medicine, 2,* 102.

MacPherson, D.W., Gurillot, F., Streiner, D.L., Ahmed, K., Gushulak, B.D., & Pardy, G. (2000). Death and dying abroad: The Canadian experience. *Journal of Travel Medicine, 7,* 227–233.

Malcolm, H. (1996). The importance of tropical medicine in north-east Tasmania. (Abstract). In: J. Koehler, R. Speare, & P.A. Leggat (Eds), *Proceedings of the fifth annual scientific meeting of the Australasian College of Tropical Medicine,* Bali, Indonesia, June 28.

Malcolm, R.L., Hanna, J.N., & Phillips, D.A. (1999). The timeliness of notification of clinically suspected cases of dengue imported into north Queensland. *Australian and New Zealand Journal of Public Health, 23,* 414–417.

Mendis, S., Yach, D., & Alwan, A. (2002). Air travel and venous thromboembolism. *Bulletin of the World Health Organization, 80,* 403–406.

Omari, A.A., Preston, C., & Garner, P. (2002). Artemether-lumefantrine for treating uncomplicated falciparum malaria. *Cochrane Database Systematic Reviews,* Issue 3, CD003125.

Prociv, P. (1995). Deaths of Australian travelers overseas. *Medical Journal of Australia, 163,* 27–30.

Reid, D., Cossar, J.H., Ako, T.I., & Dewar, R.D. (1986). Do travel brochures give adequate advice on avoiding illness? *British Medical Journal, 293,* 1472.

Seelan, S.T., & Leggat, P.A. (2003). Health advice given by general practitioners for travelers from Australia. *Travel Medicine and Infectious Disease, 1,* 47–52.

Shaw, M.T.M., Leggat, P.A., Weld, L.H., Williams, M.L., & Cetron, M.S. (2003). Illness in returned travelers presenting at GeoSentinal sites in New Zealand. *Australian and New Zealand Journal of Public Health, 27,* 82–86.

Somer Kniestedt, R.A., & Steffen, R. (2003). Travel health insurance: Indicator of serious travel health risks. *Journal of Travel Medicine, 10,* 185–189.

Steffen, R. (1991). Travel medicine: Prevention based on epidemiological data. *Transactions of the Royal Society of Tropical Medicine and Hygiene, 85,* 156–162.

Steffen, R., & DuPont, H.L. (1994). Travel medicine: What's that? *Journal of Travel Medicine, 1,* 1–3.

Steffen, R., Rickenbarh, M., Wilhelm, U., Helminger, A., & Schar M. (1987). Health problems after travel to developing countries. *Journal of Infectious Disease, 156,* 84–91.

Wilder-Smith, A., Khairullah, N.S., Song, J.H., Chen, C.Y., & Torresi, J. (2004). Travel health knowledge, attitudes and practices among Australasian travelers. *Journal of Travel Medicine, 11,* 9–15.

Wilks, J., Pendergast, D., & Wood, N. (2003). Accidental deaths of overseas visitors in Australia 1997–2000. *Journal of Hospitality and Tourism Management, 10,* 79–89.

World Health Organization (WHO). (2001). *Tuberculosis and air travel.* Geneva: WHO.

World Health Organization (WHO). (2002). *Dengue and dengue haemorrhagic fever*. Fact Sheet No. 117 (Revised 2002). Available at: http://www.who.int/mediacentre/factsheets/fs117/en/print.html (accessed 19 April 2004).

World Health Organization (WHO). (2005). *International travel and health*. Geneva: WHO. Available at: http://www.who.int/ith (last accessed 28 August 2005).

World Health Organization (WHO). (2004). *Malaria*. Fact Sheet 94. Available at: http://www.who.int/mediacentre/factsheets/fs094/en/print.html (accessed 19 April 2004).

World Tourism Organisation (2003). *Tourism highlights 2003*. Madrid: World Tourist Organisation. Available at: http://www.world-tourism.org/newsroom/Releases/2003/october/highlights.htm (Accessed 9 April 2004).

Zuckerman, J.N. (2002). Recent developments: Travel medicine. *British Medical Journal, 325*, 260–264.

Chapter 3

Travel Insurance and Aeromedical Evacuation

Peter Leggat and Peter Aitken

Introduction

Despite an improved understanding of serious injury and illness during travel, accidents, near accidents, and maladies continue to befall tourists. With knowledge of these risks, travellers should be armed with preventive strategies, emergency treatment supplies, a working knowledge of first aid, and appropriate travel insurance coverage. Travellers should know how to access appropriate care at their travel destination, ideally through the emergency assistance service of their travel insurer. The traveller should understand the indications for and logistics of emergency assistance and aeromedical evacuation.

Travel insurers normally underwrite travel, medical, and dental expenses incurred by travellers abroad, who take out "travel insurance", and provide emergency assistance and arrange aeromedical evacuation of travellers under specified conditions. Medical and dental claims make up more than two-thirds of all claims (Leggat & Leggat, 2002). Travellers should be advised to read their policies carefully to see what is covered, the level of the excesses, and to check for any exclusions. In particular, those travellers who have known pre-existing conditions, who are working long-term overseas, or who are going to undertake any form of hazardous recreational or occupational pursuit may need to obtain a special travel insurance policy, and this may attract a higher premium.

In addition, travel insurance companies normally provide a service, usually through their emergency assistance contractors, to assist travellers abroad. This may include assisting with medical care while overseas, including aeromedical evacuation. Use of the emergency telephone service provided by the travel insurance company was reported in almost one-fifth of claims in a recent study of general claims in Australia (Leggat & Leggat, 2002). In a recent Swiss study, more than two-thirds of claims made through the travel insurer's assistance centre were for illness, while the remainder were due to accidents (Somer Kniestedt & Steffen, 2003). The risk of severe injury is thought to be greater for people when travelling abroad (Bewes, 1993).

This chapter reviews the general nature of travel insurance and the mechanics and practical considerations of emergency assistance and aeromedical evacuation.

Travel Insurance

When travelling abroad, travellers are not usually covered by their health insurance, workers' compensation and third party and other personal insurance and liability policies. Few countries provide reciprocal medical and dental arrangements or free health care to travellers, even for emergency cover, and few countries provide a full range of readily accessible health care services, including aeromedical evacuation. Travel insurance for international journeys generally covers, amongst other things, the expenses of your travel, medical treatment or even evacuation in the event of misadventure or ill health. Most importantly, the travel insurer can assist in organising, co-ordinating, and, in some cases, financially guaranteeing a traveller's medical care and keeping relatives informed, which is especially important when the traveller is severely ill or injured and requiring aeromedical evacuation (see also Table 3.1).

Travellers should also consider taking out travel insurance to cover domestic travel. Like international travel, insurance for domestic travel arrangements, especially for discounted economy tickets with "no refund" or no re-routing conditions on purchase, should at least cover the traveller against unavoidable cancellation due to illness, subject to any excesses or

Table 3.1: What does appropriate travel insurance cover?

Aspects of travel misadventure normally covered by appropriate travel insurance
Aeromedical evacuation from anywhere in the world, unless specified
Repatriation of the body of the traveller back to the home country
Carriage of close family or friends to the country where the traveller is hospitalised on a longer-term basis
Liaison with the treating hospital and physician, as required
Emergency assistance, usually through a reverse charge telephone number
Advice on finding medical or dental assistance abroad
General travel health advice, possibly a booklet on travel health
Cover medical and dental expenses for problems, which are not pre-existing, and possibly for those which are pre-existing
Cover loss, theft, and damage to property, luggage, etc.
Cancellation or cessation of journey costs due to non-pre-existing illness or other specified problems
Other items specified in the policy.

Aspects of travel misadventure NOT normally covered by appropriate travel insurance
Pre-existing medical conditions
Excess on the policy — may be $50 or more
Self-inflicted injuries and some adventure sports/activities.
Items normally covered by another policy, e.g. for expensive jewellery items
Loss of wages, etc., as a result of the cancellation of trip or illness
Longer-term disability
Some other exclusions, such as war and terrorist acts, as specified by the policy

---

Source: Table reproduced with permission from Leggat and Kedjarune (2002).

prescribed conditions that may be imposed. Domestic travel insurance usually covers only travel expenses.

Raising Awareness of Travel Insurance

Travel insurance is the most important safety net for travellers in the event of misadventure, and the purchase of travel insurance should be reinforced by the tourism and travel health industry. Only 4% of general practitioners (GPs) in a late 1980s study in the United Kingdom would advise a traveller going to Turkey about travel insurance (Usherwood & Usherwood, 1989). More recent studies, however, show about 60% of GPs in New Zealand (Leggat, Heydon, & Menon, 1998), 39% of general practitioners in Australia (Seelan & Leggat, 2003), and 39% of travel clinics worldwide (Hill & Behrens, 1996) usually advised travellers concerning travel insurance. In a study by Ivatts, Plant, and Condon (1999) in Western Australia, almost all travel agents reported discussing travel insurance, but only 56% recommended that travellers seek travel health advice from a physician, where travel insurance could have been further reinforced. It is not known what proportion of airlines routinely gives advice on travel insurance.

Travel Insurance Providers

Travel insurance should be obtained well before leaving the country and application forms can be obtained from travel agents, airlines, private health insurers, doctor's surgeries, hostels, and other travel and tourism representatives. The travel insurance industry is a large dynamic industry. Some consumer organizations may help provide travellers with independent advice on which travel insurance policy represents the best value, particularly in researched reviews that may appear in consumer magazines (Anonymous, 1996).

Travel insurance policies are generally available for individual journeys or for frequent travellers as an annual policy, which should reduce the cost of the premium outlays and obviates the need for multiple travel insurance applications. Further information on travel insurance may also be available on the Internet and general reviews of travel insurance have been published in recent years in travel magazines (Ee Na Lai, 1995). Travel insurance for international travel should be taken out well before travel, and advice concerning travel insurance should be sought early by travellers, preferably at least 6–8 weeks before travel when the traveller is seeking travel health advice for their journey. It is important that travellers are advised to seek a travel insurer, which has international coverage for medical care and aeromedical evacuation, especially for the traveller's destination.

Level of Coverage

Ideally, travel insurance needs to be taken out at the top level available, which should cover as far as possible all medical, dental and surgical costs; personal liability; costs of aeromedical evacuation; costs of additional expenses associated with medical treatment, including loss of income, travel rearrangements, transport of relatives, and daily allowance; plus usual travel insurance items, such as loss of baggage; and carriage of body or ashes after death (Bewes, 1993). Travel insurers' companies may deny a traveller the right to purchase an inadequate travel insurance policy for a particular destination, for example, budget level cover for the USA, to avoid being liable for claims arising from selling an inadequate product.

The primary value of the health component in travel insurance is as a financial safety net. Cost of health care abroad can be considerable and can be demonstrated by occasional hefty hospital bills in the USA, the chartering of jet ambulances to transfer from country to country and the stretcher home on a Boeing 747. Examples of huge medical expenses incurred by injured and ill travellers abroad, occasionally appear in the popular press. Six figure accounts for hospitalisation and treatment in the USA, for example, are not unheard of.

Cost

The cost of a travel insurance premium reflects the levels of cover required and duration of time travelling, with the levels of cover required becoming more strongly linked to destination. Discounted travel insurance policies will generally have exclusions or limitations and, while policies with lower premiums for short haul destinations such as Asia may be available, the cost of seeking private medical and dental care needs to be taken into account whatever the destination. Travellers need to compare the small cost of their travel insurance premium against their total travel expenses, which, in many cases, would be less than the combined cost of airport and departure taxes for their trip. Most travel insurers, especially for international travel insurance, will require a minimum processing period for applications and travellers need to plan accordingly.

Exclusions

Even the top-level travel insurance policies usually have exclusions (Ryan, 1996). These exclusions may include claims arising from:

- travel to war zones;
- self-inflicted injuries;
- unlawful acts;
- certain infectious diseases, such as Acquired Immune Deficiency Syndrome and sexually transmitted infections;
- pregnancy; and
- participation in professional sport.

Those who are expecting to undertake any kind of hazardous pursuit should expect to pay a surcharge on their travel insurance premium, which may be assessed on a case-by-case basis by travel insurance companies. Some sporting organisations, such as those for divers, may recommend a travel insurance product. Some travel insurers may exclude pregnancy and any complications arising from pregnancy after 26 weeks, or they may restrict coverage even further, or may give no coverage for pregnancy. Excesses are also quite common these days on many aspects of claims with the various types of travel insurance policies available.

It is important also for travellers, especially old travellers, to be aware that travel insurance normally does not cover pre-existing medical or dental problems. In these cases, it may be necessary for travellers to complete further documentation of these conditions and in some cases be clinically assessed by a doctor or insurance medical representative. Many pre-existing illnesses may be covered with an additional premium (Ryan, 1996). It is possible that routine illnesses may also be excluded by the travel insurance policy. It is still important for these travellers to take out a travel insurance policy, since other conditions, not directly linked to their excluded pre-existing condition, are likely to be covered.

For those travellers who may be uninsurable because of advanced age or advanced ill health, it is important that they are advised about destinations where they could travel safely, particularly where bilateral government health agreements exist for emergency medical treatment and where airlines are prepared to uplift the traveller. It is important that travellers understand the "worst case scenario" risk and the cost to them if it occurred.

Travel insurance, provided for domestic travel by agencies such as airlines, travel agents, and automobile associations generally do not cover against medical expenses or aeromedical evacuation. However, these expenses may be covered or cost offset in other ways, for example, through their private health insurance or by their employer. Some comprehensive household insurance policies may cover some personal effects and equipment while travelling; however, the traveller should examine the policy closely. It is important that travellers do not elect to decline third party or personal liability insurance from a car rental agency in the event that they are involved in an accident, regardless of fault, as many travel insurance policies do not include claims for damage to other persons or property arising from the traveller's operation of cars, boats, jet skis, aircraft, and other motorised devices. It has also been recently discussed that not all travel insurance arrangements may be adequate for all travellers, especially those going to more remote destinations (Grace & Penny, 2004).

Credit Card Travel Insurance

Some well-known charge and credit cards include travel insurance when payments for specified travel arrangements are made with the respective card. The traveller should not assume that this cover is sufficient, and they should read the policy and the fine print well before the travel date to decide whether a standard travel insurance policy would better serve their needs. Since policies may not be issued with every travel charge made with these credit and charge cards, it is also important that travellers familiarize themselves with the relevant travel insurance documentation to determine their entitlements, preferably before they travel. Additional useful features may be provided by some travel insurance policies. Some credit card travel insurance policies may be able to be topped up to provide extra cover.

Coverage of Children

Although infants may be travelling at no charge and while they may not be old enough to have many personal belongings, it is important for children to be covered by travel insurance. Children are likely to suffer from some illness while travelling. If it is a severe illness, injury, or major dental problem, then medical or dental assistance may be needed. Those travelling with children should ensure that their travel insurance policy, usually a family policy, covers their dependent children, especially their age, while they are travelling. One parent or guardian travelling may be covered for one or more children, but travellers should be advised to check with their travel insurance company.

Travel Insurance Card

The travel insurance card is evidence of a traveller's current policy in travel insurance and the policy number to be quoted in emergencies, which may assist travellers in gaining access to medical, dental, and paramedical care in foreign countries. In addition, there is usually a 24 h toll-free contact number on the card and instructions for travellers seeking emergency assistance. The travel insurance company will usually subcontract at least some emergency assistance and aeromedical evacuation responsibilities to professional emergency assistance companies; however, it is important for travellers to ensure that the travel insurance company will co-ordinate medical care and evacuation procedures with qualified medical staff.

Travellers should take all their travel health documentation, including their travel insurance policy, with them in a waterproof plastic jacket, including their immunization record, travel insurance card, and doctor's letter for any medications carried. While travel insurance companies may keep some details of medical history, including allergies, travellers should also consider special medical alert identification for particular allergies, blood group, or medical conditions, such as diabetes, which may take the form of a special bracelet or neck chain. Some travel clinics use special cards or booklets, which can be used to write up immunisations and medications, and some publications also provide general travel health advice. Travellers should also be advised to make copies of the travel insurance policy and other important documents and keep them separately from the originals, in the event that the originals are stolen or lost.

Pre-Existing Conditions

Travellers should be advised to avoid travelling or working overseas with acute medical or dental problems, which could flare up while abroad. Known pre-existing illnesses, injuries, and disabilities may require additional coverage (Ryan, 1996). All pre-existing illnesses should be fully documented, preferably in a doctor's letter and also by means of emergency documentation, such as medical alert bracelets for some illnesses, like severe diabetes, asthma, and allergies (see also Table 3.2). Travel insurance companies may also store this type of medical information, subject to privacy issues.

Travel insurance therefore affords financial security for the traveller against what can be very costly claims for medical and related travel expenses in the event of misadventure, as well as even more costly aeromedical evacuation, occasionally requiring such things as specialized aircraft, modifications to aircraft, medical and nursing escorts, and assistance with legal, customs, and immigration procedures. One way of explaining the cost-effectiveness of travel insurance is to compare it *pro-rata* with car insurance, both private and rental car insurance, and private health insurance, which will generally be very favourable for most travellers. The bottom line is that no one should travel uninsured.

Working Overseas

Employers who have a number of employees travelling abroad on business will often take out a group travel insurance policy. Similar to "credit card" insurance, it is necessary for employees to obtain and peruse the policy documentation for their travel insurance. In

Table 3.2: Measures which should be taken for travellers with pre-existing conditions.

Take out maximum travel insurance to cover the pre-existing condition if possible

Get a full medical check-up and clearance before departure

Obtain the contact details of a physician in the countries to which they are travelling

Take and carry a doctor's letter documenting their condition and current medications or medical equipment they are carrying with them

Take a prescription, if necessary, which documents the current medication

Keep a copy of medical documentation with a third party, from whom you can access the information in an emergency

Take an adequate supply of medications for the entire journey

Advise travellers to pack at least their current medication requirements in their carry-on bags

Wear an emergency assistance bracelet for any major medical conditions or allergies

---

some cases, the employer may meet the shortfall in coverage of costs associated with mis-adventure while travelling, however this should be documented to the satisfaction of the employee. For the business traveller, these costs may include those of a replacement colleague who may have to take on the assignment of the ill or injured worker. Those about to undertake independent consulting work abroad for an employer may also not be covered by an employer's travel or workers' compensation insurance policy. Prospective consultants should be advised to consider these aspects before finalizing any contract. If the employee is in any doubt concerning coverage, they should be advised to take out appropriate additional travel insurance, whether or not the employer will cover this cost.

Travel insurance is normally provided for short-term travel only and even annual frequent or business traveller travel insurance policies do not necessarily provide continuous cover, particularly for international travel. Private insurers in the host country may provide longer-term medical insurance. It is important for all long-term travellers or workers to be aware of the location of appropriate local medical services, especially those recommended by their employer. Workers, consultants, and other long-term travellers should be advised to find out the availability of aeromedical evacuation in that area, and these travellers should be advised to register with the local embassy or consulate and workers, consultants, and other long-term travellers should give them an itinerary and/or contact address.

Medical Documentation

Many travel insurance companies and airlines will store some medical information about medical conditions and special diets of travellers. Travellers usually supply this information voluntarily. Information about medical conditions may include special travel requirements, current treatment, and allergies. If the traveller is likely to be consulting a medical practitioner overseas or where this is arranged, then the traveller should carry a doctor's letter detailing the relevant aspects of the past medical history and current treatment.

Any traveller taking medications should be advised to carry these medications onboard the aircraft with them. Travellers should have sufficient medications with them for the entire journey. If medications are lost or stolen during travel, these should be replaced with medications of the same type and manufacturer if possible. A physician should be consulted abroad for the relevant prescription. Travellers should carry separately a copy of their doctor's letter detailing their medications, which will assist them in obtaining replacement medications.

Travellers who require insulin or other injectable drugs should also carry a letter from their doctor explaining why they need to have syringes in their luggage. Ideally, this can be summarised on the doctor's letter covering all these medications. It is particularly important in this era of heightened security that travellers, travel industry, and travel health advisers liaise closely with airlines and airport security concerning travellers who may need to carry devices such as syringes onboard aircraft. Some countries may have special requirements for the importation of large quantities of medications, and relevant embassies should be contacted if in any doubt.

Travellers also need to be aware that laws describing controlled substances may be different to those in their own country. Possession of relatively common analgesics such as codeine phosphate may be regarded as a narcotics offence in some countries. Appropriate documentation may help to avoid this, but country-specific information and advice should be obtained before travel.

Documentation for Making a Claim

In serious medical cases, travellers are advised, where possible, to contact the travel insurance company as soon as possible. In some cases and in much the same way as major hotels, the medical or dental provider may request credit or charge cards as a guarantee of payment, even if the traveller has a valid travel insurance policy. In this way, credit and charge cards may be useful in medical emergencies occurring during travel. In less serious cases, or where the traveller has been unable to contact the insurer, travellers should be advised to request and keep original accounts, receipts, and medical reports for any medical or dental treatment while overseas, in case these expenses can be claimed back from a travel insurance policy, an employer, a national health service, private health insurance fund, or written-off against tax. Loss or theft of any medical or dental equipment, as with any of the travellers' belongings, should be reported to the police, usually within 24 h.

Appeals Procedures

In most cases, problems with claims are most likely to be resolved by discussing the problem with an official from the insurance company. If the traveller is not satisfied with the outcome, travel insurance companies or insurance industry associations may provide information about dispute resolution procedures in some countries. In Australia, the General Insurance Code of Practice provides for a process of dispute resolution (Anonymous, 1996). Dispute resolution procedures usually revolve around an internal system for resolving disputed claims in the first instance. An external system may also be available as a

Claims Review Panel, which may be funded by the insurance industry itself, as is the case in Australia, or by government, whose decisions may be binding in most instances. The most expensive option of dispute resolution will be taking the insurance company to court.

Emergency Assistance

Medical and dental care may not be easily accessible to travellers in the public health systems of many countries; however private clinics may be found. Even then, there may be language and financial barriers that could need to be overcome. It may be helpful before travel to provide travellers with a recommendation for suitable medical treatment services at their destinations, particularly if they are prone to medical problems. Ideally, their travel health adviser should give this recommendation, together with a letter outlining the traveller's medical history. Travellers with chronic health conditions may also elect to wear medical alert bracelets and necklaces or similar identification in case emergency health care is required while abroad. Such identification may provide critical medical information or even enable a health care professional to access medical information about the traveller in the event of an emergency.

Before travelling, recommendations concerning suitable doctors available for consultation while overseas may be obtained from travel insurers, foreign missions, hotels, private hospitals, and travel clinics. Only about half of general practitioners in New Zealand also usually advised travellers about finding medical assistance abroad and only about one-fifth of general practitioners recommended travel insurance companies as a source of medical assistance while travelling (Leggat et al., 1998).

Even life-threatening conditions are often managed surprisingly well in rather underdeveloped medical systems (Aldis, 2004). Travellers and emergency assistance companies should be prepared to make best use of overseas medical resources. Kolars (2002) suggests the following:

- Do not assume that the health care system abroad is similar to the one at home.
- Seek out health care systems that have a reputation of caring for foreigners.
- Clarify payment issues from the outset.
- Make certain the health professionals are comfortable and willing to help you.
- Avoid leveraging medical knowledge from the home country in hopes of "educating" the local providers about what needs to be done.
- Understand that in some cultures, questions from patients or family members are often perceived as challenges to the authority of the doctors.
- Decide the issues that will need to be addressed and those that are less important.
- Have "exit strategies" prepared in advance that allow travellers to depart gracefully from the care if you are dissatisfied.
- Watch for incentives for people directing health care.
- Carefully consider the fine print of travel insurance policies, especially the aeromedical evacuation provisions.

Travel insurance and other agencies often provide service to assist travellers in finding medical care while overseas and may be able to assist with providing information on the medical history of the traveller in an emergency. The most common advice required from the insurer's emergency assistance service is related to claiming and policy advice (Leggat, Griffith, & Leggat, 2005). Further, the need for emergency department review or hospitalisation was required for about one-sixth of those using the emergency assistance service (Leggat et al., 2005) (see Table 3.3). Aeromedical evacuation was an uncommon and an expensive form of emergency assistance, but was indicated for a small number of travellers (Leggat et al., 2005). Interestingly, Hochedez, Vinsentini, Ansart, and Caumes (2004) found a higher percentage (1.8%) of travellers to Nepal requiring aeromedical evacuation and a further 5% of these travellers required helicopter rescue in the Himalayas.

Aeromedical Evacuation

General Overview

Aeromedical evacuation is a planned activity, which requires careful assessment and preparation of the patient. A little time spent prior to the evacuation will make the entire procedure much smoother and less prone to complications (see Table 3.4). Escorts need to be trained health professionals, who are familiar with equipment on aircraft used for

Table 3.3: Type of emergency assistance required per 100,000 travellers that have travel insurance.

8000 will make a travel insurance claim (8%)
2000 will use emergency assistance service of travel insurer (2%)
400 will need emergency department or clinic referral (0.4%)
200 will result in hospital admissions (0.2%)
50 will need aeromedical evacuation (0.05%)

Source: Adapted from Leggat et al. (2005).

Table 3.4: Basic principles in evacuation.

The basic principles need to be adhered to in evacuation of patients by air
Transport is not an alternative to diagnosis and treatment.
Adequate stabilisation and preparation for transport is essential.
Thorough planning and communication is vital.
Mode of transport should be appropriate.
Equipment should be appropriate and checked.
Personnel should be experienced and well prepared.
Evaluation and treatment should continue during transport.
Documentation should be thorough.
Evacuation should be culturally appropriate, as far as possible.
Safety of staff is paramount.

Source: Table reproduced with permission from Graham and Putland (2002).

aeromedical evacuation. Evacuation may be performed on a conventional commercial flight or on a specially fitted out aircraft, either a fixed wing aircraft or a helicopter. The latter are usually maintained by emergency services (air ambulance), the military, multi-national companies, and also by international travellers assistance organisations. Every evacuation should be carefully considered since they are expensive both in terms of time and resources. International aeromedical evacuations can cost up to US$50,000 or more even for short flights. Hence, all travellers should take out appropriate travel insurance, which covers against this contingency, but should also use common sense to ensure that the need for aeromedical evacuation is kept to a minimum.

Air travel may not be appropriate with certain medical conditions (e.g. pneumothorax, decompression sickness, and head injuries), if other options are available. Location and transport availability may also affect choice of mode of transport. Aeromedical evacuations are also conducted on scheduled commercial aircraft, by modifying the cabin space prior to flight. Most airlines have medical policies concerning aeromedical evacuations. If, in the future, aeromedical evacuation modules are to be installed on scheduled airlines, then it might be easier to evacuate travellers using a scheduled civilian flight. A dedicated air ambulance will be used in some instances. The air ambulance selected must have adequate range, available service areas, reasonable speed, adequate cabin space, and adequate medical equipment for the journey.

Initial Clinical Assessment

The main purposes of the initial clinical assessment are to ascertain if the patient is indeed fit to travel and cannot be further stabilised in the treatment facility and to determine what medical support will be needed for the patient during the transfer. Presumably the latter is a major consideration in this case. The factors involved in making the decision to repatriate have been summarised as follows (Dewhurst & Goldstone, 2001):

- Health care facilities at the treating unit.
- Patient's condition and progress, i.e. is it urgent or time critical?
- Expected duration of treatment and level of expertise available.
- Potential detrimental effects of transport.
- Potential risk to the patient if not transferred.
- Availability of aircraft.
- Availability of beds within the receiving hospital, particularly intensive care beds.

Timing of Evacuation

There are many people involved in the decision to repatriate (after Dewhurst & Goldstone, 2001), such as:

- referring doctor;
- assistance company doctor;
- receiving doctor;
- air ambulance company;
- air ambulance escorting staff;

- patient's own general practitioner; and
- relatives, next of kin, etc.

Communication is one of the most important factors here and there may be some language barriers to overcome in this scenario. How critical the patient's transfer is will also be an important factor.

Selection of Suitable Aeromedical Attendant(s)

Aeromedical evacuation requires reasonably advanced skills in emergency medicine (Roby, 1994). The level of care should not decrease between the referral centre and the receiving hospital (ACEM, ANZCA, & JFICM, 2003). Escorts should be experienced and trained in aeromedical evacuation and may include health professionals, such as nurses, doctors, or paramedics. Some evacuations may require escorts with special skills. Evacuation should also be handled in a culturally appropriate manner and care given to preserve the patient's dignity. It would be useful if all personnel involved in aeromedical evacuation receive training in cultural safety. Escorts should be familiar with all equipment and should have checked them before evacuation; hence, they should be appropriately trained and credentialed. Some escorts prefer to take their own medical kit, so that they have equipment with which they are accustomed. Several staff or more than one shift of staff may be needed to help deal with the physical attributes of the patient as well as to share the shift during the transfer/flight. In general, medical staffs have more uniform recognition across borders than nursing, paramedic, and other potential air attendant staff (Roby, 1994; Roby, Bentley, & Munford, 1994).

The staff will need appropriate documentation, travel documents, and cash/credit cards for emergencies. Care should be taken with documentation for possession of dangerous drugs (narcotics) and visa requirements. Accommodation and transfers for medical staff in each interim stop along the way should be arranged. If necessary, staff transfers should be pre-arranged. Backup for staff will probably be available and put on standby for larger operations. Staff should have adequate insurance coverage before departure. Food and water for the flight should also be arranged.

Selection and Preparation of Equipment

Travel by commercial aircraft will necessitate bringing all equipment. Use of oxygen is also problematic as this must be organised and purchased in advance through the airline. Equipment levels available in air ambulances are inherently greater than commercial aircraft but remain variable across different providers. Air ambulances need to have (after Graham & Putland, 2002):

- Adequate lighting system (not heat producing as this is dangerous with oxygen).
- Oxygen supplies and delivery system, which need to be secured and be adequately supplied.
- Suction equipment, with oxygen or air flow dependent/compressor system.
- Monitoring equipment, including oxygen saturation monitor (pulse oximetry), end-tidal carbon dioxide (Capnograph), an electrocardiograph (ECG), blood pressure monitoring (manual/non-invasive/invasive), temperature and blood glucose monitoring.

- Defibrillation equipment and emergency drug box.
- Intravenous infusion fluids and equipment.
- Facilities for emergencies — these facilities would need to be available in this case.

More supplies than are needed should be taken, including oxygen. Attention should also be given to task-specific equipment and materials such as blood products, antivenom, pacing equipment, and neonatal transport cots and the ability to both procure these and safely secure or store them during the retrieval.

Selection of Aircraft and Flight Characteristics

Consideration of all the factors involved in the selection of aircraft is beyond the scope of this chapter but include patient characteristics (numbers, urgency, and type of care), geographical characteristics (distance, weather, and landing strips), aircraft characteristics (space, speed, ability to pressurise, and 'fit out'), and logistical characteristics (cost and availability). Flight physiology and characteristics also need to be considered as they may impact on both patient welfare and ability of the retrieval team to provide care. Flight physiology includes pressure changes with expansion of gas-filled cavities such as pneumothorax and decreasing oxygen with altitude. Flight characteristics include noise, vibration, acceleration, temperature control, and turbulence all of which may contribute to difficulties with equipment and patient care and contribute to fatigue and physical and mental discomfort to both the retrieval team and patient. Conventional commercial flights may be used but normally require modifications to enable appropriate space, use of oxygen, and other equipment. Dedicated and appropriately fitted out aircraft, either fixed wing (jet or propeller) or rotary wing, are usually maintained by emergency services (air ambulance), the military, multinational companies, and also by international travellers assistance organisations.

Logistics and Administration

Communication needs to be effective and continued communication is essential with relevant authorities, including the receiving facility and "significant others", if known. Documentation should be thorough and must accompany the patient. Communication with specialist staff is usually available over the phone and should be sought whenever necessary.

Arrangements for any transits should also be arranged in advance. The transfer should only proceed once all legal and other approvals, including customs and immigration, have been obtained and that the cost of the transfer has been authorised and documented by the relevant parties, including the travel insurance company. Privacy issues may need to be dealt with if there are passengers on the air ambulance, other than the immediate medical team.

Patient Stabilisation

This is a most important step as alluded to earlier. It is important that the patient is as stable as possible before transfer. Performing practical procedures during flight is often difficult and all interventions should be performed before flight if possible (Runcie, 1997).

All tubes that will need to be inserted should be inserted at this point and should be well secured, including intravenous access with the possibility of a central line. The staff should obtain all necessary medical and other documentation for the patient before travel and undertake a "hand-over" from a local medical staff. A checklist can be useful for this process. This process should be performed at the referring hospital, rather than at the airport or on the air ambulance (Roby et al., 1994).

Transfer to Aircraft

It may be necessary to arrange for deployment of a private ambulance to carry the patient to the aircraft. The vehicle should be well maintained and equipped. This vehicle should preferably be fitted out with appropriate monitoring equipment. Preferably, the plane should be fitted out with a slide or similar transfer device to facilitate transfer of the patient to the air ambulance. If using commercial airlines, special lifting equipment may be needed for stretcher-bound patients. Stretchers may also not fit between aisles.

In-Flight Care

If the evaluation of the patient has been thorough and the patient is fit to travel by air, then, other than the need for in-flight monitoring, in most cases, the flight should be uneventful. In those situations where an unstable patient is being transferred, the nature of the aircraft and flight as well as the skills of the medical staff can limit the ability to intervene. In-flight monitoring may include (after Shirley, 2000):

- arterial oxygen;
- ECG;
- arterial pressure;
- CO_2 monitoring and a disconnection alarm may be needed for mechanically ventilated patients; and
- temperature monitoring may also be needed for longer trips, depending on the weather and cabin temperature.

Consideration should also be given to the capability to communicate during flight. If essential, use of air ambulance is preferred, as use of satellite phones and radio is easier than with commercial flights.

Arrival at Destination

Appropriate passport and visa documentation for all crew, medical attendants, relatives and friends, and the patient are required. Liaison with port officials before arrival would be necessary, and a valid passport will be needed and possibly a visa may need to be arranged. It is important that there is a physician authorisation for any regulated medical equipment or drugs appropriate for the destination. Special customs and immigration clearance can be arranged on the tarmac if required in emergency situations.

It will be necessary to arrange for a public ambulance to meet the aircraft and assist in the transfer of the patient. The vehicle should be well maintained and equipped. Depending on the situation, the staff may hand over to the local paramedics at this point or accompany the patient to the hospital before formal transfer to the hospital staff. All appropriate medical documentation should accompany the patient and preferably have been electronically transferred or faxed before departure to the receiving medical team. A written summary of any events during the transfer should also be provided to the receiving medical team (a proforma may be used).

Conclusion

This chapter has highlighted the value to travellers of taking out appropriate travel insurance. Access to the travel insurer's emergency assistance service is a useful aspect of travel insurance coverage. In most cases, the travellers sought simple claiming and policy advice; however, the emergency assistance service also co-ordinates the provision of direct services, such as medical and dental treatment, emergency department, and hospital referral. Aeromedical evacuation is an uncommon but expensive form of emergency assistance requiring extensive logistical, administrative, and clinical planning and represents a significant health and economic risk to the uninsured traveller. In addition to travellers requiring assistance for various general medical problems, dental conditions and cancellation and curtailment, often for medical reasons, are also common precipitants leading to the use of emergency assistance service.

References

ACEM, ANZCA, & JFICM. (2003). Minimum standards for transport of critically ill patients. Policy 03. March 2003. http://www.acem.org.au (accessed 23 February 2005).

Aldis, J.W. (2004). Healthcare abroad. In: J.S. Keystone, P.E. Kozarsky, D.O. Freedman, H.D. Nothdurft, & B.A. Connor (Eds), *Travel medicine* (pp. 461–467). Mosby-Elsevier Science, Edinburgh.

Anonymous. (1996). International travel insurance. *Choice*, (November), 15–22.

Bewes, P.C. (1993). Trauma and accidents: Practical aspects of the prevention and management of trauma associated with travel. *British Medical Bulletin*, *49*, 454–464.

Dewhurst, A.T., & Goldstone, J.C. (2001). Aeromedical repatriation. In: J.N. Zuckerman (Ed.), *Principles and practice of travel medicine* (pp. 297–309). Chichester: Wiley.

Ee Na Lai. (1995). The invisible hand in travel. *Frequent Traveler*, (August–September), 28–30.

Grace, R.F., & Penny, D. (2004). Travel insurance and medical evacuation: View for the far side. *Medical Journal of Australia*, *80*, 32–35.

Graham, H., & Putland, J. (2002). Aeromedical evacuation. In: P.A. Leggat, & J.M. Goldsmid, (Eds), *Primer of travel medicine* (3rd ed., pp. 212–220). Brisbane: ACTM Publications.

Hill, D.R., & Behrens, R.H. (1996). A survey of travel clinics throughout the world. *Journal of Travel Medicine*, *3*, 46–51.

Hochedez, P., Vinsentini, P., Ansart, S., & Caumes, E. (2004). Changes in the pattern of health disorders diagnosed among two cohorts of French travelers to Nepal, 17 years apart. *Journal of Travel Medicine*, *11*, 341–346.

Ivatts, S.L., Plant, A.J., & Condon R.J. (1999). Travel health: Perceptions and practices of travel consultants. *Journal of Travel Medicine*, *6*, 76–80.

Kolars, J.C. (2002). Rules of the road: A consumer's guide for travelers seeking health care in foreign lands. *Journal of Travel Medicine, 9*, 198–203.

Leggat, P.A., Carne, J., & Kedjarune, U. (1999). Travel insurance and health. *Journal of Travel Medicine, 6*, 252–257.

Leggat, P.A., Griffith, R., & Leggat, F.W. (2005). Emergency assistance provided abroad to insured travelers from Australia. *Travel Medicine and Infectious Disease, 3*, 9–17.

Leggat, P.A., Heydon, J.L., & Menon, A. (1998). Safety advice for travelers from New Zealand. *Journal of Travel Medicine, 5*, 61–64.

Leggat, P.A., & Kedjarune, U. (2002). Travel insurance and emergency assistance. In: P.A. Leggat, & J.M. Goldsmid (Eds), *Primer of Travel Medicine* (3rd ed.). Brisbane: ACTM Publication, 62–71.

Leggat, P.A., & Leggat, F.W. (2002). Travel insurance claims made by travelers from Australia. *Journal of Travel Medicine, 9*, 59–65.

Roby, H.P. (1994) Aerial evacuation of sick travelers. *Medical Journal of Australia, 161*, 646–647.

Roby, H.P., Bentley, L., & Munford, B.J. (1994) Considerations in international air medical transport. *Air medical physician handbook* (Vol. VI, pp. 1–20). Salt Lake City: Air Medical Physician Association.

Runcie, C.J. (1997). Principles of safe transport. In: N.S. Morton, M.M. Pollack, & P.G.M. Wallace (Eds), *Stabilisation and transport of the critically ill* (1st ed.). Edinburgh: Churchill Livingstone.

Ryan, C. (1996). Linkages between holiday travel risk and insurance claims: Evidence from New Zealand. *Tourism Management, 17*, 593–601.

Seelan, S.T., & Leggat, P.A. (2003). Health advice given by general practitioners for travelers from Australia. *Travel Medicine and Infectious Disease, 1*, 47–52.

Shirley, P.J. (2000). Transportation of the critically ill and injured patient. *Hospital Medicine, 61*, 406–410.

Somer Kniestedt, R.A., & Steffen, R. (2003) Travel health insurance: Indicator of serious travel health risks. *Journal of Travel Medicine, 10*, 185–189.

Usherwood, V., & Usherwood, T.P. (1989). Survey of general practitioners' advice for travelers to Turkey. *Journal of the Royal College of General Practitioners, 39*, 148–150.

Chapter 4

Tourism and SARS

Annelies Wilder-Smith

Introduction

The Severe Acute Respiratory Syndrome (SARS) was responsible for the first pandemic of the 21st century. Within months after its emergence in Guangdong Province, mainland China, it had affected more than 8000 persons and caused 774 deaths in 26 countries on five continents. SARS illustrated dramatically the potential of air travel and globalization for the dissemination of an emerging infectious disease (Peiris, Yuen, Osterhaus, & Stohr, 2003). The history and epidemiology of the year 2003 SARS outbreak, its impact on travel and tourism and strategies to contain the international spread are discussed in this chapter.

History and Epidemiology

An unusual atypical pneumonia emerged in Foshan, Guangdong Province, mainland China, in November 2002 (Zhong et al., 2003). In February and March 2003, the disease spread to Hong Kong and then to Vietnam, Singapore, Canada and elsewhere. It was a traveller who became the vector that turned a newly emergent local virus into a global outbreak. An American businessman travelling from China via Hong Kong exported the disease to Vietnam on 23 February 2003. The resulting outbreak of this 'mysterious disease' in a Vietnamese hospital led the World Health Organization (WHO) to issue a global alert on 12 March 2003. Besides this business traveller, at least 10 other travellers to Hong Kong had stayed on the same hotel floor as the index case of SARS, a physician from Guangdong who had treated SARS patients. Together, they unmasked the problem in Southern China. From then on, SARS spread to multiple countries, always in the respiratory tract of a traveller. On 15 March, the new disease was named the Severe Acute Respiratory Syndrome, and a preliminary case definition was established. The instantaneous communication and information exchange that supported every aspect of dealing with this epidemic led to a speed of scientific discovery that has set a new standard for disease response.

A new coronavirus was identified as the causative agent and its entire genome sequenced and made publicly accessible within weeks. Coronaviruses are a family of enveloped, single-stranded RNA viruses, with SARS CoV being a new group within this family. Since seroepidemiologic data suggested that SARS CoV had not previously been endemic in humans, it seemed likely that this was a virus of animals that had crossed the species barrier to humans in the recent past. This hypothesis was further supported by anecdotal reports that some patients who had SARS in Guangdong Province in November and December 2002 reported a history of occupational exposure to live, caged animals that are used as exotic "game food", a culinary delicacy in southern China (Peiris et al., 2003). SARS-like coronaviruses were isolated from Himalayan palm civets and from raccoon dogs in one market in Guangdong Province where wild game animals are sold. In addition, persons involved in the wild animal trade in Guangdong had a higher seroprevalence of SARS CoV than unrelated controls (Guan et al., 2003). These findings support (but do not prove) that live game animals may be potential sites of interspecies transmission.

Intense shoe leather epidemiology has clearly proven transmission to be almost exclusively person to person, through direct respiratory droplets, hand contamination, and fomites (Seto et al., 2003). In some instances, fecal–oral modes of transmission may have been implicated, such as in the one well-publicized community outbreak in an apartment complex in Hong Kong. The leading hypothesis is that small virus-containing droplets from the contaminated sewage entered the bathrooms. However, other modes of transmission are the exception, although the SARS virus is hardy enough to last in the environment for several days under experimental conditions.

The spread of SARS was initially exponential, with hospital settings serving as amplifiers. SARS was transmitted primarily, but not exclusively, in healthcare settings, generally 5 or more days after the onset of disease and from patients who were severely ill (Donnelly et al., 2003). Transmission to casual and social contacts is uncommon, but has been described. Asymptomatic or mild infections are rare, and do not appear to contribute to the chain of infection.

Mathematical models have shown that SARS coronavirus, if uncontrolled, would infect the majority of people wherever it was introduced (Dye, 2003). An even more worrying phenomenon is the heterogeneity in transmission. In extreme instances of SARS, the so-called superspreading events occurred where single individuals apparently infected as many as 300 others (Dye, 2003). All the countries with major outbreaks were those that imported SARS before the disease was known and before appropriate infection control measures were instituted. With extraordinary efforts, but without a vaccine or a specific vaccine, these outbreaks were controlled once the mode of transmission was established and measures taken.

The experience of the year 2003 has taught us that although this new coronavirus is sufficiently transmissible to cause a very large epidemic, it is not so contagious as to be uncontrollable with good, basic public health measures. The basic public health measures were early identification and isolation, quarantining of contacts and a strict infection control programme based on personal protective measures, as well as travel restrictions. The WHO declared 5 July 2003 to be the date of the end of the SARS epidemic. Since then, several isolated SARS cases have been reported; none were fatal, and none resulted in a new SARS epidemic.

Travel, Tourism and SARS

SARS and travel are intricately interlinked. Travellers were among those primarily affected in the early stages of the outbreak, and they became vectors of the disease, and finally, travel and tourism themselves became the victims. The outbreak of SARS created international anxiety because of its novelty, its ease of transmission in certain settings, and the speed of its spread through jet travel, combined with extensive media coverage. By 15 March 2003, the WHO had begun to issue an unprecedented series of travel advisories (e.g. advice to postpone non-essential travel to a SARS-affected area). The purpose was to limit the spread of infection by international travel.

Impact of SARS on Tourism

Air travel to areas affected by the advisories decreased dramatically during the epidemic, although the impact of advisories compared with other sources of information to travellers, such as news media, is difficult to assess.

International tourism arrivals fell 1.2% to 694 million in 2003, according to World Tourism Organization (WTO) figures. Growth of the broader travel and tourism economy, which measures visitor spending around the world as well as capital investment, slowed to 2.9% from about 5% in previous years (http://news.bbc.co.uk/2/hi/business/3024015.stm). In East Asia, tourist arrivals dropped by 41% between April 1st and 21st compared to the same period in 2002, with the following Asian destinations suffering in particular — China, Hong Kong, Vietnam and Singapore. Over the months of the outbreak, there was a drop of 12 million arrivals in Asia and the Pacific, constituting a 9% drop compared to the previous year. According to Rick Miller, vice president of research and economics at the World Travel & Tourism Council (WTTC), the impact of SARS on these countries has been four or five times the impact of 11 September in the United States. In the first 5 months of 2003, overseas and domestic tourist arrivals in Beijing dropped by 480,000 and 8.7 million, respectively, generating losses as high as 11 billion Yuan (US$1.3 billion). The hotel occupancy rates in Beijing fell down to 10%. Four lakh foreign tourists cancelled their tours to Vietnam in 2003. The Toronto crisis cost the province of Ontario's leisure industry around Canadian $2 billion in lost revenues and 28,000 jobs, according to Ontario Ministry of Tourism figures.

SARS had major political and economic impact. The FIFA Women's World Cup, originally scheduled for China, was moved to the United States. On 30 March 2003, the International Ice Hockey Federation (IIHF) cancelled the 2003 IIHF Women's World Championship tournament, which was to take place in Beijing. On 1 April, a European airline retrenched a group of employees owing to a drop in travellers. Severe decline in customer numbers occurred for Chinese cuisine restaurants in Guangdong, Hong Kong and Chinatowns in North America; a 90% decrease in some cases. Businesses recovered considerably in some cities after promotion campaigns. Hong Kong merchants withdrew from an international jewelry and timepiece exhibition in Switzerland. Swiss officials enforced a full body check of the 1000 Hong Kong participants, which resulted in diplomatic tensions between the two countries. An estimated several hundred million HK dollars in contracts were said to be lost as a result. Some conferences and conventions scheduled for Toronto were cancelled, and the production of at least one movie was moved out of the city. The findings of the Canadian study, "Economic impact of SARS on tourism in seven selected member economies in the APEC region" can be found at www.apecsec.org.sg. WTTC estimates of the economic impacts of SARS are at www.wttc.org.

Measures at International Borders

Passive and active methods were used to provide information and screen entering and exiting travellers. These methods included signs, videos, public address announcements, distributing health alert notices, administering questionnaires to assess symptoms and possible exposure, visual inspection to detect symptoms and thermal scanning. Combined data from Canada, China, Hong Kong, Taiwan, France, Singapore, Switzerland, Thailand and the US indicate that approximately 31 million travellers entering these countries received health alert notices (Bell, 2004). Of these, approximately 1.8 million were reported as arriving from affected areas; this estimate is likely to be low given the difficulties in tracking travellers and the fact that many airline passengers change planes en route. Inadequate data exist to evaluate the effect of distribution of these notices. Mainland China reported distributing 450,000 notices and detecting four SARS cases that may have been linked to the notices. Thailand printed 1 million notices; as a result 113 cases of illness (respiratory symptoms) were detected; 24 cases were suspected or probable SARS.

Entry Screening

Entry screening was deemed necessary in response to the fact that the outbreaks in Vietnam, Singapore and Canada were due to importation of SARS via international arrivals. Visual inspections, soon replaced by temperature checks (infrared scanning), were introduced at many airports around the world. Data from a worldwide survey indicate that among 72 patients with imported probable or confirmed SARS cases, 30 (42%) had onset of symptoms before or on the same day as their entry into the country and symptoms developed in 42 patients (58%) after entry (Bell, 2004). In Singapore, there were six imported cases of SARS, of which only the first case led to secondary transmission and eventually to the large outbreak there (Wilder-Smith, Paton, & Goh, 2003a). After implementation of screening methods at the Singapore airport, no further importation of patients with SARS occurred. In total, 442,973 passengers were screened between 31 March and 31 May 2003, and of those, 136 were sent for further SARS screening and observation, but none was diagnosed as having SARS (Wilder-Smith et al., 2003a). Of 349,754 passengers arriving in Toronto, 1264 were referred for further screening, none had SARS (St John et al., 2005).

Temperature screening of 13,839,500 travellers entering or leaving Beijing by air, train or automobile identified 5907 patients with fever, of whom 12 had probable SARS (Bell, 2004). None of 275,600 international travellers who underwent temperature screening had SARS. In China–Taiwan, incoming travellers from affected areas were quarantined; probable or suspected SARS was diagnosed in 21 (0.03%) of 80,813. None of these 21 was detected by thermal scanning. Results combined from Canada, China (including the mainland and Hong Kong SAR) and Singapore indicate that no cases of SARS were detected by thermal scanning among more than 35 million international travellers scanned at entry during the SARS epidemic.

The low yield in detecting SARS is most likely due to a combination of factors, such as travel advisories, which resulted in reduced travel to and from SARS-affected areas, implementation of effective pre-departure screening at airports in SARS-hit countries, and a rapid decline in new cases at the time when screening was finally introduced (Wilder-Smith, Paton, & Goh, 2003b). An estimated Canadian $7.55 million was invested in airport screening measures in Canada (St John et al., 2005). SARS has an extremely low prevalence, and the positive predictive value of screening is essentially zero (St John et al., 2005). Screening at entry points is costly, has a low yield and is not sufficient by itself. However, one may argue that entry screening is justified in light of the major economic, social and international impact that even a single imported SARS case may have. However, new imported SARS cases need not lead to major outbreaks if systems are in place to identify and isolate them efficiently. Rather than investing in airport screening measures to detect rare infectious diseases, investments should be used to strengthen screening and infection control capacities at points of entry into the healthcare system (St John et al., 2005).

Barring the entry of travellers from SARS-affected countries is politically incorrect and scientifically unjustifiable. Saudi Arabia was one of the few countries that actually banned the entry of people who had visited or resided in China, Hong Kong, Taiwan, Singapore, Vietnam and Canada; but this measure may have been understandable given that the SARS outbreak coincided with the Hajj (Memish & Wilder-Smith, 2004). This pilgrimage attracts more than 2 million Moslems from all over the world for a month-long event that is characterized by conditions of overcrowding (Wilder-Smith & Memish, 2003). Infectious diseases that require person-to-person transmission are known to be amplified during this pilgrimage (Wilder-Smith & Memish, 2003); and it could have been conceivable that SARS could have rapidly spread under such conditions and subsequently disseminated worldwide via pilgrims returning to their countries of origin.

Exit Screening

After WHO recommended exit screening on 27 March 2003, no additional cases from airline travel were documented from countries with screening. Combined data from China (including Hong Kong SAR and Taiwan) indicate that among 1.8 million people who completed health questionnaires at exit, one probable case of SARS was detected. Combined data from Canada, China and Singapore indicate that no cases of SARS were detected among more than 7 million people who underwent thermal scanning at exit (Bell, 2004). However, exit screening may have helped dissuade ill persons from travelling by air but may have been more successful in dissuading local residents from traveling abroad than in dissuading ill travellers from attempting to return home.

Exit and entry screening may enhance the travellers' perception of security, but an unwanted side-effect may be to discourage travel for those unwilling to risk travel for the chance of being quarantined and business/holiday schedules being disrupted at a heavy cost on the presentation of fairly vague symptoms.

Passenger Contact Tracing

The Infectious Disease Act in various countries legalized quarantining of passengers who had been in contact with a SARS patient (i.e. fellow passenger). Because of the lack of internationally accepted standards for developing and retaining passenger manifests, excessive delays in obtaining the manifests from various airlines occurred (St John et al., 2005). Therefore, in addition to completing health declaration cards about symptoms, the information required also included address and flight seats, to facilitate contact tracing. According to the Canadian experience, traveller contact information forms reduced the time for securing the manifest from weeks to 2 days.

Transmission of SARS on Airplanes

Five commercial international flights were associated with the transmission of SARS from patients with symptomatic SARS to passengers and crew (Bell, 2004). Notification of exposed passengers and studies of transmission risk were greatly hampered by difficulties in identifying and tracing passenger contacts. In the most comprehensive investigation, involving three flights with extensive passenger tracing and laboratory confirmation of index and secondary cases, a wide range of risk was noted. In one extensively investigated flight, in which the secondary attack rate was 18.3%, the risk of infection was increased for persons seated close to the index patient, but most passengers who became infected were seated farther away, even though their individual risk was lower (Olsen et al., 2003; Lim et al., 2004).

On nine flights arriving in Singapore, the incidence of transmission from passengers with SARS was estimated at 1 in 156 persons (Wilder-Smith et al., 2003b). In conclusion, the overall risk to airline passengers is quite low. Aircraft ventilation systems are believed to be highly efficient at keeping the air free of pathogens, which they do by exchanging the air in passenger cabins every 3–4 min and passing the circulated air through high-efficiency particulate-arresting (HEPA) filters designed to filter out all particles larger than 0.3×1 µm (Olsen et al., 2003). The risk of aircraft transmission may have been further reduced, thanks to the implementation of safety measures and exit screening. The WHO reports that no transmission on an airline was identified after 23 March 2003. The Centers for Disease Control (CDC) have published guidelines on how to deal with airline passengers with symptoms suggestive of SARS and how to protect flight crew members and other passengers (www.cdc.gov/ncid/sars/flight_crew_guidelines.htm).

SARS Information for Travellers

Pre-travel advice for travellers should include information about symptoms and mode of transmission of SARS, and advice for early health seeking if any of these symptoms arise. Droplet precautions include frequent hand washing. A thermometer, gloves and hand sanitizers or antimicrobial hand wipes, possibly face masks should be taken along. The routine use of masks is controversial. With the exception of the Amoy Gardens cluster in Hong Kong, SARS transmission in the community from aerosols or in social settings appears to be very rare. However, isolated cases of transmission in taxis or in a large mass gathering (religious meeting in Toronto) have been reported. To minimize the possibility of infection, close contact with large number of people should be avoided, and visiting hospitals with an ongoing SARS epidemic should be strongly discouraged. Travellers are strongly recommended to be vaccinated against influenza and the rationale for this needs to be explained to them: although the influenza vaccine does not protect against SARS, it will minimize episodes of febrile illness and therefore reduce the number of misdiagnoses and lower the overall incidence of diseases that mimic SARS (Wilder-Smith & Ang, 2003). Moreover, it will reduce the risk of a febrile episode, which may be picked up at airport screening and lead to delays at the airport or even quarantining.

Travellers should regularly monitor the WHO website along with the CDC website. These institutions regularly update their websites to reflect changes in what is known about SARS, about outbreaks, and provide the latest travel guidance. Medical evacuation of SARS patients remains problematic and costly. Securing transport and locating a destination willing to accept such patients can be very difficult. Travelers should obtain information about evacuation and insurance policies with regard to SARS before departure.

Persons returning from one of the affected areas should monitor their health for 10 days. No one who has had contact with a known SARS case, whether in a SARS-affected area or elsewhere, should cross an international border for 10 days after the last contact, assuming they remain asymptomatic.

SARS and Travel Medicine

Travel medicine practitioners often constitute the first point of medical contact for ill returning travellers, and nonspecific symptoms such as fever and cough are common in them. In the pre-SARS era from January 1997 to December 2002, an estimated 5% of ill travellers worldwide who sought post-travel care from one of the 25 worldwide GeoSentinel travel clinics had pneumonia (International Society of Tropical Medicine, unpublished data, 2003). These data emphasize two things: first, it is a diagnostic challenge for clinicians trying to diagnose SARS on a background of multiple other causes of common upper respiratory infections; second, travellers are susceptible to infectious respiratory pathogens (Wilder-Smith & Freedman, 2003). This facilitates not only the spread of SARS, but also the spread of influenza and novel respiratory pathogens yet to emerge. Individual clinicians must be vigilant in detecting suspicious circumstances and reporting to appropriate authorities, especially as the heightened awareness of SARS begins to wane.

Outlook

The international spread of disease underscores the need for strong global public health systems, excellent international reporting mechanisms, robust health service infrastructures and expertise that can be mobilized quickly across national boundaries to mirror disease movements. The International Health Regulations (IHR) have not been revised since 1977 (http://www.who.int/csr/ihr/en/). SARS gave a new sense of urgency to the revision, which is (at the time of writing), now close to its completion. Revised IHR should give some teeth to a framework that will facilitate three main public health measures for the containment of SARS and other potential new respiratory pathogens: prevention of subsequent community transmission via early identification and isolation of cases, and provision of technical expertise to allow for the prevention of hospital transmission via effective infection control.

The psychological impacts of SARS, coupled with travel restrictions imposed by various national and international authorities, have diminished international travel in 2003, far beyond the limitations to truly SARS-hit areas. Governments and press, especially in non-SARS-affected areas, have been slow to strike the right balance between timely and frequent risk communication and placing risk in the proper context. Communicating clearly the content and meaning of changing travel alerts, advisories and bulletins from the WHO and national authorities is a primary task. Many countries issue alerts or bulletins to provide accurate information about the status of SARS at a destination, and these need to be distinguished from outright travel advisories against non-essential travel to the area.

The appearance and spread of SARS on a global level also raised vital legal and ethical issues. Containment strategies had three important ethical values: privacy, liberty and the duty to protect the public's health. In the context of travel this became particularly obvious for international travellers who were detained or quarantined at international airports either because of detection on airport screening (febrile illness) or because one of their fellow passengers on the aircraft was found to be a SARS patient. Development of a set of legal and ethical recommendations becomes even more essential when, as was true with SARS and will undoubtedly be the case with future epidemics, scientific uncertainty is pervasive and urgent public health action is required.

Entry screening of travellers through health declarations or thermal scanning at international borders had little documented effect on detecting SARS cases; exit screening appeared slightly more effective. The value of border screening in deterring travel by ill persons and in building public confidence remains unquantified. Interventions to control global epidemics should be based on expert advice from the WHO and national authorities. In the case of SARS, interventions at a country's border should not detract from efforts to identify and isolate infected persons within the country, monitor or quarantine their contacts, and strengthen infection control in healthcare settings. The international public health community under the direction of the WHO will need to determine when and how best to scale up or scale down screening measures at the airports.

More countries should participate in WHO networks of global surveillance in order to identify emerging pathogens of international importance. Travel medicine practitioners who want to do more can consider participation in a global provider-based surveillance network such as GeoSentinel (www.istm.org), which is an initiative of the International Society of Travel Medicine. Such networks allow for the aggregation of clinical experiences via formal data collection for analysis of trends in diagnoses and linked travel histories. In addition, official reporting systems may be constrained or delayed by national or local political considerations that can sometimes be bypassed by the informal and rapid electronic communication engendered by such professional networks.

Our hope is that, if SARS reoccurs, the subsequent outbreak will be smaller and more easily contained if the lessons learnt from the recent epidemic are applied.

References

Bell, D.M. (2004). Public health interventions and SARS spread, 2003. *Emerging Infectious Diseases*, *10*, 1900–1906.

Donnelly, C.A., Ghani, A.C., Leung, G.M., Hedley, A.J., Fraser, C., Riley, S., Abu-Raddad, L.J., Ho, L.M., Thach, T.Q., Chau, P., Chan, K.P., Lam, T.H., Tse, L.Y., Tsang, T., Liu, S.H., Kong, J.H., Lau, E.M., Ferguson, N.M., & Anderson, R.M. (2003). Epidemiological determinants of spread of causal agent of severe acute respiratory syndrome in Hong Kong. *Lancet*, *361*, 1761–1766.

Dye, C.G.N. (2003). Epidemiology. Modeling the SARS epidemic. *Science*, *300*, 1884–1885.

Guan, Y., Zheng, B.J., He, Y.Q., Liu, X.L., Zhuang, Z.X., Cheung, C.L., Luo, S.W., Li, P.H., Zhang, L.J., Guan, Y.J., Butt, K.M., Wong, K.L., Chan, K.W., Lim, W., Shortridge, K.F., Yuen, K.Y., Peiris, J.S., & Poon, L.L. (2003). Isolation and characterization of viruses related to the SARS coronavirus from animals in southern China. *Science*, *302*, 276–278.

Lim, P.L., Kurup, A., Gopalakrishna, G., Chan, K.P., Wong, C.W., Ng, L.C., Se-Thoe, S.Y., Oon, L., Bai, X., Stanton, L.W., Ruan, Y., Miller, L.D., Vega, V.B., James, L., Ooi, P.L., Kai, C.S., Olsen, S.J., Ang, B., & Leo, Y.S. (2004). Laboratory-acquired severe acute respiratory syndrome. *New England Journal of Medicine*, *350*, 1740–1745.

Memish, Z.A., & Wilder-Smith, A. (2004). Global impact of severe acute respiratory syndrome: Measures to prevent importation into Saudi Arabia. *Journal of Travel Medicine*, *11*, 127–129.

Olsen, S. J., Chang, H.L., Cheung, T.Y., Tang, A.F., Fisk, T.L., Ooi, S.P., Kuo, H.W., Jiang, D.D., Chen, K.T., Lando, J., Hsu, K.H., Chen, T.J., & Dowell, S.F. (2003). Transmission of the severe acute respiratory syndrome on aircraft. *New England Journal of Medicine*, *349*, 2416–2422.

Peiris, J.S., Yuen, K.Y., Osterhaus, A.D., & Stohr, K. (2003). The severe acute respiratory syndrome. *New England Journal of Medicine*, *349*, 2431–2441.

Seto, W.H., Tsang, D, Yung, R.W., Ching, T.Y., Ng, T.K., Ho, M., Ho, L.M., Peiris, J.S., & Advisors of Expert SARS group of Hospital Authority. (2003). Effectiveness of precautions against droplets and contact in prevention of nosocomial transmission of severe acute respiratory syndrome (SARS). *Lancet*, *361*, 1519–1520.

St John, R.K., King, A., de Jong, D., Bodie-Collins, M., Squires, S.G., & Tam, T.W. (2005). Border screening for SARS. *Emerging Infectious Diseases*, *11*, 6–10.

Wilder-Smith, A., & Ang, B. (2003). The role of influenza vaccine in healthcare workers in the era of severe acute respiratory syndrome. *Annals of the Academy of Medicine Singapore*, *32*, 573–575.

Wilder-Smith, A., & Freedman, D.O. (2003). Confronting the new challenge in travel medicine: SARS. *Journal of Travel Medicine*, *10*, 257–258.

Wilder-Smith, A., & Memish, Z. (2003). Meningococcal disease and travel. *International Journal of Antimicrobial Agents*, *21*, 102–106.

Wilder-Smith, A., Paton, N.I., & Goh, K.T. (2003a). Experience of severe acute respiratory syndrome in Singapore: Importation of cases, and defense strategies at the airport. *Journal of Travel Medicine*, *10*, 259–262.

Wilder-Smith, A., Paton, N.I., & Goh, K.T. (2003b). Low risk of transmission of severe acute respiratory syndrome on airplanes: The Singapore experience. *Tropical Medicine and International Health*, 8, 1035–1037.

Zhong, N.S., Zheng, B.J., Li, Y.M., Poon, L.L., Xie, Z.H., Chan, K.H., Li, P.H., Tan, S.Y., Chang, Q., Xie, J.P., Liu, X.Q., Xu, J., Li, D.X., Yuen, K.Y., Peiris, J.S., & Guan, Y. (2003). Epidemiology and cause of severe acute respiratory syndrome (SARS) in Guangdong, People's Republic of China, in February, 2003. *Lancet*, *362*, 1353–1358.

Chapter 5

Local Health Impacts of Tourism

Claire Schmierer and Mervyn Jackson

> Memories remind us of our successes and our failures, allow us to day-
> dream and to drift in time. In memories, we can revisit the beautiful places
> of our world, relive experiences which made us what we are today. Every
> now and then on your journey, climb from your transport, walk away, then
> stop, look and listen. Take a deep breath and savour the scents of the land.
> Look near and far. Feel the texture of trees and rock, water and sand against
> your skin (Parish, 1994, p. 158).

Introduction

Skiing, snowboarding and après ski for the winter holiday maker; sun and fun, surf and
sand for the 'beachies'; adventure, clubs, new people, new places, new experiences. These
are all thoughts, which flash through one's mind when, the words: 'travel', 'holiday',
'vacation' and 'tourist' are uttered.

   However, increasingly it seems these were the traditional tourist travel thoughts. Today,
studies have shown a small but impacting effect that accidents/illnesses have on the tourist
experience. Adventure yes, and fun and sun as well, but also an increasing number of
tourist accidents and illnesses, all having a negative effect on the tourist experience. In
order to address these issues and to contribute to safe outcomes for visitors the present
chapter briefly reviews research on the negative effects ill-health has on international travel
and the global impact some diseases have on host communities. The chapter also examines
the role of key stakeholders and the implications for future action to create and maintain a
safer tourist environment.

Global Perspective

While 11 September 2001 will forever be a landmark in terms of travel health, safety and
security, there has been a steady growth of research at national and international levels on
the broad topic of visitor health and safety over the past decade (see Wilks & Page, 2003).

Tourism in Turbulent Times
Copyright © 2006 by Elsevier Ltd.
All rights of reproduction in any form reserved.
ISBN: 0-08-044666-3

Unfortunately, this research continues to be down played, given that selling the dreams associated with tourism products is all about positive images (Wilks & Oldenburg, 1995). However, reality in terms of the ever increasing-impact of public liability has become central to tourist industry decision-making (see Chapter 20).

Previous research demonstrates that preventable accidents are accounting for between 20% and 50% of injury-related deaths for both international visitors and for domestic travellers (Schmierer & Jackson, 2003). Cossar (2003), for example, highlighted the fact that as tourist numbers increase, risks associated with death, infectious diseases and accidents also increase. The profile of vulnerable travellers includes: tourists on packaged holidays; inexperienced tourists; travellers to countries with tropical climates; summer travellers; and tourists who are younger and male (Cossar, 2003). Moreover, archival research at national and state level clearly illustrates tourists as both inpatients and outpatients are statistically over-represented in Australia's major metropolitan hospital system (Wilks & Coory, 2002; Walker et al., 1995; Wilks, Walker, Wood, Nicol, & Oldenburg, 1995a).

A previous review by Wilks and Grenfell (1997) highlighted the number of medical problems versus the number of accidents or injuries sustained by tourists in Australia. Only a sample of the studies is summarized here. Pearce (1981) analysed daily vacation diaries ($n = 96$) of tourists visiting either one of the two tropical islands. It was found that around 30% of the tourists reported medical (or viral) symptoms (colds, nausea, upset stomach, diarrhoea) and over 50% recorded an injury (or environmental shock), such as stings, bites and sunburn.

Short, May, and Hogan (1991) surveyed 689 surf rescue victims over a three-year period and found that 90.9% came from overseas and 42% could not swim. They concluded that these overseas visitors generally lacked knowledge of Australian surf conditions. More recent investigations of tourists and beach safety (see Chapter 15) show that unfamiliarity with surf conditions continues to be a major injury prevention challenge for surf lifesavers.

Segan (1994) gave post-holiday questionnaires to 202 Melbourne tourists who had travelled for a winter holiday to tropical Queensland. Thirty six per cent of the tourists reported being sunburnt. Jackson, White, and Schmierer (1996) analysed 93 tourist health case studies and found that tourist behaviours contributed to 39% of health problems (e.g., swam in tropical water in summer and was stung by a box jelly fish); another 39% arose because of a failure to use preventive health measures (e.g., traveller's diarrhoea due to the consumption of unhygienic food); and only 22% of tourist health problems were medical and not considered preventable (e.g., heart attack). In a recent survey of tourists to Magnetic Island off the north Queensland coast, only 34% of international tourists knew what the potentially deadly 'Irukandji' jelly fish was, compared to 70% of domestic tourists from outside of north Queensland and 88% of north Queensland residents (Leggat, Harrison, Fenner, Durrheim, & Swinbourne, 2005).

Salib and Brinacombe (1994) studied 225 serious incidents over 18 months at Uluru (Ayers Rock). They found 40 of the incidents were serious/life-threatening; six of the incidents were fatal, and that 41.6% were considered accidents (e.g., falls), and thus preventable. Wilks et al. (1995a) analysed 1183 visits to the tropical island resort nursing clinics and found 62% were for medical conditions (respiratory, digestive, skin, eye disorders, genitourinary) and 38% were related to injuries (lacerations, bites, stings, sprains, fractures).

White, Jackson, and Grenfell (1995) studied 150 overseas tourists presenting at general practitioner surgeries (in Melbourne, rural Victoria, coastal Queensland) and concluded that the presenting conditions were those most commonly seen in general practice. General Practitioners (GPs) reported at least one-third of these patient visits could have been avoided by pre-travel preventative care.

Finally, Nicol, Wilks, and Wood (1996) reviewed overseas and interstate tourists who were admitted to one of the seven Queensland hospitals. They reported that 37.6% of 695 overseas tourists and 15.4% of 3479 interstate tourists were admitted due to some type of injury arising from accidents. An overall summary of tourism health research in Australia can therefore only conclude that a reasonably high percentage of the ill-health reported, and a very high percentage of the injuries treated, could have been avoided. Visitors could and should have a safe tourist experience.

Following the recommendation from Wilks and Grenfell (1997) that Australia needs to gather accurate information on the types of health and safety problems experienced by tourists outside the mainstream metropolitan hospitals, studies were undertaken to address tourist ill-health in another type of health facility (a rural multi-purpose facility in a tourism-designated area). The study reported here extends the research area by comparing tourist profiles with host community profiles and focusing on the emergency department as well as admission records. Future planned research will include examining ways of informing relevant stakeholders of these findings. Opening a dialogue is vital in order to use the information for the tourism industry and tourism planners, local government and other public health service providers. It is important that they are all working towards maintaining safe experiences for visitors.

Local Community

The setting for this study is a small, rural, remote, coastal resort town on the Great Ocean Road in Victoria, Australia. This is the type of 'Locale' where many sun seekers and fun lovers plan to spend their holidays. The reported population of this town is approximately 3000 permanent residents. Like many tourist towns in Australia the reported population depends on which source of statistics is used. Town facilities include a 24-h police presence, a hospital as part of a Multi-purpose Service (MPS); fire brigade, ambulance service; vibrant late evening meals/nightlife (including two hotels). This is well beyond the services and infrastructure of comparable rural, remote non-tourist towns.

The population expands to an estimated 20,000 people during the peak summer tourist season. During the holidays and at weekends the local children amuse themselves by counting the number of tourist buses entering the town. Some of the tourists stay for a few hours, others overnight and yet others two or three days or weeks. This means the number of visitors to the town will be under-reported, with the number of actual visitors being much higher than is reported in the summer months. The town is located on a major tourist route, and although it attracts a sizeable international and interstate visitor population, its main tourist population visits from within the state.

Local Health Services

Although the town has a small population, it has an extensive health service, which is classified by the Victorian State Trauma Committee as an URGENT Care Centre. This is due to it being classed as rural and remote. This means the majority of serious health issues (trauma, accidents and injuries) are treated and stabilized at the local health service and not bypassed for a service provider in a larger populated centre.

This health service is known as a MPS but often referred to as the 'hospital'. There are also two medical practices which attend to some of the minor health issues, as do providers of other alternative/complimentary medicine, which include Reflexology, Massage, Physiotherapy, Chiropractic, Dentistry and Traditional Chinese Medicine. Some people, including tourists, prefer non-traditional remedies for illnesses and accidents, which may result in the actual numbers of tourist-related injuries/illnesses being under-reported.

The MPS provides Accident and Emergency (A&E) services to the local community and also to tourists/travellers. Information gathered from client visits to the A&E department included: date of visit; client's date of birth; permanent home postcode if Australian, or Country if from overseas; details of the presenting problem, illness/accident; location where the 'event' occurred; client care required, treatment in A&E, not admitted/admitted to the acute care ward, not transferred/transferred to a larger health service (Melbourne/Geelong); and mode of transfer: private car, road ambulance or helicopter.

The Study

Data were gathered covering visits to the A&E department during summer and winter months, and school holiday and non-school holiday times. Table 5.1 presents details of the sample ($N = 1402$), which consisted of complete data from 821 male and 581 female clients who visited the MPS over 8 months of a two-year time period.

The client data set consisted of 59% males and 41% females. The average age of the sample was 38.55 years, with an age range from less than one year to 102 years of age. The host community was defined as clients having a permanent address with either the local postcode or the adjoining postcode. This group made up 61% of the total client population. Intrastate tourists had a permanent address with a Victorian postcode (34%), interstate tourists had an Australian postcode (other than Victorian) as a permanent address (4%) and international tourists gave an overseas address as their permanent address (2%). The small numbers of interstate and overseas tourists visiting this MPS threatened the validity of most tests of statistical significance. To ensure adequate numbers in each group, all tourist data were collapsed and analysed in one group. This tourist group numbered 547 clients and constituted 39% of the total client group.

Table 5.2 shows the number of client visits by season and status of holiday. It should be noted that more clients visit A&E in the summer months and even more during the holiday season (both in summer and winter). However, further analysis indicates that the profile is different from the host community when compared to tourists. Table 5.3 presents host and tourist information for the same four quasi-experimental groups.

Table 5.1: Experimental design.

Month/Years	Experimental group	Number of cases (N)
January/2001–2002	Summer holidays	481
February/2001–2002	Summer non-holidays	283
June/2001–2002	Winter holidays	376
July/2001–2002	Winter non-holidays	262
Total		1402

Table 5.2: Client visits presented for season by holiday status.

	Holidays	Non-holidays	Total
Summer	481	283	764
Winter	376	262	638
Total	857	545	1402

Table 5.3: Hosts and tourist profiles presented for season by holiday status.

	Host	Tourist	Total
Summer holiday	188	293	481
Summer non-holiday	184	99	283
Winter holiday	284	92	376
Winter non-holiday	199	63	262
Total	855	547	1402

A χ^2 test indicated a statistically significant difference between tourists and the host community ($\chi^2 = 155.1$, df $= 3$, $p < 0.05$). The number of tourists visiting A&E is significantly greater in summer holidays and significantly less in winter (both in holiday and non-holiday periods). The number of locals visiting A&E is less in summer and more in winter. It should be noted that the winter holiday period is also the first month of winter in Victoria and is associated with higher levels of clients presenting with colds and influenza. Also of note is the finding that the rate of accidents remained constant across the four time periods surveyed.

While the clients from the host community made up the most severe category of illness (see Table 5.4), the overall results were not statistically significant ($\chi^2 = 7.2$, df $= 3$, $p = 0.06$ NS).

A χ^2 test indicated that there was an overall statistically significant difference in the cell frequencies of Table 5.5 ($\chi^2 = 73.3$, df $= 1$, $p < 0.05$). The analysis indicated that tourists are more likely to present at A&E as a result of injuries occurring through accidents, while members of the host community are more likely to attend A&E for illness.

Table 5.6 presents data on the timing of the A&E visit. A χ^2 analysis indicated an overall statistical significant difference for hosts ($\chi^2 = 5.67$, df $= 3$, $p < 0.05$). Hosts are more likely to become ill in the winter and less likely to become ill in the summer. The rate of accidents is constant across the four time periods. Similarly, a χ^2 analysis indicates a statistically significant deviation from chance for the tourist data ($\chi^2 = 5.65$, df $= 3$, $p < 0.05$). Tourists are more likely to present at A&E as a result of an accident in the summer (and more specifically, more likely to present during the summer holiday).

Two further analyses were completed: age and admissions/transfers. Hosts were significantly ($t = 7.6$, df $= 1400$, $p < 0.05$) older than tourists. The average age of the host community is 42.5 years with 18.1% of the population over 65 years of age. This coastal

Table 5.4: The numbers and percentages of hosts and tourists by illness categories.

Illness category*	Host (%)	Tourist (%)	Number (%)
5	613 (71.7)	385 (70.3)	998 (71.2)
4	178 (20.8)	104 (19.0)	282 (20.1)
3	48 (5.6)	50 (9.1)	98 (7.0)
2	13 (1.5)	7 (1.3)	20 (1.4)
1	3 (0.4)	1 (0.2)	4 (0.1)
Total	855 (100)	547 (100)	1402 (100)

*International Triage Categories, the lower the number the more severe the presenting problem.

Table 5.5: Number of hosts and tourists by presenting problem.

	Hosts (%)	Tourists (%)	Total (%)
Illness	639 (75)	288 (53)	927 (68)
Accidents	216 (25)	259 (47)	475 (32)
Total	855 (100)	547 (100)	1402 (100)

Table 5.6: Host and tourist numbers for type of presenting problem by time of year.

		Summer holiday	Summer non-holiday	Winter holiday	Winter non-holiday	Total
Host	Illness	130	141	222	146	639
	Accident	58	43	62	53	216
	Total	188	184	284	199	855
Tourist	Illness	145	57	56	30	288
	Accident	140	43	36	33	259
	Total	285	100	92	63	540

town includes a local population that is ageing and also includes a high percentage of retirees. The average age of the tourist population is 31.2 years with 7.9% of the population over 65 years. This supports previous findings that age is positively related to illness and negatively related to accidents (Cossar, 2003).

Only 74 or 5.3% of the A&E clients were admitted to the MPS or transferred to a larger hospital. There was no significant difference between hosts and tourists in terms of admissions and transfers.

Table 5.7 shows that the predominant injuries sustained by tourists are lacerations, falls and animal/insect bites/stings. Table 5.8 identifies the major locations for tourist accidents. The foreshore area (predominantly in summer) accounts for over 50% of accidents. This includes beach (21.4%), rocks (14.7%), sea (9.5%), pier (6.7%) and play equipment (4.9%). The other major category includes living/dining areas.

Table 5.7: Type of accident reported by tourists.

Type of accident	Number (%)
Lacerations	102 (35.8)
Falls	55 (19.3)
Animal/insect bites/stings	39 (13.7)
Burns (including sunburn)	29 (10.2)
Poisonings (including food)	18 (6.3)
Emergency contraception	12 (4.2)
Allergic reactions	5 (1.7)
Other	25 (8.8)
Total	285 (100)

Table 5.8: Physical site of tourist accidents.

Location	Number (%)
Beach	61 (21.4)
Private residence	49 (17.2)
Rocks	42 (14.7)
Traffic accident	38 (13.3)
Sea (surfboards, boating)	27 (9.5)
Pier (including fishing)	19 (6.7)
Retail accommodation	17 (6.0)
Play (play equipment, sport)	14 (4.9)
Hotel/restaurants	11 (3.9)
Other	7 (2.4)
Total	285 (100)

Summary of the Study Findings

The 'snapshot' of health services from this study of one community showed more visits to the A&E during holiday months, more visits during summer and a statistically greater number of tourists visiting A&E during summer holidays (compared to all other times). While the host community visits to A&E were statistically more likely to be associated with illness, tourists were more likely to visit A&E as a result of injuries occurring as a consequence of (preventable) accidents. The rates of accident presentations throughout the year remained constant for members of the host community, but there was a significant increase in absolute numbers of accidents for tourists during the summer holidays. Finally, host versus tourist clients varied in terms of age. Host community members who visited A&E tended to be older and were more prone to illness. Tourist A&E clients, however, were statistically younger and more likely to present with injuries attributable to preventable accidents.

The predominant injuries sustained by tourists in this study were lacerations, falls, animal/insect bites/stings, burns (including sunburn) and poisonings (including food). Interestingly, this is essentially the same profile as that reported by Wilks and Coory (2002) for tourist inpatient admissions in Queensland hospitals.

The physical location of more than 50% of these tourist accidents was the foreshore area (especially in summer) and included; beach, rocks, sea, pier (especially associated with fishing) and play equipment. Again these findings parallel to those of other coastal community injury studies (for example, Grenfell & Ross, 1992) suggesting that some core preventative actions might be available to address common injury concerns. The other major site for sustaining injuries was living/dining areas and included private residences (17.2%) and retail accommodation (9.9%). Traffic accidents accounted for 13.3% of tourism-related accidents.

Tourist Ill-Health: The Local Community

The benefits tourism brings to the host community are well documented. These include: income generation, employment, infrastructure development and development and maintenance of social and community services (see Walker & Page, 2003). Tourism business maintains the viability of small tourist towns such as the one depicted in this chapter.

Not so well documented are the 'side effects' or 'dis-benefits' tourist visitations have on the host community. These have their greatest impact if the tourist numbers radically increase before suitable infrastructure is put in place (Rodriguez-Garcia, 2001). It is important that the following are in place before the 'tourist invasion' occurs: adequate water supply in terms of both quality and quantity, management of sewerage, solid waste, road traffic, pedestrian traffic, supplies of consumables; services: police, healthcare, childcare, respite for the aged and emergency services.

Providing these services for tourists places a financial burden on the local community, health service, state funding body (e.g., Department of Health) and finally the tax-payer. There is a financial burden associated with all tourists, whether they are health tourists (that is, people from overseas who come for the specific reason of taking advantage of free health services) or travellers who just happen to get sick or have an accident (Evening Standard, 2003).

Over the years various studies have provided some limited insights into the financial costs involved. For example, Cossar (2003) reports that the average cost per travel related inpatient admitted to infectious disease wards in Glasgow during 1998/99 was £2136. This figure was then extrapolated to calculate a theoretical total for United Kingdom hospitalization costs from travel-related admissions. This totalled £81.95 million in 1998/99. Cossar (2003) suggests that there are clear limitations with this calculated figure. Nevertheless, it does show that the tourist health burden can be substantial.

In Australia, health authorities treat both insured and uninsured visitors, with the public system bearing the financial burden associated with tourist ill-health (Walker et al., 1995). Until a system is developed to enable the discreet identification of tourists receiving treatment, we may never be able to accurately assess the cost of tourist health services. Currently, Australian health services are well regarded by international travellers. They are relatively inexpensive even if there is a direct charge; they have much shorter waiting times than at home, and the service received in small coastal towns like the one in this study are very personalized. As the MPS is classified by the Health Department as 'Rural and Remote', it is well resourced with modern equipment and well-trained professional nursing staff. As demonstrated in this study, the staffs are in a position to gather valuable information and data to inform their practice and resource needs.

Disseminating the Information

This information should inform the host population and visitors about potential dangers while travelling, and being a 'tourist'. Recent analyses have indicated that people in the tourist role are at potentially greater risk than if they were engaging in other activities. At the general level, as 'tourists' move further away from their geographical base, they are statistically more likely to be at risk in terms of health and safety (Cohen, 1987; Messner & Blau, 1987). Cohen (1987) described the cause of this increased risk as a movement away from the 'environmental bubble'. This 'bubble' involved psycho-socio-cultural factors created by the individual to protect him/her. There are many examples of this, such as the person who generally does not ride a motorbike, but on a trip to Bali the tourist hires the motorbike, and when riding the bike does not wear a bike helmet: "it's too hot", "the local law does not require it", "it's great to have the wind blowing through my hair".

Not only are the research findings important to inform tourists, but also for travel agents (to provide accurate information so that prospective tourists can make informed decisions); the host community (to protect tourists and provide adequate health services during peak periods); the local council (to ensure the environment is safe); and State and Federal Health Departments (to provide effective health policy and infrastructure). The overall goal is to offer and provide safe and memorable tourist experiences.

Tourist Attributes

In order to achieve the goal of a positive, injury or illness-free tourist experience, the tourist needs to take responsibility for their travel and be accountable for actions taken related to the tourist experience. This does not always happen. For example, Schmierer and Jackson (1995) found that most tourists made misattributions regarding health problems arising from tourist activities. Unfortunately, tourists were not attributing the causes of pre-ventable ill-health during travel to internal/personal factors, but rather were attributing the causes to external factors (the host community, tourist industry, bad luck, fate).

Research on Australians travelling overseas has shown the negative impact ill-health has on the tourist experience, even though in most instances the tourist illness has been reported as being mild and slightly self-limiting. Grayson and McNeil (1988), and Jackson, White, and Schmierer (1993) reported that 21% of a sample of Melbourne tourists indicated that ill-health was the primary reason for their worst tourist experience.

Who Should Take Responsibility for Tourist Health?

While ultimately tourists themselves are responsible for their own health (the biopsy-chosocial view — Sarafino, 1998), local communities (including the local health facility), the tourist industry and governments, can play a role in accident prevention. A national campaign regarding preventable travel health problems would make this public health issue more visible and give key stakeholders in the industry the impetus to act in this area. At the local level, health facilities can provide sound data and advice to the community and local government regarding the types of accidents and their location. Such information allows the local community to 'design out' accidents when providing new facilities and allows warnings via signage on natural physical attractions that are associated with higher rates of injuries/accidents.

The potential health risks to the tourists when travelling are well documented, and there are many ways to reduce and in some cases eliminate the risks (for example, vacci-nation prior to travel). To be able to achieve this, there needs to be a concerted effort by the host community, local authorities and potential tourists (Organization of American States, 1997).

Tourist Ill-Health: The Emerging Public Health Problem

Tourism researchers are now proposing 'responsible tourism' (see Harrison & Husbands, 1996). Responsible tourism represents tourist planning and development in such a way that it benefits the maximum number of stakeholders and minimizes or spreads the impact across those who will be affected. In terms of health, Rodriguez-Garcia (2001, p. 96) poses some fundamental questions that need to be answered. These include: the impact of tourist travel on national and local public health sectors; the role of the public health sector in pro-tecting the health of domestic and international tourists; the interaction between tourists and the local health facility; and the responsibilities of the traveller and the tourist indus-try. Australian and international tourism health researchers have now collected sufficient information to begin implementing responsible tourism strategies in the area of health. As noted by Jackson et al. (1993), if a tourist has a poor health experience, the whole tourism venture is regarded as unsatisfactory. It is therefore important for all stakeholders to work together to ensure that the demands on health services by tourists can be met.

Conclusions

To ensure that all stakeholders are optimally involved in the delivery of timely and adequate tourist health services, the following are recommended:

First, a software package should be provided to all GPs, alternative therapists and A&E departments, which will enable immediate identification and capture of:

(1) Accident/illness types, which will help to identify the greatest risk factors for tourists visiting specific tourist destinations.
(2) The tourist/host postcode, which provides data on numbers of host versus tourists using the health service. Site/locality of the incident, as knowing the recurring locations of accidents can provide information for the development of timely promotional material, to be released prior to major holiday periods. This could be in the form of 'Handy Holiday Hints', or 'Reduce the Holiday Risk' and should be location, activity and climate specific. This information is important to inform local tourist planners, councils and other Government and planning agencies about the high-risk holiday sites.
(3) The treatment required, including whether the tourist/local required transport or admission. This information informs the government and health service providers of the costs associated with the episode of care in treating the tourist. Resources can then be allocated to the service provider to ensure that the services required can be provided (helicopter transport, paramedics and nursing staff, etc.) during peak seasons.
(4) The resources required, including A&E equipment for monitoring and treatment, staff training to ensure competence, bandages and other such consumables. Increased funding, adequate storage and sterilization of equipment and stock, and effective resources management skills will also be required.

Second, dialogue should be established between all stakeholders to ensure the optimal tourist experience for visitors, and optimal service provision from the health industry. This can be achieved by being aware of each other's roles and responsibilities. It may be better served by more formal communication and liaison.

> Home and host authorities, tourism promoters and health professionals all have important responsibilities in making tourism what it is supposed to be: a life-enriching experience with quality time spent in a quality environment recovering health and building (happy) memories forever. It must be health-oriented and diseases should be kept as far as possible from it (Organization of American States, 1997, p. 6).

The goals in providing tourists with up-to-date travel information, preparation for travel and health and safety issues related to the destination, are to maximize the safety of the tourist and minimize the risks.

References

Cohen, E. (1987). The tourist as victim and protégé of law enforcing agencies. *Leisure Studies, 6*, 181–198.

Cossar, J. (2003). Travelers' health: An epidemiological overview. In: J. Wilks, & S.J. Page (Eds), *Managing tourist health and safety in the new millennium* (pp. 19–33). Oxford: Pergamon.

Evening Standard. (2003). *Revealed: Cost of NHS tourism*, Evening Standard, 11 August, p. 5.

Grayson, M., & McNeil, J. (1988). Preventive health advice for Australian travelers to Bali. *Medical Journal of Australia, 149*, 462–466.

Grenfell, R.D., & Ross, K.N. (1992). How dangerous is that visit to the beach? A pilot study of beach injuries. *Australian Family Physician, 21*, 1145–1148.

Harrison, L., & Husbands, W. (Eds). (1996). *Practicing responsible tourism*. New York: Wiley.

Jackson, M., White, G., & Schmierer, C. (1993). The return from Xanadu. In: T. Veal, & B. Weiler (Eds), *Leisure and tourism research in Australia and New Zealand* (pp. 79–93). Sydney: ANZALS.

Jackson, M., White, G., & Schmierer, C. (1996). Tourism experiences within an attributional framework. *Annals of Tourism Research, 23*, 798–810.

Leggat, P.A., Harrison, S.L., Fenner, P.J., Durrheim, D.N., & Swinbourne, A.L. (2005). Health advice obtained by tourists traveling to Magnetic Island: A risk area for 'Irukandji' jellyfish in North Queensland, Australia. *Travel Medicine and International Health, 3*, 27–31.

Messner, S., & Blau, J. (1987). Routine leisure activities and rates of crime: A macro-level analysis. *Social Forces, 65*, 1035–1052.

Nicol, J., Wilks, J., & Wood, M. (1996). Tourists as inpatients in Queensland regional hospitals. *Australian Health Review, 19*(4), 55–72.

Organization of American States. (1997). *Proceedings of the XVII Inter-American Travel Congress*, 7–11 April, San Jose, Costa Rica: Author.

Parish, S. (1994). *Discover Australia*. Brisbane: Steve Parish Publishing.

Pearce, P. (1981). Environmental shock: A study of tourist reactions on two tropical islands. *Journal of Applied Social Psychology, 11*, 268–280.

Rodriguez-Garcia, R. (2001). The health-development link: Travel as a public health issue. *Journal of Community Health, 26*, 93–112.

Salib, M., & Brinacombe, J. (1994). A survey of emergency medical care at Uluru (Ayers Rock). *Medical Journal of Australia, 161*, 693–694.

Sarafino, E. (1998). *Health psychology: Biopsychosocial interactions* (3rd ed.). New York: Wiley.

Schmierer, C., & Jackson, M. (1995). Travel and health problems: Whom does the tourist blame? In: R. Shaw (Ed.), *Proceedings of the national tourism and hospitality conference* (pp. 266–277). Melbourne: CAUTHE.

Schmierer, C., & Jackson, M. (2003). Tourist travel as a public health issue: A local perspective. In: R. Braithwaite, & R. Braithwaite (Eds), *Riding the wave of tourism and hospitality research. Proceedings of the CAUTHE conference, Coffs Harbour.* CD-ROM. Southern Cross University, Lismore.

Segan, C. (1994). *Issues surrounding the development and dissemination of a SunSmart travel brochure*. Melbourne: Centre for Behavioural Research in Cancer.

Short, A., May, A., & Hogan, C.L. (1991). *A three year study in the circumstances behind surf based rescues*. NSW beach safety programme report, 99-1. Coastal Studies Unit, University of Sydney, Sydney.

Walker, L., & Page, S.J. (2003). Risks, rights and responsibilities in tourist well-being: Who should manage visitor well-being at the destination? In: J. Wilks, & S.J. Page (Eds), *Managing tourist health and safety in the new millennium* (pp. 215–235). Oxford: Pergamon .

Walker, S., Wilks, J., Ring, I., Nicol, J., Oldenburg, B., & Mutzelburg, C. (1995). Use of Queensland hospital services by interstate and overseas visitors. *Health Information Management, 25*(1), 12–15.

White, G., Jackson, M., & Grenfell, R. (1995). International inbound tourists: Types of travel health problems and issues. Paper presented at the 27th annual conference of Public Health Association of Australia, Cairns, 24–27 September.

Wilks, J., & Coory, M. (2002). Overseas visitor injuries in Queensland hospitals: 1996–2000. *Journal of Tourism Studies, 13*, 2–8.

Wilks, J., & Grenfell, R. (1997). Travel and health research in Australia. *Journal of Travel Medicine, 4*, 83–89.

Wilks, J., & Oldenburg, B. (1995). Tourist health: The silent factor in customer service. *Australian Journal of Hospitality Management, 2*, 13–23.

Wilks, J., & Page, S. (Eds). (2003). *Managing tourist health and safety in the new millennium*. Oxford: Pergamon.

Wilks, J., Walker, S., Wood, M., Nicol, J., & Oldenburg, B. (1995a). Remote nursing services at island tourist resorts. *Australian Journal of Rural Health, 3*, 179–185.

Wilks, J., Walker, S., Wood, M., Nicol, J., & Oldenburg, B. (1995b). Tourist health services at island tourist resorts. *Australian Health Review, 18*, 45–62.

PART 2

SAFETY AND SECURITY

Chapter 6

Terrorism and Tourism

Peter E. Tarlow

Introduction

The British Journal, *The Economist*, in 1999 reported that Yassir Arafat stated: "I formally and absolutely renounce all forms of tourism" (sic). We may assume that Arafat meant "terrorism" rather than "tourism" yet there may be more here than even he realized. Arafat, perhaps unintentionally, by his Freudian slip of the tongue connected what tourism scholars and practitioners have long known. Tourism and terrorism are linked in many more ways than about which anyone in the industry chooses to speak.

Arafat's "career" serves tourism scholars as an academic entrance into a discussion concerning the impact of terrorism on tourism. The linkage between tourism and terrorism is not accidental. Indeed, a review of the multiple acts of terrorism against many of tourism component industries during the last decades challenges both tourism scholars and practitioners to take the time to try to understand the complicated "pas à morte" that has occurred during the last 4 decades.

Terrorism is such a broad subject that no one chapter can do it justice. In fact, there is no one general consensus as to who is a terrorist or what the definition of terrorism is. This chapter recognizes these difficulties and will define terrorism not by specific verbiage but rather operationally. The chapter then will look at several operational aspects of terrorism. One way this operational definition will be developed is by distinguishing the differences between terrorism and crime. The chapter will then advance to specific parts of the tourism industry that have suffered from terrorism and finally present concepts concerning how the tourism industry can confront the terrorism risk.

Terrorism is often confused with criminal behavior. In the world of tourism, however, terrorism and crime are very different social ailments. Criminals, especially those who are businesses-people rather than criminals of passion, seek a parasitic relationship with tourism. Indeed, it may be stated that tourism criminals, be they freelancers or part of an organized group, need the tourism industry to succeed in order for them to be successful. Terrorists, on the other hand, seek to destroy nations (or governments) often through random deaths that lead to an economic collapse. Terrorists' goals are different in that they seek the destruction of a tourism industry rather than the personal/commercial benefits from a specific action. Tourism crime then is a business, while tourism terrorism is ideologically motivated. Former French President Charles De Gaul well understood "that terrorism was a religion of murderers plain and simple" (Loyola, 2004, p. 29). The goals of terrorism are destruction rather than construction. Terrorists do not seek peaceful ends to conflicts. Loyola (2004, p. 28) expresses this idea in his analysis of the Arafat era, noting that "violence was the only permissible strategy of liberation." Table 6.1 summarizes the differences between these two tourism security issues.

One of the major mistakes that tourism officials make is the belief that terrorism against the tourism industry is a recent phenomenon. In reality, terrorism has a multi-millennia recorded history, especially in the Middle East. In this modern age of terrorism, however, there has been an intensification of the use of terrorism as a weapon against civilian centers, with tourism being continually attacked. These attacks have been against all aspects of the industry: from cruise ships to hotels, from buses to airplanes. The Israeli scholar Rafael Raymond Bar-On has chronicled terrorism attacks against the tourism industry for over 30 years. His list shows that terrorism attacks against the tourism industry have taken place throughout the world (Bar-On, 2001). Among, but not including all, the nations that have suffered from terrorism attacks during the last 30 plus years are:

- Columbia
- Cuba
- Egypt
- France
- Germany
- India
- Indonesia
- Israel
- Italy
- Jordan
- Kenya
- Mexico
- Morocco
- Nepal
- Peru
- Russia
- Saudi Arabia
- Spain
- Sri Lanka
- Switzerland
- The Philippines
- The United Kingdom
- The United States
- Turkey

Table 6.1: Some terrorism basics for tourism professionals.

	Crime	**Terrorism**
Goal	Usually economic or social gain	To gain publicity and sometimes sympathy for a cause.
Usual type of victim	Person may be known to the perpetrator or selected because he/she may yield economic gain	Killing is a random act and appears to be more in line with a stochastic model. Numbers may or may not be important
Defenses in use	Often reactive, reports taken	Some pro-active devices such as radar detectors
Political ideology	Usually none	Robin Hood model
Publicity	Usually local and rarely makes the international news	Almost always is broadcast around the world
Most common forms in tourism industry are:	Crimes of distraction	Domestic terrorism
	Robbery	International terrorism
	Sexual assault	Bombings Potential for bio-chemical warfare
Statistical accuracy	Often very low, in many cases the travel and tourism industry does everything possible to hide the information	Almost impossible to hide. Numbers are reported with great accuracy and repeated often
Length of negative effects on the local tourism industry	In most cases, it is short term	In most cases, it is long term unless replaced by new positive image
Recovery strategies	New marketing plans, assumes short-term memory of traveling public.	Showing compassion Need to admit the situation and demonstrate control
	Probability ideals: "Odds are it will not happen to you."	Higher levels of observed security
	Hide information as best as one can	Highly trained (in tourism, terrorism, and customer service) security personnel

Terrorism has not targeted one specific sector within the tourism industry, though attacks on airlines have gained the greatest amount of publicity. Terrorist attacks can occur in such diverse places/means of transportation as:

- Airlines
- Buses
- Casinos
- Cruise Ships
- Hotels and places of lodging
- Major events, sporting or recreation areas
- National parks
- Places where people congregate
- Restaurants and outdoor cafes
- Wherever people are carefree and happy.

An Overview of Terrorism and Tourism

Terrorism is a form of war. Its goal is to destroy economies through random death and panic. Terrorism rarely occurs because of poverty or even as a result of social frustration. Were poverty and social frustration the causes of terrorism then it would occur wherever these social ills are located. This reality is not the case. There are many poor countries in the world in which there is no terrorism and there are a number of wealthy nations where terrorism has taken root. Even social frustration is not a basis for terrorism. For example, there was no more a frustrated group of people than Europe's Jewish population during the Nazi occupation of the 1940s. While the Jewish population did conduct military operations against the Nazis, there is no recorded incident of innocent German civilians being attacked by frustrated Jewish partisan fighters. In a like manner, most of the world's poorest countries do suffer from tourism crime, but not from acts of terrorism against the local tourism industry. Indeed, the first common mistake often made by the media is that terrorism is a result of poverty, political frustrations, and/or lack of educational opportunities. What then causes acts of terrorism and especially acts of terrorism against the tourism industry in particular? While we may never be able to explain all of the motivations that fuel terrorism, the following is a theoretical design that may help to explain this occurrence.

To begin to understand tourism's relationship with terrorism, the reader must first make a detour into some of the key elements of terrorism. Terrorism, as we know it, has existed since the 16th century. Terrorism, as distinct from crime, "celebrates" violence and terrorists often manifest what may be called a violence addiction. Terrorism also has several unique social components. These components are present in both domestic and international terrorism and are typical of what we may technically call "medieval societies."[1] As a technical term, a medieval society can exist at any point in history. These societies manifest the following sociological characteristics:

---

[1]The terms "medieval" and "modern" are used as technical terms and do not refer to their historical usage.

- The debasement of women. Medieval societies may use women as a form of gaining power, but once power is gained then women are reduced to second-class citizens. Medieval societies assume male domestic "infantilization" and female servitude.
- A xenophobic fear/hatred for the "other." Medieval societies tend to find social harmony around xenophobic hatreds. These groups reject people as individuals and instead hold their own people together by fear of the "other."
- Medieval societies are ones in which travel is made difficult. Eco (1983, p. 79) illustrates this position clearly when he writes: "Insecurity is a key word: ... In the Middle Ages, a wanderer in the woods at night saw them peopled with maleficent presences; one did not lightly venture beyond town ... This condition is close to that of the white middle-class inhabitant of New York, who doesn't set foot in Central Park after five in the afternoon, or who makes sure not to get off the subway in Harlem ... "
- The rejection of capitalism. Medieval societies have tended to see economic gain as "unholy" and have sought rewards not in this world but rather in the world(s) to come. For example, Islamic militant literature speaks consistently of the replacement of capitalism with an Islamic economic system. The same is true of other forms of terrorism around the world such as that expressed by the Senderos Iluminosos of Peru.
- The rejection of individualism. Modern societies tend to judge people as individuals rather than as part of a group. A person is expected to see him/herself as a competitor for resources and the only legal limitations placed on the individual are those of natural ability or determination. Medieval societies tend to be more proscribed societies. Positions are inherited or assigned. People are judged not by merit but rather by the group to which they belong. It is for this reason that modern societies tend to fight wars against other nation's leaders, but medieval societies tend to fight wars against "whole peoples."

Tourism is the opposite of the phenomena described above. It can be argued that using the word "modern" in its technical sense (as opposed to medieval as defined above) tourism is the most modern of industries. If terrorism is based on a medieval paradigm, then tourism is terrorism's exact opposite. It can be argued that modern mass tourism was born only after World War II. Prior to that war, tourism was an activity almost exclusively designed for the upper classes. For anyone else, it was all too easy to understand why to travel was more "work" than "pleasure." Indeed, the English word "travel" is derived from the French word "travail" (work) and which in turn was derived from the Latin word for "pitchfork." Travel, prior to WWII, was both dangerous and arduous. Post World War II society saw the development of leisure tourism as a modern industry. This modernity was not only historical in nature but also sociological.

For example, tourism is an industry in which women play a major role, not only in servant/service positions but also as leaders, CEOs, and managers. Furthermore, tourism is big business. While no one knows the exact amount of money made from the tourism industry, it is fair to say that it is one of the world's largest, if not the largest, non-bellicose industries.[2] Not only is tourism a big business, but it also holds a nation's iconic treasures.

---

[2] The economic impact of tourism will vary according to which component industries are included and according to each geographic region's definition of who is a tourist.

Thus, an attack on tourism is not only an attack on a national economy, but it often is an attack on that nation's iconic treasures. Tourism is an inviting target for other sociological reasons. For example, tourism is based on a sense of openness; it is by nature the opposite of xenophobia, a celebration of diversity. Terrorists who seek a return to medieval social paradigms then will note that tourism permits a great number of women to be employed without sexism. This return to the "days before" is what Boym (2001) calls "restorative nostalgia". Restorative nostalgia, as distinguished from Reflexive nostalgia, can become a major fuel of terrorism. Table 6.2 distinguishes the major sociological differences between these two forms of nostalgia and helps to explain part of the relationship between tourism and terrorism.

Tourism as an industry also has a number of aspects that make it highly vulnerable to terrorist attacks. For example, tourism sells a highly volatile and capricious product. Terrorists and tourism professionals alike are aware of the fact that tourism is a voluntary activity. That is, to say, that no one is forced to take a vacation or spend money on leisure travel. Thus, many leisure travelers tend to shy away from a location when there is a perceived or real sense of danger. It is important to note that a perceived act of terrorism may be as damaging from an economic standpoint as an actual threat.

Second, tourism products are open to spoilage. An airplane seat unsold is now "spoiled" and the economic loss cannot be recovered. The same is true of a hotel room, a room on a cruise line, or the lost attendance at an attraction. The opportunity-lost phenomenon also

Table 6.2: Restorative and reflexive nostalgia.

Type of nostalgia	Restorative	Reflexive
Stress	Action of going home	The longing
Push for homecoming	Quickens it	Delays it
Way it thinks of itself	Truth and tradition	Faces modernity
Dealing with absolutes	Protects the absolute truth	Questions absolute truth
Politics	National revivals	How do we inhabit two places at the same time
Emphasis on	Symbols	Details
Memory	National and linear	Social and varied
Plots	Restore national origins and conspiracy theories. A paranoiac reconstruction of "home" based on rational delusions (p. 41)	Past is dealt with, with irony and humor. Mourning mixed play pointing to the future.
Relationship to tourism industry	Negative, sees visitors as intrusion on nation	May become a basis for increased sales and holds marketing value

Adapted from Boym (2001).

occurs when terrorism warnings are increased. For example, the United States Conference of Mayors estimated that in the 15 months from September 11, 2001 until December 31, 2002 the cost of raising the code level from yellow to orange four times was over US$2.6 billion (Johnson, 2003). These estimates do not take into account lost or spoiled tourism dollars. Thus, from the perspective of terrorists who seek to create economic destruction, simply the reaction to terrorism functions as a secondary form of terrorism.

This reaction is often based on perceptions and fears. Tourism professionals know all too well that perceptions are real in their consequences. Terrorists understand that they merely have to create an atmosphere of fear in order to successfully damage a tourism industry. Fear-production is a very potent weapon in the hands of terrorists. The fear of terrorism need not even be based on terrorism. The SARS crisis in Toronto, Canada is an example of such an incorrect perception that turned into a tourism crisis (see Chapter 4). Alfred Hitchock's famous statement that: "There is no terror in the bang, only in the fear of it" well describes the Toronto SARS crisis. In reality there was no SARS tourism crisis, but due to irrational fears Toronto's tourism industry was decimated. Tourism fear is closely related to issues of terrorism. Terrorists develop fears that can continue long after the real or perceived threat has past. To accomplish this task, terrorists merely need to understand the cultural anxieties of a society and be media savvy. An informed terrorist will be aware of the fact that to travel is to have at least some anxieties and that what happens in tourism is almost always a media event. Furthermore, terrorists who seek "horror re-enforcement" through the media are well aware of the fact that a tourism scare will re-enforce itself. Tourism professionals can be sure that the media will show people suffering, and that this information will be repeated constantly on the 24-h news stations. The repetition serves to increase the fear (see Glassner, 1999). Furthermore, the scare will produce the terrorists' desired effect of economic destruction.

Still another reason why tourism is vulnerable to terrorist attacks is that tourists are hard people to track and tourism is an easy industry to attack. People on vacation often do not wish to think about the world's problems. Instead, being on holiday, they have a tendency to let down their guard, to dress strangely, to pay little attention to their surroundings and to keep strange hours. These normative social irregularities are the basis by which terrorists can easily infiltrate a tourism industry prior to an "event" and disappear after the "event."

Terrorism may seek out tourism for a number of additional reasons. For example, tourism is connected to major transportation centers. Transportation functions as the veins and arteries through which modern economies flow. If one of terrorism's goals is the destruction of these economies then attacks at airports, seaports, and bus terminals make sense. Each time a transportation center's activities are forced to cease, not only are people made aware of the terrorist's power but also great economic harm will occur. This closing of transportation centers will then become a media event serving the needs of a terrorist to broadcast his/her message. Tourism is also interconnected to a myriad of other industries. For example, there is a close relationship to the food industries and tourism (see Chapter 10). Millions of dollars are spent at restaurants each year and if restaurant sales decline so does the farmer's ability to make a profit.

Tourism is highly media oriented and terrorists, as opposed to criminals, seek publicity. Terror cannot be successful if no one has heard about the act of terror. Tourism centers tend to be places that market themselves. These are places that, with a few exceptions, want to be known. They often provide good media access and can assure a terrorist of almost instant exposure.

Furthermore, tourism centers do not take personal histories of their clients. In most cases, tourism is an industry of anonymity. People come and leave at will. Because tourists are most likely from somewhere else, no one is alerted to different accents or languages, unusual hours, or different dress codes. Such differences are the norm in tourism and often celebrated. These same differences mean that tourism can be a perfect cover for terrorist activities. Furthermore, tourists are not only often anonymous but also often in a hurry. People working in the industry are not only trained to deal with unusual behavior but accommodate such behavior as a form of good customer service. People coming to take pictures of national icons are not viewed with suspicion. The tourism business' raison d'être is based around the icon. The resulting sociological patterns make tourism an extremely easy target for someone seeking to attack the industry for reasons of terrorism.

The Post September 11 Paradigm and Air Travel

September 11th caused a great deal of damage to tourism industries around the world. If anyone ever questioned how the travel and tourism industries were united prior to September 11, 2001 there can be little doubt left after that date. Travel is an important part of tourism. In almost all cases, tourism learned that without safe travel, it too will die. While tourism and travel had been victims of terrorism prior to September 11th, it was that date that forced a major paradigm shift. The old concept that tourism security is a necessary evil that does not add to the bottom line is now over. In the ashes of September 11th, a new paradigm was born in which not only did tourism security have to become a part of a strategic marketing plan, but tourism officials had to face the fact that their industry has often been a terrorism target. The September 11th paradigm has hit the air-travel component of tourism especially hard. Part of the reasons for this reaction is based on the fact that the September 11th attacks took place from the air and there is a tendency within securities to seek to "fix" problems that have already occurred. Furthermore, the media have placed a great deal of emphasis on air-terrorism. This emphasis on air terrorism has resulted in some of the following sociological phenomena:

1. Air travel has become much more difficult. There is the need now to go through a series of screening processes that are often difficult and time consuming. In fact, some short distances are now faster to travel by car than by air.
2. In many ways, air passengers feel more out of control than ever before. The capriciousness and lack of standardization on the part of air "screeners" has meant that passengers often wonder how safe they are and how much control they have. The emphasis and resulting stress that has come about due to security concerns has also been accompanied with a decline in air service and even rudeness on the part of both flight personnel and passengers. Furthermore, the added security measures have at times resulted in flight delays or the missing of connections. These new "travel challenges" result in reality loss. The passenger is not sure if security or connections are important (or both). The greater the delay the higher the probability of stress leading to the lowering of behavioral standards and increased psychological discomfort.

3. There is now a heightened state of anomie on the part of the traveling public. People are simply confused as to what is proper. Should passengers attack a potential hijacker or cooperate, should people hide passports or other documents, is it now best to avoid the first-class cabin? Changes in regulations such as plastic versus metal knives have also caused a higher level of anomic behavior on the part of the traveling public.

4. Air travel has always had a tendency to lower some people's natural levels of inhibitions. Issues from rude behavior to excess consumption of alcoholic beverages to bizarre sexual behavior have long been a part of air travel. In the past these lowered inhibitions have not been seen as potential terrorism risks. Since September 11, 2001, however all strange or anomic behavior is now viewed through the lens of terrorism leading to higher levels of stress and passenger discomfort.

5. The current security situation has also resulted in anger displacement. This displacement means that people tend to blame those who do not have control for their frustrations. For example, flight attendants are often the brunt of anger due to flight delays that may be caused by increased security measures.

Interestingly, in a recent survey conducted by Addison Schonland in conjunction with AirguideOnline.com, more than half the people surveyed (53.2 percent) stated that they were about as concerned now regarding airline security as prior to September 11, 2001 (some 34 percent reported being more concerned). Despite this figure, some 66 percent reported that they now tend to "check out /observe" their air travel companions. Details of the survey can be found at: http://iag-inc.com/int/interview.cfm?id=27.

Cruises

Terrorism when it pertains to tourism does not even need to occur in order to succeed. A good example of this non-event success is the cruise industry. Despite the fact that there has been one attack against cruise ship passengers, the Achillie Lauro, cruise ships have not suffered from other terrorist attacks. Nevertheless, during the Northern Hemisphere's winter cruise season during 2003–2004, a number of people were sickened with a virus that most likely came from employees' lack of proper hand washing. The Norwalk virus (Chapter 10) had a major impact on the perception of cruise industry safety and has led to questions about the security of large unguarded vessels at sea. The belief that there may be a connection between the virus and terrorism spread quickly and that perceived threat may be seen as a terrorist victory despite the fact that no attack ever occurred.

Cruise tourism is also vulnerable to terrorism fears for a host of other reasons. Not only do cruise travelers manifest many of the traits of airline travelers mentioned above, but also many people who take cruises tend to be risk-adverse travelers. These people may be a bit older or they are people who seek total relaxation and a sense of security. Often cruises cater to the needs of specific groups and some of these groups may also have special security concerns. Furthermore, because cruise travel does not involve a great deal of luggage transportation and the same people are seen on board throughout the cruise, there is a tendency among cruise-ship travelers to bring greater amounts of luggage with them. This large quantity of luggage, combined with a population that seeks relaxation and often has lower levels of patience tolerance, makes baggage inspection a security challenge. Furthermore, once on board ship, many cruise passengers are convinced that due to the ship's isolation, they are safe and that nothing can happen while on the open seas.

Places of Lodging

Hotels have often been places that have acted as crime magnets. Teenagers may rent a room for a parent non-approved party or for sex, prostitutes have often worked out of hotel rooms, and hotel rooms have been used as places for illegal drug activities, and hotel rooms are the sites of robberies. Criminals know that most visitors do not spend a great deal of time in a hotel/motel room and that often valuables, laptop computers, or even cash can be found in the room when the hotel's guests are not present. In all of the cases cited above, the perpetrator of the crime followed the classical pattern of tourism criminals in that they developed an illegal action based on the fact that the hotel was a secure setting in which they could "work." In no case does the criminal or crime perpetrator seek to destroy the hotel/motel. Terrorism, however, is different. While hotels and motels may be used as places from which terrorist attacks may be planned, hotels may also be the terrorists' targets.

Attacks on hotels have occurred in such countries as Cuba, Indonesia, Israel, and Kenya. A number of victims of the September 11th attacks were staying at a hotel attached to the World Trade Center. Hotels are often highly open structures where people "feel" safe and thus let down their guard. Many hotels have lobbies that are easily attacked or open to car bombings. Hotels may also contain a restaurant that is popular with local officials or business people as well as foreigners. Because hotels often are also meeting and convention centers these buildings may be subjected to anything from intentional food poisoning to infiltration of the hotel's air heating and cooling system.

The realization that hotels may become major targets for terrorism attacks has caused a number of event planners to begin to question hotels regarding how they have updated security. For example, it is no longer unheard of for convention planners prior to accepting a convention site to want to speak with the convention hotel's security manager and ask him or her such questions as: What certifications do the hotel's security personnel have? How many security staff does the hotel employ? How is the security staff's day structured? Event and meeting planners are now asking about evacuation routes, how close the hotel's lobby's standoff distance is from the drop off points and valet parking areas, and if the security staff is required to demonstrate certain proficiencies. A common request is to review the hotel's Security Policies and Procedures Manual. The key issue is that hotels can no longer assume that they can avoid developing architectural designs that would prevent or restrict attacks, or employ staff members who are not equipped to face a world in which a terrorist can strike at any moment.

Predicting Vulnerability

Terrorists have two other major advantages, they alone know when and where they plan to attack and there is no formula to predict these attacks. Terrorists can focus their resources on the intended target while those protecting the public must assume that anything can be a target. While there is no one way to predict which areas of tourism may be targets, the following may be useful. As a predictive when referring to mass tourism there may be a relationship between these following factors and a tourism center's proclivity to become a target. These factors may be addressed in the form of interrogatives:

1. Does the site have the potential for mass casualties?
2. Does the locale offer mass publicity and good images for television?
3. Would an attack on this site result in major economic damage?
4. Is the site or does it contain a national icon which if attacked would result in national depression, anger, or fear?

The greater the number of positive responses to these questions, the higher the potential for a major terrorist attack. It should be emphasized that answering all four of the above questions in the affirmative does not mean that a terrorist attack will occur, nor do negative answers guarantee security. These answers to these questions then merely present a stochastic model that may be used as a guide.

Risk and Crisis Planning

As mentioned above, there is not a single magical formula to assure that one's locale will not be a victim of terrorism. Tourism professionals in an age of terrorism need to become much more sophisticated in issues of risk management (Wilks & Moore, 2004). While not all risk management can assure that there will be no need for crisis management, there is little doubt that the best crises are those that never occur. Despite the fact that terrorism often strikes tourism sites, tourism officials have been notoriously slow in getting beyond denial. All too often tourism professionals take the position that a terrorist attack will not happen at their locale or that even to plan for such an attack may turn into a marketing disaster. The assumption behind these positions is that the public fears security and that visible security can hurt business. For example, Rubin (2004, p. 1) notes that "since 9/11 the nature and number of risks that the U.S. faces has increased … Additionally, national concern about chem- and bio-terrorism, critical infrastructure, and cyber-terrorism threats has increased."

Tourism policy toward terrorism has often been based on what has happened rather than what may happen. An example of such a reactive policy is that of air transport security. Shoes were examined only after a potential attack was averted by an alert flight attendant. Security lines have been established based on what happened during 9/11, and new areas of airline security, such as the dangers posed to passengers as they wait to pass through the security line or upon leaving an airport are ignored. Waugh (2000, p. 24) has noted that "Policies and programs have been instituted and implemented in the aftermath of a disaster, based almost solely on that disaster experience, and with little investment in capacity building to deal with the next disaster."

Such a non-policy is not only poor planning but may also be poor marketing. The traveling public today asks about security and no matter what a particular tourism official may or may not desire, the media will speak about it. For example, very few people tend not to fly simply because airlines begin each flight with safety and security information.

Visitor Risk Analyses

While each individual tourism locale or sub-component business will have particular risks that must be evaluated on an individual basis, classically all visitor risk analysis consists of a number of standard steps. Identifying individuals, items, locales, and functions in terms of:

- Will the crisis involve a loss of life or bodily injury?
- Will the crisis involve total or temporary replacement or change of locale?
- Will there be unrecoverable , allied, or related costs due to the crisis?

Once the above questions are asked the next stage of a visitor risk analysis is to conduct a hazards and vulnerability study (site survey) of personnel, facilities, items, and functions. In this study the researcher asks questions such as: What is the probability of the negative occurrence? How or what losses can be expected? Should the negative occurrence become reality? and then a comparison of probabilities is measured against the risk in terms of criticality to the tourism component. The actual degree of risk involved depends on the following formula: "The probability of adverse effects occurring as a direct result of the threats, plus the extent to which the site or activity will be affected by the threats."

Visitor Safety Support Structures

In times of terrorism, tourism professionals must consider all facilities that supplement or make possible a visitor's stay. These may include such items as places of lodging, eating establishments, transportation arteries, medical facilities, and basic city services such as fire fighters and security professional. For example, at a hotel site, tourism security professionals will want to examine such areas as the hotel's vent system, kitchens, and loading areas.

The law enforcement/security professional community and our legal system traditionally have served as our social control process. In tourism centers, where some people exhibit low inhibition levels, social control is harder to regulate. Often, visitor security personnel also have large geographic areas to patrol. This mixture of high visitor density plus wide-open spaces leads to questions such as:

- What types of equipment are best for the specific component of the tourism industry being analyzed?
- Does the threat of punishment act as a good deterrent in visitor situations?
- How might acts of terrorism at visitor locales impact on:
  - Site disruption?
  - Damage, loss, or destruction of property?
  - Personal injury or loss of life?
  - Information security (i.e. "an inside job")?

Here are several suggestions on ways that tourism professionals can work with their tourism security professionals to lessen the chance of a terrorism attack:

- Conduct a good security analysis of all components of your tourism system. Then list weaknesses and vulnerabilities.

- Develop a working relationship between local security professionals and the various components of the visitor industry. In a like manner, develop strategic ties between the security office and the local police department(s).
- Create visitor-safety sessions for visitor industry employees
- Develop security pamphlets/signs that explain to both guests and employees things such as:

  - Best evacuation routes to take
  - People and things to avoid
  - Warning signs
  - Emergency access phones and numbers.

- Coordinate efforts with the local community as to:

  - Controlled hours and traffic flow
  - Advance notice of events
  - Consultation prior to event
  - Limitations and division of labor and resources.

The above information will be helpful in planning and managing a tourism crisis caused by terrorism. Tourism officials then need to consider planning for the next disaster. Often an easy way to plan is to think of a disaster as if it were a meal. Tourism officials will need to ask themselves what are the inherent risks of their part of the business, in a crisis what will their priorities be, and are their plans flexible? Tourism professionals need also to consider if their plans meet the needs of the people whom they are serving. For example, not every tourism commodity caters to the same clientele. Tourism centers that cater to older people or people with physical challenges will need tourism protection plans that are different from those attractions that cater to a more adventurous clientele. A tourism security plan is only as good as the people who implement it and for whom it is to serve. Tourism professionals need to have plans to take care of their caregivers. For example, in the midst of a crisis, who will feed rescue workers, where will these people sleep, and how will the first responders be protected?

For the foreseeable future, tourism and terrorism will, unfortunately, be linked. There will always be people who seek to take advantage of others for political and ideological ends. Tourism is the most modern of industries, a glimpse into a future where sexism and xenophobia are replaced with human dignity and respect. We can only hope that those who lead the tourism industry are successful in their quest to unite hearts and bring peace to the world.

References

Bar-On, R. (2001). The effects of terrorism on travel and tourism. Unpublished manuscript.

Boym, S. (2001). *The future of nostalgia*. New York: Basic Books.

Eco, H. (1983). *Travels in hyperreality*. San Diego, CA: Harcourt Brace & Co.

Glassner, B. (1999). *The culture of fear*. New York: Basic Books.

Johnson, K. (2003). In orange terror alerts, wary cities hold back. *USA Today*, 22 July, p. 1.

Loyola, M. (2004). Arafat's true legacy. *The Weekly Standard*, 27 November.

Rubin, C. (2004). Major terrorist events in the U.S. and their outcomes: Initial analysis and observations. *Journal of Homeland Security*, *1*(1), 1.

Waugh, W. Jr. (2000). *Living with hazards, dealing with disasters*. New York: M.E. Sharpe.

Wilks, J., & Moore, S. (2004). *Tourism risk management for the Asia Pacific region*. Southport, Australia: Cooperative Research Centre for Sustainable Tourism.

Chapter 7

Crime and Tourism

Peter E. Tarlow

Introduction

Just outside the gates of a major amusement park, a young woman sits crying. Someone has stolen her purse. She has not only lost her money, but also her identification card, her credit cards, her airline tickets, and her passport. Because she does not speak the local language well, she sits in agony, her vacation ruined.

The above scenario is neither 'true' nor part of an advertisement campaign. Yet this pseudo-fictitious scene, while not referring to any one specific incident, rings all too true. Indeed, there are similar press reports of crimes aimed specifically at tourists around the world. For example, a headline in the Houston Chronicle reads: "Brazil fears crime wave may wash away tourists"(Houston Chronicle, 2004). To emphasize the point, Brazil's largest newspaper, *O Estado de São Paulo* (November 21, 2004), ran a series of articles on the front page of its city section referring to crimes against tourists, especially in the city of Rio de Janeiro. A follow-up article (p. C-3) indicates that in the first 9 months of 2004, some 2553 tourists were victims of crimes, a rise of 9.6 percent over the same period in 2003.

The resulting consequences for the city of Rio have been a loss of tourism and a major decrease in the quality of life for the city's local population. As one young man in his 20s recently reported: "In Rio, the youth no longer have a night life". In reality, most locations underreport crimes against tourists. The reasons for this underreporting may vary from place to place, but the following sociological patterns that cause this trend tend to hold true wherever there are tourists:

- Immediately after a crime has been committed, some tourists may be unaware that they have been the victims of a crime. This phenomenon is especially true in cases of crimes of distraction such as pickpocketting. In these cases, tourists may not even be aware that someone has robbed them until such time as they seek to pay for something. Even then tourists may simply assume that they have left their money in the hotel room by mistake. Thus by the time victims are aware that they have been robbed, the perpetrator is long gone.

- Victims often do not know what to do when they have been assaulted. In cases where no physical harm has taken place (or even in some cases where there has been physical harm) victims may not know to whom to turn or how to report a crime. It is often easier simply to 'forget about the crime' than seek out a police station and lose a day filing police reports. This situation may especially be true if the victim does not speak the local language.
- Victims often assume that they will never receive their money/goods back. Under such an assumption, the logical thing to do is simply ignore the situation and not report it.
- Most victims may be unwilling to return to the location to testify against the perpetrator even if the perpetrator is caught. It is simpler not to report the crime.

Furthermore, many tourists fall victim to crimes in which they have been willing participants. In such cases visitor-victims may not wish the police to be aware of their actions. There are multiple forms of visitor self-induced crime. For example, young men may seek out paid sexual services. Often these 'ladies' will be part of a scam in which they 'seduce' the young man by bringing him to a room and then drug him. While he is asleep, the victim is robbed. In such cases, most visitors are unwilling to report this crime to the local police department. This form of crime is so common, and underreported, in so many large cities or tourism destinations that the Las Vegas Metropolitan Police Department has produced a training film regarding this topic.

Con artists around the world participate in another form of self-induced tourism crime. The job of the con artist is to convince their victims to part with their money willingly. For example, anyone who has ever stood outside of Harrah's Department Store in London or along New York's Fifth Avenue has witnessed street vendors convince unsuspecting visitors that they are receiving a bargain for what turns out to be merchandise that is either of little value or worthless. What is special about robberies conducted as cons is that in this case victims freely hand over their money to the perpetrator of the crime.

The examples given above demonstrate that tourism crimes (or crimes against tourists/visitors) are not easy phenomena to define. Pizam (1999, p. 5) has attempted to create "a comprehensive approach to classifying acts of crime and violence at tourism destinations". Yet, despite Pizam's work police records and interviews reveal that there is no one standard for tourism crimes. Different agencies define tourism crimes each in their own unique manner. Furthermore, as tourism rarely occurs in one specific zone or place, it can be difficult at times to determine if something is a tourism crime or merely a crime committed in a tourism area. To make the situation even murkier, it is often difficult to determine if a particular crime is a tourism crime or even who needs protection from which criminals. Whenever tourism crimes are discussed, the following caveats must be considered:

1. There is no one standard for reporting crime. Each jurisdiction uses separate reporting methods and a crime in one place may not be a crime somewhere else.
2. There is no way of knowing what we mean by a tourism district. In some communities the tourism area may be well defined; in other communities tourism attractions may be scattered throughout the community. Furthermore, locals may live within tourism districts and tourists may become involved with issues of local crimes.
3. Because the tourism geography is so fluid, tourism statistics are always suspected. Simply by redefining either crimes or boundaries, crime statistics can be manipulated to

make the numbers come out as desired. Even when there is no malice of forethought intended, all tourism crime statistics are dependent upon the social assumptions that define them.

4. Often, tourism data are reported, counted, or subsumed under the rubric of local crime data. Thus, just as a crime against a local person living in close proximity to the tourism district may be miscounted as tourism crime, at times tourism crimes may be simply classified as another form of local crime.

5. Tourism crime is often determined by X crimes per Y number of tourists. In the case of attractions, the situation becomes more difficult as we have to figure out which are crimes committed against locals who simply happen to be in the area of an attraction and which are crimes committed against visitors.

6. Because of underreporting and the fact that some crimes are self-induced or aided, there is no way of knowing how many visitors actually are victims of a tourism crime.

To understand this phenomenon better, let us return to another variation on our hypothetical case. A man on vacation loses his wallet containing US$300. The sum is not large, but it is also by no means small. The normal reaction is not to assume that one has been robbed but rather that the wallet is missing. It may have been left at the hotel room, in the pocket of his jacket, or on the counter of a restaurant where he had recently eaten. In such a scenario, many people will simply begin to retrace their steps rather than assume a robbery. The process not only increases desperation but also provides the criminal with precious time, time that is necessary to become lost in the crowd.

Continuing on with our hypothetical case, assuming that the victim (in this case, a male) decides/determines that he has been robbed, he will be subjected to distinct forms of anomie. What is he to do? Where should he go? How does he find a police department? While these questions may appear simple to someone in a less stressed situation, anomie and stress soon cloud the mind. Because tourists have been known to fake crimes or losses in order to collect insurance, police officers are obligated to ask multiple questions and take every precaution to assure themselves that our hypothetical tourist is really a victim.

Assuming that our hypothetical victim does find the police station, he may then be subjected to questioning and providing detailed information for the police records. The criminal knows that the victim will often have spotty data at best. There may be a good chance that the victim is unaware of where, when, or how he was victimized. Thus the police report may be nothing more than an exercise in frustration. The situation, however, is actually worse than the victim may at first suspect. Most police departments lack tourism safety/security units. In such cases, crimes committed against tourists may move to the bottom of the 'to do' list. Furthermore, if on the off chance that the file does get acted upon, the chances of finding the perpetrators and successfully prosecuting them are slim at best. Even if the criminal is successfully apprehended, most criminals know that the victim will be long gone, and the chances that a victim will expend resources of time and money to prosecute are almost not existent.

Criminals, most of whom are professionals, are well aware of the above scenario. They work under the assumption that visitors are easy targets for crime and that once the crime has been committed, there is very little likelihood that they will be apprehended, prosecuted, or held responsible for their actions.

No one chapter can cover all aspects of tourism crimes, so this chapter will seek to touch on some of the sociological aspects of tourism crime. Specifically, the following topics and issues will be examined:

- Tourism crime typologies and definitions — how tourism crime differs from other forms of crime;
- Who is involved in tourism crimes;
- Classical tourism crimes;
- What are crimes committed against tourists?
- What are the differences between tourism crime(s) and other types of crimes?
- What are some of the methods that have been used to keep visitors safe?
- What is the role of casinos in tourism crimes?
- Which groups are often victims to tourism crimes?
- Hotel security.

Tourism Crimes Typologies and Definitions

As noted above, tourism[1] crimes are not merely crimes committed against tourists. In fact, tourists may be the ones responsible for the crime and may commit crimes against the tourism site or personnel. Table 7.1 provides a tourism/visitor crime taxonomy.

As noted above tourism crimes are not necessarily like other types of crimes. Visitors who are victims of crime often knowingly or unknowingly collaborate with their victimizer(s). Furthermore, even when the victim is not a co-collaborator in the criminal act, there are various sociological tendencies that come into play which make tourists particularly vulnerable to criminal acts. Below is a listing of some of these vulnerabilities. It should be noted that non-tourists may suffer from these vulnerabilities at times, but tourists

Table 7.1: A tourism/visitor crime taxonomy.

Crimes committed by	Against whom	Some examples of	Goal of crime
Tourists	Other visitors or local population, or tourism personnel	Robbery, pickpockets	Usually economicor social gain
Locals	Visitors	Assaults, petty theft, con artists, crimes of distraction	Usually economic gain
Tourism industry	Visitors	Fraud, business misrepresentation	Economic

---

[1] The author is aware that the industry uses different definitions for visitor, traveler, tourist, and day-tripper. In order to avoid complications, the terms traveler, tourist, and visitor are used as synonyms. Word usage varies only for stylistic reasons.

almost always suffer from not only each of the vulnerabilities listed, but also from the interaction between them. Tourism crimes then can be committed against multiple groups, by and against tourists, by and against staff, against specific sites, and by and against representatives of the tourism industry.

Tourism Crimes

Visitors may be involved in a host of illegal activities. These activities may include the use of drugs, participation in illegal acts, such as prostitution, site destruction (both at places of lodging and at major attractions), traffic crimes, petty and major theft, and even during moments of passion, physical crimes that may end in murder. Criminals who target the tourism industry are professionals and know that tourists will suffer from the sociological phenomena stated below and will most likely never report the crime. Visitors are vulnerable both to be victims of crime and to become crime perpetrators for a number of reasons, including:

- Travelers often leave their commonsense at home. Vacationers may assume that the place to which they are traveling is safe. As such, there is a tendency to leave one's worries at home, to assume that someone else is looking out for the person traveling. The word 'vacation' gives us an insight into this phenomenon. We derive the word vacation from the French word *vacances* meaning 'vacant'. A vacation then is a time of mind-vacancy, a period when we relax and tend not to think. Examples of commonsense deprivation abound. For example, think of the large numbers of people who leave hotel doors open while going to the ice machine or how many men travel with their wallets in their back pockets rather than their front pockets. Any police officer who has worked a beat in which there are a large number of tourists will report on how bags are left unattended or cameras left on benches. Visit a buffet and one will be amazed at the number of bags, laptops and other valuable items that are left at tables while people go through the buffet lines.
- It is often easy to identify travelers. Travelers often fail to blend in with the local culture. Travelers often mark themselves not only with distinctive dress and by the fact that they may not speak the local language, but also with specific clothing items. For example, the use of 'fanny packs' is especially dangerous. Any criminal who sees a person wearing a fanny pack or 'pouch' not only assumes that the person is a visitor, but that within the fanny pack the visitor will be carrying personal documents, credit cards and money.
- Travelers are often in a state on anomie. To travel is to be confused. There are many reasons for this anomic state. For example, a person who has just made a long international voyage may have crossed multiple time zones, may have slept poorly or not at all during the trip and may well be protein deprived. Often travelers simply ache from cramped quarters. Travelers may not know the local language or may not be aware of local customs, such as who to tip or how much. Many travelers may not understand the local currency or be aware of what a particular coin or bill is worth in their own currency. This state of disorientation was first identified sociologically by David Emile Durkheim. Durkheim (1893) called this disoriented state 'anomie'. Anomic travelers are not only liable to make silly travel mistakes, to let down their guard, or simply to be careless, but those who would prey on them are well aware of this state. For example, go to any baggage claim area at an

airport. Most travelers are interested in looking for their bags on the conveyor belt rather than watching the bags that have already come off the convey belt. Taking a vacationer's bag either at check-in or as the bags leave the conveyor belt is a simple matter for most thieves. Another form of anomie is the passenger who is taken for a 'ride' by a dishonest cab driver. Dishonest cab drivers know that the visitor does not know the least expensive and most efficient way to travel around the city. Simply by making a wrong turn or choosing a less efficient route, cab drivers can create large aggregate profits while never having to worry about committing a single crime that may land them a fine or worse. Even worse, a scam involving muggings by unlicensed taxi drivers led to at least six deaths of foreign tourists arriving at Bangkok International Airport from 1998–1999 (Leggat & Leggat, 2003).

- Visitors often drop inhibitions when they travel. People tend to do things on the road that they might not try at home. This lowering of inhibitions may result in experimentation, be it with drugs or sexual, or simply being ruder than usual. There is a natural human tendency to do things that might not be acceptable in places where the visitor is not known. This tendency to experiment is one of the reasons that young men, especially between the ages 18 and 30 often become victims of tourism crime. These young men may place themselves in harm's way by willingly going to a place where they believe they will live out a sexual fantasy, the use of illegal substances, or simply taking a risk by driving under the influence of alcohol.

- Stress-related issues. To travel is to be stressed. The word travel is derived from the French word, 'travail' meaning work. In today's world, travel has once again become work, and work and stress often co-mingle. Stress-related issues in travel security mean that people tend to enter into higher levels of anomic states, tend to think in less rational ways and are often anger prone. Not everyone can manage anger. Often anger may lead beyond frustration to issues of assault. The perfect example of stress turned to anger turned to assault is the case of the passenger whose child ran down a corridor at Newark's (New Jersey) Liberty airport. Blocked by a worker for not having a proper ticket, the passenger threw the employee to the ground and broke the employee's back.

- Closely related to stress is the issue of time. Visitors seem to be able to forgive almost anything other than loss of time. One only needs to see the anger, disappointment, frustration, and stress on the faces of airline passengers to understand how powerful time is in travel. Due to lack of time, visitors will often enter into periods of stress. This stress then causes an interaction that results in lowering of inhibitions. The traveler now angry, stressed out and with lower inhibitions may also suffer from anomie and loss of common sense. The result is that travelers are often easy victims of criminals. These criminals are on their own turf, they are rested and prepared for a day's 'work'. Tourism criminals, unlike their victims, often have a great deal of time to pursue their victims and have the advantage of surprise and understanding the sociology of their victims.

Tourists are not, however, the only victims of crime. Locals and visitors may also commit crimes against those working in the tourism industry. For example, many people who may be undocumented or undereducated will seek employment in the service industries. Often these employees are deficient in the local language and are unwilling to expose themselves to the police should something happen to them. This political and ignorance-vulnerability places those in the under-classes working as tourism staff members in an awkward position. Unscrupulous guests may force staff members to do things against their will for fear of being turned in. Added to this difficulty is the fact that many women staff members may be working in places that invite sexual assault and are often under-trained in self-protection or in basic precautions. Think how many times guests enter rooms while staff members (housekeepers) are in the guest's room cleaning. Furthermore, tourism staff members often work odd hours and must use public transportation. This combination places both men and women at risk. Even when malice may not be intended, tourism staff members may inadvertently be placed in dangerous situations. For example, in a world of AIDS and other bio-hazardous illnesses, many hotel chambermaids may be exposed to articles of clothing or towels that have been contaminated by the transfer of body fluids.

Tourism crimes may also be aimed at tourism sites or specific attractions. In the post-September 11th world, site protection is often associated with acts of terrorism. This topic was examined in Chapter 6. Site protection has long been an issue prior to modern terrorism. Tourism sites may suffer, for example, from acts of vandalism and robberies. Many tourism sites, especially those with iconic or historical value, are often the targets for souvenir seekers who decide to bring home a small piece of the site. An example of such unintended vandalism is Massachusetts' Plymouth Rock. In this case, the 'rock' did not suffer from intentional harm, but so many tourists wanted a piece of it that a wall was needed to protect the rock from souvenir hunters. Graffiti is another form of site harm which tourism can produce.

Tourism sites are often places where there are large amounts of cash on hand. Tourism sites such as major amusement parks must be aware of the fact that they are targets for bandits who may seek to avail themselves of the day's receipts. Because many tourism sites are in isolated areas or empty after closing hours, these sites can become places where illegal activities occur at night. Rural tourism sites may become unintended lovers' lanes or centers for the exchange of illegal drugs. Finally, there is often a fine line between ecological illegal acts (littering or feeding animals) and simply coexistence with nature. Animal parks, zoos, and biological gardens have reported incidents where visitor behavior has resulted in the harming of even death of their animals or plants. An example of the harm to plant life is in the US State of Arizona where visitors have illegally stolen wild cactus plants for transport to their own homes.

This understanding of the sociology of tourists may be one of the reasons why all crime statistics dealing with visitors may be not only underreported but also may be irrelevant.

Classical Tourism Crimes

Tourists and visitors are exposed to the full gamut of crimes; however, some crimes are more prevalent within the tourism industry. The following are some of the more common crimes committed against tourists:

Crimes of Distraction (CoD)

The term 'crimes of distraction' refers to a whole family of crimes based on the assumption that the victim may be in an anomic state. While pickpocketting may be the most common form of a distraction crime, there are a great many crimes within this range. Distraction artists are professionals. They often train for years and may work either alone or in groups. While the media rarely notices a CoD, its victims rarely forget their experience. This simple fact represents a major challenge to the tourism industry. Tourists who are CoD victims are not only anomic, but often angry and it is not unusual for a CoD victim to blame the host community/site rather than themselves. Victims of crimes of distraction may therefore turn against the host community and the anger felt may undermine all other aspects of the vacation. While we can never go into the mind of another human being, research shows these common elements in CoD practitioners:[2]

- CoD artists feel no remorse for their victims; rather they see themselves as professionals and their victims as 'suckers'.
- They see themselves as professionals rather than as thieves, being caught is merely the price of doing business.
- They set professional goals for themselves.
- They will look for easy victims and generally avoid violence. For this reason money should be separated from victim with a minimum of difficulty.
- CoD practitioners do not wish to deal directly with victims, but instead prefer to be invisible.
- Immediate escape is foremost in the mind of a CoD practitioner.
- Distraction artists look for their victims within crowds.

While there are many forms of classical distraction theft, some of the most common are the use of a coat over the arm, in which the coat is used to take a wallet or lady's handbag and then hide it, or the spilling of something such as ketchup on the victim. While the first thief may be working to clean up the victim, his/her partner in crime is using the distraction to rob the victim without the victim knowing it.

Another form of tourism crime is airport luggage theft. Ironically, this form of crime has become easier since the war on terrorism began. Most airports have placed their security personnel at the gateways to airplanes. Criminals have taken note of this personnel reshuffling and have used the absence of guards to steal luggage not only from conveyor belts, but also as passengers wait at long check-in lines or at security lines. While waiting in lines, passengers are often in an anomic state and this absence of observation makes it easy for CoD artists to steal luggage, while passengers wait in line to check in for a flight or wait in line to pass through security lines. Restroom thefts are still another form of CoD. For example, a man or lady may hang up their jacket or purse on the backside of a lavatory door. While the person is indisposed, using the lavatory, the perpetrator simply places his/her hand over the top of the door in the hope of stealing the jacket or handbag.

White-collar crime is still another major problem in tourism since visitors often use credit cards at restaurants, hotels, transportation centers, and attractions. These credit cards are subject to being stolen. In reality, the thief may be less interested in the actual credit card than in the credit card number. A missing credit card may alert a victim, but a stolen credit card number may not be noticed for several days. In today's internet-shopping society, the possession

---

[2] This material comes from interviews between the Orange County (Florida) Police Department, the Las Vegas Metropolitan Sheriffs office and CoD practitioners (Las Vegas Metropolitan Police Department, 2003).

of another person's credit card number plus address may lead to multiple forms of theft. Credit-card theft, however, victimizes not only the tourist whose credit card has been stolen, but also the merchant who may hand over products to the person possessing the stolen card.

Credit-card thieves' goal is to take credit cards and utilize them as quickly as possible. They are aware that a savvy tourist may soon realize that their card has been stolen and therefore cancel the card. Credit-card number theft, however, is a more difficult problem. The victim may not realize that the card is being misused until a statement is received.

One of the classical reasons for travel was to go to a place where one could be anonymous. It can be said that to travel is to lose one's identity. In the past, it may have been a form of mental relaxation to lose one's identity, but in the modern world of e-commerce, identity loss has taken on a new meaning, called 'identify theft'. An identity thief seeks to assume the identity of the other person. This identification robbery may be done by stealing of documents, rummaging through trashcans, asking for identification numbers such as a United States social security number or a national identity card number along with one's mother's maiden name. The combination allows the thief to steal nothing, but rather to obtain new credit cards in the victim's name. The thief can then run up bills to thousands of dollars for which the victim must prove that he/she is not responsible. While there is no one fail-proof method to stop credit card and identity theft, there are several things that tourism personnel can do to lessen the possibilities of loss. These include:

- Keep copies of all credit card numbers and credit card cancellation numbers in a safe place that is separate from one's cards.
- Encourage employees to check signatures on credit cards. The signature on the card should look like the signature on the sales slip. Both signatures should look the same!
- Look for unusual behavior. If the person seems overly nervous, and/or is making a strange set of purchases (for example, many of the same item), this may be a sign of fraud. Another sign may be purchases made without regard to size, quantity, or color.
- Encourage personnel to seek a second form of picture identification prior to selling merchandise by means of a credit card.
- Check the date. Is the card still within its valid time period?
- In the case of foreign credit cards, ask to see a passport and check the passport's seal and the individual's photo. Be very wary of a handwritten passport.
- Be wary of customers who are unnecessarily talkative or delay a selection until the salesclerk becomes upset.
- Be wary of a person who hurries the salesperson, just as it is time to quit for the day.
- Be wary of a person who takes a credit card from his pocket rather than from a wallet or purse.
- Be wary of a person who does not carry a driver's license or does not have a photo identification card.

Casinos and Crime

One area of tourism crime that has provoked a great deal of debate is the relationship between casinos and crime. On one side of the debate is the argument that casinos lead to numerous forms of white-collar crimes and/or social crimes such as increased prostitution. The assumption behind this hypothesis is that casinos bring to an area a group of people who seek the seedier side of life, and therefore secondary crimes such as racketeering and prostitution are sure to follow. Part of the reason behind this assumption is that certain areas that first permitted gambling (often called gaming) were/are often associated with organized crime. As organized crime often ran secondary businesses such as prostitution and illegal drugs, the assumption was/is that gaming and organized crime go together and that organized crime equals social crimes.

The counter viewpoint is that in today's world, governments have placed so many restrictions on the gaming industry that gaming is no longer profitable for organized crime. This argument takes the position that most casinos are run today by very legitimate business people who have invested millions of dollars into their casino and cannot afford to permit their investment to be destroyed by any form of crime. This position also holds that because gaming centers invest large sums of money in making their guests feel comfortable, they are careful to have large, well-trained security departments. These security departments go out of their way to assure that crime stays away from the casinos and the vicinity in which they are located. From this perspective, the addition of casinos not only fails to raise the crime rate but also may play a major role in lowering the crime rate. As noted above, crime rates are not easy to define. The rise and lowering of crime rates often depends on who looks at which data. Furthermore, as in all studies of crime, there is always the issue of personal responsibility. In many of the social crimes, such as prostitution, is the fault solely with the merchant or also with the client? Can drug dealers exist if there are no buyers? While these social issues are beyond the scope of this chapter, they must be considered if we are to have an understanding of many of the crimes in which tourists are involved. Finally, can a society legislate social morality as a major issue within tourism? For example, in the case of casinos, if gaming is considered immoral the client can always gamble online or in another locale.

In the case of a specific form of tourism crime, that of the relationship between casino tourism and crime, the situation is even harder to define. Some of the reasons for this difficulty are not only those factors listed at the beginning of this chapter but also the fact that it is hard to develop one single definition of casino crime. For example, many casinos attract as many local residents as they do visitors/tourists. Do we count crime as only against one group or the other? Where do casino and casino districts end, and where is crime casino oriented versus non-casino oriented? One way that casinos are judged is by increases of social crime. On the other hand, there are multiple tourism destinations around the world where there is no gambling and social crimes exist. For example, prostitution and illegal drugs have been a major problem in Honolulu where there is no form of gambling/gaming or even lotteries allowed. This leads to the problem that it is hard or impossible to distinguish between crimes based on the social impacts of tourism versus those based on the social impact of casinos. The lack of clear definitions and imprecise data often means that the researcher can find almost any conclusion about which he/she is desirous. The tautological bias in most of these studies should be recognized.

Despite the potential for tautological bias, there does seem to be a preponderance of evidence that at least suggests that casinos do not breed crime and may in fact play a role in lowering crime. Cities such as Detroit, Michigan report no rise of the crime rate in their casino district (Christian, 2004). In fact, the Detroit Police Department's Crime Analysis Unit notes that crimes (including homicide, rape, robbery, assault, burglary, and larceny) have dropped drastically by an impressive 24 percent since casino gaming was introduced to the city. Since 1998, the year before casinos came to Detroit, homicide is down by 8 percent, assault by 12 percent, robbery by 17 percent, burglary by a whopping 30 percent, and larceny is down by an amazing 32 percent. In fact, the crime rate in Detroit has decreased in every major category since casinos were introduced to the city (http://www.ci.detroit.mi.us/police/CompStat/1990-2001stats.pdf.). Do these statistics offer proof that introducing casino gaming into a community does not increase crime? One analysis would be that casinos increased the number of people on the streets, added more and better-trained security guards to the city's downtown section, and increased employment possibilities. The other argument would be that crime fell despite the casinos, rather than because of them, that the key issues were the aging of the population, and an increase in social programs.

Other studies, however, seem to bare out the Detroit statistics. In a 1985 study of Atlantic City, Albanese, (1985) concluded: "casinos have no direct effect on the serious crime in Atlantic City, and that crime has risen due to factors other than the casinos themselves" (p. 43). Curran and Scarpitti (1991) drew the same conclusions in their follow-up study. Since 1980, data for Atlantic City, New Jersey, show that the city has experienced a significant drop in cases of violent and street crime. Its murder rate fell by 54 percent, instances of robbery by 56 percent, and reported vehicle theft fell by 86 percent. At the same time, the city saw an increase in the number of its casinos. Again, due to the social assumptions that one makes, conclusions as to the relationship between crime and casinos can be drawn.

In both cases, the researches controlled for populations at risk. In Biloxi, Mississippi, there have been two major studies. These were conducted by Giacopassi and Stitt (1993) and Chang (1996). Both studies demonstrated that there was no increase in crime due to the introduction of casinos. The Biloxi crime rate due to casinos was about the same as that experienced by the rest of the state. In a study undertaken in 2001 for the Las Vegas police department, it was determined that tourists needed police officers less in the city's casino district (the Las Vegas Strip) than in other parts of the city (Tarlow, 2002). This study is also supported by the fact that crime rate in the Las Vegas metropolitan area, which includes crimes committed by/against over 36 million annual visitors, is lower than many other major American tourist destinations. For example, if we examine the statistics for Orlando (home of Disneyworld), Florida, a non-gaming family resort, these statistics show that Orlando experienced a 3.8 percent increase in vehicle theft between 1994 and 2002, while the national rate dropped 19 percent.

No matter what statistics one chooses, the reader must always be careful not to confuse correlations with causality. Because a crime rate may have decreased in a specific locale does not mean that the cause of that decrease is known. Tourism centers have simply too many variables to determine specific causality.

Hotel safety/security is another area that presents tourism officials with a great many challenges. Places of lodging traditionally are duty bound to protect the identity of their clients. Even before terrorism touched places of lodging, hotels were used (misused) for numerous activities. Not only are hotels places in which assaults can occur (both against other guests and staff members), but people have also used hotel rooms for a number of illegitimate or illegal activities. For example, police have often had to raid hotel rooms in which illegal drugs were being used, prostitution may have been occurring, or as staging areas for illegal immigration. These police actions are not the same as those against private residence. Hoteliers may not be willing to give out the name of the person(s) whom the police are seeking, the guest may be registered under a false name, and a police raid will not only upset other guests and even cause collateral damage, but may also severely impact the hotelier's business. The traditional needs of protecting guests and staff have now acquired a new meaning. No longer do lodging guests merely worry about CoD, kidnappings, and robbery, but also are now concerned with a vast array of new issues such as food safety, biochemical poisoning, and bombings.

The hotel lodging industry knows that its clientele often suffer from higher levels of anomie than is normal, thus making their customers 'sitting ducks' for criminal elements. To add to the difficulties in providing safe and secure lodging, many people when away from home lower their moral standards thus exposing themselves to additional risks.

Hoteliers and police often have a difficult time dealing with each other. Police see their intrusions as necessary and their surprise tactics as essential for saving lives. Hoteliers on the other hand argue that they need to protect all guests along with the guest's privacy.

To lessen the burdens on the police, and to improve safety, many hoteliers have adopted methods such as:

- Be visible: The traveling public is better protected, and feels safer, when it sees uniformed employees.
- Talk to strangers: Extroverted hotel employees not only add a measure of hospitality to a property, but also have the potential to learn a great deal about who and what is on the hotel's premises. Informal conversations create the perception that the property is safe and that the employees care.
- Employee security training: Not only should hotel security have training but all members of the staff should be trained in such areas as: how to deal with a bomb threat, how to deal with a terrorist threat, how to deal with a hostile guest, and how to deal with a case of domestic violence. Dealing with such incidents does not necessarily mean becoming involved. It does mean that each employee should know what the property's policy is and whom to call in each circumstance.

References

Albanese, J. (1985). The effect of casino gambling on crime. *Federal Probation, 48*, 39–44.

Chang, S. (1996). The impact of casinos on crime: The case of Biloxi, Mississippi. *Journal of Criminal Justice, 24*, 431–436.

Christian, G. (2004). *Detroit Michigan Police Department*. Personal interview, October.

Curran, J., & Scarpitti, F. (1991). Crime in Atlantic City: Do casinos make a difference? *Deviant Behavior, 12*, 431–449.

Durkheim, E. (1893). *De La Division du travail social*. Paris: Presses Universitaires de la France.

Giacopassi, D., & Stitt, B.G. (1993). Assessing the impact of casino crime in Mississippi. *American Journal of Criminal Justice, 18*, 117–131.

Houston Chronicle. (2004). *Brazil fears crime wave may wash away tourists*. 27 November, p. A-28.

Las Vegas Metropolitan Police Department. (2003). *They call me the wiz.* Police Interviews with Donnie Jones on Crimes of Distraction, May.

Las Vegas Metropolitan Police Department. (2003). *Bang the credit card for the merchant.* Police Interviews with Gary Scott on Credit Card Theft, May.

Leggat, P.A., & Leggat, F.W. (2003). Reported fatal and non-fatal incidents involving tourists in Thailand, July 1997–June 1999. *Travel Medicine and International Health, 1,* 107–113.

O Estado de São Paulo. (2004). *Turistas Passeiam Tranquilos sem Saber de Onde de Assaltos,* 21 November, p. C-3.

Pizam, A. (1999). A comprehensive approach to classifying acts of crime and violence at tourism destinations. *Journal of Travel Research, 38*(1), 5–13.

Tarlow, P. (2002). Los problemas para la seguridad para el turismo actual. *Policia y Criminalistica, 344,* 50–56 (Buenos Aires, Argentina, Policia Federal Argentina).

Chapter 8

Current Issues in Travel and Tourism Law

David Grant, Stephen Mason, Malcolm Khan and Rob Davis

Introduction

The travel industry is no stranger to the disruption caused by the turbulence, which is the theme of this book. In fact, by its very nature, the industry may be more susceptible than most. Which other industry transports millions of people halfway around the globe and deposits them in third world countries with imperfect infrastructures, unfamiliar cultures, fragile economies, dubious political regimes, extreme weather conditions and promises them paradise — all supplied by independent foreign contractors employing untrained temporary staff on poverty line wages? The existence of the whole industry is a triumph of hope over experience and it is no surprise that occasionally that hope is misplaced.

This chapter is concerned with the legal consequences of events — political, meteorological or medical — which may cause the best of travel arrangements to fail, often disastrously, sometimes fatally. Those events are hurricanes, food poisoning, DVT and terrorism. We shall examine each of them in turn.

Hurricanes

The names, Charley, Frances, Ivan and Jeanne could not be more reassuring, rather like favourite Uncles and Aunts, but in truth these hurricanes were terrifying in their ferocity, striking the Caribbean and Florida in a period of just 6 weeks between 16 August and 26 September 2004. The destruction they wrought was of startling magnitude — buildings damaged, cars wrecked, boats blown aground, trailer parks destroyed, power lines brought down, roads swept away by floods and landslides, crops flattened, trees felled and over 100 people killed.

The damage caused to the tourism industry was equally destructive — theme parks and hotels closed, cruises re-routed, flights cancelled and holidays ruined. But what of the holidaymakers' rights in these circumstances? Do they have to stand the loss or are they entitled to refunds or even compensation? It is beyond the scope of this short section to provide comprehensive coverage but if we confine the discussion to holidaymakers departing from Europe, the largest body of outgoing tourists in the world, the discussion is more manageable. The issues can be broken down further into those who take package holidays to the regions affected and those who book flights and accommodation independently.

Package Holidaymakers

The law on package holidays is relatively straightforward. It can be found in the *European Council Directive on Package Travel, Package Holidays and Package Tours* (90/314/EEC), which has subsequently been transposed into the law of each of the Member States. Briefly, this piece of legislation provides for the rights of 'consumers' who purchase a 'package' from an 'organiser' (tour operator). A package is defined in Article 2 as:

> the pre-arranged combination of not fewer than two of the following when sold or offered for sale at an inclusive price and when the service covers a period of more than twenty-four hours or includes overnight accommodation:
>
> (a) transport;
> (b) accommodation;
> (c) other tourist services not ancillary to transport or accommodation and accounting for a significant proportion of the package.

The Directive provides extensive protection for consumers in a number of different ways including the provision of comprehensive information (Articles 3 and 4) and the establishment of a financial protection scheme in the event of an organiser's insolvency (Article 7). However, we are concerned with those parts of Article 4 that cover pre- and post-departure problems.

Articles 4.5 and 4.6, covering pre-departure problems, provide that if an organiser has to alter an essential term of the contract before departure or has to cancel the contract, then the consumer is entitled to certain remedies — the offer of alternative packages or a full refund. No compensation is payable in the event that the change or cancellation is caused by *force majeure*. *Force majeure* is defined as:

> unusual and unforeseeable circumstances beyond the control of the party by whom it is pleaded, the consequences of which could not have been avoided even if all due care had been exercised (Article 6(ii)).

In the event of a hurricane causing significant delays in departure, the change of resort or hotel, or the complete cancellation of the holiday, Article 4 would be triggered. The tour operator would either have to offer alternative packages to the holidaymakers or refund their money. However, it is unlikely that further compensation would be payable, given the definition of a *force majeure* event.

As for post-departure problems, the tour operator is governed by Article 4.7, which provides that in the event of being unable to provide a significant proportion of the services contracted for the tour operator must make suitable alternative arrangements for the continuation of the package at no extra cost, or, failing that, take the holidaymaker home again. Case law suggests that if the failure is due to a *force majeure* event then no compensation is payable. If, for example, the hotel accommodation is badly damaged by the hurricane, the tour operator must endeavour to find suitable alternatives, and if this is not possible they must take the holidaymakers home. Given the widespread destruction caused by hurricanes, it may very well be difficult for suitable alternatives to be found, but by the same token repatriating holidaymakers may be equally difficult, at least in the short term. With airports closed and airline schedules disrupted, it may be that the victims will have to endure their surroundings for some considerable time before being able to escape.

Air Travel

Although the law on package holidays may be straightforward, the position for air travellers is more complicated. Travellers who have booked flights independently of a package are partly covered by the new *Montreal Convention* (Convention for the Unification of Certain Rules for International Carriage by Air, Montreal, 28 May 1999), and partly by the contract made between the parties. The former applies if the hurricane delays the flight and the latter if the hurricane causes the flight to be cancelled altogether (although in marginal cases this distinction may be difficult to draw). The reason for this is that the Convention has specific provisions relating to delays but does not cover cancellations.

Article 19 provides that in the case of delays:

> the carrier is liable for damage occasioned by delay in the carriage by air of passengers, baggage or cargo. Nevertheless, the carrier shall not be liable for damage occasioned by delay if it proves that it and its servants and agents took all measures that could reasonably be required to avoid the damage or that it was impossible for it or them to take such measures

The real issue therefore for passengers held on the ground for hours, if not days, before being able to depart, is whether the airline did all that it could to avoid the damage. Given that the hurricane will have prevented all flights reaching the destination airport, and thus ruling out any re-scheduling of the flight, this issue would probably be decided in the airline's favour. The passenger would therefore be left uncompensated by the airline for the delay — whether at the beginning or end of the holiday. It should be observed, however, that Article 19 does not say that the *delay* should be avoided if possible; it refers to avoiding the *damage* caused by the delay. There is an argument that airlines should mitigate the damage caused by long delays by providing refreshments and accommodation for stranded passengers — even if re-routing may not be possible. (Note that under the new EU Regulation 261/2004 establishing common rules on compensation and assistance to passengers in the event of denied boarding and of cancellation or long delay of flights passengers will have to be offered assistance if their flights are delayed or cancelled — refreshments, meals, accommodation, telephone calls, as appropriate.)

Should they wish to litigate, passengers have a choice of venue under the Convention. They can bring their case before the court of the domicile of the carrier or of its principal place of business, or where it has a place of business through which the contract has been made or before the court at the place of destination (Article 33). The practical effect of this is that passengers will, in most cases, be able to litigate in their home country.

As for cancellations that are not covered by the Montreal Convention, there is no uniform set of international rules to govern the parties' rights, so recourse would have to be had to the terms and conditions of the contract between the passenger and the airline. However, before any court looked at the contractual provisions, it would first have to be decided which courts have jurisdiction, and which law would apply. If we assume that we are dealing with an EU passenger and an airline established in an EU state the position would be governed, as far as jurisdiction is concerned, by the Brussels Regulation (Council Regulation 44/2001, the 'Judgments Regulation'). The general rule under the Regulation is that defendants have to be sued in the country where they are domiciled (Article 2), but this rule is subject to a number of exceptions. The first is that in the case of contracts the defendant may be sued in the courts of the country where the contract is to be performed (Article 5). This rule is subject to a further exception where one of the parties is a consumer, in which case he is permitted to sue either in the country of domicile of the defendant or in the country where the consumer is domiciled (Article 16). Unfortunately, for air travellers this does not apply to contracts of transport (Article 15.3). However, all these rules are subject to one overriding rule, which is that if the parties have made an express choice of jurisdiction this will prevail (Article 23).

A quick glance at the conditions of carriage of two major European airlines, British Airways and KLM reveal that neither has an express jurisdiction clause, so the courts of the country where the contract was to be performed would have jurisdiction. This would probably be determined by the location of the departure airport. This in turn would favour the passenger who would, in most cases, be departing from an airport in his home jurisdiction.

As for the law that applies, this will be determined by the Rome Convention on the Law Applicable to Contractual Obligations 1980 to which EU States are party. This provides that if the parties have expressly stated the applicable law then this will prevail (Article 3). Failing that, the applicable law will be the law of the country with which the contract has the greatest connection (Article 4) — which will be determined by such factors as where the contract was made, where it was to be performed, where the parties are resident, etc. Again there is a consumer exception but as with the Brussels Regulation this does not apply to contracts of carriage (Article 5.4) although it would apply to a package holiday (Article 5.5). Neither of the contracts referred to specify a choice of law so the rules about close connection would apply.

As for the substance of the contract, both carriers have very similar clauses covering cancellations, which give passengers a range of remedies including re-routing or a refund. It is unlikely that such clauses would fall foul of the European legislation on unfair contract terms (Council Directive 93/13/EEC on Unfair Terms in Consumer Contracts) and would therefore be enforceable by the airline in almost any European jurisdiction. The passenger would therefore either have to wait for a suitable flight or accept a refund but no compensation would be available. Given that the cancellation was due to a hurricane this seems more than fair in the circumstances. In the United Kingdom under the law of frustration of contract they would be entitled to no more and in some cases considerably less.

Accommodation

If the holidaymaker has also booked accommodation independently then the situation is similar to the cancellation of the flight, there is no international convention such as the

Montreal Convention to determine the rights of the parties. They would be thrown back on the contract between them. The same issues of jurisdiction and choice of law would also arise. This is further complicated by the fact that for contracts with non-EU defendants, the Brussels Regulation and the Rome Convention may not apply. So, for example, a holidaymaker may have booked a villa in Orlando over the internet, and the contract provides that the courts of Florida (USA) will have jurisdiction and Floridian law will apply. In such a case the courts in the EU, applying the doctrine of *forum non conveniens*, may not accept jurisdiction and agree that the Florida courts may be more appropriate in the circumstances. Thus, holidaymakers who are informed just prior to travel that their villa has been destroyed will find themselves with the unenviable task of having to sue the accommodation provider in a Florida court under the US law of frustration of contract — not an enticing prospect. On the other hand, if the holidaymakers had purchased villa accommodation in the Dutch West Indies from a wholesaler/principal in Holland, the Brussels Regulation and the Rome Convention will apply.

Perhaps the most sensible solution in all these cases is for the holidaymaker to have taken out a travel insurance policy protected against the risk of hurricane damage. Litigation is not an activity, which any individual with limited resources should undertake without careful consideration, particularly where it involves a foreign element. The money would be better spent on next year's vacation rather than chasing compensation for last year's.

Food Poisoning

In this section, the term 'food poisoning' will be used as shorthand to cover a variety of agents which can have the effect of causing illness, and thereby ruining a holiday — as well as longer term consequences for a few unlucky victims (see Chapter 10). For example, the following types of outbreak are often met:

- Those most accurately described as 'food poisoning' — Salmonella in its various types, E. Coli 157, Shigella or Vibrio
- A water-borne agent such as Cryptosporidium, which can occupy the municipal water supply; but in a holiday context is most commonly associated with swimming pools
- A further water-borne bacterium, namely Legionella, causing Legionnaires disease; commonly identified with the water supply or air conditioning system of a hotel
- A virus such as Norovirus, also known as Norwalk-like virus or winter vomiting virus, which is spread person to person.

Tour Operator Liability

In English Law, the relevant legislation is the Package Travel, Package Holidays and Package Tours Regulations 1992 (SI 1992 No. 3288), based upon the EU Directive on Package Travel, Package Holidays and Package Tours (90/314/EEC) referred to above. This imposes liability on the 'organiser' of 'packages' both of which terms are defined in Regulation 2. In common parlance, it is convenient to refer to 'organisers' as 'tour operators'; but it is always important to remember that the definition captures a wide variety of businesses that put together packages; and covers business and educational travel, as well as holidays.

For our purpose the most significant regulation is Regulation 15. This provides that the organiser is liable to the consumer "for the proper performance of the obligations under the contract regardless of whether such obligations are to be performed by [the organiser] or by other suppliers of services".

What is the effect of this provision? In the event of an outbreak of food poisoning, does it impose strict or fault liability on the tour operator? On one view, it could be argued that liability should be strict; after all, if the food provided in the hotel causes illness, is that not improper performance of the holiday?

Since 2001 it has been possible to give a clear and confident answer to the question. It is fault liability. This was decided by the Court of Appeal in *Hone v Going Places* 2001 EWCA Civ 947. Longmore LJ pointed out that Regulation 15 does not deal with improper performance of the *holiday*. It deals with improper performance of the 'obligations under the contract'. He said:

> The starting point must in my view be the contract which Mr Hone made with the defendant ... in the absence of any contrary intention, the normal implication will be that the service contracted for would be rendered with reasonable skill and care. Of course absolute obligations may be assumed. If the brochure or advertisement on which the consumer relies promises a swimming pool, it will be a term of the contract that a swimming pool will be provided. But in the absence of express wording, there would not be an absolute obligation for example to ensure that the holidaymaker catches no infection whilst swimming in the swimming pool. The obligation assumed would be that reasonable skill and care will be taken to ensure that the pool is free from infection.

Prior to this decision, County Courts had been using a different route to come to much the same conclusions. In *Bedeschi and Holt v Travel Promotions Limited*, Central London County Court, January 1998, the claimants had suffered from vomiting that was attributable to the food and drink they consumed on a Nile Cruise. On the basis of expert evidence that standards of hygiene in Egypt were such that the risk of infection could not be eliminated, the court held that the claimant's illness might have been foreseeable but could not have been forestalled. The defendants therefore had a defence under Regulation 15(2).

Following *Hone*, however, it is clear that the burden of proof is on the claimant to establish negligence, and there is no burden of proof on the defendant to establish one of the defences. In the case of *Bedeschi*, the result would be the same; that may not always be the case.

Is Food Goods or Services?

The argument is sometimes heard that the meal element of a package holiday is not in fact the supply of a service, but is the supply of goods. The point being made is this: it is usual in contracts for the supply of services for the courts to impose a 'reasonable skill and care' test, as the Court of Appeal did in *Hone*. However, in the sale of goods, it is usual for strict liability to apply.

While the argument remains open, there are three reasons why it may not be very significant:

(1) It was argued by Mr Hone that Regulation 15 imposed strict liability. Although the facts are different, nonetheless it is important to remember that Longmore LJ said in response to that argument that those who drafted the Package Travel Regulations could have imposed strict liability if they had wanted to, 'but, by the use of the term improper performance, it is patent that they had not done so'.
(2) Even if there were strict liability, this would bring into play the exceptions in Regulation 15(2), for example, an event which could not have been forestalled even with all due care; or the unavoidable acts of the third party. While this switches the burden of proof to the defendant to establish reasonable skill and care, we have seen from the case of *Bedeschi* that the net result may be the same.
(3) In any event, the question is fact sensitive. Is it the actual food, which was defective? Or was it the preparation of the food, the handling of the food, the kitchen conditions, etc., which were defective? If any of the latter then the improper performance alleged would appear to be concerning a service.

Hotels

If the booking for the accommodation had been made by the guest directly with a hotel rather than through a tour operator, the problem for the guest would be the same as discussed in the sections on hurricanes and terrorism, namely, which court has jurisdiction and which law applies.

Summary

Applying the above principles, and on the basis of a factual matrix such as most commonly arises, how will our claimant fare if he brings a claim in respect of the four types of illness identified at the outset? Using the same numbering system:

(1) If there is a mass outbreak of food poisoning at a hotel, the facts, and the inferences which might reasonably be drawn from the facts, will generally make it possible for a claimant to demonstrate that the illness is the result of a lack of reasonable care and skill on the part of the hotel etc. The odds therefore favour the claimant in this situation. Where, however, the claimant is the only person affected by the illness, in a hotel where many other people are staying, it suggests that the claimant may have difficulty; even if he were to demonstrate liability (lack of reasonable care and skill), in overcoming the second great hurdle which lies in his path, namely causation? On a balance of probabilities was the hotel the source of his illness, or did he perhaps eat an ice cream bought from a kiosk on the beach?
(2) Cryptosporidium gets into swimming pool water when an already infected person has a 'faecal accident' in the pool, and the unfortunate claimant comes along shortly afterwards and swallows some of the water. If those are the facts, establishing negligence may be a problem. However, a continuing outbreak, which lasts for sometime, might well raise questions about the hotel's filtration system policies and operation.

(3) As we understand it, *Legionella* bacteria should not be in the systems of a properly run hotel; accordingly it may be possible for the claimant to establish liability, as long as the claimant is able to demonstrate causation, i.e. that the hotel was the source of the outbreak.

(4) As to Norovirus, the jury is still out. Claimants argue that these outbreaks can be avoided or stopped; defendants argue that they cannot. There is a need for more research and expert opinion in an area, which has only recently started to become the subject of litigation.

Deep-Vein Thrombosis (DVT)

In recent years, both the travelling public and the airline industry have become alerted to the medical and legal implications of passengers complaining of Deep-Vein Thrombosis (DVT) caused, as the passengers would claim, by a lack of adequate space on an aircraft, especially the space available to those in the economy class section of an airline.

So, what is DVT?

> [it] is a condition in which a small blood clot or thrombus forms mainly in the deep veins of the legs … Complications occur when a thrombus breaks away from the wall of the vein … and is carried along with the flow of the blood as an embolus. If the embolus reaches a blood vessel through which it cannot pass, it blocks the vessel, thereby producing an embolism. The most serious of these occurs in the lungs (a pulmonary embolism) … (Lord Phillips in *Re Deep Vein Thrombosis and Air Travel Group Litigation* [2004] 1 All ER 445 at 449).

The passengers' perception, supported to some extent by independent research, is that the condition of DVT is brought on by being stationary for too many hours in a sitting position in a certain kind of environment, all of which is probably a very accurate description of what normally happens in the economy section of an aeroplane on a long haul airline flight. But the relative newness of this illness combined with the fact that DVT could equally be a problem for non-airline travellers and that most if not all the claimants will have chosen, for obvious reasons, to travel economy class mean that compensation claims against the airlines in a court of law for this illness have some significant legal hurdles to overcome. For example, even if it is rightly acknowledged that a duty of care is owed to each and every passenger by the airline carrier:

- Is DVT to be classed as an accident within the terms of the Warsaw Convention (now superseded in most cases by the Montreal Convention)?
- Can it be legally established that the claimant's DVT was caused by travelling on the airline?
- If so, is it the "sitting part" of the travel, which causes the DVT? Or is the environment? Or a combination of factors?
- When did the airlines know of the DVT problem? What did they do on becoming aware there was a problem?

- In which jurisdiction do you sue?
- Does it make a difference whether you sue in contract, tort or under the terms of a particular Convention?
- Will the defendants be able to use such defences as contributory negligence, for example, that the passenger did not wear special flight socks or drank too much alcohol during the flight?

The hope was that as the case law came before the domestic courts in various jurisdictions, so definitive answers would become evident from the different decisions. What has actually happened is that although there is case law the claims have failed at what may be called the first hurdle, with the result that there has been almost no necessity for the courts to deal with the majority of the questions posed above.

In England, in *Re Deep Vein Thrombosis and Air Travel Group Litigation* [2004] 1 All ER 445, the Court of Appeal ruled that the passengers' claim was non-sustainable because it was not an 'accident' within the terms of Article 17(a) of the Warsaw Convention ("The carrier is liable for damage sustained ... if the accident which caused the damage … took place on board the aircraft or in the course of any of the operations of embarking or disembarking") since, to constitute a Convention accident the event in question had to be both unusual, unexpected or untoward and external to the passenger, whereas in the case of the DVT claimant the injury tended to result from the passenger's own internal reaction to the environment; furthermore, since the Convention was interpreted as being the sole provider of legal redress there was no scope for the claimants to pursue any alternative arguments or to seek any alternative remedy using common law concepts such as tort or contract. It must be emphasised that the Appeal Court seemed to be in no doubt whatsoever about the rightness of its approach and conclusion. Quoting with approval from the United States Supreme Court in *Air France v Saks (1985)470 US 392* and from *Shawcross and Beaumont: Air Law*, the court helpfully summed up the position this way in the words of Kay LJ:

> If one asks oneself the simple question, was there, on any recognised meaning of the word, an accident in circumstances where a person suffered a deep vein thrombosis merely because of the effect of a flight on an aeroplane without there being any triggering event, the answer in my judgment is quite simply, No (p. 466).

But on the same day that Nelson J gave his judgment in *Re Deep Vein* at first instance (the judgment which the Appeal Court approved of) the decision of the Supreme Court of Victoria in *Povey v Civil Aviation Safety Authority and others* [2002] VSC 580 was given and there Bongiorno J did uphold a claim for compensation under Article 17, ruling that the word 'accident' in Article 17 could include a failure to warn the passengers of both the known risks of DVT and the precautions that could be taken; a ruling which Lord Phillips was able to dispose of in this way:

> I cannot accept that the first two sentences [of Bongiorno J's judgment] deal adequately with the difficulty of bringing a failure to warn or advice within the definition of an accident.

Most recently in the United States Court of Appeals for the Ninth Circuit in *Rodriguez v Ansett Australia Ltd and Air New Zealand* (2004) the Court ruled that DVT was not an accident 'but instead the result of Ms Rodriguez's reaction to the aircraft's normal operations'. In the *Rodriguez* case the claimant used a variety of arguments to try and sway the court (lack of a pre-existing condition, policy considerations such as looking at the purpose of the Warsaw Convention, giving a liberal meaning to the causal link between the event and the operation of the aircraft) but to no avail.

One argument which Ms Rodriguez and her lawyers apparently did not explore is the one that says the Warsaw Convention remedies are not and should not be the sole remedies available for DVT, because of Article 24 of the Convention. The version of Article 24 of the Convention, which was relevant in the *Sidhu* case said:

> (1) In the case covered by Articles 18 and 19 … any action for damages, however founded, can only be brought subject to the conditions and limits set out in this Convention. (2) In the cases covered by Article 17, the provisions of the preceding paragraph also apply …

But this point had been considered in the House of Lords' case of *Sidhu v British Airways plc* [1997] AC 430 and there Lord Hope of Craighead summed up the court's attitude to the point this way:

> Thus the purpose is to ensure that, in all questions relating to the carrier's liability, it is the provisions of the Convention which apply and that the passenger does not have access to any other remedies, whether under the common law or otherwise, which may be available within the particular country where he chooses to raise his action. The carrier does not need to make provision for the risk of being subjected to such remedies, because the whole matter is regulated by Convention (p. 447).

In short this interpretation concentrates on ensuring that the carrier is not disadvantaged by having to defend claims under a variety of different municipal laws. But what about the rights of the passenger? Does not the *Sidhu* interpretation infringe the Human Rights Act 1998 and in particular Articles 6 and 8? No, said the House of Lords. Again as Lord Hope put it:

> The provisions of the European Convention have no bearing on the interpretation of international conventions such as the Warsaw Convention on carriage by air … (p. 443).

So, given these decisions and arguments, where in law does this leave the passenger who in future alleges that he/she is suffering from DVT and that this was caused by the cramped conditions, etc. on board the defendant's aircraft? Seemingly the claimant may only contemplate success if it can be shown that no precautions against DVT were advised by the airline either before or during the flight, such as flight socks or some form of exercise while on board the aircraft; or if it can indeed be shown that there was an 'accident' *in the form of an external event* ("… the flight crew's decision not to divert the aircraft following the plaintiff's heart attack could constitute an 'accident'" … per Circuit Judge Tashima in the *Rodriguez* case). Other than that, hoping that the Warsaw Convention is amended? Hardly likely. Forum shopping to find a jurisdiction which just might treat DVT as an *external event*? Not very practical. At present the legal picture appears bleak for the passenger/claimant with DVT.

Terrorism

Every month we receive news of terrorist attacks somewhere in the world. The nature and extent of these attacks vary depending on the objectives, resources and commitment of the perpetrators (see Chapter 6). Sometimes they involve the ransom, mutilation or execution of kidnap victims; bombings, aircraft attack, poison gas attacks and hijacking of aircraft, cruise liners, buses and even theatres.

Sometimes travellers become unintended victims of ethnic or political conflicts occurring in foreign places. It is becoming more common for travellers themselves to become the focus of violence by terrorists who regard them as representatives of enemy regimes or States.

When these attacks succeed they result in deaths and injuries to the victims, dislocation of their families, destruction of property and financial loss for survivors and their dependants. Invariably, after the initial shock of a terrorist-mediated tragedy wanes, thoughts turn to the future. Those whose lives have been ruined by injury or the loss of loved ones sometimes consider legal proceedings to assist them to regain some semblance of their prior life and to improve safety for others in the future.

The legal rights of terrorist victims vary significantly between countries, as do the avenues open to them for recompense. It is impossible in a chapter such as this to provide anything more than a general overview of the avenues open to consumers under the law and the issues commonly encountered by claimants in this type of case. The comments made in the balance of this section summarise the position that exists in much of the common law countries such as the United Kingdom, Canada and Australia, together with the USA. Analogous rights and remedies also exist in many other developed countries, though the terminology and application may differ significantly.

Litigation Issues

Requirement of a duty of care   No legal remedy exists unless the person against whom compensation is claimed owes and has breached a legal duty to the claimant. Such a duty may arise in a number of different ways. For example, the USA and most developed common law countries recognise duties to:

- exercise reasonable care to prevent harm to those who might foreseeably be injured by your conduct (negligence);
- perform obligations expressly or impliedly imposed under legal agreements (contract);
- comply with the requirements of legislation intended to provide for the safety of vulnerable citizens (statutory duty); and
- ensure that goods supplied in the course of commerce are free from defect that may cause injury (product liability).

Breach of any of these duties can enable an injured consumer or a dependant of a deceased terrorist victim to claim compensation through the courts.

For example, subsequent to the attacks on the World Trade Centre on 11 September 2001, USA class action proceedings were commenced against the airline security services responsible for screening passengers on the relevant flights; the aircraft manufacturer; the airlines concerned; and the owners of the World Trade Centre.

The proceedings alleged numerous breaches of duty against each defendant. Negligence was alleged against the airlines and their airport security companies for failing to detect the hijackers. Both negligence and product liability actions were brought against Boeing, the aircraft manufacturer for failing to ensure cockpit doors were sufficiently reinforced to prevent unauthorised entry by hijackers. The owners of the World Trade Centre were alleged to be negligent for the defective design of the buildings and the failure to design and implement systems to evacuate occupants in a timely manner.

The USA District Court found that each of the defendants owed legal duties of care to the claimants and directed that the actions proceed to trial to determine whether the defendants had, on the evidence, breached these duties.

Amount of damages recoverable   Whether, and if so, how much in damages are recoverable in a successful case will depend on a number of factors.

For example, as a general rule Courts will apply the law of the country where the attack occurred. These laws may vary widely between countries. Some countries do not limit the damages that may be recovered for personal injuries or death, whereas others limit claims involving certain types of transport, others limit damages generally, and some prevent compensation claims being litigated at all.

Where the place or circumstances in which an injury occurs involves international air transport the compensation recoverable is regulated by international treaty. For example, the liability of air carriers for injury and death (as well as loss or damage of goods) occurring during international flights is regulated by Article 17 of the *Warsaw Convention of 1929* as amended by the *Hague Protocol of 1955* and the *Montreal Protocol 1975* (collectively referred to as the 'Convention').

Most countries have enacted laws that incorporate the Convention into their domestic laws. Where this legislation exists it usually has the effect of making the Convention the exclusive remedy for accidents occurring on international flights. In the decades since the Convention was created its monetary limits on liability have failed to keep pace with inflation. Further, not all countries are parties to each amendment and some countries have failed to update their local laws to incorporate applicable amendments. To make matters worse, the liability limits under the Convention depend on both countries of origin and destination being parties to the same amendment.

This has produced a situation that ensures the lowest common denominator for damages. As a result damages under the Convention are often unacceptably low by modern standards. Consequently some countries have since enacted unlimited liability for Convention flights originating within their borders, some have imposed higher limits on their own national carriers, and some airlines have agreed to waive reliance on the damages limits imposed by the Convention itself.

More recently the *Montreal Convention 1999* was created to overcome many of the difficulties that have developed with the earlier Convention, but it has just recently received

sufficient ratifications to come into force and replace the older Convention in some jurisdictions. As a result, many international flights continue to be covered by the older regime
and a patchwork of laws and contracts intended to overcome their worst effects.

Choosing a viable defendant   A number of problems exist in identifying an appropriate
defendant in terrorism cases. These problems arise because litigation is pointless unless the
defendant owns assets that are either:

- within the jurisdiction of the deciding court; or
- in another country that permits the enforcement of the deciding court's judgement.

Clearly, the terrorists themselves are legally liable for their conduct but, for the reasons
stated, they are invariably beyond the reach of the law. Even when the individual perpetrators are apprehended and brought within a jurisdiction that permits legal recovery, they
usually have insufficient financial resources to justify proceeding against for damages.

Occasionally, it is possible to proceed against those who ordered or sponsored the terrorists but that is rarely successful or practical. Further, where the sponsors of terrorism are sovereign states they are usually immune from legal action in the courts of foreign countries.

It is not surprising therefore when victims of terrorism, if they sue, usually proceed against
local and viable defendants who ought to have foreseen the risk of attack and who had some
degree of control over and consequent responsibility for the safety of the victims of terror.

As a result, the persons and corporations most likely to become defendants following a
terrorist attack are the owners of premises, vessels or airlines in which the attack occurred,
or the providers of contracted security services responsible for screening luggage and
searching suspicious passengers.

Issues of jurisdiction, applicable law and most convenient forum   Terrorism is often
international. Terrorist attacks may be planned in one country (often without the sanction
of the government of the country concerned); financed by donations raised in other countries; and implemented by terrorists trained in countries different from those in which the
eventual terrorist attack occurs. Bombs may be placed in aircraft luggage in one country
and not explode until some considerable time later, possibly passing through other countries and involving different connecting flights in the process.

The international character of these events poses particular difficulties for courts asked
to decide claims on behalf of terrorism victims. Where terrorist attacks involve international elements courts invariably have to decide:

- whether they have jurisdiction to hear the case (the jurisdiction issue);
- what law to apply in determining the case (the choice of law issue); and
- whether, even if the court has jurisdiction, it would be more convenient for the case to
  be heard by another court (the most convenient forum issue).

If a court concludes that it lacks jurisdiction, or that it is not the most convenient forum
for deciding the case, it will usually either strike out or stay the proceedings. If a court
decides to hear the case, it is no guarantee that it will apply the law of the country where
the court is located. As a rule, courts will apply the law of the country where the wrongful
act occurred. Wrongful acts, in this context, include actionable breaches of statutes or

claims based in negligence, wrongful imprisonment, assault or other similar conduct. Where claims are based on breach of contract the courts usually apply the law of the country where the contract was formed (unless the contract itself provides to the contrary).

Locating a lawyer and legal costs   Often victims of terrorist attacks must, if they issue proceedings, rely on the advice and services of foreign lawyers. Personal injury and death claims involving issues of international law are often very complex. Care should be taken to engage lawyers with knowledge of, and hopefully prior experience in, this type of claim.

In some countries lawyers are allowed to represent clients on either a contingent or a speculative basis. Under these arrangements the lawyer assumes the financial cost of bringing the action. Where these arrangements are not available then the claimant will generally have to pay legal fees as the case progresses. Care should always be taken when engaging lawyers in other countries as legal costs and exchange rates can vary enormously.

In some countries an unsuccessful party to litigation will be required to pay legal costs to a successful party. This is often referred to as the 'loser pays' rule. This rule applies in most common law countries. In contrast, in the USA each party usually pays their own legal fees, regardless of outcome. Sometimes this is called a 'user pays' rule.

Sometimes courts will require foreign claimants to provide security for costs that may be awarded against them if they lose. This usually only occurs in those countries that apply a loser pays rule.

Conclusion

Before 11 September 2001, most insurers perceived the risk of death, injury or property damage from terrorism to be very low. Indeed the risk was considered so low in countries previously untouched by terrorism that public liability insurers provided insurance against the risk of terrorism as part of their standard public liability inclusions.

The events of 9/11 caused an immediate and profound shock to the global insurance market, coinciding as it did with depressed equity earnings and the end of sustained period of aggressive price competition within the industry. Since then many insurers have refused to provide terrorism cover. This adds yet another layer of risk and uncertainty to victims of terrorism who seek to recover damages against negligent security companies, building owners, travel agents and transport providers.

Only one thing is now certain, the law experiences as much difficulty assisting victims of terrorism as governments do at preventing terrorist attacks. As a result, people should take increased care for their own safety when travelling.

References

Legislation

International Treaties

Warsaw Convention 1929
Hague Protocol 1955

Montreal Protocol 1975
Montreal Convention 1999
Rome Convention on the Law Applicable to Contractual Obligations 1980

European Legislation

Brussels Regulation (Council Regulation 44/2001, the 'Judgments Regulation')
Council Directive 93/13/EEC on Unfair Terms in Consumer Contracts
European Council Directive on Package Travel, Package Holidays and Package Tours (90/314/EEC)

UK Legislation

Package Travel, Package Holidays and Package Tours Regulations 1992 (SI 1992 No. 3288)

Case Law

England & Wales

Bedeschi and Holt v Travel Promotions Limited, Central London County Court, January 1998
Hone v Going Places 2001 EWCA Civ 947
Re Deep Vein Thrombosis and Air Travel Group Litigation [2004] 1 All ER 445
Sidhu v British Airways plc [1997] AC 430

Australia

Povey v Civil Aviation Safety Authority and others [2002] VSC 580

USA

Air France v Saks (1985)470 US 392
Rodriguez v Ansett Australia Ltd and Air New Zealand (2004)

Chapter 9

Natural Disaster Management

Alison Specht

Introduction

Tourism is a discretionary expenditure; the primary concern of tourists is to travel to destinations that satisfy their desires, while minimising their exposure to threats to their safety (Beirman, 2003). In recent years, the attractiveness of high-risk, exotic destinations to increasingly global tourists has exposed them to greater levels of risk (Faulkner, 2001). The emergence of "adventure tourism" adds to this exposure (Ewert & Jamieson, 2003). The topic of this chapter is the threat posed to tourists from natural disasters, and how management, both in the short and long term, can reduce this threat.

The number of natural and technological disasters throughout the world has increased exponentially in recent years (Figure 9.1). The cost of such disasters to the community and regional economies is enormous. The recent tsunami (26 December 2004) in the southern Asian region illustrates the costs, in lives (more than 160,000 people perished as an immediate result of the event itself), and to the economy of the affected areas (as yet incalculable). The 20th century hurricane costs in the United States until 1985 exceeded US$12,000 million (Rogers, 1986), the tsunami in 1857 in the Virgin Islands put off the United States of America's purchase of the islands for 50 years (Palm & Hodgson, 1993), and a single season of wildfire in June and July 1998 in the St Johns River Water Management District in Florida caused total losses of at least US$600 million, of which US$140 million were to tourism alone (Butry, Mercer, Prestemon, Pye, & Holmes, 2001). With global networks having increased concurrently, many of these effects are felt well beyond the immediate location of the disaster. Good management should aim to minimise or avoid adverse effects of all events at all times, and disasters are no exception.

In this chapter, the elements of natural disasters and disaster management are introduced and discussed. The inherently variable nature of disasters and their effects mean that it would be a fallacy to develop highly specific protocols for one or another type of disaster or an industry group. The particular features of the tourism industry are also discussed, and the issues raised that could be specific to good management for the continued sustainable operations of that industry.

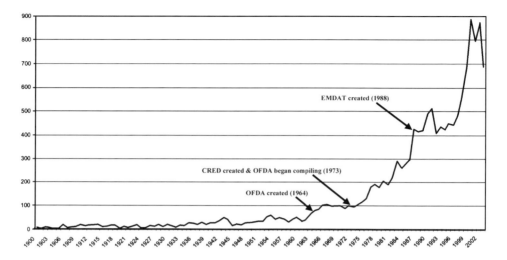

Figure 9.1: The total number of natural and technological disasters registered in EM-DAT. (From the OFDA/CRED[1] International Disaster Database, International Strategy for Disaster Reduction (ISDR), 2004a. With permission from ISDR.)

What are Natural Disasters and How do They Wreak Their Effects?

Many disturbing events, although extreme, are part of the day-to-day perambulations of a good manager. Issues continually arise which good managers deal with by using coping strategies which are incorporated into their management frameworks. Crises may arise if an event is so significant or so sudden that it (i) challenges the existing structure or routine of an organisation; (ii) there is a perception of an inability to cope among those affected, existing coping strategies not being sufficient or sufficiently flexible; or (iii) warning signs are not heeded. Faulkner (2001) took pains to distinguish a crisis from a disaster, emphasising that a crisis is something largely of one's own making (due to mismanagement and hence theoretically completely avoidable), while disasters commonly arise when "an enterprise … is confronted with sudden unpredictable catastrophic changes over which it has little control" (Faulkner, 2001, p. 136).

The definition of a disaster applied by the International Strategy for Disaster Reduction (ISDR, 2004b) is that it is a serious disruption of societal or community function where losses (human, economic, material, or environmental) are substantial, and where the ability of the "enterprise" (country or region) to cope is a critical distinguishing feature. For a

---

[1] OFDA = USAID's Office of Foreign Disaster Assistance, which sponsors CRED. CRED = Centre for Research on the Epidemiology of Disasters, based in Belgium which became a World Health Organization Collaborating Centre in 1980.

disaster to be entered into the database of the OFDA/CRED International Disasters Database (EM-DAT), for example, at least one of the following criteria must be fulfilled:

- 10 or more people reported killed;
- 100 people reported affected;
- declaration of a state of emergency; and
- a call for international assistance.

Under these definitions, the events in the United States of America of 11 September 2001 would be defined as disasters, although the USA was able to recover without external physical or monetary support. The comparison of terminologies such as crisis, catastrophe, and disaster may seem somewhat semantic, but the important point is that to be a disaster, the event has to be abrupt, somewhat unexpected (at least at the time), the loss of life and/or property considerable, and the affected community unable to cope within their own resources.

Natural disasters are a specific type of disaster defined according to their origin. They are events that are precipitated by the occurrence of natural extreme events such as earthquakes, fire, volcanic eruptions, floods, and tsunami, or are due to biotic organisms (e.g. disease outbreaks and epidemics). A natural disaster is thus the product of such an event that has a profound effect on property, life, economy, or environment, beyond the coping ability of the affected party. The occurrence of natural disasters has been increasing in recent years (Figure 9.2), particularly those in the hydrometeorological category, which includes floods and wave surges, storms, drought and related disasters such as dust storms and fires, landslides, and avalanches. In Latin America, economic losses from natural disasters were nine times as great in the 1990s as in the 1960s (Blanchard-Boehm, 2004). Natural disasters have often been viewed in the past as "acts of god", and their amelioration treated accordingly (Keys, 1999; Kempe, 2003), although even in medieval times not all disasters were viewed, nor did all people view them, as punishment from the gods (Rohr, 2003).

All of the specified extreme natural events have occurred repeatedly at various times and places throughout the centuries. Some famous instances are the volcanic eruptions in Mt Vesuvius and Krakatoa; earthquakes in Japan, Turkey, and California; tsunami in Hawaii and the Pacific Ocean generally; floods in central America, Europe, and China; hurricanes in Florida and the Caribbean, cyclones in Australia, typhoons in south-east Asia; droughts across the world in the 6th and 7th centuries, in the mid-west of the USA in the 1920s and 1930s, and somewhere in north Africa nearly all the time. All are formative historic milestones that govern the nature of many modern societies. By definition, these events only become disasters when they are interfaced with humans. When they do not, they escape notice or comment (e.g. cyclones crossing a land margin in uninhabited areas). This inter-relationship between the uncontrollable, inviolate force of nature, and the recipient humans produces the disaster. Indeed the importance of human involvement has been suggested as a reason not to use the term "natural" when referring to these sorts of disasters (Blanchard-Boehm, 2004).

Famous biological disasters (epidemics of natural disease or insect infestations) include the locust plagues of biblical (and other) times, and the plagues caused by the organism *Yersina pestis* which spread from Africa to Europe in the 6th and 7th centuries causing incalculable deaths (Keys, 1999); when it broke out again in the 14th century (Chapman, 1999)

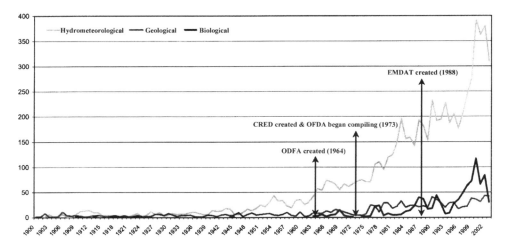

Figure 9.2: The number of natural disasters registered in EM-DAT, grouped into three types: hydro-meteorological, geological and biological. Hydrometeorological disasters include floods and wave surges, storms, drought, and related disasters such as dust storms and fires, landslides and avalanches; geological disasters include earthquakes, volcanic eruptions, and tsunami; biological disasters include epidemics and insect infestations. (Extracted from the OFDA/CRED International Disaster Database, ISDR, 2004a. With permission from ISDR.)

approximately 75 million people died. Epidemics of such organisms can often be related to physical events, such as drought, which, in the case of the plagues of the 6th and 7th centuries, appears to have precipitated a migration of rodents from failed croplands to port towns, then to trade vessels and then to Europe (Keys, 1999). Warfare breaks down barriers in disease transport as well as in hygiene and safety controls, as is the case with the Ebola virus (Chapman, 1999). The Spanish flu of 1918 killed 40 million people and hit just as the world was in the immediate recovery stage from the First World War as soldiers were most susceptible and were travelling home, providing a wonderful host and vector for the organism (Davies, 2000). The complex causes of biological hazards, their high mutability, and the very obvious role that humans play in their dissemination, places them in a special category on the boundary between a natural and a human-induced disaster, not dissimilar to pollution disasters (e.g. Bhopal). Physical natural disasters, however, are the focus of this paper.

The ISDR (2004b, p. 5) defines a hazard as "a process or phenomenon occurring in the biosphere that *may* constitute a damaging event", which may constitute a disaster. How hazardous an extreme natural event is depends on the vulnerability of the community to that event. The meaning of vulnerability is still fuzzy (Weichselgartner, 2001). Vulnerability is "susceptibility to injury or damage from a hazard" (Godschalk, 1991, p. 132; cited in McEntire & Myers, 2004, p. 144), or "the conditions determined by physical, social, economic, and environmental factors or processes, which increase the susceptibility of a community to the impact of hazards" (ISDR, 2004b, p. 8). The type or level of vulnerability is not "natural" for any community or society, but is the outcome of a complex suite of factors including affluence, education (both formal and informal), technological sophistication, and preparedness (Chapman, 1999). The importance of understanding that the creation of a disaster is as much dependent on the community being affected as the nature of the extreme natural event cannot be overstated. Vulnerability is partly the manifestation of the human tendency to defy hazard: by necessity (lack of alternatives), by default (ignorance) or by wilfulness (desire to take risks) (Alexander, 2000). People often place themselves in inherently hazardous areas, assuming that technology (e.g. warning systems, dams) will protect them, often having erased the very natural ecosystem buffers that might have protected them, and/or ignoring historical and ecological indications of the nature and extent of likely hazards, thus increasing vulnerability when the next event occurs (McEntire, 2004). Indeed, where and how development occurs can clearly determine the losses that will be suffered.

Cultural attitudes and practices can also increase vulnerability. Exposure to a hazard can vary widely depending on the type of hazard and the community it is affecting. Individual vulnerability, the personal or individual potential for loss, and the susceptibility of groups or society at large (social vulnerability) change both positively and negatively with the level of economic development. As a society becomes more developed, better planning will reduce vulnerability, while many members of such societies may become more *blasé* about the potential for a hazard to affect them (McEntire, 2004). The relationship between economic development and the number of disasters suffered is not linear. The least-developed countries suffer the least number of disasters, the most developed countries in the world the next, while a significantly greater number of disasters occur in the medium-developed countries (Figure 9.3). When these same countries are clustered according to per capita income, the frequency of disasters per year is high and very similar for the medium- and low-income countries, while the mainly Western block of high-income countries has a very low number of disasters per year.

When a country has low development and a low per capita income, the risk of a hazard producing a disaster according to the definitions of the ISDR is low: there is little property of value to be damaged, and although lives lost may be high, they are not reported or considered of sufficient importance to raise an alarm (McEntire, 2004). Education standards are commonly low, so understanding and warning may be poor. In addition, political and organisational structures in such countries are often poorly developed or supported, and not able or willing to recognise or admit disaster. As development increases, eagerness to increase income and status can take precedence over good planning, creating situations where new infrastructure and businesses are exposed in often-hazardous situations. In the most highly developed countries, protective measures are often in place to protect valuable assets, although their very value and the high density of population can make any disaster more costly than in either of the other two situations. As mentioned before, this group often feels that it can ignore warnings and development constraints when it can offset these by technological investment. Such risk-taking can often pay off, but occasionally the "one in a hundred year event" occurs more often than expected, or is greater than anticipated, resulting in a disaster (Drabek, 2000; Faulkner & Vikulov, 2001). The links between each of these development aggregates in our global community can reinforce these patterns, a matter which is discussed later in this chapter.

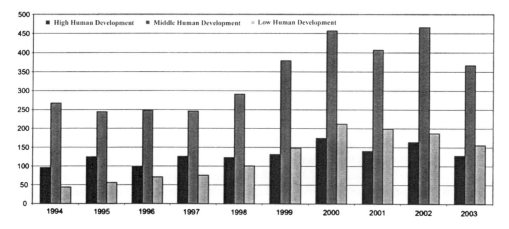

Figure 9.3: Total number of disasters per year from 1994 to 2004 according to human development aggregates. Countries belonging to the high human development aggregate include Canada, Chile, Europe, the Scandinavian countries, the Seychelles, Switzerland, the United Kingdom, and Uruguay, while those in the medium aggregate include Albania, Algeria, Brazil, Bulgaria, Guyana, Indonesia, Myanmar, Nepal, Paraguay, Sri Lanka, Thailand, Vanuatu, and Vietnam; those in the lowest aggregate include Angola, the Congo, Haiti, Kenya, Nigeria, Rwanda, Senegal, Togo, and Zimbabwe. (Sourced from the OFDA/CRED International Disaster Database, ISDR, 2004a. With permission from ISDR.)

For planners and insurance assessors, the element of risk that can be borne by the community is an important component of their work. Risk is commonly expressed as (from Alexander, 2000):

total risk $= \sum$ elements at risk $\times$ hazard $\times$ vulnerability

Natural hazard risk is dynamic and complex. Development of lands which are susceptible to hazards increases risk of life and property damage. For example, risk can be increased above the potential due to the hazard alone by inappropriate housing design (infrastructure vulnerability). A case study of natural hazards in Puerto Rico (Palm & Hodgson, 1993) highlighted the connection between housing construction and vulnerability to losses due to earthquake when compared with a similar earthquake-prone area, California. In Puerto Rico, housing is mostly of concrete or block construction, whereas in California it is of more earthquake-tolerant wood. This single fact makes Puerto Rico much more vulnerable to earthquake than California. On the other hand, it is less susceptible to fire, but fire is not as great a risk in Puerto Rico as in California. Poor education and communication can also increase vulnerability and hence risk.

The dramatic increase in the occurrence of disasters (Figures 9.1 and 9.2) has been accompanied by a similar increase in their average annual economic cost. Insurers are closely involved in covering this cost. In the past, historic claims experience has been sufficient for insurers to calculate the risk of a disaster and thence an appropriate premium for a property, but this only works if the risk is changing at a predictable rate (Crichton, 1999).

One of the ways in which insurers calculate risk in a changing environment is to use a "risk triangle" where the probability of a loss (risk) depends on three elements: hazard, vulnerability, and exposure. If the exposure of a property to a hazard is high (e.g. in earthquake-prone land), the vulnerability of that property is also high (inappropriate building materials), and an earthquake is likely to occur every 20 years (hazard), then the risk to the insurer of having to pay out is high. The insurer may decide not to cover the property, or may charge a high premium. Exposure is a calculation at the insurer level as much as at the property level, as insurers may decide to reduce their risk by limiting their exposure through limitation of the number of policies they hold in a hazardous area. Of course, risk would be removed entirely by insuring no one in the hazardous area, for example, flood cover is rarely offered for buildings situated at elevations under 100-year flood levels in Australia (Faulkner & Vikulov, 2001). When risk rises, however, insurance companies have been increasingly moving towards engagement in research and planning with the community, reducing society's exposure to risk and hence theirs (Crichton, 1999).

It should be borne in mind that crises and disasters, although they have obvious detrimental effects, can also have beneficial effects, providing an opportunity for transformational change which could not occur without such an extreme disturbance to the *status quo*. Whether the full transformational opportunities are grasped depends on the economic, temporal, and socio-political situation in which the event occurs, and the way in which decisions are made.

Management Approaches to Disasters

Once the consequences of a disaster are accepted as a component of the coping abilities of the community, management of the disaster becomes important. Good management seeks to minimise the effects of a disaster. By definition this will not be the management suitable for day-to-day, or year-to-year activities, but a management that can respond to exceptional circumstances. A resilient community will have some appreciation of the hazards likely to affect it, have put some basic strategies in place to reduce its effects when it arrives, and have good procedures in place for recovery and rebuilding after the disaster. Such management has to prevail through a situation of shock and loss, through unexpected disruption, be able to develop new ways of coping to rebuild, and be able to recognise that often the affected community was party to the extremity of a disaster and correct for it (Faulkner, 2001). It is indeed not a small task. Disaster management is a discipline in itself and the procedures and theories applied have evolved over many years.

Early modern disaster management in the mid-20th century took the following form:

(i) A strong, military-style model, often run by the military and/or government bodies (Gediz, Turkey (1970), Darwin, Australia (1974)) with a centralised command structure. This is a robust approach, with clear and un-confusing delegations of responsibilities.
(ii) Actions begin at the point of disaster (response).

By the 1970s, an increasing body of understanding was emerging that made it clear that this approach, although often efficient, was not optimal (Drabek & McEntire, 2003). In 1970, an earthquake occurred in Turkey, one of the most earthquake-prone areas of the world (Mitchell, 1976). At least 1086 people were killed and more than 1200 injured around the epicentre at Gediz. Complete towns were erased. Disaster response was swift, by the Turkish military, aid agencies and organisations, and countries throughout the world. Reconstruction works followed to rebuild villages and reinstate infrastructure, with much commitment from government planners. Several points emerged from this experience. The approach by government planners in the recovery process followed scientific and geological advice, but was not consultative, and much of the new infrastructure and housing was not, and has never been, accepted by the locals. It also became apparent that to start disaster management at the event of the disaster is reactive and avoiding some of the major responsibilities of management: avoidance and preparation.

Kates (1971) discussed the importance of "adjustment" by communities to allow them to survive and indeed benefit from the natural world. This "adjustment" was a term used for both technological and social changes that the community might make to reduce their exposure to the hazard. Mitigation in the early days often concentrated on single solutions, such as the installation of dams or levies in flood-prone areas, and this proved to be deficient in the dynamic and complex nature of the natural event itself (Ericksen, 1975). Indeed, in the case of flood cities in the USA, after a disastrous flood in 1972 in Rapid City, South Dakota, the "do nothing" approach or single, engineering solution, was finally replaced by an adoption of a suite of "adjustments" in the form of flood control works, land use regulations, and subsidised insurance, all of which were supported by scenario modelling developed with the relevant municipal decision-makers. By 1980, over 80% of flood-prone centres in the USA had some of these "adjustments" in place (Ericksen, 1975). Mitigation and preparedness has been clearly shown to significantly reduce the costs of management and restoration after a disaster (Schneider, Rao, Daneshvaran, & Perez, 1999; Alexander, 2000) and to be an integral component of comprehensive disaster management.

Two major threads form the basis of disaster management: (i) the tasks or actions inherent in a disastrous event (the "disaster cycle"), and (ii) the manner in which those tasks are to be achieved (the management structure and composition). The disaster cycle in modern times is generally understood to consist of an initial "risk assessment" (Faulkner, 2001), one part being "natural hazard analysis" (Weichselgartner, 2001), in which historical information is gathered about the nature of the hazards present in the target area, their intensity, frequency, origin, and likely locational spread. Some of this information will be quantitative, and some qualitative. Information on precipitating factors is also gathered. This procedure has been greatly facilitated by the emergence of Geographic Information Systems, which can be used as a very flexible tool for storage and illustration of past data, for analytical modelling and for decision-support (Chen, Blong, & Jacobson, 2003). The likely hazard effects are then compared with the level of vulnerability of the community or locale. This includes an assessment of the level of preparedness, any preventative actions already in place, and the amount of response-planning (Weichselgartner, 2001). Once this is done, mitigation efforts can be determined, for example, land zonation, the establishment of building construction codes, engineering works, educational activities (the surprising effectiveness of education can be illustrated by the simple example of a small girl from Britain holidaying in Sri Lanka in 2004, who having been taught about the phenomenon of tsunami at school, recognised the signs and saved her whole family while others perished), and on-the-ground training for appropriate action in the event of a disaster. Warning systems can be put in place to alert the community. When the disaster is imminent, such warning systems will have galvanised people into action. Once the disaster occurs, good preparation should reduce chaos, and minimise the loss of property and life. As the disaster passes, the recovery phase takes over, which is initially an emergency response, and then evolves as infrastructure is rebuilt and people resettled. It is at this latter stage that the transformational possibilities of the disaster can be realised.

Alexander (2003) describes the characteristic stages of the disaster cycle as: (i) mitigation — the process of reducing risks and hazards, (ii) preparation — for impending impacts (including such activities as warning and evacuation), (iii) management of, or response to, the emergency phase, (iv) recovery or restoration of major human and infrastructural systems, and (v) reconstruction of damaged buildings and structures. A final step could be added as phase (vi), evaluation and assessment, which would feed into phase (v) so pre-existing vulnerable or exposed situations are not returned, while taking an opportunity to learn from the experience.

The success of progress through the disaster cycle depends on the manner of its execution. As mentioned previously, early approaches to disaster management did not consider the planning and preparation phases to be part of the exercise, and a command and control model was used for the emergency teams. This approach assumes several things, including: (i) that people are generally confused and in a state of panic after a disaster event, and therefore need strong leadership from a single source, and (ii) that strong protocols and a hierarchical structure will be effective in a disaster. Over time, emergency management has evolved from this point. The command-control and well-planned structure has proved to be contrary to the very nature of the dynamic situation a disaster creates, where the unexpected is the norm, and flexible, rapid actions are required (Faulkner, 2001). Improvisation is an important component of disaster management (Alexander, 2000). Many of the designated (and trained) people in such a structure may well be *hors de combat* and potentially not in place in the first hours or days after a disaster (e.g. Banda Aceh had no external support in the first days post-tsunami in 2004). The latter is termed "organisational lag" (McEntire & Myers, 2004). Planning has been found to be most effective in guiding future responses if it is developed — at least in part — by the people who are going to implement it (Drabek, 1995).

A rigid structure in disaster management also ignores actual behaviour during the emergency phase of a disaster. People as a whole do not panic, and affected persons, organisations, and communities are the first to help themselves after disaster impact (Drabek & McEntire, 2003). It has become apparent that people frequently behave in a very orderly fashion, and indeed rise to the occasion and become a resource to the disaster managers themselves (Drabek & McEntire, 2003). Emergent behaviour, where new groups, roles, and social structures emerge from the community in response to a disaster in a way that could not be anticipated prior to the disaster, is a characteristic of disasters (Alexander, 2000; Drabek & McEntire, 2003). Over-preparation can stifle innovation, preventing people from responding to need, and slowing response-time, none of which is conducive to successful recovery from the event. In addition, as many experiences attest in many management arenas, collaborative management is the most successful form of management. This is demonstrated in disaster management, where inclusion of the community in the planning stage incorporates local knowledge into a management plan and mitigation measures, and serves

Table 9.1: Shifts in emergency management.

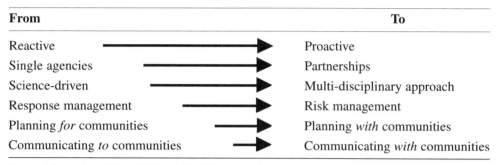

From		To
Reactive	→	Proactive
Single agencies	→	Partnerships
Science-driven	→	Multi-disciplinary approach
Response management	→	Risk management
Planning *for* communities	→	Planning *with* communities
Communicating *to* communities	→	Communicating *with* communities

Source: Adapted from Salter (1999, p. 111). With permission.

also as a component of preparation and education, equipping the very people to be affected with skills and understanding which will serve them (and their community) well in the event of a disaster. Such inclusion also avoids wastage of money in the recovery and resolution phase, as occurred in 1970 in Gediz in Turkey (see above). This evolution in emergency management is nicely summarised by Salter (1999) (Table 9.1).

Faulkner (2001) and Faulkner and Vikulov (2001) developed a disaster management framework for tourism that directly correlates the elements of the disaster cycle with that of the actions required to achieve each stage (Table 9.2). Although this is ostensibly focussed on tourism and the associated business enterprises, the elements proposed are generally applicable. The pre-event stage (assessment of risk and mitigation) is correlated with the establishment of a Disaster Management Team, with a leader and a wide range of stakeholders. This goes some way to recognising the holistic nature of the effects of a disaster (Trim, 2004), acknowledging the wide range of people and activities affected in any disaster, and the wide range of skills required to deal with it. The establishment of such a committee would avoid many of the problems resulting from lack of communication and awareness between stakeholders and experts, and provide an authoritative lobby group. As noted by Hemantha Withanage, Executive Director/Senior Environmental Scientist, Centre for Environmental Justice, Sri Lanka, on 4 January 2005 (imtiaz@travel-impact-newswire.com):

> We have a Geological Survey and Mines Bureau which only engage in mining and exploration licenses. Until this disaster happens they did not have any interest to educate public on the geological disasters and not even earthquakes. Late Professor Vithanage was worried about the unavailability of a functioning earth vibration indicator and proper use of them. All the indicators available with the Mahaweli Authority are now dead. Now we know the importance. Science and information technology would have minimized the damage.

It became clear when testing this model in a disaster operation in Australia (Faulkner & Vikulov, 2001) that there was considerable complacency in the community about the potential of a hazard, which became a major problem throughout the prodromal and emergency

Table 9.2: Disaster management framework for tourism proposed by Faulkner (2001) and modified by Faulkner and Vikulov (2001).

Phase in Disaster Process	Elements of the Disaster Management Responses	Principal Ingredients of the Disaster Management Strategies
1. Pre-event When action can be taken to prevent or mitigate the effects of potential disasters	**Precursors** • Appoint a Disaster Management Team (DMT) Leader and establish DMT. • Identify relevant public/private sector agencies/organizations. • Establish coordination/consultative framework and communication systems. • Develop, document and communicate Disaster Management Strategy. • Education of industry stakeholders, employees, customer and community. • Agreement on, and commitment to, activation protocols.	**Risk Assessment** • Assessment of potential disasters and their probability of occurrence. • Development of scenarios on the genesis and impacts of potential disasters. • Develop disaster contingency plans.
2. Prodromal When it is apparent that a disaster is imminent.	**Mobilisation** • Warning systems (including general mass media): • Establish disaster management command centre; • *Activate communication free:* • *Secure facilities and office files;* • *Switch communication systems;* • *Relocate mobile resources;* • *Relocate perishable food stocks.*	**Disaster Contingency Plans** • Identify likely impacts and groups at risk. • Assess community and visitor capabilities to cope with impacts. • Articulate the objectives of individual (disaster specific) contingency plans. • Identify actions necessary to avoid or minimize impacts at each stage. • Devise strategic priority (action) profiles for each phase.
3. Emergency The effect of the disaster is felt and action is necessary to protect people and property.	**Action** • Rescue/evacuation procedures; • Emergency accommodation and food supplies; • Medical/health services; • Monitoring and communication systems.	
4. Intermediate A point where the short-term needs of people have been addressed and the main focus of activity is to restore services and the community to normal.	**Recovery** • Damage audit/monitoring system; • Clean-up and restoration. • *Office facilities and communication support;* • *"Buddy System"/task force for operator counselling/support.* • Media communication strategy;	♦ Prodromal; ♦ Emergency; ♦ Intermediate; ♦ Long-term recovery. • On-going review and revision in the light of:
5. Long-term (Recovery) Continuation of previous phase, but items that could not be attended to quickly are attended to at this stage. Post-mortem, self-analysis, healing.	**Reconstruction and Reassessment** • Repair of damaged infrastructure. • Rehabilitation of environmentally damaged areas. • Counselling victims. • Restoration of business/consumer confidence and development of investment plans. • Debriefing to promote input to revisions of disaster strategies.	♦ Experience; ♦ Changes in organisational structures and personnel, ♦ Changes in the environment.
6. Resolution Routine restored or new improved state	**Review** *Reappraisal of marketing, planning and policy regime.*	

Note: Phrases in italics are those additions as a result of testing the model in the Katherine flood disaster reported in Faulkner and Vikulov (2001).

phase of the operation. Such complacency is understandable when the likelihood of an extreme event such as a tsunami is low, but even in areas where disasters are well known, such as hurricanes in Florida, people have been known to ignore warnings (holding a "hurricane party" in the teeth of the hurricane) and lose their lives as a consequence (World

Tourism Organization & World Meteorological Organization, 1998). This is not an uncommon feature in disaster management, and making the risk assessment phase as consultative as possible would go some way towards reducing that complacency, and ensuring education is well developed and generally available.

Despite the inherently unexpected nature of a disaster, the importance of identifying the likelihood of the types of disaster likely to affect an area will enable as much specificity to be developed as possible. It is not appropriate to have too general a disaster management plan if avalanche is the main disaster you might expect. Models are available for many areas (or can be bought at a price) that are designed to assess and model the likelihood of particular extreme events, but it must be remembered that such predictions should be viewed with some caution as there is (i) an invariably limited data set (many disasters occur at greater than 100-year intervals), (ii) uncertainty about the formulae used to calculate error, (iii) uncertainty about whether all important factors have been incorporated, and (iv) additional uncertainty brought in by the modelling process itself (Major, Carpenter, & Company, 1999; Alexander, 2000). It is wise that local knowledge is incorporated into this exercise (Cronin, Gaylord, Charley, Alloway, Wallez, & Esau, 2004).

Warning systems and communication channels in the event of a disaster are mentioned in Table 9.2 as part of the mobilisation phase. However, warnings of impending natural hazards need to be lobbied for and designed as part of the pre-event phase. A good warning system is part of mitigation. Along with ignorance and complacency ("we had the 100-year flood last year, we can not have another so high for ages"), lack of warning, and faulty communication both within the disaster team and between the team and the community are some of the greatest impediments to effective disaster management (McEntire & Myers, 2004). The recent tsunami is a case in point. Mr Withanage writes again (imtiaz@travel-impact-newswire.com):

> We have to learn lot from this disaster. Tsunami is unexpected. But there is a warning system exists in the pacific for last 60 years. They have an early warning system. Sri Lanka or even India is not a member of this warning system. They think this is expensive. But the lack of the early warning system is more expensive and not even one can estimate. We live in a world with many fast information and communication systems. It is unfortunate that the damage was increased due to lack of communication.

Tsunami warning systems exist in the Pacific and in the Caribbean, both areas where occurrence of tsunami is quite common. Indeed, the Australian geological early warning centre perceived the earthquake that gave rise to the tsunami, but mistakenly believing it was on land, did not alert anyone to the potential of a tsunami. Even if warnings are issued, their successful dissemination relies upon people "hearing" and transmitting them at the various points along the communication chain, so being aware of holidays, the range of languages likely to be encountered, and the likely location of the community will be essential (night, holiday, work and school, etc.). If the communication chain relies upon computers, or indeed satellites, any breakdown, coincidentally or by the disaster itself can paralyse the network, so planning for a variety of options is essential. The establishment of a well thought-out communication network is a major role of the Disaster Management Team.

Another important component not specifically outlined in Table 9.2, although covered in Faulkner (2001), is the need for appropriate emergency-response training for critical members of the disaster management team, the emergency services themselves, and for key stakeholders (Alexander, 2003). Although the strict, command-control approach to disaster management has fallen into some disfavour, the availability of well-trained emergency managers is an enormous asset in any disaster. At the most basic level, if all members of the community had something as simple as first aid training, a lot of the initial effects of a disaster could be reduced (life-saving courses have been incorporated into many school programs in Australia for this very reason).

One of the most valuable components of the disaster cycle proposed by Faulkner and Vikoluv (2001) is the explicit incorporation of an evaluation/review/debriefing stage. This is often talked of in management circles, but can easily be forgotten or subsumed in the closing activities of a disaster event, but can make all the difference to successful navigation of the next disaster cycle. The lack of such evaluation after the storms in southern England in 1987 failed to take advantage of an opportunity to improve the much-criticised performance of civil defence organisations and examine hazard management policy (Mitchell, Devine, & Jagger, 1989).

The role of the mass media (television, radio, and the Internet) in a disaster is many-faceted and can be positive or negative. The media can provide an educational platform for general awareness and some training, although this has not been greatly successful (Quarantelli, 1996). The media can provide a vital communication link in the prodromal stage and can provide information during the recovery stage (Faulkner, 2001). Once the disaster has struck, however, the role of the media becomes more controversial, as the demands for bite-sized chunks of information, together with the invariably dramatic nature of the events creates many opportunities for sensationalist and inaccurate reporting. It is often hard for a viewer to extract an objective reality. The reporters themselves can create a burden to overworked emergency workers and require support which might otherwise be directed to the rescue effort. Voyeurism is another negative component of mass-media coverage, which can escalate as the viewers require increasingly gory footage (Alexander, 2000). The disaster management team needs to think about the benefits and disadvantages of involvement by the media in the immediate aftermath of an event, because a lot of their time, if media management is unsuccessful, may be spent in damage control (Faulkner, 2001). The early establishment of a media communication strategy, with the establishment of a central source for media information can alleviate much of the misinformation disseminated and the time taken to deal with errant reporters. There are benefits of media coverage during an event, which can include the galvanisation of sympathy for disaster victims thereby prompting donations to aid agencies and governments. Once the immediate post-disaster phase is over, however, the mass media often turns to other things, especially if rival crises occur, as was the case in Britain in 1987 when the stock market crash pushed the news of the devastating storm across southern England off the front pages (Mitchell et al., 1989).

In recent years, the role of the Internet in providing information (albeit of extremely varying quality and authority) has increased enormously, from factual, background information for the curious about topics of interest (see www.tsunami.com); to providing reasonably factual up-to-date reports of an event; to providing a way in which family and friends of missing people can check the photographs of un-named dead from any continent in the world. The use of electronic mail has also become increasingly important as a communication tool, both for people to check each other's whereabouts in the event of a disaster, but also for transmission of news about an event and the status of recovery works. Such an email innovation is "Travel Impact Newswire", an Asia-Pacific news service established in 1998, whose utility is evidenced by the following quote from 1 January 2005 (imtiaz@travel-impact-newswire.com):

> FROM MICHAEL DUCK, SENIOR VICE PRESIDENT, CMP ASIA
> Thanks for your service it really has been of great help to understand what is going on elsewhere. I am in Krabi Ao Nang Beach and have been here for the last 10 days with my family ... we were very, very lucky to escape the tsunami and its affect ... i am staying at the Krabi Thai Village resort which is up a hill ... Krabi itself is nearly back to normal ... many tourists have gone ... most were Swedish and their Embassy told them all to leave Thailand. The Thai emergency services seem to have done miracles and over the week helicopters and planes are often to be heard. The challenge is going to be to get Tourists back here soon to ensure the economy in the area is still thriving. I leave to go back to Hong Kong tomorrow.

The Tourism Industry Subset

According to Drabek (1995, p. 86) "the tourism industry represents a disaster vulnerability of catastrophic potential". The dependency of most tourism operations on outsiders for income, and their high dependence on other components of a region for goods and services, makes tourism especially vulnerable to disasters (Murphy & Bayley, 1989). The tourism industry has particular needs and constraints which colour the nature of its participation in a regional disaster management exercise, and in the development of industry-specific disaster management plans. In today's world, with the exception of some business and cultural (opera, music, theatre) recreation travel, travel is increasingly to high-risk, exotic destinations (Murphy & Bayley, 1989). Most of the tourists to these high-risk destinations emanate from "high human development" countries, and the exotic destinations are predominantly in the middle and lower development aggregates (Figure 9.3). This pattern is evidenced by the nationalities of tourists (mostly European, British, and Australian) represented in the death tolls from the tsunami of 26 December 2004 and the Bali terrorist blasts, while the countries they were visiting which suffered the tsunami (or blast), were in the "medium human development" aggregate of countries in the world (Indonesia, Thailand, Myanmar, Sri Lanka).

Within a country, travel for recreation is also often to more inherently risky destinations than those found in the cities and towns when the tourists come: the forests near Mt St Helens (Blong, 1984), the wilderness of north-east Florida (Butry et al., 2001), the slopes of Mt Etna (Blong, 1984), and the gorges of northern Australia (Faulkner, 2001). There has also been a long history of the centres of disaster becoming tourist attractions after the disaster (Blong, 1984). Tourists can fly over rumbling volcanoes in Hawaii, tours have long been established around Mt Etna and of course Pompeii, and tours were available after the eruption of Mt St Helens (Faulkner, 2001). Some of these destinations are highly risky, but that adds to the excitement. Should the tourism operator take the risk?

One of the critical features of the tourism industry is its desire to advertise safe (albeit exciting) and dependable (a guarantee of fine weather; there will always be snow) tourism experiences. Coupled with the demand by tourists for the most attractive locations (near the beach, under a cliff but with a wonderful view), tourism operators can be tempted to provide services within quite risky areas, often contrary to (poorly regulated) planning controls. The operators, to make the tourist feel safe and hence spend time in their operation, will be tempted to play down the risk. This is especially so in low-development countries where tourists provide much-needed income. We hear again from Mr Withanage who wrote on "Travel Impact Newswire" on 1 January 2005 (imtiaz@travel-impact-newswire.com):

> We now know why we have a law to protect the coastal area. Under the Coast Conservation Act there is a set back up to 100 meters. The Coast Conservation Department has to approve any construction within this zone. But we know this is the most populated area. Coast Conservation Department failed to control building hotels and houses within this zone. They were unable to maintain any green belt. People live in the coastal zone both poor and rich destroyed the coastal resource. Green belt and corals were also destroyed by them. All politicians supported this damage. We know the coastal officers were attacked in Negombo, Matara and many other coasts. Now we know the result. If we have respect to this law more than 50 percent damage would have been avoided.

The tourism industry poses some particular difficulties for disaster management. As an entity, each tourist operation, be it a hotel, restaurant, or gift shop, has a duty of care to its customers (see Chapter 8), and under occupational health and safety regulations generally in most countries, tourist operations must adopt some disaster planning — certainly evacuation planning — into their management portfolios (Drabek, 1995). Given the busy schedule characteristic of most tourism operators, it is often hard to find time for such planning. This need is well-recognised, however, and the World Tourism Organization in association with the World Meteorological Organization compiled a Handbook (WTO/WMO, 1998) as part of the International Decade for Natural Disaster Reduction (1990–2000) in which simple, general guidance for operators and tourists for developing disaster plans is clearly given (Appendices A and B of the Handbook). Indeed, good preparedness can be a positive advertisement for a destination (Gruntfest, 1987; WTO/WMO, 1998). Data suggest that most tourism operators are very happy to prepare and provide disaster plans for their guests (Greenway, 1996; Drabek, 2000), although a response to an alert is less well accepted.

Greenway (1996) hypothesised that there is very strong within-industry feeling in tourism that, among other things, protects it from scrutiny from outsiders (whom it is trying to impress, in order to attract customers), and operators find the exposure to the wider community by evacuating in response to warnings challenging, particularly at the risk of the warning being a false alarm. Having a strong tourism industry presence in a regional disaster management team, he suggested, would be a way to overcome this reluctance, as within-industry trust and understanding is greater than between. This was supported by Faulkner and Vikulov (2001) for slightly different reasons. They suggested that being linked firmly to a disaster response organisation would enable many operators to be less isolated. Even in a highly developed country like Australia, operators can be totally unaware of a potential hazard descending on them. Emergency services are well trained to warn and save permanent residents (little old ladies and their cats), but without advocacy by the tourism industry, intervention in tourist operations is of low priority. This is encouraged by the often large and multi-tasking staff of a tourist operation, with a reasonably good internal capability for response themselves, giving a perception of self-sufficiency. Sometimes this perception is correct, but sometimes the operation becomes invisible to the emergency personnel with sad consequences.

It is well established that strong relationships within staff of an organisation and between organisations are of great benefit in times of stress (Paton, Johnston, & Houghton, 1998). This has been a clear outcome of studies by the author of tourism businesses in times of stress: good staff morale leads to effective responses and consequent swift recovery. The tourism industry has a large proportion of highly mobile staff, so the development of this vital attribute is continually challenged. A high mobility of staff also creates problems with the development of relationships between the tourist operator/executive and other organisations in the region. Tourism is highly dependent on the effective functioning of other components of the region in which it takes place, and in times of emergency this relationship is even more vital. An ecotourism operation offering wilderness experiences does well to foster a good relationship with its relevant parks service; in times of emergency it will need that co-operation to ensure successful evacuation from remote and difficult areas (e.g. heart attack victims along a rainforest trail, fire outbreaks). Good relationships with local police and emergency service personnel are also required. These take time to develop, as do strong community relationships (preferably by active membership of the disaster management committee). This is more effectively achieved at a personal level, which is difficult if staff members are changing regularly. Maintaining an appropriate level of emergency training in tourist organisations is problematic: with mobile staff, training sessions could be a year-round activity, making them difficult to fit into a busy schedule. Development of *esprit de corps* takes time and a stable workforce, but both are very important in event of disaster. Unfortunately, the majority of operators are very occupied running the business leaving them little time to participate in outside organisations or to develop a relationship with others, short of their immediate service providers, but it must become higher on the list of priorities if they are to successfully survive the unexpected.

Tourists themselves offer some unique challenges which have to be incorporated into the disaster management plan of a tourist operation and certainly into the regional disaster plan. The number of tourists varies considerably from time to time (e.g. season), and in many locales the actual numbers are not known at any given time. This produces simple logistical problems: knowing how many people need to be evacuated and from where, and how many need to be accommodated in emergency shelters, and so on. Tourists at any one location are often without a common language, especially with that of the host country, meaning that warnings may not be understood. Tourists are usually unfamiliar with the local environment and the geography of the area (the location of the main road, the police station, the evacuation centre). Unlike locals, however, travellers can pack up easily and have few possessions to linger over (Faulkner & Vikulov, 2001).

The media is very significant to the tourism industry in the case of a disaster. Because the tourism industry depends on discretionary spending, it is easy for tourists to change their plans if a destination is put in doubt by the media. The vagueness common in the fast, bite-sized media report at the time of a disaster, accompanied by sensational coverage, can be very damaging to the industry. The supervision of media coverage during a disaster is especially important for the tourism industry (Beirman, 2003). "Disastrous fires in the north coast: 10 people dead" on a news report can make people who do not know the area change their holiday plans. What they might find, if they searched a little further, is that the fires were in a very small area of the "north coast" and nowhere near the destination that they were intending to visit. But the damage is done. It takes some effort of marketing to re-assure the client-base that things are all right, although being over-zealous to re-assure travellers can backfire (Faulkner, 2001). The World Tourism Organization/World Metrological Organization Handbook (WTO/WMO, 1998) includes a section on data gathering by regional tourist organisations in the post-disaster stage (Appendix E), which appears to have been applied via the email service "Travel Impact Newswire" in the 26 December tsunami disaster in at least one country (imtiaz@travel-impact-newswire.com). Once such a collation is made, and infrastructure, health, and service availability are determined to be satisfactory, a regional tourism organisation (at whatever level) can take responsibility for marketing the status of a destination for tourism with much more authority than an individual operation.

The disaster recovery phase is very important for tourism. As mentioned before, the reliance of tourism on non-permanent residents for income makes it imperative that business is restored as soon as possible, while being sensitive to the trauma recovery time required for the service providers. When a destination is unavailable to tourists they will find alternative destinations, and they need to be re-introduced to that destination for them to return (Durocher, 1994). Such marketing can be very effective. Within a month of the Izmit earthquake in August 1999, Turkish tourism authorities began the task of rebuilding the market. They used several approaches, including visits by travel industry and tourism journalists to see the recovery first hand. This proactive response enabled tourist numbers to recover to pre-earthquake levels within a year. This is just one example of many instances of recovery marketing being of considerable value to the industry (Beirman, 2003).

Conclusion

Natural disaster management for the tourism industry has much in common with that for the community at large. The nature of tourism, however, exposes the industry to high risk from a natural disaster through its very charter, the location of tourist operations, the nature of tourists, and the structure of the industry itself. The tourism industry exists to facilitate tourists in their quest for a safe and pleasant experience in a (possibly exotic) location with opportunity for a variety of recreation activities. Such locations are commonly highly vulnerable to natural hazards: alpine regions, rivers, wilderness areas, tropical coasts, islands, and so on. The tension between being "safe" and the desire for the recreational experience by the tourist exposes the operator to risk. The industry tries to present a very positive face to the world, sometimes to a state of denial of the potential for natural disasters. Tourists themselves are vulnerable to natural disasters because of their lack of familiarity with signals, which the local environment may be giving those more familiar with their surroundings. Tourists are, however, accepting of information and can be a valuable resource.

The tourism industry is highly dependent on the health and good function of the environment in which it is placed, and as such for its survival must engage actively with that environment. The negative effects of a natural disaster can be minimised by ensuring a high level of staff morale is maintained, providing good staff training to ensure good staff preparedness, and developing good communication within the industry and between the industry and the community as a whole. Active participation on regional planning and disaster management teams will ensure the needs of the tourism industry are understood and incorporated sensibly in planning. A strong, effective, regional (world, country, state, or smaller) tourism industry body, which actively engages with its members and with other organisations can be an insurance policy in itself.

Understanding and listening to the environment on which tourism depends and from which the tourist derives many pleasures is a key ingredient in the mitigation of the effects of disaster. Do not push the envelope of desire beyond nature's limits: it can claim a heavy price.

References

Alexander, D.E. (2000). *Confronting catastrophe: New perspectives on natural disasters.* Harpenden, England: Oxford University Press.

Alexander, D.E. (2003). Towards the development of standards in emergency management training and education. *Disaster Prevention and Management, 12*(2), 113–123.

Beirman, D. (2003). *Restoring tourism destinations in crisis — a strategic marketing approach.* Sydney: Allen & Unwin.

Blanchard-Boehm, R.D. (2004). Natural hazards in Latin America: Tectonic forces and storm fury. *The Social Studies, 95*(3), 93–105.

Blong, R.J. (1984). *Volcanic hazards: A sourcebook on the effects of eruptions.* Sydney: Academic Press.

Butry, D.T., Mercer, D.E., Prestemon, J.P., Pye, J.M., & Holmes, T.P. (2001). What is the price of catastrophic wildfire? *Journal of Forestry, 99*(1), 9–17.

Chapman, D.M. (1999). *Natural hazards* (2nd ed.). Melbourne: Oxford University Press.

Chen, K., Blong, R., & Jacobson, C. (2003). Towards and integrated approach to natural hazards risk assessment using GIS: With reference to bushfires. *Environmental Management, 31*(4), 546–560.

Crichton, D. (1999). The risk triangle. In: J. Ingleton (Ed.), *Natural disaster management* (pp. 102–103). Leicester, England: Tudor Rose.

Cronin, S.J., Gaylord, D.R., Charley, D., Alloway, B.V., Wallez, S., & Esau, J.W. (2004). Participatory methods of incorporating scientific with traditional knowledge for volcanic hazard management on Ambae Island, Vanuatu. *Bulletin of Vulcanology, 66*(7), 652–668.

Davies, P. (2000). *The Devil's Flu: The world's deadliest influenza epidemic and the scientific hunt for the virus that caused it.* New York: Henry Holt & Co.

Drabek, T.E. (1995). Disaster planning and response by tourism business executives. *Cornell Hotel and Restaurant Administration Quarterly*, *36*(3), 86–96.

Drabek, T.E. (2000). Disaster evacuations: Tourist-business managers rarely act as customers expect. *Cornell Hotel and Restaurant Administration Quarterly*, *41*(4), 48–57.

Drabek, T.E., & McEntire, D.A. (2003). Emergent phenomena and the sociology of disaster: Lessons, trends and opportunities from the research literature. *Disaster Prevention and Management*, *12*(2), 97–112.

Durocher, J. (1994). Recovery marketing: What to do after a natural disaster? *Cornell Hotel and Restaurant Administration Quarterly*, *35*(2), 66–70.

Ericksen, N.J. (1975). A tale of two cities: Flood history and the prophetic past of Rapid City, South Dakota. *Economic Geography*, *51*(4), 305–313.

Ewert, A., & Jamieson, L. (2003). Current status and future directions in the adventure tourism industry. In: J. Wilks, & S.J. Page (Eds), *Managing tourist health and safety in the new millenium* (pp. 67–83). Oxford: Pergamon.

Faulkner, B. (2001). Towards a framework for tourism disaster management. *Tourism Management*, *22*, 135–147.

Faulkner, B., & Vikulov, S. (2001). Katherine, washed out one day, back on track the next: A post-mortem of a tourist disaster. *Tourism Management*, *22*, 331–344.

Greenway, R.J. (1996). Natural hazard management and tourism. In: R.L. Heathcote, C. Cuttler, & J. Koetz (Eds), *NDR96 conference on natural disaster reduction*, 29 September–2 October 1996, Gold Coast, Australia (pp. 195–199). Barton, ACT: Institution of Engineers, Australia.

Gruntfest, E. (1987). Pre-flood/post-flood mitigation planning: The Manitou Springs, Colorado Case. *International Journal of Mass Emergencies and Disasters*, *5*(1), 89–93.

International Strategy for Disaster Reduction. (2004a). Disaster statistics 1994–2004. http://www.unisdr.org/disaster-statistics/introduction.htm.

International Strategy for Disaster Reduction. (2004b). Terminology: Basic terms of disaster risk reduction. http://www.unisdr.org/eng/library/lib-terminology-eng-p.htm.

Kates, R.W. (1971). Natural hazard in human ecological perspective: Hypotheses and models. *Economic Geography*, *47*(3), 438–451.

Kempe M. (2003). Noah's Flood: The genesis story and natural disaster in early modern times. *Environment and History*, *6*(2), 151–173.

Keys, D. (1999). *Catastrophe: An investigation into the origins of the modern world*. London: Random House.

McEntire, D.A. (2004). Development, disasters and vulnerability: A discussion of divergent theories and the need for their integration. *Disaster Prevention and Management*, *13*(3), 193–198.

McEntire, D.A., & Myers, A. (2004). Preparing communities for disasters: Issues and processes for government readiness. *Disaster Prevention and Management*, *13*(2), 140–152.

Major, J., Carpenter, G., & Company. (1999). The uncertain nature of catastrophe modelling. In: J. Ingleton (Ed.), *Natural disaster management* (pp. 104–105). Leicester, England: Tudor Rose.

Mitchell, W.A. (1976). Reconstruction after disaster: The Gediz earthquake of 1970. *Geographical Review*, *66*(3), 296–313.

Mitchell, J.K., Devine, N., & Jagger, K. (1989). A contextual model of natural hazard. *Geographical Review*, *79*(4), 391–409.

Murphy, P.E., & Bayley, R. (1989). Tourism and disaster planning. *Geographical Review*, *79*(1), 36–46.

Palm, R., & Hodgson, M.E. (1993). Natural hazards in Puerto Rico. *Geographical Review*, *83*(3), 280–289.

Paton, D., Johnston, D., & Houghton, B.F. (1998). Organisational response to a volcanic eruption. *Disaster Prevention and Management*, *7*(1), 5–15.

Quarantelli, E.L. (1996). Local mass media operations in disasters in the USA. *Disaster Prevention and Management, 5*(5), 5–10.

Rohr, C. (2003). Man and natural disaster in the middle ages. *Environment and History, 9*(2), 127–151.

Rogers, P. (1986). The social and economic impact of tropical cyclones. In: R.H. Maybury (Ed.), *Violent forces of nature* (pp. 195–203). Airy, Maryland: Lomond Publications Inc.

Salter, J. (1999). A risk management approach to disaster management. In: J. Ingleton (Ed.), *Natural disaster management* (pp. 111–113). Leicester, England: Tudor Rose.

Schneider J., Rao, G., Daneshvaran, S., & Perez, J. (1999). Mitigating property and business losses. In: J. Ingleton (Ed.), *Natural disaster management* (pp. 254–256). Leicester, England: Tudor Rose.

Trim, P.R.J. (2004). An integrative approach to disaster management and planning. *Disaster Prevention and Management, 13*(3), 218–225.

Weichselgartner, J. (2001). Disaster mitigation: The concept of vulnerability revisited. *Disaster Prevention and Management, 10*(2), 85–94.

World Tourism Organization & World Meteorological Organization. (1998). *Handbook on natural disaster reduction in tourist areas*. Madrid: World Tourism Organization.

Chapter 10

Tourist Gut Reaction: Food Safety and Hygiene Issues

Donna Pendergast

Introduction

While scrambled eggs, cold chicken and water sound like relatively innocuous and typical foods consumed by many tourists every day around the world, they are potentially lethal unless enormous care is taken by food handlers to prevent contamination or deterioration of the foodstuffs. It happens that innocent sounding eggs, chicken and water — like many food products — are ideal hosts to some potentially nasty food-borne illnesses, which cause symptoms ranging from mild gastrointestinal discomfort to severe vomiting, diarrhea and pain; possibly requiring hospitalization and potentially leading to death in cases affecting high-risk groups, such as the young and the elderly.

Food safety is gaining prominence as a consideration by concerned tourists and the wider tourism industry, as awareness of newly emerging food safety issues such as Bovine Spongiform Encephalopathy (BSE — sometimes referred to as 'mad cow' disease) are raised through heightened media attention. As noted in Chapter 1 of this book, food safety is recognized as one of the three primary concerns raised by participants at the 1998 Think Tank on Safety and Security (International Hotel & Restaurant Association, 1998). This chapter sets out to explore: the nature of food-borne illness; the extent that it strikes the tourism market; the potential for genuine partnerships to make a difference; and how being an active agent, including knowing which foodstuffs to avoid, might be a useful strategy for minimizing the potential time spent engaged with a pedestal, rather than in more appealing tourist activities!

Unlike many risk-taking activities in which tourists might keenly and knowingly engage — bungy jumping, trail riding, scuba diving, parachuting, running the bulls in Pamploma — eating a meal may seem like an everyday event that does not rate a mention. This cuts both ways; for example, I have yet to be presented with a disclaimer to sign before eating a meal at a tourist venue! Sure, it is possible to increase the risk by experimenting with foods such as the very expensive and prized delicacy Fugu (pufferfish) in

Tourism in Turbulent Times
Copyright © 2006 by Elsevier Ltd.
All rights of reproduction in any form reserved.
ISBN: 0-08-044666-3

Japan, which is poisonous if not correctly prepared, leading to death from tetradotoxin; or Cassava, which contains a toxin that can be converted into cyanide in the human body if it is not properly prepared; but generally speaking, eating food during a tourist experience is not intended to be a potentially life-threatening activity and typically is presented as a soft cultural experience. Yet, food consumption might well be the very activity with the highest potential risk for loss of enjoyment, illness or even worse, that tourists will unwittingly engage in because very often food that makes us sick looks, smells and tastes normal. There are few, if any, clues to trigger caution. And, it may take up to 3 days or longer after eating contaminated food before there are signs of illness, so it is often difficult to pinpoint the cause of the problem.

Extent of the Problem of Food-Borne Illness in Tourism

There is no shortage of detail about episodes of food-borne illness involving tourists. Take for example *Gastro cuts short South Pacific Cruise* — the Australian Broadcasting Commission (ABC) news story that documents the misery of 140 passengers with vomiting and diarrhea, on the seventh day of their eleven night cruise (ABC, 2004). Then there is *Onshore catering increases the risk of diarrheal illness among cruise ship passengers*, a journal article that investigates one voyage where 91 of 134 passengers on a cruise reported various illnesses including 41 with diarrhea (Pugh, Selvey, Crome, & Beers, 2001). The authors found that passengers were significantly at risk of developing diarrhea when they ate onshore while undertaking a tour compared to those who did not participate in tours, leading them to recommend caution in food selection and consumption while onshore. Most significant is the comprehensive analysis undertaken by Rooney et al. (2004), *A review of outbreaks of food-borne disease associated with passenger ships: evidence for risk management*, which reviews 50 outbreaks of food-borne diseases on passenger ships, affecting nearly 10,000 people. For each outbreak a range of data were investigated, including pathogens/toxins, type of ship, factors contributing to outbreaks, mortality and morbidity. The findings of this review show that in many cases prevention would have been possible "if measures had been taken to ensure adequate temperature control, avoidance of cross-contamination, reliable food sources, adequate heat treatment, and exclusion of infected food handlers from work" (p. 427).

Airlines also have considerable problems with food-borne illnesses. For example, Hatakka and Asplund (1993) investigated the occurrence of Salmonella in airline meals between 1989 and 1992. Over 2000 samples of food were collected from flight kitchens in 29 countries. The material consisted of 400 cold dishes and 1288 hot dishes as well as salads, cheese plates and desserts. Salmonella were isolated from 6 samples; one prepared in Bangkok (which was found to be connected with an outbreak to passengers in Finland), one in Mombasa and the remaining four in Beijing. These figures might seem small, but they are very significant in their potential impact. As Burslem, Kelly, and Preston (1990) argue, airline food is a "major threat" to airline operations. They document a serious food poisoning outbreak of Salmonella where 1000 passengers and crew were affected, throwing an airline into a crisis paralleling a major aircraft disaster. Given that there are now 1 billion passengers who travel by air each year, the potential effects are enormous (Ryan & Kain, 2000).

While this literature reports on passenger ship and airline scenarios, it is the day-to-day tourist visiting restaurants and eateries of various kinds where the majority of food-borne illness occurs, the extent of which is difficult to ascertain. Simple logic tells us that those people who are eating out in restaurants, hotels and the like are at a greater risk of contracting a food-borne illness than those eating at home. This is confirmed by Tambling (1999) who estimates that 80% of food-borne illness is the result of food-handling practices outside the home. This places tourists in a particularly vulnerable position. Added to this increased exposure is the general acceptance that the incidence of food-borne illness is increasing. The World Health Organization (WHO) agrees with this assessment, and surprisingly, particularly for developed countries (Food Standards Australia New Zealand – FSANZ, 2005). Curson (2004), for example, claims that "[F]ood poisoning is rampant in Australia as it is in all developed countries and increasing at an alarming rate." In 1999 it was estimated that on any one day there are 5700–8600 new cases of food poisoning in Australia, with an estimated 2.1–3.5 million cases of food-borne illness every year (Tambling, 1999). The total cost burden of food-borne illness in Australia is estimated to be in the vicinity of $4 and $7 billion every year (Tambling, 1999). But what do we know about tourists as a subset of this total number? And what about food-borne illness on a worldwide platform? One way of beginning to gain a useful picture is to consider the epidemiology of traveler's diarrhea (one possible symptom of food-borne illness), which is consistently identified as the most common travel-related health problem (Brewster & Taylor, 2004). Even so, there is a lot of guesswork, as the incidence of many illnesses among travelers is unknown because they frequently go unreported. However, as Ryan, Wilson, and Kain (2002) note, new surveillance systems are beginning to yield useful data to better understand the real impact of illnesses for travelers. By way of informed guesswork, Ryan and Kain (2000, p. 1716) state that:

> Ten to 60 percent of travelers to developing nations have diarrhea; at least 20 percent of affected travelers are bedridden for part of their trip, and 40 percent change their itinerary because of diarrhea.

In making this claim, Ryan and Kain (2000) use the figure of 50 million as the number of people from industrialized nations visiting the developing world each year. So, using their estimates for travelers to developing countries only, a minimum of 5 million visitors experience diarrhea each year. Of these, at least 1 million are bedridden for part of the trip, and at least 2 million change their itinerary because of diarrhea. Similar figures are confirmed as an acceptable estimation by Brewster and Taylor (2004). And this is just the tip of the iceberg. As already noted, diarrhea is only one possible symptom of food-borne illness. And, added to this, food poisoning is on the increase in developed countries. The loss of potential revenue from bedridden tourists highlights just one aspect of the economic burden of this illness (Brewster & Taylor, 2004).

In part, the escalation in food-borne illness in developed countries has been attributed to the growing demand for 'healthy' food alternatives, which typically undergo less processing, contain fewer additives and preservatives, and hence are keen targets for bacteria and microorganisms which cause food deterioration and spoilage. In addition, there are new and emerging pathogenic bacteria to contend with. It seems ironic that those making a conscious effort with healthy food choices may in fact be increasing their vulnerability to food-borne illnesses. There is also growing evidence that "food poisoning can lead to a range of chronic conditions, including reactive arthritis and Guillian-Barre syndrome" (Tambling, 1999), which is an "inflammatory disorder ... characterized by the rapid onset of weakness and, often, paralysis of the legs, arms, breathing muscles and face" (Guillain-Barre Syndrome Foundation International, 2005). There is also speculation that having experienced a bout of food poisoning, a person is henceforth more vulnerable to future episodes.

What's in Our Food?

A sickness caused by eating contaminated food is often called 'food poisoning', or more correctly, 'food-borne illness'. In almost all cases, this illness can be easily prevented with the use of careful food-handling and storage techniques, personal hygiene practices and cleaning processes, particularly in mass catering settings such as restaurants, hotels and takeaways, thereby reducing the opportunity for food-borne illnesses to occur. Food handlers should handle food in ways to ensure it does not become contaminated; and growth of microorganisms is stopped or slowed down. Following a number of simple rules aids in the prevention of food-borne illness:

* keep hands and fingernails clean;
* keep food preparation surfaces and equipment clean and free of pests;
* handle food safely;
* cook high-risk food thoroughly; and
* keep hot food hot and cold food cold — always check temperatures using a thermometer (Queensland Health and the Home Economics Institute of Australia, 2000).

These simple practices of course elaborate into more detailed procedures, but the principles in and of themselves are the key to preventing food-borne illness. Given that prevention seems to be relatively straightforward, how does food contamination occur and why is prevention a problem? Food-borne illnesses occur because of some form of contamination that can be categorized as:

* Chemical, e.g., cleaning products, burner fuel
* Foreign matter, e.g., hair, jewelry, dead insects, metal, glass
* Natural toxin, e.g., ciguatera in seafood
* Microorganisms, e.g., viruses, fungi, parasites, bacteria

Chemical contamination typically occurs due to spillages, leaking equipment and accidental inclusion of the chemical during cleaning or other similar events. It may also be the result of biological magnification, where chemicals become increasingly concentrated, as food sources are higher up the food chain. The unintentional inclusion of foreign matter, such as insects (sometimes alive!), fingernails, band-aids, hair and glass can happen due to lack of vigilance during food storage, preparation and handling. In some cases, this foreign matter causes little effect in terms of direct ill-health effects, however psychosomatic effects can be quite damaging. In the year 2000, FSANZ reported that 66% of food recalls in Australia comprised of food contaminated by chemicals, nails, shards of glass or metal pieces, which could be considered to be potentially serious in their impact on health (Harty, 2000).

Of the contaminants, microorganisms and particularly bacteria cause the most concern for food-borne illness. Bacteria live all around us — in the air, soil, water, on plants, animals and food products, and on our bodies. All people carry bacteria that have the potential to cause illness when given the right opportunity to multiply to large numbers. Some bacteria make us sick, while others make food deteriorate. It is not only the bacteria themselves, but the waste they produce. This waste, or toxin, can be poisonous and in large amounts can make us sick. Many toxins are not destroyed when food is cooked. In order to grow, bacteria need time, food, water or moisture and warmth. They multiply by splitting in two, doubling their number every 10–30 min. If we start with one bacterium that splits every 20 min, we would have over 2 million bacteria in 7 h — more than enough to cause illness from certain bacterial types. And food usually contains more than one bacterium. Temperature control is one of the most effective means of controlling bacterium growth to maintain a rate where the number of bacteria and/or the toxins they produce in foodstuffs does not cause illness.

There are many bacteria keen to invade our food and the following section outlines just a few of these potential contaminants. According to FSANZ, Campylobacter is the most common food-borne illness. The United States Food and Drug Administration (FDA) also identifies this food-borne pathogen as the most common bacterial cause of diarrhea in the United States, resulting in 1–6 million illnesses each year. Sources include: raw milk, untreated water, and raw and undercooked meat, poultry, or shellfish. The incubation period for illness to emerge is 2–5 days after ingestion, and symptoms include: diarrhea, abdominal cramps, fever, muscle pain, headache, and nausea, which lasts between 7 and 10 days (United States FDA, 2005). Another bacterium, Salmonella, is found in a variety of foodstuffs but is frequently associated with undercooked poultry, meat, eggs and unpasteurised milk. The incubation period for onset of symptoms is 12–72 h after eating contaminated food, and symptoms typically include diarrhoea, fever, and abdominal cramps which can last 4–7 days. In severe cases death can occur. Staphylococcus (commonly known as Staph) is carried by humans in the nose and throat and also on infected skin. Regular cooking and reheating does not achieve temperatures to kill Staphylococcus toxins, which explains the importance of personal hygiene for those involved in food preparation.

Foodstuffs often contain natural toxins, which, when inappropriately handled and/or stored, can become dangerous to humans. For example, *Escherichia coli* (commonly known as *E. coli*) is a bacterium that lives in the intestines and hence faeces of humans and some animals in large numbers, and while most types of *E. coli* are harmless, some can produce a deadly toxin. Foods in which this may be a problem include undercooked hamburger mince, unpasteurised milk and contaminated water. Incubation for the onset of symptoms is usually 3–4 days after ingestion, but may occur anywhere from 1 to 10 days after consumption and symptoms are severe abdominal cramps, bloody diarrhoea and nausea. In severe cases this pathogen can cause kidney damage that can lead to death.

More recently, there have been some food-borne illnesses that have caused hysteria in the international community, including the tourist community, such as the BSE epidemic in cattle in England and parts of Europe in the mid-1990s, which led to the slaughter of over 5 million cattle. BSE is a chronic degenerative disease affecting the central nervous system of cattle. Of concern is the knowledge that "the same infective agent that causes BSE in cattle, results in variant Creutzfeldt–Jakob disease (vCJD) in people" (Australian

Government, Department of Agriculture, Fisheries and Forestry, 2005). There have been 147 definite and probable cases of vCJD as at July 2003, but the incubation period is very long, possibly 10 years or more, so these diagnoses would not have resulted from the current epidemic in cattle (Ansdell, 2004). Symptoms of vCJD include forgetfulness, clumsiness, poor eyesight, fatigue and rapid weight loss which develops into blindness, inability to swallow, loss of motor skills, dementia and eventual death (Australian Government, Department of Agriculture, Fisheries and Forestry, 2005). vCJD "probably occurs mainly as a result of ingestion of beef on the bone and ground beef products such as beef burgers and sausages" (Ansdell, 2004, p. 448), a fact leading to a worldwide scare about eating beef and the slaughter of millions of cattle without physical signs of BSE but that had been on a ruminant diet (an apparent causative factor for spreading the infection), in an attempt to remove BSE from the food chain. Reassuringly, to date "no cases of vCJD have been reported in travelers and the risk of vCJD for current travelers is considered to be extremely small" (Ansdell, 2004, p. 449).

With just a taste of some of the current food-borne illnesses and their potential severity, it is timely to reflect again on the basic principles of prevention for the vast majority of these potential contaminants: keep hands and fingernails clean; keep food preparation surfaces and equipment clean and free of pests; handle food safely; cook high-risk food thoroughly; and keep hot food hot and cold food cold — always check temperatures using a thermometer (Queensland Health and the Home Economics Institute of Australia, 2000). Why is it that these simple rules are not applied throughout the world, and why might prevention be a problem?

In order to respond to the question of the implementation of basic food safety practices, it is useful to revisit food preparation sites. A look at the Australian context begins this journey.

What's Happening in Australia?

Australia is generally considered to be a relatively low-risk destination in terms of food safety. Yet, findings from the *National Food Handling Benchmark Survey* on food-handling practices in Australian food businesses, such as food manufacturers, food retailers, child care centres, schools, hospitals, cafés and restaurants released in 2001 by the FSANZ has findings that suggest there is plenty of room for improvement. The study was undertaken prior to the introduction of new food safety standards, which require businesses to have safe food-handling practices, premises and equipment. Selected findings from the telephone survey of awareness and knowledge of food businesses of safe food-handling practices included the following:

- 21% of businesses did not know the correct temperature to store chilled food (5°C or under) so that food poisoning bacteria cannot grow;
- 23% did not know that hot food must be held at or above 60°C to prevent food poisoning bacteria growing;
- 26% of food businesses reported they did not offer staff food safety training.

Key findings from the on-site survey of actual food-handling practices included:

- only 19% of food businesses had a written food safety program;
- a considerable number of businesses used 'touch' (43%) and/or 'sight' (57%), rather than a thermometer, to assess food temperature;
- 9% of food businesses had staff who didn't wash their hands when necessary;
- 17% of businesses did not have sufficient hand washing facilities, 7% no soap or hand cleanser available for staff and 14% no warm running water (FSANZ, 2005).

These figures demonstrate that there is potential for some gut wrenching effects — food-borne illness has the opportunity to occur in many establishments with less than ideal food safety practices. Following this benchmarking study, the States and Territories of Australia introduced three new national Food Safety Standards, developed by FSANZ, that require businesses to have safe food-handling practices, premises and equipment. To accompany the Standards, guidelines and fact sheets on the new Food Safety Standards have been developed, including translated fact sheets into 15 languages (see www.food standards.gov.au). In the future, studies will be conducted to determine the effect of these Standards on food safety practices. Certainly, if the benefits are as projected, this should see far fewer people — including tourists — being affected by food-borne illnesses.

What's Happening in Some Other Parts of the World

A travel guide for a south-east Asian country states the following:

> Vegetables and fruit should be washed with purified water or peeled where possible. Beware of ice cream that is sold in the street or anywhere it might have been melted and refrozen; if there's any doubt (e.g., a power cut in the last day or two), steer well clear. Shellfish such as mussels, oysters and clams should be avoided as well as undercooked meat, particularly in the form of mince. Steaming does not make shellfish safe for eating … (Cummings, 1999, pp. 108–109).

One of the charming features of many south-east Asian destinations is the practice of street vending, and of small side street cafes and restaurants with amazing offerings of food, including fried grasshoppers, skewered rats, and the like. While it might be easy to avoid the obvious risks for an unseasoned stomach (yes, stomachs do adjust — the micro flora of stomachs 'toughen' as they become familiar with different bacterium), even the more recognizable foodstuffs such as ice cream and indeed water potentially pose a threat to health. It is the very character of such venues that adds to their risk — potentially a lack of reliable electricity for heating and cooling in hot, humid climates; lack of access to running, pure water for cleaning both foodstuffs and food preparation tools, not to mention personal hygiene; lack of protection from potential pest (such as cockroaches and flies) invasion; knowledge about food handling, storage and preparation practices, and so on.

This site for food-borne illness was identified in the project *Streetfood Safety Training* conducted in Quezon City, Philippines (see Dumelod & Gatchalian, 2001).

In this project, it was noted that there is a rapidly growing popularity of streetfoods by both local residents and tourists in major cities in south-east Asia. Streetfoods are highly attractive and saleable because of their variety in terms of taste, color, form, nutritional quality, affordability and accessibility. They are also considered by many tourists to represent the true culinary experience of a culture. However, food safety is often ignored by street vendors, leading to reduced food quality and sometimes food-borne illness episodes. Streetfoods may be considered to be more risky than hotel and restaurant food and have been associated with typhoid fever, hepatitis A, cholera and intestinal diseases. Microbial analyses of some popular street-vended foods have shown that they may contain high levels of coliform, yeasts, molds, Staphylococcus aureus, Salmonella and Vibrio. The health risks associated with the consumption of streetfoods may be attributed partly to the vendors' lack of awareness of the importance of food hygiene, ignorance about good manufacturing practices, lack of concern for consumers well-being, and malpractices of food handlers (Dumelod & Gatchalian, 2001).

To this end, WHO has revised the document entitled *Essential Safety Requirements for Street-Vended Food*, which considers practical and flexible approaches for improving the safety of street-vended food in a variety of settings and conditions. The text can be used as the basis for training and education programs, for food inspectors and street-food vendors, as well as for developing codes of practice for street-vended food (WHO/FNU/FOS/96.7). The increasing popularity of street-vended foods, coupled with an increase in local outbreaks of food-borne illnesses, prompted the Quezon City Government, the Technical Education and Skills Development Authority and the University of Philippines to embark on a program to ensure the safety of streetfoods in Quezon City in the Philippines. The four-phase program included:

Phase 1: Survey. A survey of food safety knowledge and practices among 326 streetfood vendors in Quezon City. The findings revealed that the respondents were fairly aware of food safety but had misconceptions about major aspects of food preparation, storage and general handling. Most importantly, it was widely thought that food is not a good medium for growth of microorganisms, a serious misconception.

Phase 2: Module development. Five teaching modules each in English, Filipino, and a cartoon version for illiterate participants were prepared based on the survey findings. The topics were:

1. Food contamination and spoilage
2. Good manufacturing practices
3. Food handler health and hygiene
4. Facilities and equipment management
5. Food laws and regulations.

Phase 3: Training and certification of trainers. Training of 41 prospective instructors to help in the dissemination of the principles, procedures and techniques in safe food handling was conducted over a 5-day period. These instructors were street vendors.

Phase 4: Pilot training and certification of trainees. A pilot food safety training and certification course among 85 street-food vendors and officials from Quezon City was conducted. Participants acknowledged the significance of the training. The trainees suggested that incentives be provided to encourage greater awareness and practice of food safety, such as giving rewards to outstanding street-food vendors.

The project recommendations made clear that the training of street vendors is essential to ensure that the safety of streetfood can be improved, and that the popularity of street-food continues to grow and be an increasingly safe alternative for locals and tourists alike (Dumelod & Gatchalian, 2001).

In another part of the world, the Federation of Tour Operators (FTO) has developed a *Preferred Code of Practice* (FTO, 2003) which provides advice regarding a range of elements at tourist destinations including those related to: fire safety, pool safety, beach safety, children's clubs; and importantly, food safety. The document has been "issued to 18,000 accommodation providers in destination, and is the criteria that our members and experts use to measure acquiescence" (FTO, 2005). The food hygiene component of the Code of Practice commences with a note about the lack of an acceptable code against which an audit of food hygiene practices might be conducted, thereby setting a firm justification for the guidelines provided. It then details the use of the Hazard Analysis Critical Control Point (HACCP) approach that informs the development of the comprehensive guidelines. Essentially, HACCP involves seven principles:

- *Analyze hazards.* Potential hazards associated with a food and measures to control those hazards are identified. The hazard could be biological, such as a microbe; chemical, such as a toxin; or physical, such as ground glass or metal fragments.
- *Identify critical control points.* These are points in a food's production — from its raw state through processing and shipping to consumption by the consumer — at which the potential hazard can be controlled or eliminated. Examples are cooking, cooling, packaging and metal detection.
- *Establish preventive measures with critical limits for each control point.* For a cooked food, for example, this might include setting the minimum cooking temperature and time required to ensure the elimination of any harmful microbes.
- *Establish procedures to monitor the critical control points.* Such procedures might include determining how and by whom cooking time and temperature should be monitored.
- *Establish corrective actions to be taken when monitoring shows that a critical limit has not been met.* For example, reprocessing or disposing of food if the minimum cooking temperature is not met.
- *Establish procedures to verify that the system is working properly.* For example, testing time- and temperature-recording devices to verify that a cooking unit is working properly.
- *Establish effective record keeping to document the HACCP system.* This would include records of hazards and their control methods, the monitoring of safety requirements and action taken to correct potential problems. Each of these principles must be backed by sound scientific knowledge: for example, published microbiological studies on time and temperature factors for controlling food-borne pathogens (United States FDA, 2005).

The HACCP approach underpins the FTO food hygiene code of practice, and provides a sound set of guidelines for member organizations. This is an example of an effective partnership between FTO and member organizations, with the FTO providing solid guidelines that aid in the education of members, along with the provision of practical measures for prevention.

Being an Active Agent in Prevention — "Boil it, Cook it, Peel it or Forget it"

There is some solid advice that can help tourists to minimize their risk of experiencing food-borne illnesses on the basis that prudent avoidance of high-risk foods cuts the odds of falling victim, and the travelers adage cited above is an example of a simple one. In fact, education and behavior modification are regarded as the "cornerstone of prevention" for traveler's diarrhea — one of the possible symptoms of food-borne illness. However, compliance becomes a problem for many once the momentum and temptations of travel surround them (Ostrosky-Zeichner & Ericsson, 2004, p. 186). Peltola and Gorbach (1997, p. 78) concur with this assessment, lamenting that "many cases are preventable by precautions regarding food and drink, but great motivational problems exist."

Many travel medicine practitioners, researchers, food hygienists and others with an interest in this field have specified foods to avoid, and advice regarding water consumption. For example, Ryan and Kain (2000, p. 1717) provide clear guidelines of what is to be avoided by travelers to the developing world:

> Avoid uncooked food (other than peeled fruit and vegetables), nonbottled beverages, and unpasteurised dairy products. Eat well-cooked, hot foods. Do not eat food purchased from street vendors. Use bottled water for drinking, making ice cubes, and brushing teeth. Wash hands with soap and water frequently, especially before each meal.

Most travel guides contain a list of tips for travelers, often destination specific, and these are generally useful for highlighting key risks. There is no doubt that as an informed tourist making intelligent food choices, the chance of suffering the ill effects of food-borne illness can be reduced. But this does require careful and consistent vigilance. Total eradication of the problem does rely on a cooperative effort, including at a minimum the education and training of food handlers and the development and enforcement of government standards for food safety and hygiene — an enormous challenge for the tourism industry and government authorities.

Nevertheless, here are some tips for all travelers, anywhere in the world, who wish to be an active agent in minimizing their risk of suffering from food-borne illness:

- Avoid the following foodstuffs, each of which are very risky: tap water, ice, milk, fresh fruits and vegetables, seafood, rare meat dishes, chicken and undercooked eggs. Be vigilant about these foodstuffs — choose them only if you are confident about their storage, preparation and handling. This can be country or region specific.
- Choose eating venues that are well patronaged. This will lead to a greater chance that food is not stored for long periods, is likely to be fresh, and less vulnerable to microbial attack or contamination. Ideally look for establishments with regular power supplies, running water, and sanitation services that provide hand washing facilities for visitors and staff.
- Select cooked dishes that are prepared on demand. Buffet-style meals which may sit at warm temperatures for several hours create an ideal environment for microbial growth

and should be avoided unless there is volume turnover. If buffet meals are the only choice, avoid foods that are high risk, such as rare meats, chicken, seafood.
* Safe food is hot, dry and peeled.
* Request that beverages are poured in your presence from untampered bottles and cans. Check the seals first.
* Safe drinks are carbonated and water in a container with a sealed top.
* Do not become complacent about food choices while traveling, **ever**.

References

Ansdell, V. (2004). Food-borne illness. In: J. Keystone, P. Kozarsky, H.D. Nothdurft, D.O. Freedman, & B. Connor (Eds), *Travel medicine* (pp. 443–452). London: Mosby.

Australian Broadcasting Commission News On-line (ABC). (2004). *Gastro cuts short South Pacific Cruise*. Saturday, May 8, 2004. 2:34pm (AEST). http://www.abc.net.au/news/newsitems/s1104199.htm (accessed 18 March 2005).

Australian Government, Department of Agriculture, Fisheries and Forestry. (2005). http://www.affa.gov.au/ (accessed 21 March 2005).

Brewster, S., & Taylor, D. (2004). Epidemiology of traveler's diarrhea. In: J. Keystone, P. Kozarsky, H.D. Nothdurft, D.O. Freedman, & B. Connor (Eds), *Travel medicine* (pp. 175–184). London: Mosby.

Burslem, C., Kelly, M., & Preston F. (1990). Food poisoning – a major threat to airline operations. *Journal of Social and Occupational Medicine*, *40*(3), 97–100.

Cummings, J. (1999). *Lonely planet guide: Thailand*. Melbourne: Lonely Planet Publications.

Curson, P. (2004). Gut reaction to food-borne disease. *Courier Mail*, 12 October.

Dumelod, D., & Gatchalian, C. (2001). Streetfood safety training and certificate program: A collaborative experience. In: C.F. Gatchalian, V.C.S. Heung, & R.G. Cruz, (Eds), *Mix, match and move: Shaping the future of tourism. Proceedings of the 7th annual conference of the Asia Pacific tourism association* (pp. 140–143). Makati City, Philippines: Asia Pacific Tourism Association.

Federation of Tour Operators (FTO). (2003). *Preferred code of practice*. Lewes, United Kingdom: Federation of Tour Operators.

Federation of Tour Operators. (2005). http://www.fto.co.uk/health_safety.php?a=198 (accessed 21 March 2005).

Food Standards Australia New Zealand. (2005). http://www.foodstandards.gov.au (accessed 19 March 2005).

Guillain-Barre Syndrome Foundation International. (2005). http://www.guillain-barre.com/overview.html (accessed 18 March 2005).

Harty, C. (2000). Food poisoning costing the nation $2.6 million. *Retail World*, *20* (December), 9.

Hatakka, M., & Asplund, K. (1993). The occurrence of Salmonella in airline meals. *Acta Veterinaria Scandinavica*, *34*(4), 391–396.

International Hotel & Restaurant Association. (1998). *Think-tank findings on safety and security. Executive summary*. Unpublished Report, Orlando, FL, 18 and 19 August.

Ostrosky-Zeichner, L., & Ericsson, C. (2004). Prevention of traveler's diarrhea. In: J. Keystone, P. Kozarsky, H.D. Nothdurft, D.O. Freedman, & B. Connor (Eds), *Travel medicine* (pp. 185–189). London: Mosby.

Peltola, H., & Gorbach, S. (1997). Traveler's diarrhea. In: H. DuPont, & R. Steffen (Eds), *Textbook of travel medicine and health* (pp. 78–86). Ontario: B.C. Decker.

Pugh, R., Selvey, L., Crome, M., & Beers, M. (2001). Onshore catering increases the risk of diarrhoeal illness amongst cruise ship passengers. *Communicable Disease Intelligence*, *25*(1), 15–17.

Queensland Health and the Home Economics Institute of Australia. (2000). *Food Safety Matters.* Brisbane: Queensland Health.

Rooney, R., Cramer, E., Mantha, S., Nichols, G., Bartram, J., Farber, J., & Benembarek, P. (2004), A review of outbreaks of food-borne disease associated with passenger ships: Evidence for risk management. *Public Health Reports*, *119*(4), 427–434.

Ryan, E., & Kain, K. (2000). Health advice and immunizations for travelers. *New England Journal of Medicine*, *342*(23), 1716–1725.

Ryan, E., Wilson, M., & Kain, K. (2002). Illness after international travel. *New England Journal of Medicine*, *347*(7), 505–516.

Tambling, G. (1999). Costs of food poisoning cannot be underestimated. Media Release. 14 February. Available on FSANZ. Website http://www.foodstandards.gov.au (accessed 19 March 2005).

United States Food and Drug Administration (FDA). (2005). http://www.cfsan.fda.gov (accessed 19 March 2005).

World Health Organization (WHO). (2005). Essential Safety Requirements for Street-Vended Foods (WHO/FNU/FOS/96.7). http://www.who.int/foodsafety/publications/fs_management/street_vend/en (accessed 28 March 2005).

Chapter 11

Tourist Injury

Tim A. Bentley and Stephen J. Page

Introduction

The importance of the safety and well-being of tourists has become a global issue and one of the primary concerns of the tourism industry (Frangialli, 2003; Wilks & Page, 2003). Indeed, the welfare of tourists is a growing area of interest for researchers from a range of disciplines including tourism, ergonomics, safety science, travel medicine and health (Page, Bentley, & Meyer, 2003). Importantly, researchers from these areas have begun to recognise the advantages of collaboration in multi-disciplinary research, where the complexity of the tourist safety problem is reflected in the range of expertise of the research team (e.g. Bentley & Page, 2001). These initiatives have occurred despite a serious lack of funding from government and industry internationally for research in the tourist health and safety area. Such a situation is surprising, given the considerable impacts tourist fatalities and injuries can potentially have on the image of both the industry and regional and national destinations (World Tourism Organization, 1996). New Zealand, for example, a country with an economy highly dependent upon its two-plus million overseas visitors per year, has been host to a large number of high-profile fatality cases involving overseas visitors taking part in adventure and recreational tourism activities, including major incidents and fatalities involving scenic flights, white water rafting, jet boating and tramping and mountaineering. While the impact of these and other serious incidents in terms of visitor perceptions and travel behaviour have not been meaningfully quantified, there is anecdotal evidence that the travel behaviour of potential visitors from lucrative markets such as the US and Japan may be affected by news of serious incidents involving fellow nationals. For example, a survey reported in the New Zealand press (Bentley & Page, 2001), found safety concerns to be the major hindrance to Japanese travel to New Zealand, with New Zealand ranked behind Hawaii, Australia, Switzerland, Canada, Singapore, UK and Guam as a safe destination. It is likely these perceptions were strongly related to media reports in Japan concerning scenic flight crashes in which Japanese tourists were killed (also see Greenaway, 1996; Page & Meyer, 1996; Page, 1997).

One important reason for the lack of serious interest in this phenomenon from governments, industry and researchers is that the extent of the tourism health and safety problem is unknown in most countries. Without national tourism injury databases or surveillance systems, and/or any one body reliably collating and reporting national or industry injury statistics, the true extent of the tourist injury problem is masked. As a consequence it is hard for researchers to mount a case for funding to address the problem, and visitor safety never gets onto funding priority lists. Likewise, there is likely to be only limited political and public awareness of the problem where tourist injury numbers are effectively hidden.

Research into tourist safety that has been conducted to date has been mainly non-strategic, that is to say the studies reported in the tourism, sport and recreation, medical and safety literature have been piecemeal in nature and independent of each other rather than part of an ongoing programme of research with longer-term aims around the prevention of tourist injuries in a particular industry sector or destination. An exception to this is the research into adventure and recreational tourism safety that has been conducted in New Zealand over a number of years, and more recently Scotland, by these authors, where an attempt has been made to establish a baseline of visitor injuries and to understand their causes using both primary and secondary data sources. Findings from this research will provide the focus for this chapter, as adventure tourism is by far the highest risk sector for the international tourism industry.

Adventure Tourism Safety in New Zealand

While the issue of risk is a key phenomenon in terms of adventure tourism safety, risk *per se* is not the central focus of this chapter (this issue is covered by Morgan in Chapter 12, also see Ryan, 2003). The research reported here, however, does impact upon the perception of this sector as one characterised by risk dependent upon the activity one engages in. The research undertaken by these authors to date has taken a more macro approach to the problem of tourist injuries, with its major aims being to determine the extent of the problem in New Zealand; identify high-risk activity sectors; and determine key risk factors for adventure and recreational tourism injuries. This information was considered an essential foundation to more focused research concerned with the prevention of injuries for high-risk activities.

Figure 11.1 provides a breakdown of what is now an established definition of the scope of activities within adventure tourism used in numerous studies internationally; organised under land, water- and air-based environments.

Millington, Locke, and Locke (2001, p. 67) define adventure travel as:

> ... a leisure activity that takes place in an unusual, exotic, remote or wilderness destination. It tends to be associated with high levels of activity by the participant, most of it outdoors. Adventure travellers expect to experience various levels of risk, excitement and tranquillity, and be personally tested. In particular they are explorers of unspoilt, exotic parts of the planet and also seek personal challenges.

The New Zealand adventure tourism sector

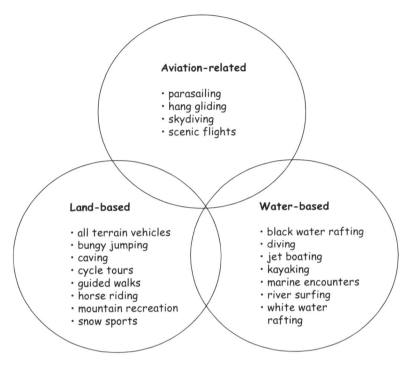

Figure 11.1: The adventure tourism sector in New Zealand.

This definition highlights several potential areas of risk to the adventure tourism participant, including unfamiliar environments, remote locations, risk-taking and the opportunity to be personally tested or challenged. Indeed, the importance of unfamiliar marine and road environments and activities in which the visitor lacks experience has been implicated in tourist morbidity and mortality by previous research (Wilks & Atherton, 1994; Wilks & Oldenburg, 1995; Wilks & Watson, 1998).

There is evidence too that some New Zealand adventure activities, notably white water rafting, scenic flights and mountain recreation, present significant risks of serious and fatal injury to clients (Hall & McArthur, 1991; Johnston, 1989; McLaughlan, 1995; Greenaway, 1996; Bentley, Meyer, Page, & Chalmers, 2001a). Bentley et al. (2001a), from an analysis of overseas visitor hospitalisation data in New Zealand for the period, 1982–1996, identified some 1027 overseas visitor hospitalisations where adventure tourism activity of some form was being undertaken at the time of the injury. This figure represents 17% of all overseas visitor injuries during this period, and corresponds to an injury-incidence rate of approximately eight hospitalised injuries per 100,000 overseas visitors for the period of the analysis. A further 99 (22%) fatalities due to participation in adventure pursuits were found for the same period. Highest counts of adventure tourism-related injuries and fatalities were sustained by recreationalists engaged in unguided, independent adventure activities, notably skiing and mountaineering. Highest counts of commercial adventure tourism injuries were found for horse riding and cycling. Unsurprisingly, aviation and water-based incidents resulted in injuries of greatest severity.

A survey of 142 New Zealand adventure tourism operators (Bentley, Page, & Laird, 2001b) allowed analysis of client injuries and their primary causes among a wider range of commercial adventure activities. This study found relatively high-reported client injury rates among cycle tour and horse-riding operators, these findings being in line with those of the hospitalisation data analysis. It was noted that these activities, which arguably have a low level of 'perceived risk' associated with them, had greater 'actual risk' than activities with higher levels of perceived risk (e.g. white water rafting, skydiving and bungee jumping). The authors note that "the perception of risk held by the clients participating in adventure tourism activities may be an important moderator of client behaviour, and thus a significant factor in injury risk" (CM Research, 1995). These findings can also be misleading, however, as those organisations that report a very high ratio of minor to serious harm injuries may simply have superior injury reporting systems (i.e. they are good at reporting and recording injuries); a positive indicator in terms of safety management practice, as the reporting of minor injuries and near miss-events are essential to a good injury prevention system. This appears not to be the case with activities such as cycle touring/mountain biking and horse riding, however, as these operators reported a low ratio of minor to serious harm injuries.

Bentley et al. (2001a, b) identified falls as the most frequent cause of injury for adventure tourism clients, comprising 65% of all adventure tourism-related injuries among overseas visitors. These findings were supported by the responses of adventure tourism operators surveyed, with most reporting slips, trips and falls on the level to be events commonly leading to client injuries. This finding suggests that adventure tourism injuries most commonly involve minor, relatively low hazard events, rather than catastrophic events such as those that commonly attract the attention of the news media.

Operators reported risk factors for adventure tourism client injuries to include a wide range of client, equipment, environment and organisational factors. These were organised into a conceptual model for adventure tourism client injury risk (Figure 11.2), useful in assisting operator risk assessment and other safety management activities where information about potential risk factors for adventure tourism activities is of benefit. The most important contribution of this model is that it illustrates the multi-causal nature of adventure tourism injuries, involving interactions between human, task, environmental and social contributory factors. An important implication of this approach to adventure tourism injury and tourist safety more generally is that injuries are increasingly likely where environmental risks (such as unfamiliar marine environments or fast changing weather conditions) are present at the same time as human factors (such as fatigue, inexperience, risk-taking and shortcuts). Latent factors related to the organisation of work (such as policy, time pressures, work scheduling and training), and design of task and equipment, often underlying human and task factors, can play an even more important role in adventure tourism injuries. Indeed, latent factors can often be the most effective target for prevention as it is often easier to design-out a risk through design or organisational means 'upstream', rather than try and change a multitude of client and staff behaviours 'downstream'.

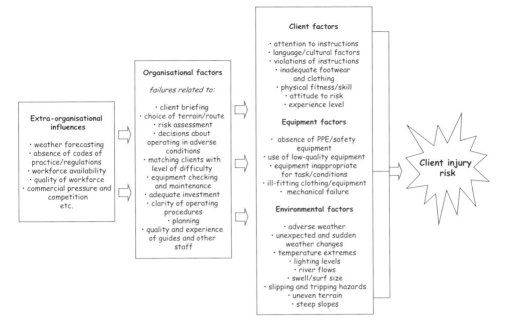

Figure 11.2: Risk factors for adventure tourism client injury.

The 2003 New Zealand and Scotland Adventure Tourism Safety Experience Survey

This study sought to build upon the 1999 studies on adventure tourism safety in New Zealand (see Bentley et al., 2001b), the results of which are described above. The aims of the 2003 study were broadened to assist the establishment of priorities for intervention to reduce adventure tourism risk, and identification of client injury control measures currently in place (or absent) in the New Zealand adventure tourism industry, with a view to establishing guidelines for the development of effective adventure tourism safety management. The 2003 adventure tourism safety experience survey was also administered in Scotland. Scotland was chosen as a comparative destination since it exhibited many of the inherent environmental qualities which characterise adventure tourism operations in New Zealand: it has a degree of rural remoteness and a relatively scenic backdrop for adventure tourism participants; its volume of international and domestic tourism flair are not too dissimilar to permit valid comparisons.

Method

The 1999 survey involved the use of an initial survey instrument, which was devised as a self-completion questionnaire, being four pages in length with a series of open- and closed questions. The instrument was piloted among a sample of 10 operators in 1998 after preliminary scoping interviews with key operators and NGOs in 1998 to establish the principal issues to examine. The questionnaire was then mailed out to the entire known population of adventure operators during the winter season. In 2003, this survey instrument was revisited, with revisions made to the questionnaire structure to incorporate questions that allowed the researchers to examine the risk management practices of operators.

An extensive review of secondary sources was undertaken, including listings in trade journals and activity magazines, trade associations, regional and national tourist boards as well as listings in the Yellow Pages to identify the scope of this sector. In New Zealand, some 301 companies were identified after 59 business closures/database duplications were removed and in Scotland, some 389 companies were located, which was modified after an initial mail out to 351 operators from a known total of 960 'activity' operators who operate adventure through to non-adventure-related holidays/activities (System Three, 1998). This provided two sample populations of almost equal size, illustrating one of the similarities between the two countries in terms of the size and importance of this niche sector.

The questionnaire comprised three discrete sections: the business, its characteristics and volume and nature of clients; a much lengthier section on injuries and risk factor perceptions and a third section inviting operators to expand or elaborate upon their experiences. Each respondent was provided with a reply-paid envelope and the survey was addressed to the business owner or operations manager.

Response Rate and Operator Demographics

A total of 96 New Zealand operators responded to the survey, equating to a 31.9% response rate. The low response rate in New Zealand may be attributed to the timing of the survey in the winter period, and the sensitive nature of this type of study, seeking data on client injury experiences. In Scotland, 132 operators responded, providing a response rate of 37.6%. This is, by international standards for postal surveys of small tourism businesses, a reasonable outcome given that response rates for this type of survey rarely exceed 40%.

In both countries, the majority of businesses responding to the survey were owned by individuals or jointly owned (Scotland, 44.7%; New Zealand, 41%). In Scotland, the average number of full-time employees was 4.61, while in New Zealand the numbers were markedly lower at two employees per operator, and only 5–10 employees in 27% of businesses. Many Scottish and New Zealand adventure tourism businesses were not only very small in terms of full-time equivalents, but relatively newly formed, with over 20% being in operation for less than 6 years.

Locations of Operators

In New Zealand, the majority of operators included in the sample were located in the known major adventure tourism centres at Queenstown and Wanaka, in and around Auckland, Rotorua, Taupo, Nelson and the West Coast. In Scotland, the sample reflected the three broad geographical groupings by Tourist Board region: First, in Central Scotland, the Argyll, the Isles, Loch Lomond, Stirling and Trossachs (AILLST) area which is adjacent to the main gateways of Glasgow and Edinburgh and major sources of domestic visitors, also containing over 50% of Scotland's population. It also includes Scotland's first National Park. Second, the Perthshire region, to the north of the AILLST area, with a series of lochs and glens which are accessible but deemed remoter adventure activity sites. Lastly, the Highlands of Scotland with its historical associations with mountain climbing and outdoor pursuits, focused on Aviemore (skiing), Fort William and the Lochaber district (climbing) and a number of smaller clusters on islands (e.g. Ullapool).

Activities Represented in the Sample and Clients of Adventure Tourism Activities

Activities provided by operators spanned 27 activity sectors, ranging from soft to hard, active to passive and being high and low in risk. The most commonly reported activities provided by New Zealand operators were: scenic flights (15%), Kayaking (14%), mountain guiding (6%), white water rafting (6%) and horse riding (6%). Land-based activities dominated the Scotland sample (54.69%), followed by water-borne (25%), air-based (1.56%) or those offering a mixed portfolio of activities across these categories (11.72%). Horse riding (15.15%), boat-based trips (9.85%), multi-activity centres (8.33%), canoeing/rafting (6%), land-based ecotours (5.3%), outward-bound educational trips (5.3%), mountaineering (6%), snow sports (4%) and off-road driving/quad biking (4.55%) were the most common activities provided, with 25 categories of activities listed.

In New Zealand, operators reported 643,167 clients in the period January–December 2002 and a mean number of clients of 7479 ranging from 20 to 128,000 per annum. In Scotland, the sample reported 599,088 clients with a mean of 5301 clients per annum, ranging from 50 to 200,000 per annum. In terms of client mix, 51% of New Zealand clients were male and 14% of the market were children aged less than 16 years of age. In Scotland, 52% of clients were male and 10–20% of their market were children, which is not unexpected given the number of activity centres and tradition of outward bound activities. The largest age group for participants in adventure tourism activities was 25–40 years for both countries. The major client demographical difference between Scotland and New Zealand was the principal market for such activities. In Scotland, the volume of clients was estimated by operators as 14% overseas (83,872), 62% domestic (371,434) and 24% day trips/leisure (143,781), while in New Zealand the market was estimated to be 53% overseas (340,878), 30% domestic (192,950) and 17% leisure/day trip traffic (109,338). The two countries have distinctly different markets, therefore, with New Zealand viewing adventure tourism as a well-developed international visitor product and, in contrast, Scotland focusing on the less lucrative domestic and day trip/leisure traffic. From a safety management perspective, however, the New Zealand industry has a far greater potential for language and cultural barriers in the management of client safety due to the overseas markets it targets, particularly Asia.

Operator Perspectives on Client Safety

Operators were asked to rank a list of factors they perceived as threats that impacted upon client safety in terms of client factors, environment factors, task and equipment factors, work organisation and management. Both sets of respondents ranked environmental factors as a key threat to client safety, combined with unfamiliar environments, which also feature prominently in the 'excitement' factor for such activities. For example, New Zealand operators ranked weather conditions and changes as the number one risk factor in 28% of cases and as a top five ranked risk in 90% of cases (Table 11.1). Unfamiliar operating environments,

Table 11.1: Perceived risk factors for adventure tourism operations.

Risk factor	Number of times ranked as number one risk factor (n)	Number of times ranked in top five risk factors (n)	Proportion of respondents ranking factor (%)
Client/behavioural factors			
Horseplay/ignoring instructions	12	41	44
Client knowledge and abilities	9	43	46
Language/cultural factors	3	27	29
Shortcuts/risk-taking by clients	3	30	32
Environmental factors			
Weather conditions/changes	28	90	97
Unfamiliar operating environments	10	33	35
Slipping/tripping hazards	7	38	41
Exposure to water/drowning risk	14	33	35
Task and equipment factors			
Equipment failure	7	26	28
Equipment use/suitability	1	17	18
Operating at heights	3	17	18
Operating at high speeds	3	14	15
Degree of task difficulty	2	22	24
Work organisation and management			
Staff experience/quality	7	38	41
Financial considerations	2	10	11
Operational decisions	6	24	26
Client/guide ratio	2	17	18
Absence of safety management systems	8	24	26

exposure to water/drowning risk and slipping and tripping hazards were also ranked as the number one threat by a marked proportion of operators, further highlighting the importance of the New Zealand outdoor environment as the primary area of risk from the perspective of the operator. The ranking of client factors was matched in magnitude, perhaps surprisingly, by rankings for work organisation and management factors, where staff experience and quality, operational decisions and absence of safety management systems were recognised as key threats to safety by a notable proportion of operators.

In line with previous research, slips, trips and falls were the major threat to injury for adventure tourism clients in both countries (Scotland, 60%; New Zealand, 49%), with other underfoot injuries, including stepping on/in or twisting ankle injuries also highly ranked. Other frequently reported hazards in New Zealand included striking an object (30%), falls from a height (26%) and drowning or non-fatal submersion (18%). In contrast, exposure to water and risk of drowning accounted for just 4.8% of responses in Scotland.

Client Injuries Reported by Operators

Operators were asked to record the number of injuries from their accident book over the last 12 months. In New Zealand, 87 businesses responded to this request and 125 in Scotland. Some 1095 injury incidents were recorded by New Zealand operators, compared to 1030 in Scotland as shown in Table 11.2.

Just 148 (16% of all incidents) serious harm incidents requiring hospitalisation, at an average of 1.6 per operator, were reported by New Zealand operators. In Scotland, 116 (11%) such incidents occurred, the majority occurring with land-based activities. A surprisingly large proportion of operators in both countries reported no injuries (New Zealand, 44%; Scotland, 51%), suggesting a serious injury under-reporting problem in both countries. Table 2 also shows mean client injury incidence rate per million participation

Table 11.2: Distribution of client injuries by activity sector in New Zealand and Scotland.

Activity sector in New Zealand	Client injuries (all) (n)	Serious harm injuries (n)	Mean client injury incidence rate (PMPH)
Black water rafting	40	2	280.0
Bungee jumping	62	3	477.0
Cycle tours/mountain biking	19	1	304.0
Ecotourism activities	9	0	58.5
Education/personal and social development	7	4	3.0
Horse riding/pony trekking	35	13	759.5
Indoor climbing	13	0	250.0
Kayaking/canoeing	16	1	241.3
Multi-activity	24	1	247.5
Scenic flights	15	3	3.2
Snow sports	796	112	2229.3
Walking/tramping	19	0	195.6
White water rafting	14	1	191.4
Activity sector in Scotland			
Accommodation/holidays	5	1	3.0
Boating/sailing	12	0	79.8
Ecotours	1	1	20.8
Education/personal and social development	77	0	584.2
Horse riding/pony trekking	275	12	2397.4
Kayaking/canoeing	12	1	625.0
Mountaineering/climbing	20	2	2152.2
Multi-activity	293	10	1456.2
Off-road driving/quad biking	24	24	—
Snow sports	267	61	1031.0
Walking/hiking	9	0	640.6

hours for each activity sector. This statistic provides a measure of exposure, as it takes account of the amount of time participants are exposed to any risks associated with the activity by multiplying annual number of clients with duration of activity and dividing by total injuries recorded (multiplied by 1 million). Highest incidence rates for the New Zealand sector were observed for snow sports and horse riding, while these activities are also prominent in terms of incident rates in Scotland. In Scotland, snow sports accounted for 53% of all serious harm injuries, with 53.4 incidents per operator. In the high-profile sector in New Zealand, bungee jumping recorded 62 injuries, although only three led to serious harm to a client. This represents an increase on the injury rates reported by Bentley, Page, and Laird (2000), with a rate of 117 PMPH compared to 477 in the present study. In contrast to Scotland, the educational and personal development activity providers (which correspond to pursuits marketed by many multi-activity centres) had low client injury rates, which could suggest that this sector has a low level of reporting in New Zealand. The Scottish multi-activity operators reported relatively high levels of injury to clients. Here the problem of fatigue, unfamiliar tasks and different environments can increase injury risk. The youngest and smallest businesses in both countries reported relatively low levels of injuries, with many recently established businesses in this sector found to have better safety management.

Client Safety Management and Barriers to Safety Improvements

Operators were asked to describe their safety systems or measures they had in place to reduce risk injury to clients. In New Zealand, the situation is less straightforward, since minor injuries and accidents to visitors are covered by the Accident Compensation Corporation Scheme (Page & Meyer, 1996; Callander & Page, 2003). This fact does not, however, remove the legal duty of care to provide a safe environment for employees and clients. A disappointingly low proportion of operators in each country reported having a formal risk management programme in place. In New Zealand, 30 businesses reported a safe operating plan, clear operational guidelines or regulatory Codes of Practice as the principal safety measures taken. Only 16 businesses reported a risk assessment procedure, while 34 businesses used staff training and selection as a preventive measure, with 25 businesses giving safety training or talks prior to, or during activities and 20 undertook regular equipment checks.

In Scotland, 36 businesses had a risk assessment procedure, reflecting the much higher importance attached to operating and regulatory procedures in EU countries but particularly in the UK following numerous high-profile law suits against school teachers following catastrophic events during outward bound courses. Other frequently reported prevention factors were adherence to Codes of Practice, regular equipment checks, provision of safety information and guidance as well as close supervision of clients due to a much more litigious environment in relation to health and safety. External bodies such as the Adventure Activity Licensing Authority (AALA) and other regulatory bodies were cited as imposing stringent conditions related to licencing, particularly as it was imperative to have risk assessment procedures for all forms of activity provision where AALA approval was sought.

Barriers to Safety Improvements

Businesses feedback on continuous safety improvements were sought, particularly in terms of perceived barriers to their safety management practices. The cost of compliance in implementing safety measures was cited in both countries as a major barrier to safety. Safety management efforts also had to be counterbalanced with the requirement to maintain a degree of realism in the natural environment in relation to perceived risk and excitement. Operators also highlighted the problem of recruiting staff with adequate competence and depth of experience as important, and commonly reported that finding time to remain ahead of such issues was a problem due to the wide range of tasks facing SMEs. Operators from both countries pointed to participants who often overestimated their own ability, particularly with horse riding, as an important barrier to safety efforts. If clients do not heed safety warnings, or horseplay occurs in individual or group situations, it can lead to an incident in which guides can lose control of the activity and injury is likely. While all operators acknowledged the dangers posed by changeable and unpredictable weather, client lack of preparation or awareness of the level of challenge posed by activities in each country was a major barrier to safety.

Discussion and Conclusions

This study, in line with others discussed earlier in this chapter, has highlighted the fact that relatively few serious harm incidents occur in adventure tourism, which is reassuring for the commercial sector (i.e. operator-led sector). This is in contrast to the informal recreational sector (i.e. unguided tramping and mountain climbing) which has a history of serious incident and injury in New Zealand (e.g. Johnston, 1989; Bentley et al., 2001a) and Scotland (Sharp, 2001). As found in earlier studies, a considerable number of minor injuries were reported by operators in each country, with a large proportion of operators reporting no injuries. However, from a safety management perspective, these findings are unfortunate as minor injuries and near-miss events provide important organisational learning opportunities for operators seeking to better understand risk factors associated with their activities, and indicate many operators possess inadequate safety management systems to control client safety adequately. The relatively high ratio of serious harm injuries to all injuries reported for some sectors (e.g. horse riding, quad biking, scenic flights) further emphasises this point.

Land-based operators reported highest client injury numbers, especially in the snow sports and horse-riding sector, and in Scotland, within the multi-activity sector. This finding is reflected in the injury types most frequently reported, with slips, trips, and falls (STF) and underfoot injuries the dominant minor-injury category. Contributory risk factors for occupational STF are reported by Bentley and Haslam (1998), with environmental factors (i.e. slippery underfoot conditions), weather contingent situations (i.e. wet/frozen), individual risk-taking (rushing and shortcuts), task-related factors (i.e. carrying kayaks) and work organisation and management factors (e.g. route and task decisions, work scheduling, policy and training) interacting to produce increased STF risk. Consideration of these factors in risk management can help identify and address some of these problem scenarios, which is now becoming a global process, which many tourism businesses have to consider when dealing with visitors. At a more generic level, Figure 2 introduced earlier in the chapter, provides a more holistic assessment of the interactions which may contribute to adventure tourism incidents and illustrates how each of these different factors are inter-related.

The use of Codes of Practice to help operators to focus on best practice to reduce client injuries is an important development in Scotland. Codes of Practice also assist the development of the sector's potential, through continuous improvements, so that short-term events such as client injuries do not damage the long-term objectives that adventure activities are relatively safe to undertake, when accounting for the risk factors which participants face to increase the thrill and excitement associated with an activity.

The studies reported in this chapter raise concerns about the lack of consensus among operators concerning the use of formal risk management practices as a mandatory process that all must endorse. It is important, therefore, that interventions targeting safety improvements across the sector should include improved knowledge of effective risk management practices. Reliance on alternative injury prevention activities such as client briefings to address this weakness is unsatisfactory, particularly in stressful conditions (e.g. a raft turnover), where language and stress factors will be a major barrier to communication. Greater supervision and better client/supervisor ratios are required, particularly where English is not the first language (i.e. among overseas visitors), as are instructions, verbal and written, in the main languages spoken by an activity's clients. Recent changes in New Zealand's occupational health and safety legislation (Health and Safety in Employment Amendment Act, 2002), which has been extended to provide coverage for maritime and aviation environments and to reflect the situation of small businesses, will provide further impetus for the industry to place client safety as a top business priority.

It is crucial, however, that these issues be set in context: adventure tourism is a sector experiencing growth at a global level (Swarbrooke, Beard, Leckie, & Pomfret, 2003), with increasing participation, making injury risk a key element of the adventure-participating experience. It is not desirable to sanitise these experiences, through a global harmonisation of experiences already evidenced in the hospitality sector. Locations, products and visitor experiences must be different, stimulating and challenging for them to compete and add to the visitor experience. Recognising this, however, does not remove the responsibility of operators that clients be advised of likely risks associated with the activity they wish to participate in, given their personal capabilities, and of how to react in situations during their activity experience, so operators are responsible and transparent.

Future research should focus upon those areas of concern raised in this chapter. Specifically, a better understanding of safety and risk management systems currently in place in the adventure sector and development of models of best practice in respect to safety need to be achieved for high-risk activities. As a precursor to this, basic baseline data are needed to establish the extent of the adventure tourism safety problem in other countries where the client risk must be understood and managed due to the rapid growth in visitor participation in outdoor recreation, and in particular the commercial sector of the adventure tourism industry. It seems likely that this will occur soon through the use of similar methodologies to those used to date in the New Zealand and Scotland studies. These studies will allow benchmarking of safety management practices internationally, and the opportunity to raise awareness of the nature of the tourism injury problem on a more global platform.

References

Bentley, T.A., & Haslam, R.A. (1998). Slip, trip and fall accidents occurring during the delivery of mail. *Ergonomics, 41*, 859–872.

Bentley, T.A., Meyer, D., Page, S.J., & Chalmers, D. (2001a). Recreational tourism injuries among visitors to New Zealand: An exploratory analysis using hospital discharge data. *Tourism Management, 22*, 373–381.

Bentley, T. A., & Page, S.J. (2001). Scoping the extent of accidents in adventure tourism. *Annals of Tourism Research, 28*, 705–726.

Bentley, T.A., Page, S.J., & Laird, I. (2000). Safety in New Zealand's adventure tourism industry: The client accident experience of adventure tourism operators. *Journal of Travel Medicine, 7*, 239–245.

Bentley, T.A., Page, S.J., & Laird, I. (2001b). Accidents in the New Zealand adventure tourism industry. *Safety Science, 38*, 31–48.

Callander, M., & Page, S.J. (2003). Managing risk in adventure tourism operations: A review of the legal case history and potential for litigation. *Tourism Management, 24*, 13–24.

CM Research. (1995). *White water rafting customer research: Qualitative and quantitative research findings.* Report prepared for the Maritime Safety Authority White Water Rafting Safety Advisory Group. Wellington, New Zealand.

Frangialli, F. (2003). Foreword. In: D. Glaesser (Ed.), *Crisis management in the tourism industry* (pp. xi–xii). Oxford: Butterworth Heinemann.

Greenaway, R. (1996). Thrilling not killing: Managing the risk tourism business. *Management*, (May), 46–49.

Hall, C., & McArthur, S. (1991). Commercial white water rafting in Australia. *Australian Journal of Leisure and Recreation, 1*, 25–30.

Johnston, M. (1989). Accidents in mountain recreation: The experiences of international and domestic visitors in New Zealand. *GeoJournal, 19*, 323–328.

McLaughlan, M. (1995). White water death: Why is the Shotover New Zealand's most lethal river? *North and South*, (December), 70–81.

Millington, K., Locke, A., & Locke, T. (2001). Occasional studies: Adventure travel. *Travel and Tourism Analyst, 4*, 65–97.

Page, S.J. (1997). *The cost of accidents in the New Zealand adventure tourism industry.* Report for Tourism Policy Group, Ministry of Commerce. Wellington, New Zealand.

Page, S.J., Bentley, T.A., & Meyer, D. (2003). Evaluating the nature, scope and extent of tourist accidents: The New Zealand experience. In: J. Wilks, & S.J. Page (Eds), *Managing tourist health and safety in the new millennium* (pp. 35–52). Oxford: Pergamon.

Page, S.J., & Meyer, D. (1996). Tourist accidents: An exploratory analysis. *Annals of Tourism Research, 23*, 666–690.

Ryan, C. (2003). Risk acceptance in adventure tourism – paradox and content. In: J. Wilks, & S.J. Page (Eds), *Managing tourist health and safety in the new millennium* (pp. 55–66) Oxford: Pergamon.

Sharp, B. (2001). *Strategies for improving mountain safety: Analysis of Scottish mountain incidents 1996–1999.* Glasgow: University of Strathclyde.

Swarbrooke, J., Beard, C., Leckie, S., & Pomfret, G. (2003). *Adventure tourism: The new frontier.* Oxford: Butterworth Heinemann.

System Three. (1998). *Activity holidays in Scotland: A survey of operators' views and opinion.* Edinburgh: System Three.

Wilks, J., & Atherton, T. (1994). Health and safety in marine tourism: A social, medical and legal appraisal. *Journal of Tourism Studies, 5*, 2–16.

Wilks, J., & Oldenburg, B. (1995). Tourist health: The silent factor in customer service. *Australian Journal of Hospitality Management, 2,* 13–23.

Wilks, J., & Page, S.J. (Eds). (2003). *Managing tourist health and safety in the new millennium.* Oxford: Pergamon.

Wilks, J., & Watson, B. (1998). Road safety and international visitors in Australia: Looking beyond the tip of the iceberg. *Travel Medicine International, 16*(5), 194–198.

World Tourism Organization. (1996). *Tourist safety.* Madrid: World Tourism Organization.

PART 3

ADVENTURE

Chapter 12

Risk Management in Outdoor Adventure Tourism

Damian Morgan and Kay Dimmock

Introduction

Risk management is mandatory practice for operators of outdoor adventure tourist activities. In many instances the outdoor adventure tourism operator must demonstrate the ability to manage risk before gaining access to activity settings, qualifying for public liability insurance, and gaining accreditation through recognised industry organisations. Of equal importance to the outdoor adventure tourism operator is the role of risk management in ensuring business viability. This is achieved by providing clients with appropriate and safe outdoor adventure tourism experiences. Later in this chapter, we explain a risk management process that can be used to facilitate safe outdoor adventure tourism activities. Before this, we discuss two topics that underpin the development of this sector of the tourism industry: the factors that have encouraged the growth and scope of outdoor adventure tourist activities; and, the experience provided by outdoor adventure activities.

Outdoor Adventures are a Special Type of Tourism

Tourism researchers have long recognised positive and negative relationships between tourism and the natural environment (e.g., Budowski, 1976). This relationship, and implications arising from it, will depend on a range of factors including the type of environmental setting (e.g., arid, mountainous, or aquatic), the type of activity pursued, equipment used, and the behaviour, expertise, and experience of participants. The phenomenon of outdoor adventure tourism presents a *special* relationship between tourism and the environment. In outdoor adventure tourism activities, participants' engagement with the environment provides a unique personal and social experience. Moreover, hazards found in the environment place the onus on outdoor adventure tourism operators to manage risk to ensure safe client experiences.

Tourism in Turbulent Times
Copyright © 2006 by Elsevier Ltd.
All rights of reproduction in any form reserved.
ISBN: 0-08-044666-3

The outdoor adventure tourism industry is a diverse phenomenon (Ewert & Jamieson, 2003). For the purpose of this chapter, we deem outdoor adventure tourism activities to be commercial operations in largely or wholly natural areas offered primarily to tourists. In these activities, the outdoor adventure tourism operator routinely provides participants with the required equipment and access to the location in which it occurs (Morgan & Fluker, 2003). Some common outdoor adventure tourism activities are presented in Table 12.1.

Participants in outdoor adventure tourism activities are aware of, enthralled, and often challenged by the natural surroundings. Furthermore, participants in these activities become exposed to a range of potentially hazardous environmental features. Examples of environmental hazards range from white water eddies and waves along New Zealand's rivers to extreme cold and ice found in the Canadian Rockies. Importantly, participants' negotiations of these kinds of environmental hazards are a key defining feature of the outdoor adventure tourism experience.

Outdoor adventure tourists are required to be *active* players in the adventure; the level of effort, behaviour, and *style* of participation will help create a unique and distinct experience of the activity. Interestingly, participant surveys of adventure tourism indicate that safety is a fundamental desire held by adventure tourists and they rate the competence of the instructor and standard of equipment among the most important activity features (Hall & McArthur, 1994; Morgan, 1998). In short, participants do not expect to be injured during their adventure experience and would not participate if this was a probable outcome. Hence, it is the responsibility of the adventure tourism operator to provide and facilitate a

Table 12.1: Examples of common adventure tourism activities across settings.

Setting	Activity
Air	Hang gliding
	Sky diving
Land	Skiing
	Sand boarding
	Abseiling
	Trekking
	Climbing
	Mountain biking
Water	River rafting
	Surfing
	Wind surfing
	Wake boarding
	Scuba diving
	Kayaking
	Sailing
	Snorkelling

safe opportunity for participants to negotiate the anticipated range of environmental hazards found in the activity.

Trends Promoting Outdoor Adventures

For much of the twentieth century, remote and environmentally challenging locations catered to only small numbers of dedicated participants in their pursuit of high-risk activities and adventures. Over recent decades, social change has encouraged tourists to more often seek novel and stimulating experiences (Gartner & Lime, 2000). In step with this change, attention by the visual media has encouraged a growing interest in nature-based and adventurous activities. Indeed, a growing public fascination with risky activities helps to create unmet desires among the general tourism markets, reflected in the popularity of adventure-related fashions and short films (Buckley, 2003).

Technical advances help realise the demand for adventure tourism experiences. Through the development of transport options, such as all terrain vehicles and helicopters, tourists can enter hitherto inaccessible locations with relatively little effort (Parker, 2001). Advances in equipment and clothing have complemented improved access to natural locations. Equipment in many activities is now easier to use and more portable than was previously the case, making self-organised adventures more readily available. Snowboarders, surfers, windsurfers, scuba divers, for example, may travel with their own personal equipment. These developments have made outdoor adventure activities cheaper, safer, and more reliable for both self-organised tourists and organised commercial-based adventures. In the latter case, outdoor adventure operators may offer a range of product options including equipment hire for experienced clients.

Mass tourist access to new locations and the emergence of commercial outdoor adventure activities have changed the profile and image of many locations. Examples include surf tourism at previously remote destinations such as in the Indo-Pacific region, camping trips to Antarctica, or maximum packaged adventure available in Queenstown, New Zealand (Buckley, 2002; Stonehouse, 2001; Berno, Moore, Simmons, & Hart, 1996). Akin to safety management, environmental management remains an important responsibility for the outdoor adventure tourism industry.

Adventure as Both a Special Interest and Mass Tourist Product

Commercial outdoor adventure tourism activities cater for a wide array of clientele. Many operators will cater to novice and inexperienced participants enticed from a number of countries and cultural backgrounds. Most of these tourists will be seeking out nature-based adventures as just one component of their broad tourism experiences and travels (Wight, 1996). To attract this market, outdoor adventure operators typically advertise their adventures through market channels directed towards an undifferentiated mass tourism market. Examples include brochures at visitor centres or transport hubs, internet links from general tourism web sites, and advertisements in regional tourism promotion literature.

In contrast, some outdoor adventure tourism operators will cater to special interest tourist markets. Examples of special interest markets include corporate groups racing performance yachts and experienced divers on shipwreck night tours. Not surprisingly, operations catering to special interest markets can be longer in duration and present a relatively high objective level of risk. Compared to mass market adventures, the operator catering to special interest markets may require that clients have existing skills and previous training in the activity (Morgan, Moore, & Mansell, 2000). Despite the diversity in adventure activities and clients, the fundamental concept of adventure will provide similar experiences to both the novice and experienced participants.

The Outdoor Adventure Experience

Engaging with the outdoor environments provide people with novel and stimulating experiences (Wagner, undated) and can meet their spiritual and emotional needs (Heintzman & Mannell, 2003). A large body of research supports the benefits of experiencing nature. For example, Catton (1971) described national parks as *social playgrounds* demonstrated by the significant human use of wildlands for recreational activities; while in Australia, beach and national parks continue to be among the most popular locations visited by international tourists (Tourism Australia, 2003). Settings that include national parks, reserves, and protected areas offer the would-be outdoor adventure tourist an opportunity to *connect* with and experience remote and often pristine locations.

Outdoor adventure tourism is a new and emerging form of tourism so a clear understanding and knowledge of the phenomena is at an early stage (Beedie, 2003; Buckley, 2004). Much current knowledge has been sourced from studies of the adventure experience had by recreationists. For example, Hamilton-Smith (1993) argued that adventure was *serious* leisure because of the risk involved and the physical demands required in the activity. Similarly, Ewert (1989) distinguished outdoor adventurers by their level of commitment when engaging in high-risk activities.

As we have discussed, the demand for adventure tourism activities is not confined to experienced and involved adventurers (Millington, Locke, & Locke, 2001). By providing necessary equipment, training, and instructor or guide expertise, the outdoor adventure tourist operator is better able to manage participants' experience level and skill in the activity. Managed adventure tourism activities still provide immediate thrills and challenge, even for novices undertaking a highly controlled experience. Likewise, novice adventure tourists are routinely aware of dangers and experience fear and anxiousness (Morgan, 2002). It has also been suggested that adventure tourists can gain unanticipated benefits from the experience, such as self-insight and personal growth (Walle, 2001).

Risk Perceptions and Safety

The outdoor adventure tourism operator understands that the expectation and experience of the risk perceived by participants, and their feelings of control over those risk perceptions, is the critical antecedent of clients' outdoor adventure experiences (Morgan, 2000).

A body of empirical research has demonstrated that an optimal psychological experience can be had where success in an activity requires participants to perform at or close to the limit of their abilities, in order to negotiate or overcome perceptions of risk and inherent challenge (e.g., Jones, Hollenhorst, & Perna, 2003). Participants taking an optimal experience from the outdoor adventure tourism activity will more likely report feelings of excitement, arousal, challenge, and fun (Morgan, 1998).

The real or objective risk stemming from environmental hazards in the activity may not be clearly understood or assessed by participants, and in any case, this risk is controlled by the activity operator. The outdoor adventure tourism operator manages objective risk to the level that is safe for participants while delivering the risk perceptions appropriate to the intended client experience. This requires the operator to achieve a balance between safety and participants' exposure to real risk. Therefore, the level of real or objective risk inherent to an activity plays two significant roles; being a determinant of an adventure participant's experience and the fundamental element in safety management.

Based on the level of objective inherent risk, outdoor adventure tourism is categorised as soft or hard adventure (e.g., Swarbrooke, Beard, Leckie, & Pomfret, 2003). Of course, the level of risk within any outdoor adventure activity will vary depending on the environmental conditions, nature and quantity of hazards, as well as the standards of participants' training, skills and equipment. Under this categorisation, soft (low-objective risk) adventures will appeal to a broad range of tourists; activities such as rafting on flat water rivers or horse trekking along beaches can be easily managed by first time participants with little instruction.

Hard adventures offer greater uncertainty and risk during the activity. These activities may be sought by tourists with greater experience or by those less averse to taking risks (Creyer, Ross, & Evers, 2003). A hard adventure is likely to test the skill level of the participant, especially where the activity requires a level of participation on the *edge* of one's ability to control the risks. Examples include white-water rafting, scuba diving, spelunking, and mountain climbing (Swarbrooke et al., 2003). Regardless of the level of real or objective risk, a primary challenge for adventure tourism managers is to ensure client safety.

Managing Tourists in Outdoor Adventures

Given the nature of the adventure experience, it follows that definitions of outdoor adventure tourist activities routinely include the element of risk being either real or perceived by clients (e.g., Ewert & Jamieson, 2003; Fluker & Turner, 2000; Sung, Morrison, & O'Leary, 1997; Swarbrooke et al., 2003; Walle, 2001). As we have discussed, the client's perceived risk, stemming from operator management of real risk, determines the level of challenge fundamental to the adventure experience. More generally, definitions of *risk* typically encompass two concepts: uncertainty of the outcome; and the possibility of an outcome that entails loss (Vaughan, 1997). From the perspective of the outdoor adventure tourist, loss during the activity can manifest in a number of ways including a lack of enjoyment or boredom, an incident leading to social embarrassment, or not getting value for money.

A more serious form of loss occurs when outdoor adventure tourists or their guides sustain physical injury. Although severe injuries appear uncommon across the industry, statistics and operator reports indicate injuries to tourists do occur during outdoor adventure activities (e.g., Bentley & Page, 2001; Bentley, Page, & Walker, 2004; Wilks & Coory, 2000). Safety management is therefore an important component of risk management planning. Safe outdoor adventure tourism operations not only protect clients but also guard operators against damaging publicity, loss of the company's reputation, financial compensation claims, and/or legal prosecution. Safe operations also reinforce the outdoor adventure industry profile as a *bona fide* product for the tourism marketplace.

Yet the outdoor adventure tourism operator cannot remove all risk from an activity. Activities without risk will, by definition, lack challenge and uncertainty and so would cease to provide clients with adequate arousal, feelings of control and competence, and hence, satisfaction. In short, while the activity might provide thrills and high stimulation (e.g., a roller coaster ride or bungy jump), strictly speaking, the activity would no longer be an *adventure* because the client has no scope to exert control during participation. Fortunately, most soft and hard adventure activities can readily retain sufficient uncertainty through active client participation, even though the real risk of injury (as known to the operator) is negligible. This outcome is achieved through suitable safety management practices and processes delivered within overall risk management strategies.

Risk Management Concepts

Humans have been managing risk since the earliest times and the concept of risk management has been studied and discussed by scholars for nearly half a century (Vaughan, 1997). In his well-known text, Vaughan recognises that risk management is both a science and an art. In outdoor adventure activities, scientific methods can be applied to gather data that identifies, evaluates, and quantifies the foreseeable risks posed by natural hazards. Nonetheless, the astute outdoor risk manager still needs to make judgements and decisions about the management of risk (Haddock, 2004). In outdoor adventure tourism activities, these judgements and decisions may draw upon known factual information, but also make use of the manager's experience in and knowledge of the activity and environment, the equipment used, the setting and conditions in which the activity takes place, and the ability and behaviour of participants who engage in it.

Research on Adventure Tourism

From the standpoint of scientific knowledge, the academic study of outdoor adventure tourism has received increased attention over the last decade. The industry, and sectors within it have been analysed conceptually (e.g., Ewert & Jameison, 2003; Walle, 2001), the experience has been empirically evaluated (e.g., Fluker & Turner, 2000), and injury statistics and related data have been reported in a range of academic journals (e.g., Bently, Page, & Walker, 2004; Wilks & Coory, 2000, 2002).

In Chapter 11, Bentley and Page provide a detailed outline of the occurrence of injury and incidents in New Zealand and Scotland's adventure tourism industries. This information is valuable as studies of injury patterns and rates identify risk factors for various activities (see also Page, Bentley, & Walker, 2005). Where risk factors are identified and quantified, interventions can be proposed and trialled to reduce or remove unacceptable risk.

Often detailed information is required to determine the nature and quantity of risk. For example, based on outdoor adventure tourism operator reports, Bentley et al.'s (2004) study indicated a relatively high client injury rate for horse riding/pony trekking activities. Further study of this activity will be warranted where the rate of injuries (and risk) is judged unacceptably high by the industry or industry stakeholders (e.g., government). Such studies would involve identifying the causal factors that result in the injury and assessing whether these can be modified to reduce the risk.

Studies designed to identify and quantify risk factors can be complex. This is because the risk of injury is normally associated with many factors, or combination of factors, linked to the client, equipment, operator practices, or the environment (Page et al., 2005). Identifying the role played by each risk factor for common injury can be obtained through rigorous scientific design. However, the cost, effort, and time needed to obtain required data on hazards, incidents, risks, and risk exposure has (so far) precluded detailed epidemiological studies of injury risk factors in adventure tourism activities. Even where science can provide detailed knowledge of the operation of risk in these activities, identified risk factors may not be modifiable, or removal of the risk posed by them may be impractical.

Nevertheless, studies of outdoor adventure tourism activities support an evolving knowledge base of safe industry practices. This knowledge base is supplemented by studies and reports of outdoor adventure and risk management undertaken across a range of fields including applied economics, recreation and leisure studies, medicine, and outdoor education. Adventure-related study and research has in turn been underpinned and informed by the development of outdoor recreation standards and industry practices across a range of activities.

The management of risk and safety should therefore be based on *all* available information, guidelines and knowledge found in the outdoor adventure tourism operating environment. Reviews of the industry have identified this environment to be composed of a range of elements (Cloutier, 2003; Morgan & Fluker, 2003). These elements include those for which the *safe* operator is not directly responsible but would likely adhere to, such as the legal requirements, industry standards, and accreditation requirements. Other elements are directly linked to the adventure tourist activity and so require direct management by the operator through a risk management process. These elements include the setting in which the activity occurs, operational decisions, information provided to clients, the training and competency of employees, and equipment used. These elements will now be discussed with respect to managing a safe experience in outdoor adventure tourism activities.

Legal Requirements

Legal requirements form part of a minimum standard of safety adherence for operators (Dickson & Tugwell, 2000). A range of laws and statutes are in place across countries that provide access to outdoor settings, activity operation guidelines, health and safety procedures, employee training, and equipment standards pertaining to various industry sectors.

A fundamental legal requirement is that outdoor adventure tourism operators provide a *standard of care* to their clients. Where a client is injured as a result of an outdoor adventure tourism operation failing to meet the standard of care, the operator may be found negligent and face the legal consequences (Hicks, 2000).

The legal consequences of client injury provides (at the minimum) a financial rationale for outdoor adventure tourism operators to meet the standard of care owed to their clients. To achieve the standard of care, the operator will meet or exceed the standard of care more widely practiced (or reasonably expected) for the particular outdoor adventure activity. Common sources used to discern the standard of care are the known industry standards and accreditation guidelines.

Industry Standards and Accreditation

Legal requirements provide a general guide to the safety requirements for outdoor adventure tourism operators. Even so, the outdoor adventure tourism industry offers a diverse array of products. Because of this diversity, it is not feasible to develop a detailed and all encompassing set of standards relevant to the whole industry. Instead, adventure activity sectors within many countries have developed tailored activity standards or codes of practice. For example, in Victoria, Australia, the Outdoor Recreation Centre Inc. (2005), in conjunction with government and industry associations, has developed a set of adventure activity standards (AAS) for a range of activities. The intention of the AAS is to promote safe operator practices, afford legal protection for operators, and facilitate access to insurance coverage. The specific role of the AAS is provided at the Outdoor Recreation Centre Inc. website:

> AAS ensure those who lead and participate in group-based activities have an opportunity to be appropriately informed of the legal expectations and responsibilities that they accept. That in conducting such activities, organisations and leaders know what is expected of them and as such, helping to ensure that the appropriate duty of care for self, others and the environment is afforded (Outdoor Recreation Centre Inc, 2005).

Each AAS begins with a review of legal guidelines and then provides detailed information tailored to the particular activity addressed. This information covers planning (including documentation, hazard identification, and emergency strategies), responsibilities of the trip leader/guide (including required minimum competencies, responsibilities, and group sizes), equipment (including standard use and maintenance), activity conduct, and definition of terms. The Outdoor Recreation Centre Inc. (2005) recognises that AAS are not static; they are designed as documents to be reviewed and amended over time.

In addition to conforming to standards, outdoor adventure tourism operators and their employees may be accredited in the activity. Accreditation is provided by industry bodies or government authorities to confer that the operator meets specified standards, competencies, experience, or principles. Industry bodies or training authorities will also accredit competencies in activities for individual instructors and guides. This accreditation may be internationally recognised, such as PADI (2005) qualifications awarded to scuba divers or be a national system such as Australian Canoeing Inc. (2005) coaching awards. Accredited instructors or guides also have access to public liability insurance and professional indemnity provided by the accrediting authority.

Industry standards and accreditation provide the means for outdoor adventure tourism operators to benchmark their operations against industry recognised best practice. Where standards do not exist, or they are out of date, the outdoor adventure tourism operator should contact peers or relevant national bodies to determine current best practice (and standard of care) expected in the activity (Haddock, 2004).

Risk Management Process

With knowledge of the legal responsibilities and industry best practice, the outdoor adventure tourism operator will develop a risk management process to meet the legal standard of care. The Australian/New Zealand Standard for risk management (Standards Australia, 2004) is a relevant framework that can be applied to a broad range of risk situations (see Chapter 1). The standard specifies seven elements that comprise the risk management process (Figure 12.1). These are: establish the risk context; identify risks; analyse risks; evaluate risks; treat risks; monitor and review; and communication and consultation. The difference between the 1999 version of the Standard (Figure 1.2, Chapter 1) and the 2004 version of Figure 12.1 is the inclusion of a specific assessment element between evaluation and treatment of risks.

The first element of the risk management process requires the operator to establish the risk management context. This element involves analysing the organisation, the operating environment, the activity, and importantly, establishing criteria for defining risk, including its acceptability and management. Here the operator will make an assessment of the organisational goals and capabilities. Also, the *safe* operator would develop criteria that reduce the risk of client and employee injury from environmental hazards to a minimum practical level.

The second element of the risk management process is risk identification. Broadly speaking, the outdoor adventure tourism operator faces a range of risks. With respect to safety, these risks will stem from environmental hazards. Hazards will include relatively more permanent features of the environment found in an activity, such as low tree branches facing trail riders, sharp river drops crossed by rafters, or reefs crossed by surfers. Other hazards that may be less predictable include fallen trees in flooded rivers, rock falls, storms, slippery tracks, or other adverse weather and ground conditions. It is important for the outdoor adventure operator to be aware of existing and potential hazards and the ensuing risk posed by them.

Analysis of the identified risk comprises the third element of the risk management process. Detailed methods have been developed to analyse and quantify risk (Standards Australia, 2004). As we have mentioned earlier, there remain knowledge gaps concerning the operation of risk factors in adventure tourism activities. It is therefore difficult for operators to obtain objective data on the true risk posed by environmental hazards. However, risk from existing hazards can be estimated using the best data available. This

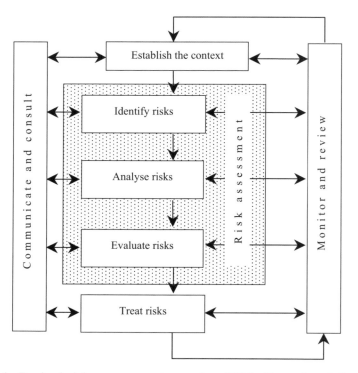

Figure 12.1: Revised risk management overview 2004. (Reproduced from Australian Standard AS/NZS 4360:2004 *Risk management.* Full details on the use and application of this diagram are available in the Standard and in its supporting publication HB 435 — 2004 *Risk Management Guidelines.)*

knowledge can be included when developing a risk management matrix based on the frequency of occurrence and the severity of injury, such as that shown in Figure 12.2 (see also Wilks & Davis, 2000).

To evaluate and treat risk (elements 4 and 5, respectively, of the risk management process), the likelihood and severity of consequence is compared with the criteria for acceptable injury (developed in element 1). Minor injuries such as slight bruising or chafing requiring little or no medical intervention may be an inherent activity risk. By applying the risk management matrix, occurrence of these injuries may be infrequent, and when they do occur, have minimal effect on the individual's experience of the adventure activity. Where it is not practical to minimise or eliminate this risk, it should be retained as part of the activity. Nevertheless, the operator should inform participants before the activity of the possibility of this type of injury and take steps to minimise its occurrence.

Frequent injuries of low severity, such as blisters from paddling and non-venomous insect stings, can be minimised through protective gloves and clothing. High-severity risk should be eliminated, regardless of frequency (Davidson, 2004). For example, the risk of severe sunburn inflicted while sea kayaking in tropical areas should be removed through protective clothing and sunscreen, and the potential for hypothermia in surfing activities can be controlled by using wetsuits and monitoring participants.

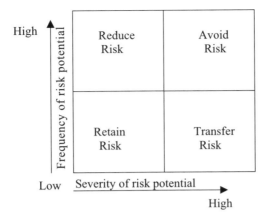

Figure 12 2: The risk evaluation matrix (Wilks & Davis, 2000, p. 595).

In short, to retain a high level of safety the outdoor tourism operator must identify and eliminate all but minor risks. Even so, following the risk management process can never entirely rule out potential for client injury. For instance, it may be difficult to predict and remove the risk of bone fractures from falls on slippery tracks or eye-piercing injuries from broken tree branches during *soft adventure* bushwalks. Risk management plans must assume that these occurrences, even if very unlikely, will happen and hence develop training and procedures to manage injuries and crises.

Understanding the risk potential from environmental hazards also assists outdoor adventure operators to protect themselves and their business. For example, operators will transfer to an insurer infrequent but severe risk by way of professional indemnity and public liability insurance. Clients may be required to agree to legally binding releases or waivers and so carry responsibility themselves for the risk involved. This may be particularly useful in activities where participants have scope to vary the level of risk they face (Cloutier, 2000).

The Risk Management Standard for Australia/New Zealand (Standards Australia, 2004) has two final elements in the risk management process: monitoring and review; and communication and consultation. Both elements recognise that risk management is a dynamic process and so link to other elements (Figure 12.1). For example, a useful risk management practice is to initiate regular reviews and evaluations of the process by company or outside individuals and organisations. This practice will keep the operator abreast of developments in the activity and provide a check to ensure the appropriate standard of care is being met. Similarly, communication and consultation within the organisation and to external stakeholders at all stages of the risk management process will assist in the development of effective and inclusive safety plans.

Other Safety Considerations

Safe operations will be demonstrated by documenting the risk management process. Documentation provides a number of benefits. Indeed, detailed documents assist in demonstrating to other parties the outdoor adventure tourism operator's adherence to the required standard of care. Nevertheless, the development of documents can be time consuming and as Haddock (2004, p. 112) points out, "to meet statutory health and safety requirements, organisations must be able to show that their practices, not their paperwork, meet standards of safety".

Documentation does not negate an operator's role in making judgement decisions before and during adventures. Advanced outdoor leadership qualities have been coined "meta skills" by Priest (2000, p. 38). Part of the meta skill is making good judgements. Priest (p. 55) explains; "good judgement is an indispensable tool for estimating uncertainty, substituting for missing information, guessing about the vague, and predicting in the place of the unknown".

Meta skills build on the outdoor adventure tourism instructor's hard (technical, safety, and environmental) skills and soft (organisational, instructional, and facilitation) skills (Priest, 2000). The development of these skills in outdoor adventure tourism leaders is vital to ensure a safe experience. This is not only because of the need to negotiate hazards, but also because of the potential variation among clients. Adventure tourists will vary in their levels of ability in the activity. In addition, an adventure participant's facility to understand instructions and communicate with the instructor may be limited by the time available and because of language ability or cultural misunderstandings.

It is important for the outdoor adventure tourism instructor or guide to be able to accurately assess clients' abilities, understanding, and affective responses. This understanding allows the instructor or guide to adjust the level of risk faced by clients to a suitable level. Of course, the requirement for tailoring an adventure to particular clients will vary according to the activity and participant characteristics. Where implemented, this dynamic and mindful process will assist the operator in providing to their clients a safe and rewarding adventure experience.

Conclusion

The purpose of this chapter was to explain the risk management process, and concepts that underpin it, as this pertains to operators of outdoor adventure tourism activities. The chapter is not intended as a *risk management tool kit*, and for this purpose, interested readers should begin by consulting the references at the end of this chapter. The key message that emerges is the importance of safe experiences for adventure tourists. Safe experiences will not only lead to happy and satisfied clients, but also encourage the development of a strong and profitable adventure tourism sector that will have ongoing benefits for operators, their employees, and participants.

References

Australian Canoeing Inc. (2005). Instructor education. Australian canoeing online. [Retrieved 30 January, 2005 from http://www.canoe.org.au/.].
Beedie, P. (2003). Adventure tourism. In: S. Hudson (Ed.), *Sport and adventure tourism* (pp. 203–237). New York: Howarth Hospitality Press.
Bentley, T. A., & Page, S. J. (2001). Scoping the extent of adventure tourism accidents. *Annals of Tourism Research*, 28(3), 705–726.

Bentley, T. A., Page, S., & Walker, L. (2004). The safety experience of New Zealand adventure tourism operators. *Journal of Travel Medicine, 11*(5), 280–286.

Berno, T., Moore, K., Simmons, D., & Hart, V. (1996). The nature of the adventure tourism experience in Queenstown, New Zealand. *Australian Leisure, 7*(2), 21–25.

Buckley, R. (2002). Surf tourism and sustainable development in Indo Pacific Islands. *Journal of Sustainable Tourism, 10*(5), 405–424.

Buckley, R. (2003). Adventure tourism and the clothing, fashion and entertainment industries. *Journal of Ecotourism, 2*(2), 126–134.

Buckley, R. (2004). Skilled commercial adventure: The edge of tourism. In: T. V. Singh (Ed.), *New horizons in tourism* (pp. 37–48). Lucknow, India: CABI Publishing.

Budowski, G. (1976). Tourism and environmental conservation: Conflict, coexistence, or symbiosis? *Environmental Conservation, 3*(1), 27–31.

Catton, W. (1971). The wildland recreation boom and sociology. *Pacific Sociological Review, 14*(Jul), 339–357.

Cloutier, R. (2000). *Legal liability and risk management in adventure tourism.* British Columbia: Bhudak Consultants.

Cloutier, R. (2003). The business of adventure tourism. In: S. Hudson (Ed.), *Sport and adventure tourism* (pp. 241–271). Howarth Hospitality Press: New York.

Creyer, E. H., Ross Jr, W. H., & Evers, D. (2003). Risky recreation: An exploration of factors influencing the likelihood of participation and the effects of experience. *Leisure Studies, 22*(3), 239–253.

Davidson, G. (2004). Fact of folklore? Exploring "myths" about outdoor education accidents: Some evidence from New Zealand. *Journal of Outdoor Education and Outdoor Learning, 4*(1), 13–38.

Dickson, T. J., & Tugwell, M. (2000). *The risk management document: Strategies for risk management in outdoor and experiential learning.* Sydney: Outdoor Recreation Industry Council of NSW.

Ewert, A. (1989). *Outdoor adventure pursuits: Foundations, models and theories.* Scottsdale, AZ: Publishing Horizons Inc.

Ewert, A., & Jamieson, L. (2003). Current status and future directions in the adventure tourism industry. In: J. Wilks, & S. Page (Eds), *Managing tourist health and safety in the new millennium* (pp. 67–83). Amsterdam: Pergamon.

Fluker, M., & Turner, L. (2000). Needs, motivations, and expectations of a whitewater rafting experience. *Journal of Travel Research, 38*(4), 380–389.

Gartner, W., & Lime, D. (2000). The big picture: A synopsis of contributions. In: W. Gartner, & D. Lime (Eds), *Trends in outdoor recreation, leisure and tourism* (pp. 1–15). St. Paul: CABI Publishing.

Haddock, C. (2004). *Outdoor safety: Risk management for outdoor leaders.* Wellington: New Zealand Mountain Safety Council.

Hall, C. M., & McArthur, S. (1994). Commercial white water rafting in Australia. In: D. Mercer (Ed.), *New viewpoints in Australian outdoor recreation research and planning* (pp. 109–118). Australia: Harper Marriott and Associates.

Hamilton-Smith, E. (1993). In the Australian bush: Some reflections on serious leisure. *World Recreation and Leisure, 35*(1), 10–13.

Heintzman, P., & Mannell, R. C. (2003). Spiritual functions of leisure and spiritual well-being: Coping with time pressure. *Leisure Sciences, 25*(2/3), 207–230.

Hicks, R. E. (2000). The jury's in: A defense lawyer's perspective on risk management and crisis response. In: *Lessons learned: A guide to accident prevention and crisis response* (pp. 103–137). Anchorage: University of Alaska-Anchorage.

Jones, C. D., Hollenhorst, S. J., & Perna, F. (2003). An empirical comparison of the four channel flow model and adventure experience paradigm. *Leisure Sciences, 25*(1), 17–31.

Millington, K., Locke, T., & Locke, A. (2001). Adventure travel. *Travel and Tourism Analyst, 4*, 59–88.

Morgan, D. J. (1998). *An analysis of perceptions of risk and competence of instructors and partici-pants in three water-based adventure tourism activities.* Unpublished master's thesis. Lincoln University, New Zealand.

Morgan, D. J. (2000). Adventure tourism activities in New Zealand: Perceptions and management of client risk. *Tourism Recreation Research, 25*(3), 79–89.

Morgan, D. J. (2002). Risk, competence and adventure tourists: Applying the adventure experience paradigm to white-water rafters. *Leisure, 26*(1–2), 107–127.

Morgan, D. J., & Fluker, M. (2003). Risk management for Australian commercial adventure tourism operations. *Journal of Hospitality and Tourism Management, 10*(1), 46–59.

Morgan, D. J., Moore, K., & Mansell, R. (2000). Adventure tourists on water: Linking expectations, affect, achievement and enjoyment to the adventure. *Journal of Sports Tourism, 6*(1), [online].

Outdoor Recreation Centre Inc. (2005). Adventure activity standards. *Outdoor Recreation Centre Inc. website.* [Retrieved 30 January, 2005 from http://www.orc.org.au/aas/index.htm.].

PADI. (2005). Go Pro. *PADI website.* [Retrieved 30 January, 2005 from http://www.orc.org.au/aas/index.htm.].

Page, S. J., Bentley, T. A., & Walker, L. (2005). Scoping the nature and extent of adventure tourism operations in Scotland: How safe are they? *Tourism Management, 26*, 381–397.

Parker, S. (2001). Marine tourism and environmental management on the Great Barrier Reef. In: V. Smith, & M. Brent (Eds), *Hosts and guests revisited: Tourism issues of the 21st century* (pp. 232–241). New York: Cognizant Communication Corporation.

Priest, S. (2000). Effective outdoor leadership. In: *Lessons learned: A guide to accident prevention and crisis response* (pp. 33–64). Anchorage: University of Alaska-Anchorage.

Standards Australia. (2004). *Risk management AS/NZS 4360:2004.* Sydney, Australia: Standards Association of Australia.

Stonehouse, B. (2001). Polar environments. In: D. B. Weaver (Ed.), *The encyclopaedia of ecotourism* (pp. 219–234). New York: CABI Publishing.

Sung, H. H., Morrison, A. M., & O'Leary, J. T. (1997). Definition of adventure travel: Conceptual framework for empirical application from the providers' perspective. *Asia Pacific Journal of Tourism Research, 1*(2), 47–67 [Retrieved 30 January, 2005 from http://www.hotel-online.com/Neo/Trends/ AsiaPacificJournal/index.html.].

Swarbrooke, J., Beard, C., Leckie, S., & Pomfret, G. (2003). *Adventure tourism: The new frontier.* Oxford: Butterworth-Heinemann.

Tourism Australia. (2003). Top ten activities. *Market Insights Tourism Facts.* (December). [Retrieved 2 September, 2005 from http://www.tourism.australia.com/content/Research/ Factsheets/activi-ties_fact_sheet_ dec2003.pdf].

Vaughan, E. J. (1997). *Risk management.* New York: Wiley.

Wagner, F. H. (undated). Outdoor recreation and tourism. In: R. Peters, & T. Lovejoy (Eds), *Rocky mountains great basic regional climate change assessment.* [Retrieved 30 January, 2005 from http://www.cnr.usu.edu/publications/Chapter-6.pdf accessed 18.1.05.].

Walle, K. (2001). Outdoor adventure tourism: A review of research approaches. *Annals of Tourism Research, 28*(2), 360–377.

Wight, P. A. (1996). North American ecotourism markets: Motivations, preferences, and destina-tions. *Journal of Travel Research, 35*(1), 3–10.

Wilks, J., & Coory, M. (2000). Overseas visitors admitted to Queensland hospitals for water-related injuries. *Medical Journal of Australia, 173*(5), 244–246.

Wilks, J., & Coory, M. (2002). Overseas visitor injuries in Queensland hospitals: 1996–2000. *Journal of Tourism Studies, 13*, 2–8.

Wilks, J., & Davis, R. J. (2000). Risk management for scuba diving operators on Australia's Great Barrier Reef. *Tourism Management, 21*, 591–599.

Chapter 13

Tourist Trauma in National Parks

Travis W. Heggie

Introduction

The date was 19 July 1998. I was 2 h into my first shift as a park ranger assigned to eruption duty in Hawaii Volcanoes National Park when a panic-stricken Japanese tourist and her son came running up to me. I could not understand a word they were speaking, but from the exhausted look on their face and the desperate urgency in their voice, it was obvious that something was wrong. It did not take long to figure out that the concern was directed towards a husband and father who was hurt or possibly dead somewhere out on the lava field. With only two rangers on location, a land search for the missing tourist would take hours if not days. Fortunately, a helicopter working a nearby forest fire was able to search for and rescue the missing tourist within 45 min. At the time of his rescue, the 29-year-old Japanese male was severely dehydrated and wandering in a confused state only a couple of metres from an ocean cliff. There is little doubt that the availability of a helicopter and a quick medical response by park staff prevented his core body temperature from reaching dangerously high levels and ultimately saved the life of this tourist. Unfortunately, the official incident report described a scenario I would see repeat itself numerous times over the next few years. Wearing tennis shoes and sandals, and carrying only 1 litre of water between them, this family had ignored warning signs and hiked 4–6 km over difficult and uneven basaltic terrain in an attempt to view active lava flows. What these tourists failed to realise, however, is that the temperature of the lava flows can reach 1000°C on the surface and instantly turn the human body into a raisin.

Tourism in National Parks

The development of the 386 national parks, monuments, recreation areas, historic sites, preserves, seashores, rivers, and scenic trails under the administration of the United States National Park Service has been closely tied to the development of tourism (Towner & Wall, 1991). In fact, total visitation to these destinations reached 277 million in 2002 with popular destinations such as the Grand Canyon reporting international tourists to comprise as high as 40% of their total visitation. Nevertheless, aside from the postcards and the stories of scenic grandeur, the untold story of national parks is that of visitor injuries. We occasionally hear media reports of unsuspecting tourists finding themselves caught in sudden snowstorms in Yosemite National Park, animals attacking tourists in Yellowstone National Park, and mountain climbers needing rescue from the slopes of Mt. Rainier and Mt. McKinley. However, what is missing from these reports are details about the frequency and severity of injuries in national parks, the contributing factors behind these injuries, and the increasing number of lawsuits filed against national parks as a result of these injuries.

Tourist Injury and Illness in National Parks

Three years, 38 search and rescue (SAR) missions, and thousands of first-aid incidents after my first encounter with the Japanese tourists, I again found myself working eruption duty. This time, however, I was kneeling over a 52-year-old female tourist from Florida, who had suffered a closed head injury after losing her balance while operating her video camera. As I looked into the confused and pained eyes that you often see in a person with a concussion, I began to wonder how many tourists to this and other national parks are injured each year. A search I later conducted of visitor fatality records kept by the Risk Management Division of the U.S. National Park Service shed some light on the issue. From 1971 to 2000 there were 4680 recorded visitor fatalities in U.S. National Parks with motor vehicle accidents and drowning incidents being the most frequent cause of fatality. In addition, in 2003 the park service conducted 3108 SAR operations at a cost of U.S. $3.4 million and 69,749 personnel hours.

While the identification of motor vehicle and drowning-related incidents as the most frequent cause of death to tourists visiting U.S. National Parks mirrors the findings of Wilks, Pendergast, and Wood, (2002) and McInnes, Williamson, and Morrison, (2002) on tourist populations in general, a search of the academic literature investigating fatal and non-fatal tourist incidents, specifically, within national parks is somewhat limited. However, the literature that does exist tends to be focused on the environment that tourists visit, the activities that tourists participate in, and the knowledge and behaviour of tourists. For example, in a study of tourist encounters with wild animals in parks and reserves in South Africa, Durrheim and Leggat (1999) report that fatal and non-fatal encounters largely occur as the result of tourists carelessly approaching prides of lions on foot, tourists ignoring established rules, and a general ignorance of animal behaviour on the part of the tourist. In addition, Boulware (2004) identifies poor hygiene and a willingness to drink untreated surface water as a frequent cause of diarrhoea among wilderness travellers on the Appalachian Trail and Bauer (2002) reports that the vast majority of tourists visiting Manu National Park in Peru are unaware of leishmaniasis (parasitic disease) despite seeking travel advice prior to their visit.

Two specific studies by Mackie (1999) and Dingwall, Fitzharris, and Owens (1989) highlight the role the environment can play in injuries to tourists in national parks. In a study reporting the pattern of drowning fatalities in Australia from 1992 to 1997, Mackie (1999) reports that 26% of all drowning incidents in Australia occur at surfing beaches and ocean/tidal sites that are considered part of the Australian National Park system. Likewise, in a landmark paper discussing the interface between natural hazards and visitor safety in New Zealand's national parks, Dingwall et al. (1989) suggest that the scenic and rugged geographic features that attract visitors to national parks are often the exact features that place visitors at higher levels of risk. Dingwall et al. (1989) specifically points out that the congregation of people on ski slopes, the flanks of volcanoes, glacial moraines, and in high alpine areas makes them more susceptible to storms, avalanches, landslides, floods, and earthquakes. Similar sentiments were expressed by Johnston (1989) in her report on mountain recreation and the experiences of international and domestic visitors in New Zealand, and by Heggie and Heggie (2004) in their documentation of injuries sustained by tourists hiking in Hawaii Volcanoes National Park. Johnston (1989) specifically found climbing activities in New Zealand's national parks (especially Aoraki/Mount Cook National Park) to be a high-risk activity for international tourists whereas Heggie and Heggie (2004) point to the inexperience of tourists in wilderness areas and an overall lack of preparedness as significant factors contributing to the high rate of injuries and illnesses sustained by the tourists.

More recent studies carried out by Golding, Tuler, and Krueger (2002) for the U.S. National Park Service Social Science Program at Yosemite National Park in California, Lake Mead National Recreation Area near Las Vegas, Nevada, and the Statue of Liberty (Ellis Island National Monument) in New York highlight the role that tourist activities and the natural environment play in injuries to tourists in wilderness, water, and urban-based parks. Between 1993 and 1998 a total of 67 tourists died, while visiting Yosemite National Park and 4114 tourists suffered non-fatal injuries and illnesses. Out of all the fatalities at Yosemite, 54 involved domestic tourists from the United States and the rest involved visitors from Germany, France, the United Kingdom, Croatia, the Czech Republic, India, Japan, South Korea, Norway, and Spain. Thirty of the fatalities were the result of falls while hiking, climbing, and walking and 10 of the fatalities were the result of motor vehicle accidents. Figures 13.1 and 13.2 display the activities and types of injuries and illnesses associated with visitor incidents in Yosemite National Park and indicate that cuts and abrasions, breaks and fractures, head injuries, joint injuries, and cardiovascular incidents are the most common injuries and illnesses in Yosemite. Moreover, motor vehicle accidents, skiing-related activities, and falls while hiking, climbing, and walking are the most frequent activities associated with these injuries. The majority of the injured tourists in Yosemite were from the United States. However, 144 injured tourists were from the United Kingdom, 48 were from Holland, and 180 were from Australia, France, Germany, India, Israel, Italy, Latvia, Mexico, Spain, and Switzerland.

In contrast to Yosemite National Park, Figures 13.3, 13.4, and 13.5 display the primary activities and causal events associated with non-fatal injuries and illnesses at Lake Mead National Recreation Area, the visitor activities associated with non-fatal injuries and illnesses at the Statue of Liberty, and the nature of visitor injuries and illnesses at the Statue of Liberty. Between 1993 and 1998 there were 106 fatalities recorded at Lake Mead and between 1995 and 1998 there were 3560 recorded non-fatal injuries and illnesses. All but two of the fatalities involved domestic tourists and occurred while visitors were boating, swimming, operating motor vehicles, or participating in other water-related activities. Out of the 3560 visitor injuries and illnesses recorded at Lake Mead, the majority of incidents were associated with boating accidents (41%), motor vehicle accidents (29%), and swimming-related incidents (8%).

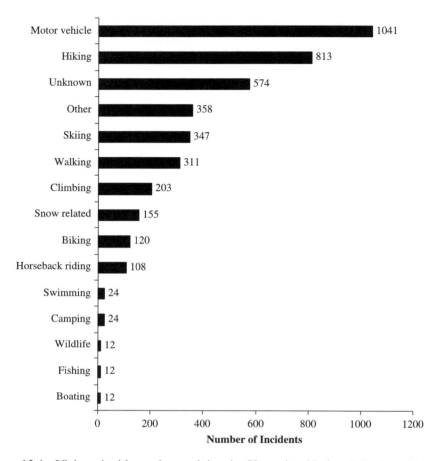

Figure 13.1: Visitor incidents by activity in Yosemite National Park, 1993–1998 (*N* = 4114).

During a similar period, there were only two fatalities but 5302 non-fatal injuries and ill-nesses recorded at the Statue of Liberty. Both fatalities were Americans involved in motor vehicle and pedestrian incidents. In addition, out of the total 5302 recorded incidents, 4930 involved domestic tourists, 54 involved tourists from Japan, 53 involved tourists from the United Kingdom, and 265 involved tourists from Australia, Belgium, Canada, China, France, Germany, Ireland, Italy, South Korea, Mexico, Sweden, and Venezuela. Cuts and abrasions are by far the most frequent type of non-fatal injury at the Statue of Liberty fol-lowed by joint injuries and cardiovascular-related events. Moreover, walking is the activity most frequently associated with visitor incidents at the Statue of Liberty. It is interesting to note that the peak injury age at Yosemite National Park is 20–50 years of age, the peak injury age at Lake Mead National Recreation Area is 20–40 years of age, and the peak injury age at the Statue of Liberty is 11–15 years of age. As well, 54% of the victims at Lake Mead were injured between 1200 and 1800 hours, 22% were injured between 0600 and 1200 hours, and 17% were injured between 1800 and 2400 hours.

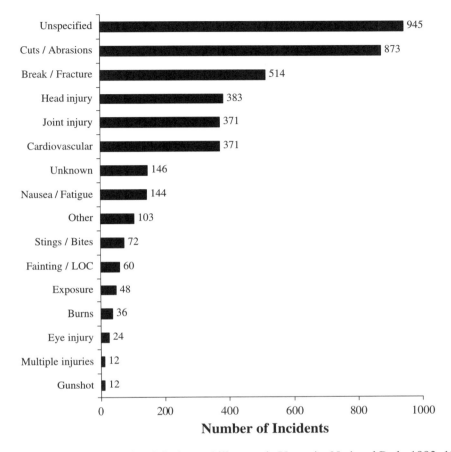

Figure 13.2: Nature of visitor injuries and illnesses in Yosemite National Park, 1993–1998 ($N = 4114$).

Safety Policy in U.S. National Parks

With visitation to national parks increasing, and health and safety issues playing a more prominent role in the selection of holiday and recreation destinations (Bentley & Page, 2001), the U.S. National Park Service has recognised visitor safety as a critical component of protected area management and expressed concern for visitor safety. In Section 8.2.5.1 of the 2001 National Park Service Management Policy, the National Park Service states that:

> The saving of human life will take precedence over all other management activities. The National Park Service and its concessionaires, contractors, and cooperators will seek to provide a safe and healthful environment for visitors and employees. The Park Service will work cooperatively with other federal, state, and local agencies, organizations, and individuals to carry out this responsibility. However, park visitors assume a certain degree of risk and

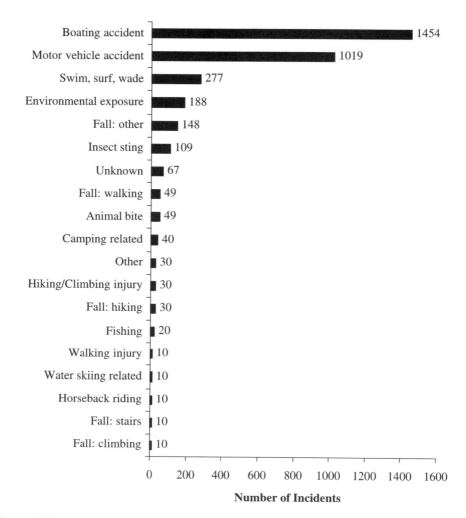

Figure 13.3: Primary activities and causal events associated with non-fatal injuries and illnesses at Lake Mead National Recreation Area, 1993–1998 (*N* = 3560).

responsibility for their own safety when visiting areas that are managed and maintained as natural, cultural, or recreational environments (2001, p. 85).

In order to provide direct support for this policy, the National Park Service (1999) refers to Director's Order and Reference Manual #50B on Occupational Safety and Health. Even though this order primarily addresses occupational safety and health issues, Section 14 of the reference manual specifically addresses public health and safety. This order states that:

The National Park Service holds the safety and health of the visiting public, its employees, contractors, and volunteers to be a core value of the National

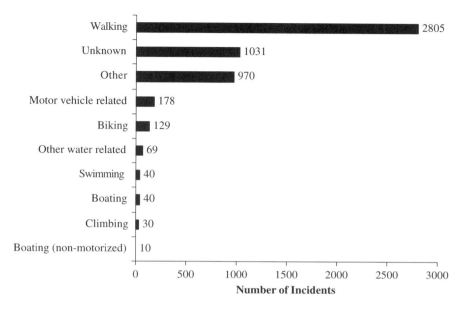

Figure 13.4: Visitor activities associated with non-fatal injuries and illnesses at the Statue of Liberty/Ellis Island National Monument, 1993–1998 ($N = 5302$).

Park Service. As well, the National Park Service has a continuing concern about the health and safety of its employees and others who spend time in the parks — whether as visitors, volunteers, contractors, concession employees, or in any other capacity. Those who participate in work or recreational activities in the parks are always, to some extent, exposed to the risk of accident, injury or illness. In recognizing this, the National Park Service is committed to reducing these risks and the associated pain, suffering, and financial expense (p. 3).

Director's Order and Reference Manual #50B additionally states that:

The overall purposes of the National Park Service Risk Management Program are to establish and implement a continuously improving and measurable risk management process that: (1) provides for the occupational safety and health of NPS employees; (2) provides for the safety and health of the visiting public; and (3) maximizes the utilization of NPS human and physical resources, and minimizes monetary losses through effective workers' compensation case management (p. 4).

Director's Order and Reference Manual #50C establishing the policies and procedures of the National Public Risk Management Program was in preparation at the time of this writing.

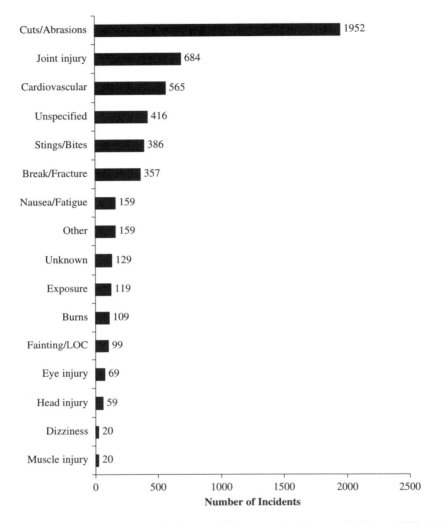

Figure 13.5: Nature of visitor injuries and illness at the Statue of Liberty/Ellis Island National Monument, 1993–1998 ($N = 5302$).

Injury Reporting in National Parks

The U.S. National Park Service has recently turned to the field of injury epidemiology in order to better understand and control injuries in national parks. For example, the National Park Service recognises the identification of injuries as the first step in determining the cause of injuries. This has proven to be a challenge, however, because aside from the most serious incidents and fatalities reported in *Morning Reports*, there is no national injury surveillance or reporting system established for national parks. Instead, each individual park keeps track of visitor incidents on *Case Incident Reports*. Park personnel who respond to visitor incidents will typically complete an *Emergency Medical System Report* at the scene of the incident reporting the nature and location of the incident, the basic medical and demographic information pertaining to the injured party, and a summary of park personnel responses to the incident. This information is then transferred to *Case Incident Reports* and includes information about the date, time, and location of the incident; the age, gender, race, nationality, place of residence, and number of visitors involved in the incident; a description of the environment and conditions at the scene of the incident; the nature of the activity in which the visitor was engaged at the time of the incident; the type and severity of the injury incurred by the visitor, and the actions taken in response to the incident by park personnel and others. Case incident reports also provide space for narrative descriptions of the incident, cost summaries of major incidents, photos of the injury scene and injury, and include emergency medical log records, emergency medical service (EMS) reports filled out by paramedics or wilderness emergency medical technicians, SAR reports, coroners' reports, and follow-up reports with hospital personnel.

Injury Epidemiology and the Haddon Matrix Framework

Once the *Case Incident Report* data is collected from individual parks, the National Park Service has started analysing the injury data using a conceptual model known as the *Haddon Matrix*. One of the most utilized frameworks in injury control research, the Haddon Matrix is used to conceptualise the aetiologic factors for injury and to identify potential preventive strategies (Runyan, 2003; Lett, Kobusingye, & Sethi, 2002). Developed by Dr. William Haddon Jr. in the late 1960s, Haddon grounded his matrix on the foundation of the epidemiologic model that involves the core concepts of the *agent*, *host*, and *environment* (Runyan, 2003). Just like an infectious disease, Haddon theorised that injuries are the product of the interaction between the host, agent, and the environment (Runyan, 1998, 2003; Lett et al., 2002). Moreover, Haddon defined the *host* as the person injured or the person at risk of being injured, the *environment* as the elements of the physical surroundings that contribute to the occurrence of injury, and the *agent* as injury-producing energy transferred to the host by either an inanimate vehicle or animate vector (Runyan, 2003). In describing the *agent*, Haddon built on the work of Gibson (1964), who recognised that injury is due to the transfer of mechanical/kinetic energy, thermal energy, radiant energy, chemical energy, or electrical energy to a host in an amount exceeding or below the threshold for tissue damage.

In order to create an awareness of the factors contributing to injuries, Haddon (1972, 1980a, 1980b) devised a two-dimensional matrix consisting of three columns and three rows (Figure 13.6).

The columns in the matrix represent the host, agent, and environmental factors that contribute to the injury process and the rows in the matrix represent time phases (pre-injury, injury and post-injury). During the *pre-injury phase*, individual host, agent, and environmental factors contribute to the increase in exposure to potentially damaging energy. This is followed by the *event phase* in which an excessive amount of energy is transferred to the individual host resulting in injury. The *post-injury phase* begins directly after the energy transfer and encompasses emergency care, transport, and other attempts made to restore the injured host to pre-injury functioning.

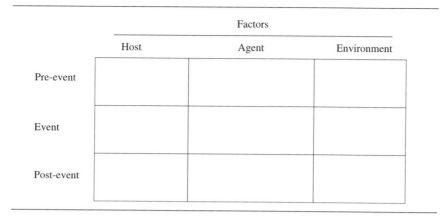

Figure 13.6: The Haddon Matrix. *Source*: Runyan (2003).

Applying the Haddon Matrix Framework to National Parks

Applying the Haddon framework to a setting such as a national park requires park management to view the Haddon Matrix within a recreational tourism activity system. For example, within this system the host factors would consist of visitor characteristics such as the type of tourist visiting the park (age, gender, race, and nationality), their level of experience in the type of setting they are visiting, their actions, and behaviour while visiting the park (non-compliant behaviour/ignoring safety information, judgment error, participating in an activity despite having a pre-existing health condition that could hinder their health during the activity, faulty behaviour such as the consumption of alcohol), and their level of preparedness (wearing appropriate clothing, having the appropriate equipment and supplies, participating in activities they are not physically prepared for). Moreover, environmental factors within this system would consist of both natural factors (geological hazards, wildlife and insect hazards, meteorological hazards, floral hazards, topographical/terrain hazards) and built factors (type of hiking trail, roadway conditions, building and infrastructure hazards, maintenance hazards). The agent factor or type of energy transfer in this system would depend on the type of activity the tourist participates in or the type of energy to which they are exposed to during their activity. For instance, injuries sustained from motor vehicle accidents, skiing incidents, tour helicopter crashes, and falls, while hiking or climbing would be considered a mechanical/kinetic energy transfer, insect stings and contact with toxic plants would be a form a chemical energy transfer, injuries resulting from contact with power lines or lightning would be a form of electrical energy transfer, exposure to the sun resulting in sunburns or dehydration would be a form of radiative energy transfer, and injuries resulting from contact with fire, steam, or hot water would be a form of thermal energy transfer. It is important to note that the transfer of mechanical/kinetic energy tends to originate from physical events such as an impact, breakage, shear, and flow. In addition, injuries may also result from the sudden absence of essentials such as heat or oxygen. Examples of this type of situation could be hypothermia and drowning incidents.

The ultimate goal of aetiologic studies using the Haddon Matrix is not to create an endless list of risk factors that contribute to tourist injuries in national parks. Instead, the focus should be on understanding the factors resulting in an injury in order to develop effective injury prevention strategies. This can be challenging given the diverse nature of national parks and the chronic funding, training, and staffing problems faced by most parks. However, despite these challenges, the National Park Service has adopted three fundamental injury prevention strategies in order to reduce visitor injuries. These strategies involve: (1) informing visitors to national parks of the risks they face and encouraging them to alter their behaviour accordingly; (2) requiring visitor behaviour change by law or administrative rule; and (3) providing protection through maintenance and environmental design. It is generally felt among injury researchers that while each of the above strategies plays a role in any comprehensive injury prevention programme, the second strategy requiring visitor behaviour change by law or administrative rule is more effective than the other two strategies. From a park management perspective, this strategy could involve developing gates and other barriers that restrict access into high-risk areas, increasing the presence of law enforcement rangers, or requiring visitors to receive direct permission from the park prior to entering a wilderness area. As we have witnessed with the recent debates and legal action surrounding snowmobiling activities in Yellowstone National Park, a problem with this approach is that many visitors complain when access to areas of the park is denied or their ability to participate in a particular activity is restricted. This has also been a particular challenge for park managers in Hawaii Volcanoes National Park where tourists wanting to access active lava flows have literally climbed over barriers, ignored strict warning signs, and entered restricted areas at night after park staff have exited the area.

As a result of the challenges presented by the second strategy, the National Park Service is placing more of an emphasis on informing visitors to national parks of the risks they face and by providing as much protection as possible through their maintenance programmes. Individual parks are in the process of identifying injury hot spots within their park with an emphasis on identifying patterns involving the most frequent and the most severe injuries. Injuries such as minor scrapes, abrasions, and cuts tend to occur in circumstances that are substantially different from those resulting in more severe injuries. Therefore, concentrating solely on injury frequency will only serve to misdirect prevention resources from the most severe and costly injuries. Once these hot spots are identified, improvements such as decreasing the gradient of trails and improving the surface friction of trails and roadways are being made by maintenance teams. A particular problem spot for many national parks are their parking areas in front of visitor centres and museums where numerous visitors have incurred serious injury from tripping over speed bumps and tall curbs constructed to blend in with the natural environment. As a result, maintenance teams are making an effort to improve sidewalk access and paint speed bumps and curbs with slip-resistant yellow paint that does not hide the characteristics of the surface. Park managers are also making efforts to: (1) collaborate with local tourism authorities to promote safe tourism in their marketing campaigns; (2) increase the number of park staff in high-risk areas; (3) upgrade staff training from basic first aid to first responder status; (4) design signs and brochures in multiple languages and with both English and metric units; (5) place safety messages in visitor centres and other educational settings; (6) include safety messages in radio and phone information sources; and (7) place safety information on all park websites. National parks such as the Grand Canyon have reported success using a "Heat Kills, Hike Smart" campaign that involves handing safety information to all visitors entering the park and placing information posters at each trailhead (Stewart et al., 2000). As well, given the transient nature of tourists visiting national parks and the difficulties associated with embarking on a large-scale public education campaign, safety information placed on websites is also proving to be an effective instrument in preparing domestic and international tourists for their visit to a national park.

Conclusion

Injuries are not random events. Likewise, injuries are one of the oldest human problems that accounts for an enormous loss of life and disability worldwide. Over the last 15 years, a number of respectable injury research programmes have been established in countries such as Australia, Canada, France, New Zealand, the United Kingdom, and the United States. However, while many of these programmes pay attention to recreational injuries, very few of them concentrate on injuries unique to tourist populations. As the demand for outdoor recreation opportunities increases, the number of recreational visits to national parks and the number of injuries is also expected to increase. The injury control programme established within the U.S. National Park Service is a young and developing programme with the aim of improving the experience of each visitor to a national park by making their visit as safe as possible. Each national park is different and presents a unique challenge requiring adaptable injury-control measures. However, even though it is virtually impossible to prevent all injuries, the Haddon Matrix provides a conceptual framework that can improve our understanding of the causal factors behind tourist injuries in national parks and ultimately guide the development of preventive strategies.

References

Bauer, I. (2002). Knowledge and behavior of tourists to Manu National Park, Peru, in relation to Leishmaniasis. *Journal of Travel Medicine, 9*, 173–179.

Bentley, T.A., & Page, S.J. (2001). Scoping the extent of adventure tourism accidents. *Annals of Tourism Research, 28*, 705–726.

Boulware, D.R. (2004). Influence of hygiene on gastrointestinal illness among wilderness backpackers. *Journal of Travel Medicine, 11*, 27–33.

Dingwall, P.R., Fitzharris, B.B., & Owens, I.F. (1989). Natural hazards and visitor safety in New Zealand's National Parks. *New Zealand Geographer, 45*, 68–79.

Durrheim, D.N., & Leggat P.A. (1999). Risk to tourists posed by wild mammals in South Africa. *Journal of Travel Medicine, 6*, 172–179.

Gibson, J.J. (1964). The contribution of experimental psychology to the formulation of the problem of safety: A brief for basic research. In: W. Haddon, E.A. Suchman, & D. Klein (Eds), *Accident research: Methods and approaches* (pp. 296–304). New York, NY: Harper & Row.

Golding, D., Tuler, S., & Krueger, R.J. (2002). An analysis of visitor risk in the national park system. United States National Park Service Social Science Program. http://www.nature.nps.gov/socialscience/docs/Safety_Risk.pdf. (last accessed 10 December, 2004).

Haddon, W. (1972). A logical framework for categorizing highway safety phenomena and activity. *The Journal of Trauma, 12*, 193–207.

Haddon, W. (1980a). Options for the prevention of motor vehicle crash injury. *Israel Journal of Medical Sciences, 16*, 45–68.

Haddon, W. (1980b). Advances in the epidemiology of injuries as a basis for public policy. *Public Health Reports, 95*, 411–421.

Heggie, T.W., & Heggie, T.M. (2004). Viewing lava safely: An epidemiology of hiker injury and illness in Hawaii Volcanoes National Park. *Wilderness & Environmental Medicine, 15*, 77–81.

Johnston, M. (1989). Accidents in mountain recreation: The experiences of international and domestic visitors in New Zealand. *GeoJournal, 19*, 323–328.

Lett, R., Kobusingye, O., & Sethi, D. (2002). A unified framework for injury control: The public health approach and Haddon's matrix combined. *Injury Control and Safety Promotion, 9*, 199–205.

Mackie, I.J. (1999). Patterns of drowning in Australia, 1992–1997. *Medical Journal of Australia, 171*, 587–590.

McInnes, R.J., Williamson, L.M., & Morrison, A. (2002). Unintentional injury during foreign travel: A review. *Journal of Travel Medicine, 9*, 297–307.

National Park Service. (1999). National Park Service Director's Order #50B and reference manual #50B: Occupational health and safety program. United States National Park Service, Washington, DC. http://www.nps.gov/policy/DOrders/DO50BRM.doc. (last accessed 15 December, 2004).

National Park Service. (2001). National Park Service Management Policies. United States National Park Service, Washington, DC. http://www.nps.gov/policy/mp/chapter8.htm. (last accessed 15 December, 2004).

Runyan, C.W. (1998). Using the Haddon matrix: Introducing the third dimension. *Injury Prevention, 4*, 302–307.

Runyan, C.W. (2003). Back to the future: Revisiting Haddon's conceptualization of injury epidemiology and prevention. *Epdemiologic Reviews, 25*, 60–64.

Stewart, W., Cole, D., Manning, R., Valliere, W., Taylor, J., & Lee, M. (2000). Preparing for a day hike at Grand Canyon: What information is useful? *United States Department of Agriculture Forest Service, Rocky Mountain Research Proceedings, 15*, 221–225.

Towner, J., & Wall, G. (1991). History and tourism. *Annals of Tourism Research, 18*, 71–84.

Wilks, J., Pendergast, D.L., & Wood, M.T. (2002). Overseas visitor deaths in Australia: 1997–2000. *Current Issues in Tourism, 5*, 550–557.

Chapter 14

Safety in the Dive Tourism Industry of Australia

Christopher Coxon[1]

International Dive Tourism

Scuba diving is one of the dominant activity-based tourism options found in tropical and temperate waters worldwide. The major recreational diver training agencies recorded 1,73,476 new diver certifications in 2003. Each certification supports dive travel, accommodation, equipment sales and a range of marine facilities. Despite this role the global industry is in something of a crisis where, after many years of sustained growth, certification rates for new divers show signs of decline (Dive Equipment Manufacturer's Association, 2004).

Since mistakes made in the marine environment can have very serious consequences, safety has always been of particular concern to dive tourism operators and government agencies charged with protecting visitors. The recent release of the movie 'Open Water' describing two American tourist scuba divers left at sea by a charter operator has increased public interest and attention to safety in dive tourism. This chapter details the challenges and responses for dive tourism drawing on Australian experiences.

Water Safety in Australia

The Australian National Water Safety Plan confirms that over 300 Australians drown annually, making it the nation's third highest cause of accidental death (Australian Water Safety Council, 1998). This has been despite the considerable efforts of water safety organisations, governments, statutory authorities, facility operators and individuals. To address this alarming figure, the Plan identifies four key result areas for future action. These are:

- Water safety research,
- Management of aquatic locations,

---

[1] The opinions expressed in this paper are those of the author and do not necessarily represent the opinions or policies of the Department of Industrial Relations or the Government of Queensland.

- Water safety education, and
- Targeting of drowning demographics.

The safety of recreational scuba divers is identified as a focus for water safety education. Reference is made to Australian Standards **www.standards.org.au** and the provision of training by recreational diver training organisations. In-bound tourists, in general, are also identified as a key demographic accounting for 3.9% of the total number of drownings (5-year average). Between 1992 and 1998 there were 119 tourist deaths due to drowning in Australia. Of these, 50.4% occurred in Queensland with a further 25.2% in New South Wales (Australian Water Safety Council, 2000).

Tourists differ from the wider community in that their lack of awareness of the risks of Australian water conditions may be combined with a lower level of water skills. A number of studies have highlighted the implications of these two risk factors (Edmonds & Walker, 1999; Mackie, 1999; Walker, 1999). Walker (1999, pp. 584–585), for example, describes individual risk factors such as the inability to speak English and the unlikely prospect that "most tourists on a day trip to the reef will consider their pre-existing medical factors and physical fitness levels". She also illustrates environmental variables — "Australian ocean conditions are deceptively treacherous and may change from minute to minute".

This chapter seeks to explore these concerning trends with regard to the dive tourism industry. To do this, an outline of the structure of the tourist diving industry in Australia is provided, with a particular emphasis on the important position of Queensland both in terms of incidents and standards development. The relevant research is considered and certain inadequacies identified. The impact of the media is discussed and from there the development of self-regulatory and government regulation approaches to tourist diver safety are mapped out and reviewed.

The Structure of Dive Tourism in Australia

The current structure of the Australian recreational diving industry reflects its historic development and the regional growth of marine tourism across a number of geographically favoured sites. However it is not homogenous in structure or growth, making generalisations difficult.

In the various regions the importance of a wider and varied marine tourism industry is considerable. Nowhere is this more apparent than in Queensland with the marine attractions provided by the Great Barrier Reef. A detailed study of the structure and economics of the marine tourism industry in the Cairns region of the Great Barrier Reef (Coopers & Lybrand, 1996) made a number of findings, which illustrate this. Other marine tourism "hot spots" around the world may likewise have a similar role in regional economies. The key findings included:

- The marine tourism industry consists of operators of commercial passenger vessels and associated businesses that provide a nature-based experience to visitors.
- The marine tourism industry provides substantial economic benefits to the regional economy, which in turn supports corresponding infrastructure development, other tourism services and attractions.

- Tourism contributes a significant proportion (AUD$0.8 billion or 25%) to the gross regional product of AUD$3.2 billion (in 1992).
- Marine tourism activities on the Great Barrier Reef are a major drawcard to both the Cairns region and to Australia more generally.
- Approximately 75% of visitors to the Cairns region engaged in marine tourism. Visitor growth rates averaged approximately 9% in the 1990s.
- The industry is vulnerable to external influences due to its remote nature and highly sensitive ecosystem. It has a limited ability to influence the factors that may affect the industry.

More recent studies again indicate the considerable economic contribution both of the reef tourism industry and of the variety of contributions through taxes and other charges to government funds. Mules (2004) reports total expenditure by Great Barrier Reef tourism as AUD$1.36 billion in 2004 prices. However, the growth trends are neither consistent nor necessarily positive. Returns for the environmental management charge collected from commercial reef visitors from 1994 to 2003 show declining visitation rates for the Cairns section of the Great Barrier Reef Marine Park, rising visitation in the Whitsundays region and static rates for Port Douglas (Hocking Research and Consulting, 2004).

According to Cater (2004) key threats and opportunities for the sustained growth of the marine recreation industry are identified as:

- Economic:
  - global economic outlook;
  - changes in key source markets;
  - aviation changes.
- Social:
  - global political uncertainty;
  - severe acute respiratory syndrome (SARS);
  - media coverage.
- Environmental:
  - crown of thorns;
  - coral bleaching.

The negative impact of tourist diver incidents is discussed in a later section with a view to the media coverage generated and as such is a key factor able to impact on the industry's viability. Diver safety is an issue the industry cannot neglect.

The diving industry is a major sector of the broader recreational marine industry, which also includes non water-based activities such as fishing, cruising, whale watching and resort destinations.

Within the diving industry, there is no standard operator profile. Instead, it is varied according to the services that are offered. Across Australia there are distinct differences between the diving industry sectors, which service tourist divers as opposed to those servicing domestic markets. Table 14.1 illustrates typical contrasting features:

The tourist diving industry also has a number of distinct operational types, which cater for client variables such as cost and nature of experience. The services offered are not always compatible, for example combining beginner divers with more experienced divers, and so individual operators tend to focus on certain client types.

This parallels common distinctions used in the wider adventure travel industry between hard and soft activities (Ewert & Jamieson, 2003). Some larger companies have developed separately marketed and operated vessels to deal with this. Some of the major tourist diving operational types are shown in Table 14.2. The tourist diving industry is both internally and externally competitive, with aggressive marketing both domestically and overseas. The industry is very price driven with many operators offering similar products and customers easily able to substitute one dive product for another. This is exacerbated by the relative strength of dive product wholesalers and retailers who have a high degree of control on the customer flow to preferred operators and very low switching costs between products (Coopers & Lybrand, 1996).

Table 14.1: Typical features of tourist and domestic diving.

Tourist diving	Domestic diving
Visiting clientele	Local clientele
One off visitation	Repeated visitation
Tropical and sub-tropical waters	Sub-tropical and temperate waters
Entry-level training	Training at all levels
Introductory experiences	Ongoing training
Extended certificated dive trips	Weekend or short trips
Small- to large-scale operators	Small- to medium-scale operators
Tourism high and low seasons	Summer and holiday seasons

Table 14.2: Major tourist diving operational types.

Operational type	Typical features
The dive school	Focussing on training divers from entry-level certification upwards. They may be mainland, offshore or vessel based. May be live-in or separately accommodated
The live-aboard certificated dive vessel	Offering adventurous diving for certificated divers over several days
The day trip	A variety of dive and other activities may be offered from a vessel. Focussing on the occasional or time limited certificated diver, introductory diving and snorkelling
Limited diving	Diving activities are not the focus of an operation but offered as a part of a wider marine package. For example beach hire, cruise ships, sail charters, island resorts. Catering for a similar group as the day trip vessels

A small number of operators have been able to develop and market differentiated products. Primarily these are by providing higher service and facility standards, or offering unique environmental and adventure experiences.

The implications for tourist diver safety of this variation in structure may be summarised as:

- The economic importance of marine tourism, particularly in certain regional contexts, ensures that there is a broad community and government interest in diving safety issues.
- Analysis of diving incident data does not always make reference to the variations shown within the industry between regions and sectors.
- Safety standards must be flexible enough to recognise and be adapted to both regional and sector variations within the diving tourist industry.
- There are intense competitive features of the regional, national and international diving tourist industries. These make any differentiation of product that affects price or a customer's experience a grave concern to operators.

How Safe is Tourist Diving in Australia?

> If you can't measure it — you can't manage it.

There have been a number of discreet and some ongoing studies that provide a great deal of diving mortality and morbidity data within Australia and across its states. In part this has been ably supported by two major research and advisory organisations that support the diving industry. The South Pacific Underwater Medical Society (SPUMS) aims to promote and facilitate the study of all aspects of underwater and hyperbaric medicine. The Divers Alert Network (DAN) is an international group of autonomous non-profit scuba diving associations with branches throughout the world whose mission is to improve the safety of recreational scuba diving.

However, analysis of recreational diving incident data in Australia is unfortunately bedevilled by the lack of meaningful and differentiating denominator figures. The incident literature is dominated by descriptive case study and cross-sectional reports. These are extremely useful studies and assist in identifying the nature and mechanisms of injury, but do not allow any evaluation of ongoing diver safety *per se* or the impact of specific safety strategies.

Worldwide there is a considerable reported range in mortality rates amongst divers and allegations that diving industry sponsored studies have inflated the alleged population at risk so as to reduce the overall death rate (Edmonds, Lowry, Pennefather, & Walker, 2002).

Two of the better Australian studies (Monaghan, 1988, 1989) assessed the rate as 16.7 deaths per 1,00,000 for recreational divers but this fell to between 5.8 and 6.5 per 1,00,000 when the population expanded to include those who have had any diving experience. These fall within ranges found overseas; for example, 17.5 per 1,00,000 divers found in Japan (Ikeda & Ashida, 2000).

It is probable that studies reflecting different locations or sectors within the industry would show varying results and would hence be of great interest to those sectors. A study based on Stoney Cove Quarry (Hart, White, Conboy et al., 1999), an inland freshwater diver training site in Great Britain was able to accurately measure diver numbers as its denominator, in that all divers are required to register at the site. This study showed a relatively low fatality rate of 2.9 per 1,00,000 divers per year.

Queensland is particularly poorly served with studies of this kind. Still the most widely quoted study (Santoro, 1996) into the number of dives in Queensland dates from 1994 (Windsor, 1996). This study, which emanated from within the recreational dive industry, concludes that 1,290,500 dives were undertaken on the Great Barrier Reef in 1994. However, the rounded figures quoted (to the nearest 500 or 1000), indicate that the calculations are approximations. The mortality rate concluded by this study was an extremely low 1 per 4,30,000 (or 0.23 per 1,00,000) dives in Queensland. Unfortunately, this study has not been updated or externally corroborated. Even the national rate (for drownings of divers only) is only marginally lower, 0.08 per 1,00,000 of the overall population (Australian Water Safety Council, 1998).

Australia has been well served by the highly descriptive reports by Dr Douglas Walker commencing in 1972 and detailing approximately 400 diving and snorkelling deaths since that time (Walker, 1998, 2002). The trend shown here is disturbing, with an increasing average annual number of diving deaths over the study period. This contrasts with the US experience, for scuba divers only, showing a fall from a high of 147 in 1972 to 66 in 1988 and an average of approximately 80 deaths per year since that time (Divers Alert Network, 2000).

Although it is not clear if the Australian increase is due to increased participation or reporting there is only cold comfort to be drawn from an examination of these case studies, leading Edmonds and Walker to conclude "the real tragedy of this survey was that it shows that the lessons and teachings of yesterday are still not sufficiently appreciated today" (Edmonds & Walker, 1989). One wonders if they would make the same comment today?

Studies into recreational diver morbidity also paint a concerning picture. The preponderance of admissions of overseas visitors to Queensland hospitals for water-related injuries has been noted (Wilks, Coory, & Pendergast, 2004). This study showed that, for the three financial years 1998/1999–2000/2001, 59.6% of these admissions (162 patients) were using diving equipment. Of the diving incidents, the dominant cause of admissions was for decompression illness, accounting for 54.8% (149 patients). Sadly, comparisons with an earlier study (Wilks & Coory, 2000) conducted for the previous 3-year period (1995/1996–1997/1998) revealed that decompression illness continued to be the main condition treated, and that the proportion of patients treated had not changed over 6 years. This led the authors to recommend that scuba diving safety in Queensland requires further targeted attention. Specifically, that it is important to know which international visitor groups are experiencing problems and whether education and injury prevention initiatives are being delivered appropriately and in the correct languages.

In contrast, recent reports from the Townsville General Hospital Hyperbaric Unit (the main treatment facility for the Great Barrier Reef) show a drop in the numbers of divers being treated between 1997 and 2002 (Table 14.3). Possible explanations proposed by the treating physicians include the increased use of dive computers, calibrated for slow ascent rates and fitted with warning alarms as well as "tougher workplace health and safety laws"

Table 14.3: Divers treated in the Townsville General Hospital Hyperbaric Unit 1997–2002.

	Total divers	Recreational divers	Recreational dive instructors
1997–1998	89	76	8
1998–1999	98	80	15
1999–2000	84	70	8
2000–2001	64	48	6
2001–2002	65	59	5

Source: personal communications.

(ABC, 2004). However, declining visitor numbers in some sections of the marine park may equally be contributing to this decline (Hocking Research and Consulting, 2004).

Overseas, the US figures for decompression illness also show a recent decline. The DAN figures record increasing treatment rates from 1987 to 1994 but declining numbers since then (Divers Alert Network, 2000).

Tragically though; tourist divers who visit Australia to dive continue to die and be injured each year. The circumstances are rarely novel and the mechanisms usually identifiable. A better understanding of sector- and location-specific incidence rates would be useful not only to help identify preventative strategies but also to evaluate their success.

The Influence of the Media on Perceptions of Tourist Diving Safety

There is an ongoing morbid media interest in human suffering. Even with the positive market projections for marine tourism generally, and the hugely supportive international audience for the movie Finding Nemo, the popular media continues to monitor marine tourism activities very closely (see for example, Moore, 2004).

Certain factors appear to excite more than the usual media interest. There seems to be an increased level of interest in incidents where the combinations of the following factors are present:

• Youth
• Female
• Overseas
• Inexperience
• Time of life (holidays, gap year, honeymoon)
• Exotic locations
• Adventure activities

The tourist diving industry can provide each of these factors. For example, Wilks (2000) showed that British, American and German tourists are the most frequently represented overseas nationalities in diving and snorkelling fatalities in Queensland.

The emotive impact this can have on the industry is illustrated in the following extract from a book written to assist tourist dive operators deal with the media after an incident:

> An aggressive journalist can skew the true facts about diving to paint a picture of an opportunistic industry more concerned with profit than it is with safety. It's an increasingly more commonplace attitude; one in which accountability has now been replaced the notion of self responsibility. None of which helps a dive operator faced with a crisis situation where they might have to deal with the loss, injury or death of a customer, whatever the cause or reason. And who faces a barrage of questions from a media driven by the mantra "if it bleeds, it leads" (Strike, 2004).

However the longer term implications are less clear. There is some evidence to suggest that negative portrayal of environmental damage does not significantly impact on visitation numbers (Cater, 2004). Discussion of safety issues, such as recently occurred with the release of the film 'Open Water' also gives the tourist diving industry an opportunity to promote innovation and change in their safety systems. Perhaps there is no such thing as bad publicity!

Heightened media interest may also have the effect of sparking political and hence regulatory interest. Two coronial matters discussed below involved female Japanese divers and both had intense local media interest when the incidents occurred. The furore (Reid, 1998) surrounding the disappearance of the Lonergans in Queensland in 1998 went worldwide and has continued with the release of both books and a film based on the incident.

Self-Governance and Recreational Dive Training Agencies

Self-regulation is popular with tourist diving operators seeking freedom to engage in their business without legislative restraint. The diving industry in Australia has an extensive experience with self-regulation, particularly through the recreational diving training agencies. However in response to the ongoing mortality rates discussed above, self-regulation has repeatedly been subject to criticism, particularly from the various state coroners and sections of the media.

Since its inception in the 1940s and 1950s, the organisation of recreational diver training in Australia has followed a similar path to the rest of the world. After a period without regular formal training extending into the 1960s, diver training agencies developed either regionally or nationally in the 1960s and 1970s. The impact of these agencies has been extensive and today the major organisations are dominant fixtures in the recreational diving world.

Australia has seen the decline of local agencies, such as the Federation of Australian Underwater Instructors (FAUI), and the rise of the mainly US based agencies such as the Professional Association of Diving Instructors (PADI) and Scuba Schools International (SSI).

Affiliations between these and other agencies have led to a degree of standardisation of training, equipment and diving practice across the globe. Each agency practices a degree of risk management, quality assurance, legal advice and group insurance for members

(Nimb, 2004). The limitations facing these training agencies however are the same as those facing the dive operators themselves. In a competitive diver training marketplace where operators are able to transfer between agencies at will, the incentive to enforce onerous and costly safety requirements on members may be limited.

This may be contrasted with other adventure tourism sectors, such as the Australian Parachuting Federation where a single non-government agency dominates the activity. They are able to provide safety control of the industry's operators through both recognition of its status by the relevant regulatory authority, in this case the Civil Aviation Safety Authority, and by providing a gatekeeping mechanism, such as access to insurance.

The self-regulation of the diving industry in Australia has also been attempted through the development of employer groupings and associations. Nationally, these have tended to be short lived and characterised by internal division or marginalisation rather than by achievement. Associations such as Dive Australia have come and gone leaving no representational employer group currently on the national stage, while the Australian Underwater Federation focuses primarily on sport applications of diving and has little active association with the tourist diving sector.

Regional associations such as Dive Queensland or the Association of Marine Park Tourism Operators have tended to be focussed on particular issues and acted both as an industry apologists and advocates. With the development of a government regulatory approach to tourist diving safety, these organisations have moved towards an advocacy and consultative role rather than developing a self-regulatory approach. In the late 1980s, continuing high-profile incidents prompted the beginning of this more regulatory approach to diving safety.

Regulation of Diving Safety

Standards Australia

Standards Australia is a non-government independent body, which is recognised by the Commonwealth government as Australia's peak national standards agency. These standards may be called up by different state legislators or used as references to "best practice" in civil and other matters.

Standards Australia has long had an interest in occupational diving. This devolved, with consent from within sections of the recreational diving industry, into the development of Australian Standard 4005 (1992) Training and certification of recreational divers. Part 1: minimum entry level SCUBA diving. A revised version was released in 2000. This important document formed a benchmark for this level of diver training and helped set a number of standards, for example, the medical evaluation of divers which has become a national norm despite the fact that a medical consultation is not required by most of the diver training agencies.

After this tentative beginning, Standards Australia has more recently been prompted into taking a considerably more proactive role with regard the recreational diving industry. This has seen both the development of further training standards and with the release of Australian and New Zealand Standard 2299 (2003) Occupational Diving Operations.

Part 3: Recreational industry diving and snorkelling operations. The impact of this standard on tourist diver safety is still to be evaluated but will no doubt be referenced by regulatory agencies in all states in the future.

Queensland's Workplace Health and Safety

Queensland, unsurprisingly in view of its dominance of marine tourism in Australia, first began to experiment with a regulatory approach towards enforcing certain safety standards on the tourist diving industry in 1989. As with other jurisdictions worldwide, the task of regulation was given to the occupational health and safety agency, in this case being Workplace Health and Safety Queensland, a part of the Department of Industrial Relations. The health and safety of others, the diving customer, is to be protected in as far as it may be affected by the conduct of the diving operator.

A succession of fatal recreational diving incidents in the late 1980s that attracted considerable media and coronial interest prompted Workplace Health and Safety to release part 36 of the Workplace Health and Safety Regulation 1989 "Dive shops, self-employed scuba instructors and dive charter vessels". This regulation marked the beginning of a succession of evolving standards for the recreational dive and snorkelling industry, summarised in Table 14.4.

This original regulatory part prescribed standards for dive equipment, air purity, equipment available on dive vessels and operational requirements to be ensured by the dive master. In some cases the regulations can now only be described as arbitrary, where the outcome appears to have more to do with measuring compliance than improving health and safety. For example, regulation 264(3) (j) limits any diver to undertaking no more than four dives in any 1 day. As a control measure to limit the risk of a diver developing decompression illness this control is demonstrably illogical in that there is no reference to individual dive profiles.

The reaction from the Queensland tourism diving industry to these regulations was negative, loud and long (Spencer, 1990). The prescriptive nature of regulation and lack of

Table 14.4: Queensland recreational diving and snorkelling standards.

Workplace Health and Safety Regulation 1989-Part 36 Dive Shops, Self-employed SCUBA Instructors and Dive Charter Vessels — Repealed
Code of Practice for Recreational Diving at a Workplace 1992 — Repealed
Code of Practice for Recreational Diving and Recreational Snorkelling at a Workplace 1995 — Repealed
Workplace Health and Safety Regulation 1997-Part 12 Underwater Diving Work — Current
The Compressed Air Recreational Diving and Recreational Snorkelling Industry Code of Practice 2000 — Current-under review
The Industry Code of Practice for Recreational Technical Diving 2002 — Current

flexibility when applied to the different sectors found within the industry made its effectiveness as a risk management tool questionable. With limited resources applied to this new area; compliance, monitoring and enforcement efforts were also low.

However, the underlying need for a standard supported by Workplace Health and Safety was recognised by the peak recreational diving employer's organization, the Queensland Dive Tourism Association of Australia, later to become Dive Queensland (Heywood, 1996). In partnership these two organizations developed the 1992 Code of Practice. This new standard provided a much more extensive document in a more flexible code of practice format. Specific sections applied differing standards to differing risk groups so that sections were developed catering for the differing needs of resort divers, divers in training and certified divers.

Workplace Health and Safety had by this stage recruited specialist diving inspectors and begun compliance monitoring and enforcement activities. The following years from 1992 until 1998 saw the Code of Practice revised reactively following a number of significant incidents.

The disappearance of Thomas and Eileen Lonergan while diving from the vessel Outer Edge near St Crisper's Reef in January 1998 prompted the largest and first holistic review of the legislation since the original 1992 Code of Practice.

Coroner Noel Nunan made extensive findings but a limited set of recommendations following the inquest into the disappearance. The recommendations were aimed at preventing a recurrence of the event, with specific comments made on lookouts, counting procedures and signalling devices to be incorporated into the then ongoing review of the Queensland Code of Practice (Nunan, 1998).

This incident prompted the then Minister for Employment Training and Industrial Relations to set up a Diving Industry Taskforce to examine and report back on the overall approach to managing health and safety within the recreational diving and snorkelling industry in Queensland. This taskforce started a process of consultation with a variety of stakeholder groups against a background of intense media interest (Metcalf, 1998), broader tourism industry concerns, a coronial investigation and the unlawful killing (manslaughter) charge brought against the master of the Outer Edge.

This matter was also prosecuted under the Workplace Health and Safety Act 1995 and a guilty plea was entered by the employer. This resulted in the then largest fine for a recreational diving matter of AUD$27 500.

The ensuing report of the taskforce (Division of Workplace Health and Safety, 1999) recommended that the existing Code of Practice be reviewed in both content and legislative basis. A further recommendation led to the appointment of another specialist diving inspector. Following an extensive program of face-to-face and written industry consultation, the results were amendments to Part 12 Underwater Diving Work of the Workplace Health and Safety Regulation 1997, and the release of the Compressed Air Recreational Diving and Recreational Snorkelling Industry Code of Practice 2000.

By combining regulatory and industry code of practice provisions, flexibility is maintained while improving the robustness of monitoring and enforcement activities. The first state-wide audit program was conducted in 2001. A total of 59 tourist diving and snorkelling operators were audited and 169 Improvement Notices issued. This outcome was achieved with a high degree of operator support (Thompson, 2002). Enforcement activities have also led to a number of prosecutions based on breaches of these standards. For example, in 2003 a Cairns dive operator was fined AUD$10,000 following a further incident where a crew member was left behind in the water for 25 min.

As with the 1992 Code, subsequent incidents have prompted further amendments to the standards. A fatal incident involving a recreational dive worker using a semi-enclosed enriched air nitrox rebreather off Cooktown was outside the scope of the existing standards, so a new standard was developed commencing in February 2002. The Industry Code of Practice for Recreational Technical Diving 2002 incorporates diving using both open circuit and rebreather SCUBA systems for gases other than air as well as decompression stop diving on all gases.

Workplace Health and Safety Queensland has also taken a proactive advisory and educational role to enhance industry use and understanding of the relevant standards. Most recently, translations into 10 languages of medical advice for prospective resort divers and snorkellers, as well as briefings for certified divers and snorkellers, were produced in a waterproof format and provided to assist all Queensland dive operators.

The evolution of these regulatory standards in Queensland has had a considerable impact in other jurisdictions. The relevant Australian Standard, AS/NZS 2299.3 (2003) makes extensive use of the Queensland standards as the basis for its own text.

Western Australia

Following the death of Kaori Adachi on 1 December 1998 at Exmouth in Western Australia on a night dive, the coroner made comments specifically regarding rescue tenders, qualifications of divers and out of water supervision (Hope, 2001). The coroner concluded with the following comments to encourage the development of a regulatory code of practice for recreational dive operators:

> I note that a draft Code of Practice has been prepared for approval pursuant to section 57 of the Occupational Health and safety Act 1984 relating to recreational diving using compressed air and recreational snorkelling. That draft code of practice does deal with the issue of supervision of divers in open water and the requirement of a lookout. The Code of Practice also provides that the dive supervisor should manage the dive operation and remain at the surface of the dive site while the diving is taking place. It is important that safety issues of this type should be covered by such a code of practice (Hope, 2001, pp. 31–32).

Following these recommendations, the Department of Sport and Recreation published the 'Recreational Diving and Snorkelling Codes for Western Australia'. Interesting and unlike most other jurisdictions, this standard was not made under the relevant occupational health and safety legislation but contains the following reference:

> All workplaces are covered by the Occupational Health and Safety Act (1984) and this document attempts to benchmark minimal acceptable standards for assisting achieving compliance as well as best practice for industry.... The

regulatory function under the Occupational Health and Safety Act (WA) will be undertaken by Worksafe WA with reference to this code whilst the Department of Sport and Recreation provides an advisory role (Department of Sport and Recreation, Government of Western Australia, 2003, p. 1).

New South Wales

In New South Wales, the coroner, Mr Elwyn Elms, made extensive recommendations regarding regulation of the recreational dive industry following the inquest into the deaths of Midori Takano and Nicola Sheen. The recommendations are highly critical of self-regulation within the industry and of PADI in particular. The coroner makes reference to another six fatalities in NSW between 1994 and 2001. He states:

> Why make recommendations? The short answer is to minimise risk and to avoid needless waste of life which this court has had to concern itself over the years. Particularly concerning is the needless waste of life involving young inexperienced divers, who fall into a statistical bracket which shows they are more likely to succumb to injury or death in view of their inexperience and low skill levels (Elms, 2002, p. 4).

And:

> To my mind, it is no answer to say that this is an adventure sport that the participant is qualified and takes the risk, that if they don't know what to do, they shouldn't be there in the first place, and that in such a sport deaths are going to occur from time to time. The young people I am concerned with in these inquests comprise the industry's most vulnerable participants (Elms, 2002, p. 4).

In conclusion, the coroner makes reference to both the Queensland Code of Practice and the, then, draft Australian Standard. He advocates the adoption of a suitable standard, which can be enforced by an appropriate regulatory body (Elms, 2002).

Overseas Comparisons

In many countries there appears to have been a reluctance both from operators and the authorities to become entangled with diver safety at a regulatory level. However as in Australia, this has in certain cases been overcome by continuing incidents, media concern and stern coronial recommendations, which have all combined to prompt the regulatory or standards authorities into action.

In several cases the outcome and response seem to have mirrored the Queensland experiences. Overtly regulatory regimes have differentiated local diving tourism products to their detriment and zealous enforcement creates a combative rather than a supportive relationship between government and industry.

Malta, for example, has specific regulations including requiring divers to obtain permits to dive from licensed dive centres. These are only issued when the diver has produced acceptable evidence of their certification and current diving medical certificates. Spain likewise requires divers to produce current medical certificates. However, these and other restrictions differentiate the local product from regional competitors and are consequently resisted by some operators (Anonymous, 2004).

Great Britain has also prescriptively legislated for its recreational dive industry, producing a range of information products and engaging in high-profile enforcement activities including audits and prosecutions of operators.

Other European nations have pursued the development of consensual standards, similar in scope to those of Standards Australia, to include competency, medical assessment and tourism services including dive operators and dive training schools (Wendling & Muller, 2004).

The USA has largely been an exception to this trend perhaps reflecting a generally stronger self-regulatory approach. Again though, when significant or repeated incidents have occurred, regulatory authorities have sought a role.

In 2000 two US divers were left behind by a dive charter vessel from Key Largo, Florida. Fortunately they swam to a light and remained there until they were rescued, *before* their disappearance was reported by the dive operator. The company involved in this matter was fined US$1000 under local maritime safety legislation and required to adopt a safe accounting system (Warren, 2004).

Most recently, a diver was left behind at a dive site off California by the dive operator but was eventually spotted from an offshore platform. Following this the US Coastguard directed PADI to take steps to improve counting procedures. PADI then sent out a Diver Accounting Procedures Reminder to all members worldwide. This included reference to a tagging board developed by Divers Alert Network (PADI, 2004).

The Future

The nature of tourist diving as an adventure activity in a marine environment unfortunately precludes the likelihood of any strategy absolutely removing the incidence of death and injury among divers. However, in an increasingly litigious society one can anticipate that morbidity and mortality are now likely to be followed by demands for compensation for an unfortunate outcome. These outcomes will continue to attract intense media interest.

Notwithstanding this there remains much room for improvement in strategies to reduce both the incidence and rate of tourist diver morbidity and death. There is likely to be a continuation of a cycle of incident, media interest and investigation, possibly leading to reactive developments in both self-regulatory and government regulatory regimes.

All those stakeholders with an interest in diving safety are therefore faced with the challenge of working within this reality to develop outcomes that can genuinely improve diver safety without having the effect of imposing conditions that are overtly unworkable for the tourist diving industry.

Systems of self-regulation in a competitive environment will continue to only have a limited value in ensuring improvements in diver safety. Dive tourism operators would be better served to develop a single national body with close links to government regulators that is able to formulate and implement well-researched safe systems and perform an effective education, assessment and quality control function for its members. The development of Australian Standards provides a basis for this but to date there has been insufficient leadership regarding implementation from within the stakeholder group.

Without this leadership there continues to be an erosion of confidence in the self-regulatory approach and government regulators have moved slowly in to fill this gap. Tensions have developed where the resulting systems appear to create unreasonable reactive standards that differentiate the local dive industry rather than any measurable improvements in safety.

Queensland's relatively long experience in this process has resulted in a more flexible and dynamic regulatory approach, which combines a measure of industry acceptance with a regulatory program balancing consultation, education, assessment and enforcement. Other jurisdictions confronted with similar problems have used this as a model for their own approaches. Ongoing analysis of trends in diving incidents is required to provide a better picture not only of emerging issues but also to assess the impacts of safety strategies.

References

ABC seven o'clock news. (2004). [*television*]. Brisbane: Australian Broadcasting Corporation.

Anonymous. (2004). Diver requirements eased for Malta and Spain. *Diver Magazine*, July, 23.

Australian Water Safety Council. (1998). *National water safety plan*. Sydney: Author.

Australian Water Safety Council. (2000). *Analysis of drowning in Australia and pilot analysis of near-drowning in New South Wales*. Sydney: NSW Injury Risk Management Research Centre, University of New South Wales.

Cater, C. (2004). *The Great Barrier Reef tourism industry (Draft October 2004)*. Brisbane: Queensland Tourism Industry Council.

Coopers & Lybrand. (1996). *Reef tourism 2005 — Structure and economics of the marine tourism industry in the Cairns section of the Great Barrier Reef*. Cairns: Author.

Department of Sport and Recreation, Western Australia. (2003). *The diving and snorkelling codes of practice — recreational diving using compressed gas and recreational snorkelling*. Perth: Author.

Dive Equipment Manufacturer's Association. (2004). *2003 Certified open water level diver count*. Retrieved October 26 2004, from http://www.dem.org/associations/1017/files

Divers Alert Network. (2000). *DAN report on decompression illness and diving fatalities — 2000 Edition*. Durham, NC: Author.

Division of Workplace Health and Safety. (1999). *Review of workplace health and safety arrangements for recreational diving and snorkelling. Final report to the Minister of Employment Training and Industrial Relations*. Brisbane: Author.

Edmonds, C.W., Lowry, C., Pennefather, J., & Walker, R. (2002). *Diving and subaquatic medicine* (4th ed.). London: Arnold.

Edmonds, C. W., & Walker, D.G. (1989). Scuba diving fatalities in Australia and New Zealand: 1. The human factor. *South Pacific Underwater Medicine Society Journal*, *19*, 94–104.

Edmonds, C. W., & Walker, D.G. (1999). Snorkelling deaths in Australia 1987–1996. *Medical Journal of Australia*, *171*, 591–594.

Elms, E. (2002). *Inquest into the deaths of Midori Takano and Nicola Sheen. Recommendations pursuant to section 22A of the Coroners Act 1980*. Sydney: Coroners Court of New South Wales.

Ewert, A., & Jamieson, L. (2003). Current status and future directions in the adventure tourism industry. In: J. Wilks, & S.J. Page (Eds), *Managing tourist health and safety in the new millennium* (pp. 67–83). Oxford: Pergamon.

Hart, A.J., White, S.A., & Conboy, P.J. (1999). Open water scuba diving accidents at Leicester: Five years experience. *Journal of Accident and Emergency Medicine, 16*, 198–200.

Heywood, L. (1996). Divers back new safety regulations. *The Cairns Post*, 6 July, p. 7.

Hocking Research and Consulting. (2004). *Visitation to the Great Barrier Reef Marine Park*. Report for the Tourism and Recreation Group, Tourism and Recreation Reef Advisory Committee, Great Barrier Reef Marine Park Authority. Brisbane: Author.

Hope, A. N. (2001). *Inquest into the death of Kaori Adachi*. Perth: Coroners Court of Western Australia.

Ikeda, T., & Ashida, H. (2000). Is recreational diving safe? *Undersea Hyperbaric Medicine, 27* (Suppl.), 138 (abstract).

Mackie, I.J. (1999). Patterns of drowning in Australia, 1992–1997. *Medical Journal of Australia, 171*, 587–590.

Metcalf, F. (1998). Lawyers call for dive industry overhaul. *Brisbane Courier Mail*, 27 June, p. 3.

Monaghan, R. (1988). The risks of sport diving. *South Pacific Underwater Medicine Society Journal, 18*(1), 53–60.

Monaghan, R. (1989). Australian diving death rates: Comparison with USA and Japan. *South Pacific Underwater Medicine Society Journal, 19*(1), 24–25.

Moore, T. (2004). US tourist dies snorkelling. *Brisbane Courier Mail*, 25 November, p. 8.

Mules, T. (2004). *The economic contribution of tourism to the management of the Great Barrier Reef Marine Park*. Brisbane: Queensland Tourism Industry Council.

Nimb, H.C. (2004). Risk management in recreational diving: The PADI approach. *South Pacific Underwater Medicine Society Journal, 34*(2), 90–93.

Nunan, N. (1998). *Inquest into the cause and circumstances surrounding the disappearance of Thomas Joseph Lonergan and Eileen Cassidy Lonergan*. Brisbane: Queensland Coroners Court, No 52 of 1998.

PADI. (2004). *Training bulletin — A training and education update for PADI members worldwide, 3rd Quarter 04, Product No 01224* (Vol. 5). San Diego: International PADI.

Reid, R. (1998). Deep doubts. *The Australian Magazine*, 7 November, pp. 7–8.

Santoro, S. (1996). Ministerial statement. Workplace health and safety in the diving industry. In: *Queensland Parliamentary Debates*. Brisbane: Queensland Legislative Assembly, 1997–1998 (6 August).

Spencer, R. (1990). NQ calls to repeal new Qld dive law. *The Cairns Post*, 25 August, p. 5.

Standards Australia. (2000). *AS/NZS 2299.3 2003 Occupational diving operations — Part 3: Recreational industry diving and snorkelling*. Sydney: Author.

Standards Australia. (2003). *AS 4005.1 2000 Training and certification of recreational divers. Part 1: Minimum entry SCUBA diving*. Sydney: Author.

Strike, D. (2004). *Diving and the media: A survival guide*. Sydney: Strikeinc Pty Ltd.

Thompson, C. (2002). Dive audit good news. *The Cairns Post*, 25 February, p. 5.

Walker, D. (1998). *Report on Australian diving deaths 1972–1993*. Ashburton, Victoria: JL Publications.

Walker, D. (2002). *Report on Australian diving deaths 1994–1998*. Ashburton, Victoria: DAN SE Asia Pacific Ltd.

Walker, R. (1999). Dead in the water: How safe are our water sports? *Medical Journal of Australia, 171*, 584–586.

Warren, S. (2004). Dead calm. *Diver Magazine*, July, pp. 28–36.

Wendling, J., & Muller, P.H.J. (2004). Standards for diving in Europe — the present situation. *South Pacific Underwater Medicine Society Journal, 34*(3), 141–144.

Wilks, J. (2000). Scuba diving and snorkelling safety on Australia's Great Barrier Reef. *Journal of Travel Medicine, 7*, 283–289.

Wilks, J., & Coory, M. (2000). Overseas visitors admitted to Queensland hospitals for water-related injuries. *Medical Journal of Australia, 173,* 244–246.

Wilks, J., Coory, M., & Pendergast, D. (2004). Tourists still getting the bends. *Tourism in Marine Environments, 1,* 61–62.

Wilks, J., & Davis, R. (2000). Risk management for scuba diving operators on Australia's Great Barrier Reef. *Tourism Management, 21,* 591–599

Windsor, D. (1996) A study into the number of dives conducted on the Great Barrier Reef in 1994. *South Pacific Underwater Medicine Society Journal,* 26(2), 72–74.

Chapter 15

Surf Beach Risk and Safety

Damian Morgan

Introduction

According to Raban (1992, p. 1), the sea is a significant topic in English literature because "people generally write about things that give them the most difficulty in their lives, and maritime peoples are chronically oppressed and fascinated by the sea". Humans have a longstanding association with water and the sea. The earliest known depictions of human swimming have been dated at 9000 B.C., and history records swimming as a common recreational activity among many cultures (Freas, 1999).

In many parts of the world, the beach is a place for leisure and provider of pleasure to swimmers and those engaged in other activities. Dutton (1985, p. 13), for example, acknowledges the pleasurable experiences offered by Australian beaches, and notes the ease of access for the majority of residents:

> Of all the countries in the world, none presents greater opportunity for this hedonism [manifest at the beach] than Australia. Not only are there hundreds of miles of marvellous beaches all around the continent, with climates to invite people to them, but the cities spill onto the beach ….

The beach is a well-known and culturally laden natural attraction for tourists and visitors (Wearing, 2003). It is also an environment that comprises numerous hazards and consequent dangers. This chapter focuses on the dangers of the beach and methods used to mitigate potential risks of injury and death. Information contained in the chapter is related primarily to Australian beaches, but also includes examples and beach-related research from other countries. We begin the chapter with a description of two significant beach-drowning incidents and outline other dangers presented by beach environments. Following this, the use of the beach environment is explained. The chapter concludes with a review of beach hazards and risk minimization strategies including the role of life-saving services.

Tourism in Turbulent Times
Copyright © 2006 by Elsevier Ltd.
All rights of reproduction in any form reserved.
ISBN: 0-08-044666-3

Beach Drowning Tragedies

In response to drowning at popular surf beach locations, surf life-saving clubs were founded in Australia from the first decade of the 20th century, propelling the formation of the Australian Surf Life Saving Movement (Huntsman, 2001). The Australian Surf Life Saving Movement encouraged surf life saving clubs across the country to adopt equivalent practices and techniques for swimmer supervision, surf rescue and resuscitation practices. Huntsman notes the success of this historic prevention strategy given that no drownings were reported at surf beach locations during life-saving patrol times up to 1938.

The situation changed on 'Black Sunday', the 6th of February 1938, and emphasised clearly to an Australian public the potential danger of the surf beach. The following account of this tragic day was drawn from records held at Sydney's Waverly Library (2001). On a hot summer afternoon at Sydney's Bondi beach, approximately 300 bathers were swimming and wading between the patrol flags (supervised swimming area) on a submerged sandbar in shallow (waist deep) water. Soon after a series of larger-than-average waves, bathers were swept off the sandbar as the increased volume of water surged back out to sea through rip current feeder channels. The surging water carried the bathers into deep water and away from the beach. Luckily, there was more than the usual number of lifesavers present on the beach at the time of this incident, as there was a surf carnival that day plus a changeover of lifesaver shifts. Some 60–80 lifesavers assisted approximately 250 bathers back to shore. In total, 150 bathers were reported as being rescued unharmed, 60 as suffering from the effects of immersion but remaining conscious, 35 as being revived from an unconscious condition, and five persons unable to be revived.

Waters and Ellis (2003) relate the events leading to a more recent drowning tragedy at Australia's Gunnamatta beach in January 1998. On this day, two families comprising some 11 children arrived at the car park of a beach they had assumed was patrolled by lifesavers. The patrolled area was actually located adjacent to a second car park, about 800 m further along the access road. Believing that they were supervised, seven of the children entered the water but were quickly washed seaward in a rip current. While three were rescued, two children from each family died as a result of this horrific event.

These two surf beach drowning tragedies, separated by some 60 years, illustrate the serious danger presented by rip currents, an ever-present hazard inherent to surf beaches. In Australia as well as other countries, supervision and assisted rescue has been the primary drowning prevention strategy for surf beach patrons. Additionally, child-age swimming training has been in place for over a half a century in the Australian community (Ozanne-Smith & Wigglesworth, 2002).

Surf Beach Hazards

In addition to drowning, surf beach injuries can be sustained through a range of hazards found in these environments. Examples of hazards and potential injuries are listed in Table 15.1. To gain a full understanding of this problem, research studies or reports from beach management agencies are required to gauge the frequency and severity of these injuries.

Table 15.1 Examples of hazards and potential injury in surf beach environments.

Hazard type	Potential injury	Example of mechanism
Water	Immersion	Drowning
Marine animal	Bite or sting	Blue-ring octopus
Litter/rubbish	Cuts	Broken glass
Wave action	Broken bones	Broken collarbone from dumping
Equipment	Head injury	Hit by surfboard
Cliffs	Fall	Trip on cliff edge
Water pollution	Infection	Gastroenteritis from faecal contamination
Underwater object	Spinal cord injury	Diving into sandbar
Criminal activity	Assault	Robbery

Unfortunately, this evidence base is somewhat limited as injury surveillance systems are not sufficiently developed to assess the true risk posed by surf beach environments.

Before discussing hazard research in more detail, the next section describes the range of surf beach types, motivations for visiting surf beaches, and patterns of beach use. This information is important as it provides an insight to how and why surf beaches are utilised, as well as features inherent in these environments. Beach managers can then employ this information to develop and implement strategies and practices that promote a safe experience for beach users.

Surf Beach Types, Usage and Visitor Management

The surf beach is distinguished from other swimming sites by its dynamic natural environment. This environment is a transition zone between land and open sea, developed and characterised by the continual breaking of high-energy ocean swell (surf) onto the accumulated fine sediment (sand) (Short, 1999). Beach images are used commonly in tourism brochures, indicating the popularity of these locations for recreation and leisure. The appearance and uses of beaches vary greatly around the world, exacerbated in many locations by human-made structures such as hotels and marinas situated close to or on the beach frontage.

A range of beach classification systems has been developed to capture these variations in beach types and characteristics. These are often based on environmental features, amenities, or beach quality, such as the blue flag system (e.g., Mihalic, 2002). Of direct relevance to beach safety is a beach classification system developed by Short (2002).

Short's (2002) system allocates a beach hazard rating (from a low of 1 to a high of 10) based on beach *morphodynamics*. This system has been applied to all identifiable coastal beaches in Australia. Outlined in Figure 15.1, the system was developed from an earlier classification system originally proposed by Wright and Short (1984) and enhanced by Short and Hogan (1995). The beach hazard rating implicitly assumes that exposure to submersion injury (drowning) at beaches is determined, at least in part, by the level of relatively constant

WAVE DOMINATED BEACH TYPES

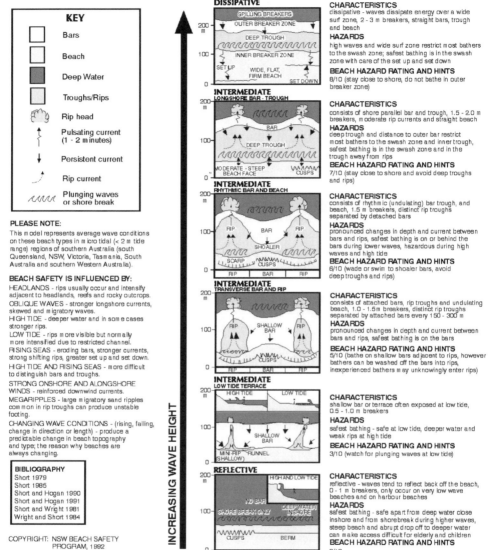

Figure 15.1: Wave-dominated beach characteristics and hazards. Reproduced with permission: Short (1993).

physical hazards. Beaches are given a modal beach hazard rating based on average wave height measured in the general vicinity. At any given time, a surf beach's prevailing hazard rating will depend on the type and height of breaking waves in operation; this rating can be above or below the modal rating.

Under this system, reflective beaches offer the safest bathing (rating up to two out of ten), with waves rising to 1 m. At the other end of the scale, dissipative beaches (rating of eight to ten out of ten) are the most dangerous due to the presence of 2–3 m breaking waves (see Figure 15.1). At higher ratings, rips currents will be faster flowing and drag the unaware swimmer farther seaward.

Short's (2002) beach hazard rating provides an objective measure of the drowning risk inherent to a surf beach at any particular time. Nevertheless, risks faced by beach users will vary according to the activities undertaken and the experience of those undertaking them. For example, a weak swimmer with little surf beach experience would be foolhardy to bath unsupervised at a surf beach carrying a high beach hazard rating. Conversely, experienced surfers with specialised equipment (e.g., surfboard) might safely seek out good sized waves while avoiding crowded surf spots.

As discussed earlier, understanding why people visit beaches and how they use beaches will impact on coastal management strategies, including those employed to mitigate beach hazards and increase safety. Studies of beach users' choice of beaches and preferences for particular beach attributes provide a useful starting point by providing an insight into visitor motivations. For example, studies based on self-reports from beach users have documented the relative offensiveness of beach litter (Nelson, Botterill, & Williams, 2000), adolescent females' higher propensity for visiting a beach to tan their skin relative to other groups (Pratt & Borland, 1994), the likelihood of near shore beach use as opposed to back of beach dune use predicted from selected sociodemographic, psychological, and behavioural variables (Williams, Winiarski-Jones, Davies, & Curr, 1992), and beach users' predilections for a *beach climate* based on reported preferences or thermal index systems (Becker, 1997; Morgan et al., 2000). Safety factors are also likely to influence beach choice. For example, some people will prefer to use a beach that has shark netting, even though the effectiveness of this protective devise is unknown (Meerman, 2002). Swimming in a patrolled (supervised) area has also been reported as an attractive aspect of the beach among the Australian population (Breitkreutz, 2000; Kellogg's & Newspoll, 2000).

International studies have examined the relative preferences for multiple beach attributes. For example, studies of beach users in Europe (including the United Kingdom), South Africa, and California have evaluated the importance of attributes including the knowledge of beach award systems, physical factors, biological factors including pollution, physical use factors, access factors, on site facilities, user conflicts, and level of development (De Ruyck, Soares, & McLachlan, 1995; Leatherman, 1997; MacLoed, Silva, & Cooper, 2002; Morgan, 1999a, b; Nelson & Botterill, 2002; Pendleton, 2001). The research indicates that preferences for particular beach attributes will vary among users. That is, there are a range of motivations for visiting the beach. Beach goers will be likely to make their choice based on a range of spatial and temporal characteristics including accessibility (and cost), environmental quality and features, amenities, and climate.

In both Australia and the United States, beach usage is monitored by land managers (e.g., Parks Victoria) and life saving authorities (e.g., Surf Life Saving Victoria). Estimates of beach use are normally based on user counts (or proxy measures such as number of vehicles parked close by) at the point of beach entry or on the beach area itself. However, these counts will not provide an accurate picture of total use, given that not all beaches or access points will be monitored at all times along a given coastline. This is not surprising as obtaining accurate estimates of beach use is difficult and costly (Deacon & Kolstad, 2000).

When estimating beach usage, the alternative to counting actual user numbers on site is through population-based surveys. For example, in the Australian state of Victoria, local residents have been estimated to undertake some 69 million visits to the coast each year, averaging 14.9 visits per person (TQA Research, 2000). In addition to these visits, surveys indicate that international tourist to Australia make in the vicinity of two and half million trips to the beach with domestic tourists making a further 17 million (Bureau of Tourism Research, 1999a, b). Clearly, surf beaches are very popular in Australia but no doubt beach patronage is many times higher at beaches located in more populated regions around the world.

Beaches are used for a host of water- and land-based activities. Land-based activities range from active recreational pursuits such as fishing, ball sports, walking, jogging, and exploring or fossicking to passive leisure activities such as sun bathing, sightseeing, and socializing. Water-based activities include swimming, surfing, windsurfing, kite surfing, jet skiing, snorkeling, and scuba diving. Each of these activities will present a specific risk profile. For example, sunbathers risk sunburn whereas scuba divers risk drowning in the event of equipment failure. The risk profile of beach users is made more complex given that the rate of participation in various activities will vary according to time of day, characteristics of the beach, and the season. For example, in temperate zones, the number of beach bathers will be higher in the warmer parts of the year and during the middle part of the day (Tower & Kain, 1993).

Surf Beach Drowning

Published research studies indicate that drowning is a significant injury problem at beaches around the world. For example, Steensberg (1998) examined 349 unintentional drownings or coolings in water (*immersio frigida*) from death certificates occurring from 1989 to 1993 in Denmark (excluding foreigner drowning deaths). Thirty-six (10.3 per cent) of these cases occurred at a beach location. This ranked as the fourth most frequent location behind 113 (32.4 per cent) open sea cases, 71 (20.3 per cent) harbour cases, and 48 (13.8 per cent) lake/watercourse cases. In Bell et al.'s (2001) study of 352 drowning deaths among U.S. active duty army soldiers, 52 (14.8 per cent) occurred at an ocean location. Unfortunately, comparing drowning rates in these studies is problematic given the different criteria used to identify the *beach* within the category location. Further, drowning studies often do not report cross tabulation of location with factors such as age or sex.

An exception is Gomez, Saywell, Zollinger, Schmit, and Donahue's (1992) study of drowning for 1989 in Dade County, FL, USA. Twenty-three (25.8 per cent) of the sample drowned at an ocean beach location. Where data were available for the 23 deaths, 20 (87.0 per cent) were found to be unintentional, 12 (52.2 per cent) were swimming prior to the incident, 12 (52.2 per cent) were known swimmers and 3 (13.0 per cent) were known non-swimmers. Resuscitation was attempted in 14 (60.1 per cent) cases. For the beach victims tested, 5 (25.0 per cent) had a blood alcohol concentration (BAC) greater than 10 per cent (using the criteria specified by Wintemute, Teret, Kraus, & Wright, 1990). Three (14.3 per cent) of the tested beach drownings were found to have consumed drugs following screening for intake (drug screened for included cocaine, tranquillisers, dilantin, pheno-barbituate, and marijuana).

Reports from life-saving services do focus exclusively on beach and ocean drownings. For example, the United States Lifesaving Association (2002) has reported beach drownings in the USA from 1996–2000. On average 86.4 people drowned per year over these 5 years with 87.5 per cent of these incidents occurring in unguarded areas. From the published beach attendance figures (reported for guarded beaches only), the present author calculated an average drowning rate of 0.033 per 100,000 beach attendances. In Australia, Williamson and Schmertmann (2000) have reported and analysed surf beach drowning patterns for the period 1992–1998 using drowning statistics drawn from the Australian Bureau of Statistics (ABS). In this study, the majority of victims were males aged over 14 years. Williamson and Schmertmann also analysed drowning according to geographic location (p. 39) and found that the majority of victims resided on the coastline with most drownings occurring close to a coastal city.

Research data suggest that person-related characteristics can *mark* a swimmer as being at relatively greater risk of drowning at a surf beach (e.g., adult and male). Whether this is in fact the case, or whether it is merely a reflection of swimmer patterns, remains to be determined. Nevertheless, many causal risk factors can be deduced from safety tips provided by surf life-saving organisations. Table 15.2 includes examples of 10 safety tips drawn from beach safety websites in Australia, the United States, and Great Britain. Common messages include swimming under supervision, awareness of conditions, avoiding alcohol or drugs, and understanding the limits of one's swimming ability.

Research has an important role here by contributing to a better understanding through quantifying the contribution made by causal risk factors to a specified injury (e.g., drowning). For example, Lushine, Fletemeyer, and Dean (1999) reported an ambitious study of surf beach drowning that attempted to identify rip currents as a risk factor. The authors examined 148 surf beach drownings in Florida from 1979–1988 drawn from newspaper clippings. Ninety-eight (66.2 per cent) of beach drownings were classified as "rip current related" (p. 289) based on eyewitness reports, daily beach reports, or environmental conditions indicating that a rip current would be operating on the day and at the specific beach where the drowning event occurred. Similar findings have associated rip currents with drowning for Australian beaches (see Ballantyne, Carr, & Hughes, 2005). These studies suggest that public awareness campaigns highlighting the dangers posed by rip currents and the safety provided by supervised (patrolled) swimming location are key elements for drowning prevention. This awareness is particularly important for visitors and tourists unfamiliar with surf beach environments.

Smaller scale studies in Australia have examined the role of alcohol as a potential risk factor in surf beach drowning. Plueckhahn (1984) reported a prospective study examining the relationship between unintentional drowning and alcohol for persons aged 15 years and over from 1959–1983 in Geelong and the surrounding district within the Australian state of Victoria. Plueckhahn's sample comprised 122 males and 13 females where valid BAC values at the time of death could be established. The study examined a sub sample of 35 male victims who were drowned while either swimming or surfing. Many of these deaths presumably occurred at a surf beach, although the actual location of the drowning death was not reported. Sixteen (45.7 per cent) of this sub sample had consumed alcohol prior

Table 15.2 Selected safety tips listed by selected surf life saving organisations.

Surf Life Saving Australia (2005)	United States Life Saving Association (2005)	Surf Life Saving Association of Great Britain (2005)
1 Always swim or surf at places patrolled by surf lifesavers or lifeguards.	Swim near a lifeguard.	Always swim or surf at a beach patrolled by life savers or lifeguards.
2 Swim between the red and yellow flags. They mark the safest area to swim.	Learn to swim.	Swim between the red and yellow flags. They mark the safest areas to swim.
3 Always swim under supervision or with a friend.	Never swim alone.	Avoid swimming alone or unsupervised.
4 Read and obey the signs.	Don't fight the current.	Read the signs. If a beach is closed, don't swim there.
5 Don't swim directly after a meal.	Swim sober.	If you are unsure of the surf conditions ask a lifeguard or lifesaver.
6 Don't swim under the influence of drugs or alcohol.	Leash your board.	Don't swim directly after a meal.
7 If you are unsure of surf conditions, ask a lifesaver or lifeguard.	Don't float where you can't swim.	Don't swim under the influence of alcohol or drugs.
8 Never run and dive in the water. Even if you have checked before, conditions can change.	Life jackets = boating safety.	Don't run or dive in the water, always check the conditions, they might have changed.
9 If you get into trouble in the water, don't panic. Raise your arm for help, float and wait for assistance.	Don't dive head first. Protect you're neck.	If you get in trouble in the water, don't panic, raise one arm up and float until help arrives.
10 Float with a current or undertow. Stay calm. Don't try to swim against it. Signal for help and wait for assistance.	At home you're the lifeguard.	Float with a rip current or undertow, don't swim against it.

to swimming or surfing (BAC greater than 3.0 mmol/l); of these 16, 10 (62.5 per cent) were in the 30–64-year-old age group.

In conjunction with supervision, resuscitation is a demonstrated surf beach drowning prevention measure. For example, Manolios and Mackie (1988) examined resuscitation report forms for 262 cases of immersion completed by attending lifesavers across Australia from 1 July 1973–30 June 1983. Of the 262 cases, 100 (38.2 per cent) died as a result of the immersion. Of the 162 survivors, 72 (44.4 per cent) had breathing absent, pulse absent, or both vital signs absent at initial assessment. Fenner, Harrison, Williamson, and Williamson (1995) also analysed resuscitation success based on 171 resuscitation report forms, with the sample being limited to Queensland between 1973 and 1992. Outcome measures in the study were distance from patrolled area, victim's age, sex, facial colour on presentation, occurrence of vomiting, airway difficulties, and involvement of alcohol (identified by smell of breath). One hundred and nine cases were immersion victims of which 35 (32 percent) died. Based on statistical analysis, resuscitation was reported as more likely to be successful for the immersion subgroup were commenced on victims swimming in patrolled (supervised) areas during normal patrol hours.

Surf Beach Hazard Research

Water immersion injuries occur relatively frequently at surf beaches and obviously hold serious consequences for the victims. The nature of this injury gives rise to drowning as the predominant risk in surf beach settings. Even so, an array of other prevalent surf beach hazards (see Table 15.1) lead to various injuries of ranging severities. For example, Taylor, Ashby, and Winkel (2002) reported that Victorian hospital presentations resulting from injuries inflicted by sea creatures are infrequent but often severe events. Injuries reported in this study included lacerations, spikes, stings, and bites from creatures including stingrays, sharks, other fish species, jellyfish, and shell fish. Likewise in Victoria, Grenfell and Ross (1992) have reported a range of beach injuries presenting to surf clubs and local medical services. In this study, cuts to the feet from litter were a frequent injury cause.

Beach-related activities also carry a range of injury risks. Water-based surf sports, for example, have been shown to cause injuries ranging from open wounds to dislocations and fractures (Ashby & Morgan, 2004; Taylor, Bennet, Carter, Garewal, & Finch, 2004). Coastal rock fishing has also been demonstrated as a risky activity. Jones' (2003) study of Australian rock fishing fatalities indicated that victims did not expect to find themselves falling or being washed into the water, given that approximately one-quarter were non swimmers and none were wearing a personal flotation device (e.g., lifejacket).

A recent study by Staines, Morgan, and Ozanne-Smith (2005) reviewed available data related to tourism and visitor safety on Victorian beaches. Aside from common beach injuries mentioned above, this study documented a number of deaths at beach locations resulting from natural causes (e.g., heart failure following excercise) or intentional self-harm (e.g., suicide). In addition, crime was found to be common at beach locations. This included assault and robbery against the person and theft against property.

Taken together, the range of hazards found at surf beach locations may lead one to believe that beaches are very dangerous. Given the absence of more precise injury and risk exposure data, the actual risk posed by the gamut of hazards at surf beaches can neither be determined nor readily compared to the risks from hazards in other popular tourist and visitor locations. It is clear, however, that surf beaches continue to attract high use even though horrifying and debilitating incidents (such as shark attacks or shallow dive spinal injuries) can attract extensive media attention and/or result in high profile legal cases (see, for example, Charrington, 2002).

Surf Beach Management

In many countries, surf beaches are public land managed by government bodies (Morgan, 2003). Although this is the case for Australia, a raft of government, non-government, and private organisations form a complex web of stakeholders in coastal environments. These organisations influence public policy on a range of issues including coastal development and environmental management (James, 2000). More specifically, a range of dedicated organisations and services ensure the opportunity for safe surf beach experiences for the majority of visitors.

Australia's foremost surf beach safety organisation is Surf Life Saving Australia (SLSA). SLSA provides surveillance by volunteer and professional lifesavers for more than 300 beaches across Australia and each year carries out 11,000 rescues and 48,000 first-aid treatments (Surf Life Saving Australia, n. d.). In addition, SLSA provide surf safety training, education programmes, and research. The organisation enjoys a high public awareness of their services among Australians and has established specialised awareness campaigns promoting surf beach safety for international tourists (Wilks, Dawes, & Williamson, 2005). SLSA maintains operational links with land managers and emergency services to ensure a coordinated approach to beach safety management.

Conclusion

The surf beach is a dynamic environment that provides pleasure and enjoyment to millions of visitors and tourists around the world each day. Nevertheless, hazards found in beach environments can place beach patrons at risk of sustaining injuries ranging from minor cuts or bruising to death. Fortunately, surf life-saving organisations around the world are dedicated to preventing injury and reducing fatalities through education and awareness programmes and the provision of on site beach supervision. In this capacity, these organisations form an important component of the tourism industry in promoting beach safety and supervising beach goers.

References

Ashby, K., & Morgan, D. (2004). Surfing related injuries. *Hazard, 56,* 16–17.
Ballantyne, R., Carr, N., & Hughes, K. (2005). Between the flags: An assessment of domestic and international university students' knowledge of beach safety in Australia. *Tourism Management, 26,* 617–622.

Becker, S. (1997). Beach comfort index — a new approach to evaluate the thermal conditions of beach holiday resorts using a South African example. *GeoJournal, 44*(4), 297–307.

Bell, N. S., Amoroso, P. J., Yore, M. M., Senier, L., Williams, J. O., Smith, G. S., & Theriault, A. (2001). Alcohol and other risk factors for drowning among male active duty U.S. army soldiers. *Aviation, Space, and Environmental Medicine, 72*(12), 1086–1095.

Breitkreutz, G. (2000). Beachgoers willing to pay for safety: Study. *The Age* (July 4).

Bureau of Tourism Research. (1999a). *International visitors survey*. Canberra: Bureau of Tourism Research.

Bureau of Tourism Research. (1999b). *National visitors survey, 1998*. Canberra: Bureau of Tourism Research.

Charrington, B. (2002). Surf related litigation: Keeping your case between the flags. *Plaintiff, 53*, 6–14.

Deacon, R. T., & Kolstad, C. D. (2000). Valuing beach recreation lost in environmental accidents. *Journal of Water Resources Planning and Management, 126*(6), 374–381.

DeRuyck, A. M. C., Soares, A. G., & McLachlan, A. (1995). Factors influencing human beach choice on three South African beaches: A multivariate analysis. *GeoJournal, 36*(4), 345–352.

Dutton, G. (1985). *Sun, sea, surf and sand — the myth of the beach*. Melbourne: Oxford University Press.

Fenner, P. J., Harrison, S. L., Williamson, J. A., & Williamson, B. D. (1995). Success of surf lifesaving resuscitations in Queensland, 1973–1992. *Medical Journal of Australia, 163*(11–12), 580–583.

Freas, S. J. (1999). A history of drowning and resuscitation. In: J. R. Fletemeyer, & S. J. Freas (Eds), *Drowning: New perspectives on drowning intervention and prevention* (pp. 1–19). Boco Raton, FL: CRC Press LLC.

Gomez, D. A., Saywell, R. M., Zollinger, T. W., Schmit, T. M., & Donahue, R. (1992). Factors related to adult drowning. *Journal of Safety Research, 23*, 1–8.

Grenfell, R., & Ross, K. N. (1992). How dangerous is that visit to the beach? A pilot study of beach injuries. *Australian Family Physician, 21*(8), 1145–1148.

Huntsman, L. (2001). *Sand in our souls: The beach in Australian history*. Melbourne: Melbourne University Press.

James, R. J. (2000). The first step for the environmental management of Australian beaches: Establishing an effective policy framework. *Coastal Management, 28*, 149–160.

Jones, M. (2003). *Investigation into coronial files of rock fishing fatalities that have occurred in NSW between 1992 and 2000*. Sydney: NSW Water Safety Taskforce.

Kellogg's, & Newspoll. (2000). *National surf safety audit*. Sydney: Hausmann Communications.

Leatherman, S. P. (1997). Beach rating: A methodological approach. *Journal of Coastal Research, 13*(1), 253–258.

Lushine, J. B., Fletemeyer, J. R., & Dean, R. G. (1999). Towards a predictive model for rip currents and their impact on public safety with emphasis on physical, demographic, and cultural considerations. In: J. R. Fletemeyer, & S. J. Freas (Eds), *Drowning: New perspectives on drowning intervention and prevention* (pp. 281–303). Boco Raton, FL: CRC Press LLC.

MacLeod, M., Silva, C. P. D., & Cooper, J. A. G. (2002). A comparative study of the perception and value of beaches in rural Ireland and Portugal: Implications for coastal zone management. *Journal of Coastal Research, 18*(1), 14–24.

Manolios, N., & Mackie, I. (1988). Drowning and near-drowning on Australia beaches patrolled by life-savers: A 10-year study, 1973–1983. *Medical Journal of Australia, 148*, 165–167, 170–171.

Meerman, R. (2002). *Shark nets*. ABC website. Retrieved 8/3/2002, from http://www.abc.net.au/science/slab/sharknets/.

Mihalic, T. (2002). The European Blue Flag campaign for beaches in Slovenia: A programme for raising environmental awareness. In: Harris, R., Griffin, T., & Williams, P. (Eds), *Sustainable tourism: A global perspective*. Great Britain: Butterworth-Heinemann.

Morgan, D. (2003). Public lands. In: J. M. Jenkins, & J. J. Pigram (Eds), *Encyclopedia of leisure and outdoor recreation* (pp. 397–398). London: Routledge.

Morgan, R. (1999a). A novel, user-based rating system for tourist beaches. *Tourism Management, 20*, 393–410.

Morgan, R. (1999b). Preferences and priorities of recreational beach users in Wales, UK. *Journal of Coastal Research, 15*(3), 653–667.

Morgan, R., Gatell, E., Junyent, R., Micallef, A., Ozhan, E., & Williams, A. T. (2000). An improved user-based beach climate index. *Journal of Coastal Conservation, 6*, 41–50.

Nelson, C., & Botterill, D. (2002). Evaluating the contribution of beach quality awards to the local tourism industry in Wales — the Green Coast Award. *Ocean and Coastal Management, 45*, 157–170.

Nelson, C., Botterill, D., & Williams, A. (2000). The beach as leisure resource: Measuring user perceptions of beach debris pollution. *World Leisure and Recreation, 42*(1), 38–43.

Ozanne-Smith, J., & Wigglesworth, E. (2002). Childhood drowning prevention [Summary]. *Proceedings of the world congress on drowning*, 33. The Netherlands, Stichting Foundation.

Pendleton, L. (2001). Managing beach amenities to reduce exposure to coastal hazards: Storm water pollution. *Coastal Management, 29*, 239–252.

Plueckhahn, V. D. (1984). Alcohol and accidental drowning. *Medical Journal of Australian, 141*(1), 22–25.

Pratt, K., & Borland, R. (1994). Predictors of sun protection among adolescents at the beach. *Australian Psychologist, 29*(2), 135–139.

Raban, J. (1992). *The Oxford book of the sea*. Oxford: Oxford University Press.

Short, A. D. (1993). *Beaches of New South Wales coast: A guide to their nature, characteristics, surf and safety*. Sydney: Australian Beach Safety and Management Program.

Short, A. D. (1999). Beaches. In: A. D. Short (Ed.), *Handbook of beach and shoreface morphodynamics* (pp. 3–20). West Sussex: Wiley.

Short, A. D. (2002). Beach hazards and risk assessment. Paper presented at the world congress on drowning, Amsterdam, 27 June.

Short, A. D., & Hogan, C. L. (1995). Rip currents and beach hazards: Their impact on public safety and implications for coastal management. *Journal of Coastal Research*, Special Issue No. 12, 197–209.

Staines, C., Morgan, D., & Ozanne-Smith, J. (2005). Threats to tourist and visitor safety at beaches in Victoria. *Tourism in Marine Environments, 1*(2), 97–104.

Steensberg, J. (1998). Epidemiology of accidental drowning in Denmark 1989–1993. *Accident Analysis and Prevention, 30*(6), 755–762.

Surf Life Saving Australia (2005) *Surf and beach safety*. Website. Retrieved 24 March 2005 from http://www.slsa.asn.au/doc_display.asp?document_id=103.

Surf Life Saving Australia (n.d.) *Service profile* (Pamplet). Sydney: Surf Life saving Australia.

Surf Life Saving Association of Great Britain (2005) *Beach Safety*. Website. [Retrived 24 March 2005 from http://www.surflifesavers.org.uk/safetyrescue.htm.]

Taylor, D. McD., Ashby, K., & Winkel, K. D. (2002). An analysis of marine animal injuries presenting to emergency departments in Victoria, Australia. *Wilderness and Environmental Medicine, 13*, 106–112.

Taylor, D. McD., Bennet, D., Carter, M., Garewal, D., & Finch, C. F. (2004). Acute injury and chronic disability resulting from surfboard riding. *Journal of Science and Medicine in Sport, 7*(4), 429–437.

Tower, J., & Kain, A. (1993). *Victorian coastal recreation study*. Melbourne: Sport and Recreation Victoria and Surf Life Saving Victoria.

TQA Research. (2000). *Market research report: Victorian coastal and marine environment community attitudes and behaviour (Wave 2) — Executive summary*. Melbourne: Department of Natural Resources and Environment.

United States Lifesaving Association. (2002). *The Official Website of the United States Lifesaving Association.* Website. [Retrived 15 August 2003 from http://www.usla.org/index.shtml.]

United States Lifesaving Association. (2005). *USLA's top ten (safety) tips.* Website. [Retrieved 25 March 2005 from http://www.usla.org/index.shtml.]

Waters, W., & Ellis, B. (2003). Water safety signage: Trails, evaluation, and lessons learnt. *Proceedings of the 2003 water safety conference*, Sydney: Australian Water safety Council (pp. 177–181).

Waverly Library. (2001). *Bondi's black Sunday.* Website. [Retrieved 16 July 2001, from http://www.waverly.nsw.gov/Library/about/historical/black.htm.]

Wearing, S. (2003). Beach. In: J. M. Jenkins, & J. J. Pigram (Eds), *Encyclopedia of leisure and outdoor recreation* (pp. 28–29). London: Routledge.

Wilks, J., Dawes, P., & Williamson, B. (2005). Patrol smart 7/52: Queensland's integrated surf life saving program. *Australian Journal of Emergency Management, 20*(1), 38–45.

Williams, A. T., Winiarski-Jones, T. C., Davies, P., & Curr, R. (1992). Psychological profile of the beach/dune user in South Wales, U.K. *Shore and Beach, 60*(2), 26–30.

Williamson, A., & Schmertmann, M. (2000). *Analysis of drowning in Australia and pilot analysis of near-drowning in New South Wales.* Sydney: NSW Injury Risk Management Research Centre, University of New South Wales for the Australian Water Safety Council.

Wintemute, G. J., Teret, S. P., Kraus, J. F., & Wright, M. (1990). Alcohol and drowning: An analysis of contributing factors and a discussion of criteria for case selection. *Accident Analysis and Prevention, 22*(3), 291–296.

Wright, L. D., & Short, A. D. (1984). Morphodynamic variability of surf zones and beaches: A synthesis. *Marine Geology, 56*, 93–118.

PART 4

GOVERNMENT AND INDUSTRY INITIATIVES

Chapter 16

The World Tourism Organization Safety and Security Program[1]

Jeff Wilks and Henryk Handszuh

Introduction

As the leading international body in the field of tourism, the World Tourism Organization (WTO) is the United Nation's specialized agency entrusted with its promotion and development. The WTO serves as a global forum for tourism policy issues and as a practical source of tourism know-how. Membership currently consists of 145 countries, 7 territories and around 300 Affiliate Members representing the private sector, education institutions, tourism associations and local tourism authorities (www.world-tourism.org).

   Since its establishment, safety and security has been a central pillar of WTO activities. Members and non-Members have approached the Secretary-General of WTO and its Secretariat on many occasions requesting assistance to solve tourism safety and security problems, particularly:

- When countries, destinations or sub-sectors of the tourism industry experience chronic safety and security problems or are victims of continuous bad image due to past safety and security incidents.
- At times of crises, which occur in countries from time to time, such as epidemics, social unrest, sudden increases in common delinquency and crime, terrorism, natural and man-made disasters and other disasters affecting tourism.
- When foreign governments issue recommendations or prohibitions advising their citizens to avoid certain destinations considered dangerous or unsafe.

---

[1] This chapter includes material developed by Jeff Wilks as a Consultant on Tourism Safety and Security to the World Tourism Organization.

Over the years WTO has undertaken a wide range of activities on safety and security issues. The following list highlights some of these key activities:

1989 Decision of the Executive Council to increase activities in safety and security
1991 *Recommended Measures for Tourism Safety* (WTO General Assembly resolution, A/RES/284(IX), Buenos Aires, Argentina)
1991 *Travelers' Health Abroad* (booklet)
1991 *Creating Tourism Opportunities for Handicapped People in the Nineties* (GA resolution, A/RES/284 (IX))
1993 *Health Information and Formalities in International Travel* (GA resolution A/RES/ 310(X), Bali, Indonesia)
1993 *Sustainable Tourism Development: A Guide for Local Planners* (book)
1994 Experts Meeting on Tourist Safety and Security
1996 *Tourist Safety and Security: Practical Measures for Destinations* (book, first edition)
1997 Regional seminars for Africa and Europe (Addis Ababa and Warsaw)
1997 *Tourist Safety and Security: Practical Measures for Destinations* (book, second edition in French and Spanish)
1998 ESCAP seminar (Phuket); Russia Far East seminar (Vladivostok); Central American course on hotel security and tourist police (Santo Domingo)
1998 Mediterranean and Middle East Food Safety Conference
1999 ECOWAS seminar (Cotonou); Middle East seminar (Amman)
1999 Provisions on tourist safety and security in the Global Code of Ethics for Tourism (GA resolution A/RES/406(XIII), Santiago, Chile, 27 September–1 October 1999), endorsed by resolution A/RES/56/212 of the United Nations (21 December 2001) (http://www.un.org/documents/ecosoc/docs/2001/e2001-61.pdf)
2001 September 11th Tourism Recovery Committee Meeting at World Travel Market in London (report and strategy)
2002 Tourist Safety and Security seminar at FITUR (International Tourism Fair, Madrid)
2002 September 11th Tourism Recovery Committee Meetings (Berlin and London)
2002 Tourism Recovery Committee for the Mediterranean Region (2 meetings and report)
2003 September 11th Tourism Recovery Committee Meetings (Berlin and Beijing)
2003 SARS monitoring (survey and Executive Council)
2003 WTO Crisis Summit, Manila, Philippines
2003 *Crisis Guidelines for the Tourism* Industry (booklet)
2004 *Tourism Risk Management for the Asia Pacific Region* (book, WTO joint sponsor)
2004 Three pilot missions to Cameroon, Nigeria and Seychelles
2004 Presentation of the SAFE project at the 35th session of ICAO (www.world-tourism.org)
2004 "Travel Advisories" discussed with ICAO (Facilitation Division), regional commissions (Middle East, Africa) and the Executive Council (India, Brazil) leading to formulating *Recommendations for Responsible Travel Advisories*
2005 Emergency Task Force on the Consequences of the Tsunami on the Tourism Sector, Phuket, Thailand (meeting and Action Plan)
2005 Second meeting of the WTO Emergency Task Force at ITB in Berlin.

The WTO's involvement in the area of safety and security, including health, has been traditionally led by the Quality and Trade in Tourism program. While acknowledging the significant contribution of other programmes in the organization, especially the Education Council, the Business Council, the Regional Commissions and direct global leadership from the Secretary-General, this chapter mainly provides an overview of tourism safety and security from a quality perspective. This is in keeping with the theme of the book. There are two key WTO initiatives in this area:

1. Recommended measures for tourism safety.
2. The safety and security network and task force for tourism.

Recommended Measures for Tourism Safety (Recommended Measures)

As resolution A/RES/284(IX) adopted by the General Assembly at its ninth session (Buenos Aires, Argentina, 30 September–4 October 1991), the recommended measures are designed to guide WTO Members in ensuring safety of international tourists and excursionists (same-day visitors) in particular, although it is understood that such measures equally benefit national tourists and other users of tourist facilities. Because the recommended measures are essentially the 'foundation' of the WTO tourism safety and security program it is worth expanding a little on their detail, as a number of elements have subsequently been developed as independent initiatives.

For the purpose of the recommended measures the term 'international tourist', hereafter just referred to as a 'tourist', means a person:

- who travels to a country other than that in which they usually reside;
- whose main purpose of travel is a tourist visit or stay not exceeding 1 year;
- who does not engage in remunerated activity in the country visited; and
- who, at the end of the visit or stay leaves the country visited, either to return to the country where they usually reside or to travel to another country (WTO, 1991).

The term 'tourist' here does not include persons who, after entering the country for a tourist visit or stay seek to prolong their length of visit or stay, so as to establish residence and/or to engage in a remunerated activity there.

In order to be very clear about what was and what was not intended in the recommended measures the WTO also provided that:

- The recommended measures should not be interpreted to benefit persons who abuse their tourist status, particularly by committing serious criminal offences, such as attempts against the physical security of other persons, participation in organized crime, terrorist activities, drug trafficking or theft of cultural property.
- Nothing in the recommended measures should be interpreted as putting at a disadvantage or restricting the interests and rights to security and protection of internal tourists, the suppliers of tourism services or the host communities of tourists.
- No provision of the recommended measures should be interpreted in a manner that limits or invalidates national legislation and international agreements regarding the rights,

privileges and duties of foreigners, the prevention of crime and the treatment of offenders, including tourists accused of crime or imprisoned in foreign countries.

Preventive Measures

The recommended measures then propose that every State should assess and monitor the scope and degree of threat to the life and health, property and economic interests of tourists within its territory and should develop a national policy on tourism safety commensurate with the prevention of tourist risks.

Specifically, every State should undertake the necessary measures to:

- identify potential tourist risks in specific types of travel, specific tourism receiving sectors and specific tourism sites; safeguard tourist health; suppress illicit drug abuse and trafficking relating to tourism;
- cooperate in the event of unlawful acts against the safety of tourism facilities; and
- undertake to cooperate in ensuring that a tourist who is a victim of an unlawful act against the safety of tourism facilities, including any means of tourist transport, receives all the necessary assistance and compensation for damages, which such acts may entail. This recommended measure takes due account of the fact that a number of States are already a party to relevant international instruments providing for such assistance, as those adopted under the auspices of the International Civil Aviation Organization (ICAO) and the International Maritime Organization (IMO).

The WTO General Assembly Resolution Adopting the 'Recommended Measures'

For those readers unfamiliar with the language and protocols adopted by the United Nations, the following resolution may seem very formal. However, the coverage and detail in the resolution are very worthwhile reporting since they established the context (to use the risk management terminology from Chapter 1) for tourist safety and security programs in many countries over the following decade.

Drawing inspiration from the Manila Declaration on World Tourism (1980), the Acapulco Document (1982), the Tourism Bill of Rights and Tourist Code (Sofia, 1985) and The Hague Declaration on Tourism (1989):

- aware that safety is a basic need in all spheres of human activity, including tourism;
- considering that ensuring tourism safety arises from the traditional notion of hospitality, which is shared by all peoples;
- solemnly affirming that safe tourism for all contributes to accomplishing the social and cultural objectives of tourism, and serves international understanding, confidence, peace and universal respect for, and observance of, all human rights and freedoms;
- convinced that safety of tourism should be enhanced in tourism planning and promotion;
- further convinced that contemporary mass tourism requires the definition of a set of basic measures, which should be commonly followed so as to make tourism development more

stable and harmonious in the interest of all those who travel, those who supply tourism services and the populations of the host communities;
* agreeing that tourists are particularly vulnerable to hazards on their trips abroad and that common measures for tourism safety are mutually beneficial to all countries, both tourism receiving and generating ones;
* desirous that such measures generate international cooperation and solidarity with a view, in particular, to assisting less developed countries in attaining adequate tourism safety standards; and
* noting the need for periodical review of such measures.

   Adopts the *Recommended Measures for Tourism Safety* set forth in the Annex to this Resolution and invites the States to apply them in accordance with the procedures prescribed in the legislation and regulations of their own countries.

WTO's Global Code of Ethics for Tourism

The second critical set of guidelines for the WTO tourist safety and security program comes from the Global Code of Ethics for Tourism, adopted at the WTO General Assembly in Santiago, Chile in 1999 (www.world-tourism.org/code_ethics/eng.html). According to the resolution introducing the Code, it should "guide tourism development … and serve as a frame of reference for the different stakeholders in the tourism sector (p. 2)". The relevant provisions consider the security and safety of host populations and visitors alike. Here are some of the most important points:

   Article 1 of the Code advocates tourism's contribution to peace and understanding among nations and between hosts and visitors.

   Article 2 explains that tourism should be a vehicle for individual and collective fulfillment, respecting equality of men and women, promoting human rights, and the rights of the most vulnerable groups in society. It should not be used to exploit human beings in any form, and in particular the sexual exploitation of children should be battled vigorously.

   Article 3 considers the sustainability of tourism and encourages the adoption of policies to minimize damage to the environment, society and culture and to enhance tourism's beneficial impacts on industry and the local economy.

   Article 4 highlights the need to control the cultural and social impacts of tourism development, recognizing that tourism is both a user of the cultural heritage of mankind and a contributor to its enhancement.

   Article 5 states that tourism should be a beneficial activity for host countries and communities, with equitable participation in the economic, social and cultural benefits that it generates, in particular direct and indirect employment.

Article 6 considers the obligations of stakeholders in the development of tourism, the security, health and food safety protection of tourists, insurance and compensation in cases of difficulty and the contribution of tourism professionals to the cultural and social fulfillment of tourists. It also requires governments to inform their citizens of the dangers associated with traveling abroad and the press to provide accurate and honest information, particularly in times of crisis.

Article 7 declares that tourism must be a right for all the world's inhabitants and highlights social tourism as a particular form of tourism that should be encouraged.

Article 8 relates the liberty of tourist movement to article 13 of the Universal Declaration of Human Rights and states that tourists should be allowed to travel without being subject to discrimination or excessive formalities. Tourist rights should include prompt and easy access to local administrative, legal and health services, immediate and easy contact with consular representatives of their countries and the same data protection as citizens of the country visited.

Article 9 advocates the rights of workers and entrepreneurs in the tourism industry including social protection, job security and initial and continuous training.

Essentially, the WTO Global Code of Ethics provides the philosophical principles guiding the sustainable and responsible development of world tourism. It also specifically identifies host and guest responsibilities for safety and security. For example, taking one item from Article 2, that "the sexual exploitation of children should be battled vigorously", WTO has established a child prostitution and tourism task force and worked tirelessly with other international agencies in this area (see the WTO Statement on the Prevention of Organized Sex Tourism, available on the WTO website).

Safety and Security at a National Level

The *Recommended Measures for Tourism Safety* are specifically directed to Member States, so it is at the national government level that action on tourism safety and security needs to occur. Indeed, the WTO recognizes the importance of partnerships for this to be successful (WTO, 1997; Beatson, 1997) and suggests that the way forward is through formation of a National Tourism Council. The Council should then organize a National Safety and Security Committee. In many countries, coordination of safety, and particularly security activities, is only carried out among government agencies. However, in tourism it makes sense to form a mixed-sector council with government and industry participants, since many of the actions can and should be implemented by the private sector (Handszuh,

1997). Government agencies and tourism industry sectors to consider for membership on the National Safety and Security Committee include:

- National tourism administration (NTA)/tourist board
- National police
- Immigration
- Judiciary
- Customs
- Transportation
- Health
- Foreign affairs
- Civil defence
- Airlines and transportation company associations
- Hotel associations
- Tour operators' associations
- Travel agents' associations
- Other travel and tourism representatives
- Consumer groups
- Retail trade organizations
- Tourism safety and security oriented research and documentation centres.

National Tourism Safety and Security Plan

The National Tourism Safety and Security Plan is a logical consequence of the development of a national committee and subsequent policy on this subject. WTO suggests that such a plan should address the following main areas:

- Identification of potential tourist risks according to types of travel, affected tourism sectors and locations.
- Detection and prevention of offences against tourists.
- Protection of tourists and residents from illicit drug trafficking.
- Protection of tourist sites and facilities against unlawful interference.
- Establishment of guidelines for operators of tourist facilities in the event of unlawful interference.
- Responsibilities for dealing with the press and other media, at home and abroad.
- Information to be provided to the international travel trade on safety and security issues.
- Organization of crisis management in the event of a natural disaster or other emergency.
- Adoption of safety standards and practices in tourist facilities and sites with reference to fire protection, theft, sanitary and health requirements.
- Development of liability rules in tourist establishments.
- Safety and security aspects of licensing for accommodation establishments, restaurants, taxi companies and tour guides.
- Provision of appropriate documentation and information on tourist safety to the public, for both outgoing and incoming travellers.

- Development of national policies with regard to tourist health, including reporting systems on health problems of tourists.
- Development of tourist insurance and travel assistance insurance.
- Promotion, collection and dissemination of reliable research statistics on crimes against travellers.

Implementation of a safety and security plan will, in turn, be enhanced by setting up a database of model programmes, useful practices and reliable data on problems affecting tourists. It is in this area of strategic support that the WTO has perhaps made its most significant contribution to tourism safety and security. Recognizing that no one destination has in place all the proposed measures and systems of a National Tourism Safety and Security Program (Wilks, 2003), the WTO has developed a Safety and Security Network and Task Force for Tourism to assist its members.

The Safety and Security Network and Task Force for Tourism

In responding to requests for assistance from member countries, and in the light of incidents around the world, the WTO examined the feasibility of developing an international safety and security network (Handszuh, 1999). It was initiated in July 2002 and currently features basic safety and security information and contact points on some 60 Full (States) and Associate Members (territories), as well as safety and security links. It is envisaged that this initiative would bring together organizations and experts from around the world who are concerned with safety and security, provide a forum for the exchange of ideas, create an information link to all organizations in the network, encourage and undertake research on burning issues and supply services to network beneficiaries and interested stakeholders.

The project was met with great interest at meetings organized by other professional bodies (e.g. Aviation Security — AvSec, Minneapolis, 1998 and Healthy Tourism Conferences — Simrishamn, Sweden, 1998 and 1999). It was also presented to the *Think Tank on Safety and Security* organized by the International Hotel and Restaurant Association in Orlando, USA, in 1998. It continues to enjoy renewed interest in the light of current safety and security events affecting tourism. Accordingly, this topic features in the WTO's current work programme as "tourist safety and security information-consultation service" and "tourist safety, security and facilitation task force" and is being gradually implemented. The following framework for the Network, as described on the WTO website, is presented in future tense to reflect the gradual implementation process.

Network Scope and Activities

The virtual network organization or coalition will be based on voluntary participation. Each party's contribution to the network activity will be clearly defined and limited to its recognized competence in the field concerned. Importantly, the network and resulting services will not overlap or compete with existing services and activities, but will rather provide the following advantages:

- Transparency with regard to the activities of existing organizations in this field. As members of the network, they will be recognized by user groups, referred to and contacted when the need for their information, services or actions arises. They will also share their output (information, expertise) with other members in the network.
- The generation of additional services to users because of network synergy.
- The systematization and streamlining of work in the safety and security area.
- A practical tool for tourism policymakers and professionals to discuss and solve current safety and security problems.
- Privileged access for tourism policymakers and professionals to a comprehensive and authoritative body of knowledge on safety and security in tourism.
- The mobilization of the tourism sector to meet safety and security standards and to cooperate with other sectors.
- The creation of priority links between network members for expediency, professional accuracy and objectivity.
- Help in generating funds and sponsorships for research and fieldwork.

The scope of the network's activities is based on the comprehensive definition of tourism and tourism characteristic activities as defined by the WTO and the United Nations Statistical Commission (http://www.world-tourism.org/statistics/tsa_project/basic_references/index-en.htm).

The issues under review by the network will be those featured in the *Recommended Measures for Tourism Safety*.

A major task for the proposed network going forward will be to define a body of safety and security indicators and standards for tourism destinations as benchmarks for 'safe destinations'. It was tested in 2004 in the WTO pilot safety and security missions mentioned above. The network will offer technical assistance to destinations to help them identify the causes of safety and security problems (chronic and current), propose curative measures and mobilize sources to achieve improvements. An early detection system will also be implemented to uncover symptoms of new, emerging and re-emerging diseases and outbreaks. This system would also cover impending natural disasters and identify tourism channels used for drug trafficking, and other crimes such as the sexual exploitation of children. A consultation system will be designed to allow destinations that have had travel warnings issued against them by tourist-generating countries to be at least informed before the caution is made public so that they could act positively to 'undo' the causes of the warnings. A mechanism will be established to ensure that during critical safety and security situations, information and advice is made available and warnings issued to industry and the public. This would in fact bring together all the sources of information that are already provided by the many organizations working in the field and present them in a coherent and comprehensive way. Finally, the network will identify issues for research and seek funding.

The network will work through an executive facility or secretariat. Depending on the resources available, it could be physically located in the WTO Secretariat in Madrid. The executive facility will operate its own website. Access to the main pages of the site would be open to the general public and certain areas will be available by means of passwords to privileged network members. Contributing network members would be free to amend/update their information content on the web. Finally, the Task Force, or various task forces, to result from the network will be called upon by the WTO to provide specific public and customized services to the network beneficiaries.

While much of the network development is still being established, recent 'shocks' to the global tourism industry have accelerated some processes. For example, WTO's *Crisis Guidelines for the Tourism Industry* was released in 2003 at the WTO Crisis Summit in Manila. It contains a list of Crisis Management Experts identified by the WTO. Emergency Task Forces have also been quickly formed in response to the terrorist attacks of 11 September 2001 and the more recent tsunami crisis. So, some of the network activities are already in progress. However, one area that is progressing in a more ordered and systematic manner is the collection of core national tourism safety and security information from Member States.

National Tourist Safety and Security Sheets

As the first stage in generally opening up its safety and security network for tourism, the WTO has made available on its website the national data sheets of 61 Member States. Table 16.1 lists the participants as at March 2005. The sheets include basic facts on safety and security for tourism in countries, territories and other tourist destinations. The scope of the information covered varies from sheet to sheet and may undergo constant updates and modifications, in particular by including additional data. The number of national sheets may also vary over time.

Most national sheets indicate the person who has been designated by the NTA as the NTA Focal Point to respond to queries or otherwise guide inquirers and network users on issues relating to safety and security in tourism in their country, territory or destination. In asking for the designation of the NTA Focal Point, the WTO Secretariat has proposed some of their tasks and duties to be as follows:

- To keep on record basic facts on tourist safety and security in their country or territory (rules and regulations, identification of tourist risks, travel warnings, research and publications on the tourist safety and security status and incidents, relevant statistics, experts, etc.).
- To be familiar with facilities and institutions, both public and private, assisting international visitors and outgoing nationals in safety and security problems (police, first-aid, insurance, travel assistance, consulates, etc.).
- To establish and maintain a working relationship with other government departments competent in tourist safety and security matters (interior, health, consumer affairs, judiciary, foreign affairs, civil aviation, civil defence, etc.);
- To establish and maintain a working relationship with safety and security focal points at national tourism industry organizations.
- To be the NTA spokesman before the media and general public on national tourist safety and security issues.

Table 16.1: Member States providing National Tourist Safety and Security Sheets on the WTO website (as at 24 March 2005).

Angola	Lao P.D.R
Argentina	Lebanon
Austria	Macau
Bolivia	Madagascar
Brazil	Malaysia
Bulgaria	Malta
Burkina Faso	Mauritius
Cameroon	Mexico
Chad	Namibia
China	Nigeria
Colombia	Pakistan
Congo	Palestine
Côte D'ivoire	Paraguay
Croatia	Peru
Cuba	Philippines
Cyprus	Portugal
Czech Rep.	Rep. of Korea
Dominican Rep.	Romania
Ethiopia	Serbia and Montenegro
Finland	Seychelles
French Polynesia	Sierra Leone
Gabon	Slovak Republic
Georgia	Slovenia
Guatemala	Solomon Islands
Honduras	South Africa
Hungary	Swaziland
Israel	Togo
Italy	Tunisia
Jamaica	Turkey
Kazakhstan	Vietnam
Kyrgyzstan	

Information in the national sheets is provided under the responsibility of the NTA concerned or its Focal Point. The WTO Secretariat responsibility is limited to the proper processing and presentation of this information. Its publication on the WTO website is not to be construed as an expression of opinion or endorsement by the WTO or its Secretariat with respect to the tourist safety and security status of the countries, territories and other destinations concerned, but as a statement of objective facts with a view to achieving more transparency in this area and the current 61 members contributing to this initiative should be congratulated for their participation.

Strategic Partnerships

Strategic partnerships with other international organizations have also provided new opportunities for the WTO. For example, as reported on the Quality and Trade in Tourism webpage, WTO has joined the Board of Simplifying Passenger Travel (SPT), a joint initiative by various air transport-related organizations aimed at ensuring that essential increases in security are matched by parallel actions to improve travel comfort for passengers (www.simplifying-travel.org). The SPT's objective is to promote the use of biometrics and other new technologies and to share information among service providers, thus enabling controls and services to be carried out more efficiently. The ultimate goal is a streamlined system built around a passport/visa-linked passenger travel card that will facilitate all stages of a journey from initial reservation to ground transfer at the final destination.

SAFE — WTO Strategy on Security and Facilitation Enhancement

Another initiative currently reported on the Quality and Trade in Tourism webpage is that of the SAFE strategy, which was presented at the 35th Session of the Assembly — ICAO, Montreal, 28 September–8 October, 2004. While this particular presentation focused on aviation security and tourism, the four key components of the strategy are clearly applicable across all areas of tourism. The four components are:

- *Establishing benchmarks* with the aim of ensuring the cohesion, currency and dissemination of WTO safety/security/facilitation parameters and guidance.
- *Building capacity* with a goal of enabling best safety/security/facilitation practice worldwide, WTO will:

  (a) Develop dedicated educational/training modules aimed at achievement of the Benchmarks by States and industry; and
  (b) In partnership with other institutions, develop and obtain funding for projects and equipment to enable States and industry to achieve the Benchmarks.

- *Assessing performance and identifying remedial projects* with a goal of ensuring that best facilitated safety/security/facilitation practice is in place worldwide, WTO is assembling a group of experts to carry out audits in States against the Benchmarks, focusing on the Least Developed Countries.
- *Building confidence*, an important and integral component of SAFE is an ongoing promotional campaign and use of the WTO website (www.world-tourism.org) with the aim of enhancing confidence of the public, tourism entities and investors in facilitated security of tourist destinations.

What the SAFE initiative captures is an acknowledgment of the range of expertise that already exists within the WTO, and that is now required to develop international best practice. The frameworks for best practice have been in place since the *Recommended Measures* in 1991, but the difficulty has always been providing the specialist assistance to help tourism industry members to meet quality standards. SAFE will require coordination and integration by various WTO programmes that are already contributing in different ways to the area of tourism safety and security. For example, in 'building capacity' the Education Council has particular expertise in developing training programmes and providing quality education certification through the Themis Foundation. Most recently the Education Council released an Action Plan for Tsunami Recovery with seven distinct initiatives aimed at strengthening human resource capacity and creating new tourism products and strategies for areas affected by the tsunami. A Think Tank Meeting on Security Issues in Tourism, followed by a conference on the topic, is planned for mid-2005.

In terms of 'building confidence', considered an integral component of SAFE, the WTO Market Intelligence and Promotion Program has considerable expertise in crisis work through managing the Tourism Recovery Committee's high profile role over 2 years, and as a key support for the personal leadership provided by the Secretary-General across a number of international crisis responses.

Quality in Tourism

While the development and implementation of the WTO Safety and Security Network, and extension initiatives such as SAFE will take some time, it is encouraging to see tourism legitimizing health, safety and security as core elements of quality service. The current recognition and appreciation of this area, long before it became topical or even good business practice, is largely due to the long-term efforts of the WTO. In its current work programme WTO is guided by the understanding of quality in tourism as:

> ... the result of a process which implies the satisfaction of all the legitimate product and service needs, requirements and expectations of the consumer, at an acceptable price, in conformity with mutually accepted contractual conditions and the underlying quality determinants such as safety and security, hygiene, accessibility, transparency, authenticity and harmony of the tourism activity concerned with its human and natural environment [Defined and modified by the WTO Quality Support Committee at its Sixth Meeting (Varadero, Cuba, 9–10 May 2003)].

Specifically in relation to the Safety and Security element, the Quality definition states:

> A tourism product or service cannot represent danger to life, damage to health and other vital interests and integrity of the consumer (even if we talk about "adventure tourism"). Safety and security standards are normally established by law (e.g. by fire prevention regulations) and should be considered as quality standards *per se* (www.world-tourism.org/quality/E/main.htm).

In Chapter 1, a number of current issues were identified for tourist health, safety and security. One of these was the critical importance of having genuine partnerships in place. In revisiting the WTO Recommended Measures from 1991 it is enlightening to note that under the heading of International Cooperation all of our current 'new millennium' issues had already been captured. Specifically, the Recommended Measures provide (www.world-tourism.org/quality/E/main.htm):

> Having due regard to national legislation and international agreements and arrangements pertaining to safety, crime prevention, and the treatment of offenders and to the general procedures established in countries to deal with emergencies, States should undertake to cooperate, on a bilateral and multilateral basis, and, if possible, within the already existing legal framework, in the areas of:
>
> (a) Exchange of information on tourism safety
> (b) International compatibility of safety standards and practices in tourism facilities and sites
> (c) Training of staff for tourism safety
> (d) Travel assistance, tourist insurance and civil liabilities
> (e) Consumer protection of tourists
> (f) Assistance to tourists in emergencies
> (g) Tourist health
> (h) Suppression of illicit drug abuse and trafficking relating to tourism.

To some readers this consistency of purpose over more than a decade may come as no surprise from a United Nations specialized agency. However, during that time there have been huge changes in tourism and the global economies it serves. In terms of providing safe experiences for visitors, the main concern of this book, the consistency of focus and the importance assigned to safety and security by the WTO underline its established role as the leading international organization in the field of tourism.

Conclusions

The WTO has already provided the detailed frameworks for visitor safety and security to be achieved, and to some extent the operational mechanisms required by its 145 member countries. Current initiatives aim to further refine benchmarks so that definitive criteria for a 'safe destination' will be available. Through education, training, enforcement and genuine partnerships with other concerned stakeholders there will be no legitimate reason for tourism groups in the future not to include visitor health, safety and security as a key element in quality service.

References

Beatson, M. (1997). A partnership approach to the management and regulation of risk. Paper presented to the WTO European Seminar on Tourist Safety and Security, Warsaw, 11–12 September.
Handszuh, H. (1997). Tourism facilitation and security councils. Paper presented at the Seminar on Safety and Security for African Quality Tourism, Addis Ababa, Ethiopia, 24–25 April.

Handszuh, H. (1999). Safety and security in tourism: The problem of responsibilities. Paper presented at the Seminar on Safety and Security of Persons and Goods in the Tourism Sector, Cotonou, Benin, 22–24 March.

Wilks, J. (2003). Safety and security for destinations: WTO case studies. In: J. Wilks, & S.J. Page, (Eds), *Managing tourist health and safety in the new millennium* (pp. 127–139). Oxford: Pergamon.

World Tourism Organization (WTO). (1991). *Recommended measures for tourism safety*. Madrid: WTO.

World Tourism Organization (WTO). (1997). *Tourist safety and security: Practical measures for destinations* (2nd ed.). Madrid: WTO.

Chapter 17

Developing Tourism Safety and Security in the Kingdom of Saudi Arabia[1]

Jeff Wilks and Faisal Al-Mubarak

Introduction

The Council of Ministers Resolution No 9 dated 19/1/1421 H (14 April 2000 G) established the Supreme Commission for Tourism (SCT) in the Kingdom of Saudi Arabia. The Commission's brief is to stimulate the development of tourism in a controlled and sustainable manner, always recognising that Saudi Arabia has a unique culture and considerable natural and heritage attractions that must be protected.

A comprehensive Sustainable Tourism Development Plan has been developed (SCT, 2002a,b), including a 20-year Tourism Master Plan and a 5-year Action Plan (2003–2007). The SCT Master Plan prioritises the following target markets:

- Saudi domestic leisure tourism;
- Gulf Cooperative Council (GCC) and neighbouring Arab country visitors;
- international Umrah;[2]
- the Muslim community worldwide; and
- specialised foreign niche markets based on activities such as eco-tourism, heritage and cultural tourism.

---

[1] This chapter draws on material developed by Jeff Wilks as a Consultant on Tourism Safety and Security to the Supreme Commission for Tourism.

[2] Hajj is the once-in-a-lifetime obligatory pilgrimage of Muslims to Makkah, Saudi Arabia during Dhul Hijjah (month for Hajj). Hajj, the Fifth Pillar of Islam, is absolutely required of all capable Muslims. Umrah, when performed independent of Hajj, is the optional lesser pilgrimage and may be accomplished anytime during the year.

The SCT Master Plan notes that tourism in the Kingdom is not an objective in itself, but rather a vehicle for realising the comprehensive targets of national development. This is well summarised in the tourism Mission:

> The Kingdom of Saudi Arabia will harness its unique endowments to develop tourism in a sustainable manner, providing quality experience, while contributing to economic diversification, employment creation, environmental and heritage preservation, cultural awareness and community enrichment (SCT, 2002a, p. B)

Figures collected for the Master Plan show that in the year 2000 domestic tourism in Saudi Arabia was estimated at 14.5 million trips worth SR22.4 billion (at the time of writing the conversion rate was 3.75 Saudi Riyals (SR) to the United States Dollar — Expedia.com visited 27 December 2004). Of these domestic trips, 44% were for holiday/leisure purposes, 27.5% for performing Umrah and 19% for visiting friends and relatives (VFR) (SCT, 2002a). In the same year, around 6.3 million foreign tourists are estimated to have visited the Kingdom for religious (Umrah 36%, Hajj 22%) and other purposes (VFR 19%).

Economically, tourism is very important to Saudi Arabia. For example, total expenditure on tourism in the year 2000 amounted to SR35 billion or 5.4% of the Kingdom's Gross Domestic Product (GDP) and generated 638,000 jobs. At present there are more than 95,000 hotel rooms (73% of these are in the Holy City of Makkah) and more than 40,000 bedrooms in furnished apartments available within the Kingdom.

Tourism safety and security is discussed throughout the SCT Master Plan and some developmental activities have already occurred, including the establishment of a Tourism Safety and Security Unit within the SCT. However, to date there has been no large-scale investigation and reporting on safety and security related to tourism in Saudi Arabia. The present chapter outlines the steps taken so far to develop a programme of partnerships and activities for safety and security that are integrated with the overall SCT Master Plan.

Developing a Framework for Tourism Safety and Security

In July 2003, the SCT commenced the Tourism Safety and Security Project. Initially, the project focus was on tourism and security, and a specific outcome was the development of a Terms of Reference (TOR) for a major investigation. As the project progressed it was recognised that there was a range of safety issues affecting tourism that needed to be included, in addition to security. For example, fire safety is a major concern for all accommodation providers. This reflected international best practice (e.g., Federation of Tour Operators, 1999); the adoption of which was a guiding principle of the SCT project.

In keeping with a best practice approach, the project adopted the World Tourism Organization's (WTO) framework for understanding where risks to the safety and security of visitors, tourism employees and host communities might originate (Wilks, 2002). As outlined in Chapter 1, the WTO four source areas are:

1. The Human and Institutional Environment outside the Tourism Sector (e.g., crime, terrorism, social conflicts, political and religious unrest).

2. The Tourism Sector and Related Commercial Sectors (e.g., poor safety standards in tourism establishments, fraud in commercial transactions).
3. The Individual Traveller (e.g., personal risks such as dangerous sport and leisure activities, criminal activities, causing conflict and friction with local residents).
4. Physical and Environmental Risks (e.g., visitor exposure to natural disasters, visitors causing environmental problems such as pollution).

In addition to the above, a fifth specific category was identified as critically important for tourism safety and security in Saudi Arabia. This was:

5. Sociocultural and Religious Values, and Cultural and Heritage Sites (e.g., protection of Saudi values and sites from any direct or indirect effect from tourism activities).

The importance of each source area, and the individual elements within each area, was tested and validated by way of two brainstorming sessions and focus group meetings initially with SCT internal stakeholders, then in January 2003 by way of a major conference held in Riyadh with other government agencies. Material from existing literature, research and reports that had been reviewed to provide context at the commencement of the project (e.g., Prince Naif Academy for Security Sciences, 2002) was incorporated into the framework finally adopted (Wilks, 2003).

Of particular note for other governments and destinations undertaking a similar project was the detailed discussion that was had on the distinction between safety and security for tourism, and whether the SCT project should be restricted to security. Traditionally, tourism does not directly involve itself in security issues, leaving this to other specialist agencies within government and the private sector. Safety, on the other hand, is very much within the domain of tourism, having day-to-day relevance to the broad activities of the world's largest industry. The chapters of this book reflect the relationship tourism has with safety issues, while at the same time recognising that partnerships must be developed to protect tourism interests from security threats (Wilks & Moore, 2004). In the SCT project, both safety and security were included and the following vision developed:

Vision

> To provide world-class tourism safety and security services in the Kingdom of Saudi Arabia through partnerships across government and private sector agencies.

A series of steps was then established in order to work towards this vision. The first step involved examining the activities and direction taken by other countries to address similar issues as those faced by Saudi Arabia. Two examples are presented below.

ASEAN: Within the Association of South East Asian Nations (ASEAN) group, all countries share similar concerns about safety and security in tourism. Many of these countries are of the Muslim faith, with developing economies heavily reliant on a stable tourism industry.

The Tourism Ministers of ASEAN held their Sixth Meeting on 24 January 2002 in Phnom Penh, Cambodia in conjunction with the ASEAN Tourism Forum 2003. The theme of the Forum was "ASEAN Unity: Ensuring a Brighter Future".

The Ministers signed the ASEAN Tourism Agreement and noted that the signing of this landmark agreement by the leaders reflects a high priority placed on tourism development within Southeast Asia. It was also a re-affirmation at the highest political level that the tourism industry is a key factor in promoting peace and economic stability.

The Ministers then issued the following *Declaration on Tourism Safety and Security* (www.aseansec.org/14028.htm)

Recognising the importance of tourism as a significant industry in the promotion of economic benefits and social unity, which among others, provides job opportunities thereby alleviating poverty, improves the quality of lives among the ASEAN citizens and promotes friendliness, networking and widens perspectives among nations;

Realising that terrorism is a direct challenge to tourism development in ASEAN;

Reiterating our commitment to work in close partnership to build travellers' confidence in ASEAN; and

Desiring the endorsement of peace and stability through tourism in the region

HEREBY DECLARE AND COMMIT OURSELVES TO:

1. Stand united in ensuring the safety and security of travellers in ASEAN. As safety and security is the heart of tourism, we are committed to work together with the relevant government bodies in combating terrorism, including preventive and repressive actions to ensure the safety and security of travellers in this region.
2. Carry out specific measures to ensure travellers' safety as mandated by the ASEAN Leaders in the ASEAN Tourism Agreement.
3. Work closely with the relevant ASEAN Bodies in reviewing existing polices and adopting appropriate measures to prevent tourism related threats.
4. Work closely with the law enforcement agencies to ensure the strengthening of security in airports, seaports and all tourists' sites.
5. Strengthen information sharing networks among ASEAN Member Countries and between ASEAN and China, Japan and Korea and other countries.
6. Create an ASEAN webpage to provide precise and timely information on tourism safety and security. This Tourism Safety webpage will provide the official information on safety and security for public and private media as well as foreign governments.

7. Encourage the private sector such as the travel agencies, airlines, hotels and tourism-related establishments to work in partnership with Member Countries to implement the safety and security measures, including information sharing co-operation.
8. Work closely to build capacity throughout the region by enhancing human resources competency in tourism safety and security.

The ASEAN group (http://www.aseansec.org) includes the following nations: Brunei Darussalam, Cambodia, Indonesia, Laos, Malaysia, Myanmar, Philippines, Singapore, Thailand and Vietnam.

The special relevance of the ASEAN Declaration on Tourism Safety and Security to the SCT project was the emphasis other countries are placing on partnerships in this area. In particular, point 4 about working closely with law enforcement agencies to ensure the strengthening of security in airports, seaports and all tourists' sites was a key recommendation highlighted for discussion across Saudi government agencies.

Arab Nations: A response somewhat similar to that of the ASEAN Declaration was more recently provided by delegates to the Scientific Symposium for Tourism Security held in Beirut, Lebanon 18–20 August 2003. The symposium was sponsored by the Prince Naif Arab Academy for Security Sciences (now the Naif University) and resulted in the following recommendations from delegates (translated from Arabic by the SCT):

1. We call on all specialised bodies in Arab countries to work towards spreading total security awareness in the domain of protection for tourism and tourists.
2. We urge Arab countries for consolidation in relation to arrangements, and exchange experiences between them in the domain of tourism security.
3. We call on all specialised bodies in Arab countries for necessity of integrating public and private sectors to improve the requirements for exercising tourism activities in the shadow of robust and sustainable security status within the frame of comprehensive development plans.
4. We request the Naif Arab Academy for Security Sciences to do a study about Quality Standards related to security in tourism activities.
5. We request the Naif Arab Academy for Security Sciences, in collaboration with Universities and Colleges that deal with tourism, to formulate a training curriculum for workers in specialised bodies for tourism and tourist security, as well as introduce more training courses and scientific symposium in all subjects that directly effect tourism activities and tourism security.

The similarities in interest and suggested directions are apparent across the two declarations, and indeed share a common theme with the recommendations of the recent Asia Pacific Economic Cooperation (APEC) report (Wilks & Moore, 2004) of partnerships across government and private sector agencies. Of particular note is point 4 (above) concerning the need to understand and promote quality standards in relation to tourism safety and security. The link between safety and quality service is a central theme of this book, and is also recognised as a critical issue in the SCT Master Plan. For example, in relation to registration and licensing of all tourism establishments in the Kingdom, the Master Plan states:

> Internationally compatible minimum standards in respect of safety and security, hygiene and sanitation must be prescribed and met for the purposes of licensing and registration (SCT, 2002a, p. D).

Best Available Practice

The value of examining the activities of other countries and international groups in the area of tourism safety and security was that it provided a perspective on "best practice" to be adopted by the Saudi project. In particular, the directions emphasised by WTO, ASEAN, APEC and Arab Nation initiatives all support the importance of genuine partnerships across government agencies and with the private sector.

Such partnerships cannot be established overnight. They are an incremental process based on respect, understanding of roles and responsibilities and a willingness to work through issues together. The SCT Tourism Safety and Security Conference held in Riyadh with other government agencies in January 2003 was a positive step towards establishing these key partnerships.

A related point that emerged from the review of international best practice was that partnerships across government agencies, and with the private sector, need to be formalised at the highest level. An executive-level committee, in the case of Saudi Arabia the SCT Board of Governors which already exists, can then direct the development of a National Safety and Security Plan for Tourism. Following the WTO tourism safety and security framework (Chapter 16) the composition of key agencies and organisations that might contribute to such a plan in Saudi Arabia were identified as:

- Supreme Commission for Tourism
- Ministry of Interior
- Ministry of Hajj
- Ministry of Foreign Affairs
- Ministry of Health
- Ministry of Transportation
- Presidency of Civil Aviation
- Commission for the Promotion of Virtue and Prevention of Vice.

This list is not intended to be exhaustive; but rather identifies a core group that might work together to develop the five areas where risks related to tourism might originate.

A Risk Management Approach

The most common failure in effectively managing any crisis in tourism is lack of preparation and not including key partners at each step in the process. This common failing has recently been confirmed for tourism by the Pacific Asia Travel Association (PATA, 2003).

The intention of the SCT project was to avoid this problem by adopting a structured risk management framework. The Australian and New Zealand Standard for Risk Management (Standards Australia and Standards New Zealand, 1999) was chosen to guide this process. The Standard follows the same principles as those employed by the United Nations for Disaster Management (International Strategy for Disaster Reduction, 2002). It is also used to guide national emergency programmes (Emergency Management Australia, 2000) and has most recently been applied to tourism through the WTO (Wilks, 2003) and APEC (Wilks & Moore, 2004) in the Asia Pacific region.

As discussed in Chapter 1, the first step in the risk management process is focused on the environment in which any tourism destination operates. This is the point where basic parameters or boundaries are set within which risks must be managed. This step requires an understanding of crucial elements that will support or impair the risk management process. Among the crucial elements are internal and external stakeholders. In the case of tourism, without the support of senior government officials there is little point in continuing the process.

A critical decision at this first stage is which group or agency should be given the lead role in risk management/crisis or disaster response. This is where an understanding of definitions is important (Chapter 1). Traditionally, risk planning and low-level problems are retained by tourism authorities (e.g., Code of Conduct programmes for tourists about appropriate behaviour). A crisis response is traditionally coordinated by police (eg., a hotel fire), whereas a disaster (e.g., a major flood) is managed by emergency services. In establishing the risk management context for any tourism destination the roles and responsibilities of various stakeholders must be made clear at the outset. This should be documented as part of national policy, and linked to any wider government disaster management plan.

In Saudi Arabia the above distinctions were considered very important in order to define roles and responsibilities for various government agencies, both for safety areas and for security areas. The view of the SCT project team was that where there are existing safety and security roles and responsibilities in place for a government department, these should continue with the support and involvement of tourism, where appropriate. This pertains mostly to security services, where current expertise determines the agency with the lead role. This same approach was successfully adopted by the Department of Foreign Affairs and Trade in managing the Australian government response to the Bali bombings (see Chapter 19).

In the area of safety, tourism should most often take a lead role, especially where licensing and permit requirements for tourist operators contain safety requirements (see Federation of Tour Operators, 2003). In broader areas, such as protection of cultural and heritage sites (often referred to as Visitor Impact Management), tourism should work in close partnership with the relevant authorities and take a coordinating role.

Establishing partnerships across government agencies and the private sector may sometimes seem slow and frustrating, but without the foundations in place none of the subsequent activities will be successful. The project team concluded that the SCT has a major responsibility to ensure that policies, plans and partnerships are in place across the tourism sector to support the active role of the security services. This responsibility was progressed through the development of the TOR for a tourism safety and security plan for the Kingdom, directly addressing the second step in the risk management process; that is, identifying risks.

Development of a Tourism Safety and Security Plan

The TOR document sought to identify risks and threats to tourism (actual and perceived) through a complete and accurate assessment of the present tourism safety and security situation in Saudi Arabia, along with identification of current and future opportunities and impediments (Wilks, 2004). The outcomes of this comprehensive assessment proposal included a national policy document and operational plans for developing key programmes in tourism safety and security. The outcomes were consistent with the overall social, economic and cultural objectives of the SCT Master Plan.

Initial drafts of the TOR included a detailed 10-year Master Plan and a 5-year Action Plan, following the format of the SCT overall Master Plan. However, stakeholder feedback suggested that this approach was too detailed. The final submitted proposal instead focused only on the Master Plan: Phase 1 and, in particular, the development of a national policy document that would guide the subsequent targeted projects. The critical importance of having a documented risk or crisis management plan is highlighted throughout the professional literature (e.g., Beirman, 2003; Drabek, 1995; Mitroff & Pearson, 1993; Peterson & Hronek, 2003), so a key outcome of the TOR was an operational plan for tourism. By way of example, the Objective of the TOR Master Plan and Output 1.4 are presented below. Output 1.4 relates to Tourism Related Sectors under the WTO threat area framework.

TOR Phase 1: Master Plan Objective

- To prepare a comprehensive medium-term (10 years) tourism safety and security Master Plan. The plan shall be structured so as to be actionable at both the national and provincial levels. The plan will also contain a national policy document that outlines roles, responsibilities and lines of authority for tourism safety and security activities. The plan will address both current and future safety and security issues for tourism.

Output 1.4 Inventory and Evaluation of Tourism and Related Sectors

Undertake an inventory and evaluation of the existing and potential tourism safety and security threats and concerns arising from within the tourism and related sectors in the Kingdom of Saudi Arabia.

This Output draws on the second risk category identified by the WTO as well as the work of the Federation of Tour Operators and the International Hotel and Restaurant Association.

Activities

1. Determine the nature and extent of tourism safety and security threats arising from activities within the tourism and related sectors based on the following categories:

   - Poor safety standards in tourism establishments (fire, construction errors, lack of anti-seismic protection).
   - Food handling and hygiene.

- Poor sanitation and disrespect for the environment's sustainability.
- The absence of protection against unlawful interference, crime and delinquency at tourism facilities.
- Fraud in commercial transactions.
- Non-compliance with contracts.
- Strikes by staff.

For each of these categories, provide detailed facts and figures about the actual and perceived threats, based on field surveys, document research and data collection undertaken in partnership with relevant government and private sector agencies.

2. Provide a detailed assessment of how each category of threat above might impact on the SCT target markets of Saudi domestic leisure tourism, GCC and neighbouring Arab country visitors, international Umrah visitors, the Muslim community worldwide, and specialised foreign niche markets based on activities such as eco-tourism, adventure, sport, heritage and cultural tourism.
3. Review the risk management programmes and prevention activities of the relevant government and private sector agencies to document existing policies, plans and resources. Also identify opportunities where tourism might contribute to safety and security in the categories above.
4. Identify the scope of further field surveys, document research and data collection that should be undertaken in partnership with relevant government and private sector agencies in order to maximise the integration and value of tourism safety and security.
5. Produce a detailed report that documents and evaluates the existing and potential tourism safety and security threats and concerns arising from activities within the tourism industry and related sectors in the Kingdom of Saudi Arabia. The report should specifically include the current activities and initiatives of SCT programmes, such as the Hotel Accommodation and Furnished Apartment Task Force in order to synthesise existing work. The report should also recommend minimum standards that must be put in place for the Saudi tourism industry to compete on quality with foreign destinations.

As this extract demonstrates, the task of benchmarking tourism safety and security for any one destination across numerous categories is quite daunting (Wilks, 2004). The original TOR for Saudi Arabia was a very detailed proposal — in retrospect, too detailed and complex, especially in relation to engaging partners from other government agencies and integrating roles and responsibilities. In developing an operational crisis management plan for tourism other destinations have opted for a more generic approach (Wilks & Moore, 2004), which has the benefit of avoiding detail and responding to any particular crisis in a general way. The downside of a generic approach is that often the operations manual produced is little more than a telephone directory of who to contact and in which order to achieve an adequate response. As noted with the unfortunate events of the recent Asian Tsunami, without a comprehensive policy in place to support an emergency plan the links between various agencies may not be well established or maintained. In the Asian Tsunami case, the United States monitoring station in Hawaii was unable to effectively warn authorities in Asia about the impending crisis, there being no formal communication path in place across agencies (Janega, 2004).

A second consideration in developing a national tourism safety and security plan for any destination is that there must be some short-term tangible outcomes produced by tourism in order to engage other groups. Success breeds success. This is particularly true when tourism proposes a partnership with security services. The latter know their job well and legitimately ask what value or benefit tourism brings to the relationship. Positive outcomes can be achieved for tourism through partnerships with emergency (Wilks, Dawes, & Williamson, 2005) and security services (Handszuh, 1997) but these outcomes do not happen overnight, they are the result of concerted efforts and close cooperation.

In view of the need for short-term tangible outcomes the SCT project team recommended an immediate focus on areas where tourism can deliver valuable results. The areas were:

1. Establishment of a Tourism Safety and Security Unit within the SCT — this small unit would be available to liaise with other government agencies and private sector groups, collect information, provide reports and work with external consultants to develop the national tourism safety and security plan. At the time of writing the unit has been formally established, with a Manager and two support staff.

2. Production of a comprehensive briefing paper, outlining progress of the tourism safety and security project so far, and detailing next steps. This paper has been completed and recommends the short- and medium-term directions discussed below.

3. Development of a preliminary crisis management plan for the SCT. Modelled on the Australian National Tourism Incident Response Plan (Department of Industry Tourism and Resources, 2004) the plan would initially include roles and responsibilities of SCT and other agency stakeholders, activation and notification protocols, coordination mechanisms, and response and recovery programmes. A particular focus would be on active communication channels between the SCT and its partners. Over time the plan would be expanded to include policy material and specific responses to different types of threat, rather than the initial generic response framework. This proposal is currently being considered.

4. Expansion of the current SCT National Tourism Research and Information Centre (NTRIC) computer capability and operations brief to include gathering safety and security information. This would support the preliminary crisis management plan (above) and immediately provide value to key partners through the development of a tourism safety and security monitoring system. This proposal is currently being considered.

5. Finally, an audit and synthesis of all existing SCT programmes and activities that have a safety and/or security component. The resulting material could then be placed in the NTRIC computer system to allow sharing and development across agencies. A medium-term goal would be to extend this audit nationally under the five WTO risk source areas, as proposed in the TOR described earlier. This proposal is currently being considered.

Taking point 5 a step further, there is considerable value in undertaking at least one "best practice demonstration program" in tourism safety and security for the benefit of both internal and external stakeholders. The project team identified marine tourism, and specifically scuba diving, as an ideal target activity because:

• it is an activity that can be enjoyed by adult people of all ages (minimum starting age is 12 years);

- participants need to be reasonably healthy, but no standard fitness level is required (disabled persons can participate with proper instruction and facilities);
- it is a sustainable, nature-based and non-competitive activity;
- it appears compatible with Islamic Values;
- safety and security are key elements in the activity;
- it fits with promotional directions identified in the SCT Action Plan by promoting Saudi Arabia as a destination; supports regional destinations; and helps create a tourism image for the Kingdom; and finally
- scuba diving is very popular among Muslim groups in South-East Asia so it will be an attractive recreational option for Umrah Plus visitors (SCT, 2000b).

While the market is still relatively small, scuba diving on the Red Sea coast off Jeddah is a tourism product that is already recognised as world-class. Scuba diving is also an activity where internationally recognised safety standards are critical (see Chapter 14). The best practice demonstration programme recommended by the project team involves an audit of existing scuba diving services and facilities provided by operators in Saudi Arabia, while simultaneously working with SCT legal advisors to draft a set of "best practice" regulations for the Kingdom's scuba diving industry. These regulations will be based on Queensland (Australia) Workplace Health and Safety legislation, which is considered to be the world benchmark in this area (Chapter 14). The resulting regulations for scuba diving would provide a safety template for other eco-tourism and adventure tourism programmes within the Kingdom, since regulation, licensing and accreditation are all key elements for achieving quality standards in the tourism industry. Again, this proposal is currently under consideration.

Conclusions

There is no denying the current pockets of political unrest and sporadic incidents of terrorist cell activity within the Kingdom of Saudi Arabia (Qusti & Hassan, 2004). However, to date these incidents appear to have had little impact on tourism and remain the domain of the security services (in Saudi Arabia the lead agency is the Ministry of Interior). Over time tourism can assist counter terrorism efforts by sharing database information routinely collected as travellers move in and out of the country. Interestingly, this information is usually collected by customs and immigration agencies so there are several partnerships involved. Moreover, tourism can take a lead role in the area of safety through licensing, regulation and accreditation of operators.

Safety issues related to fire, food, buildings, swimming pools and other recreational facilities are all the legitimate concerns of tourism internationally (see Federation of Tour Operators, 2003). Again, these are areas where tourism needs to form partnerships with local government authorities, police, health and emergency services in order to ensure that quality standards are adopted and maintained. Should there be an emergency, these established partnerships would be available and actioned through a crisis management plan.

The SCT now has a Tourism Safety and Security Unit in place to develop programmes and liaise with other government agencies and private sector groups. Short-term goals are to produce the preliminary crisis management plan that links key stakeholders, and to demonstrate the value of safety and security for the growing tourism industry. This can best be achieved by concentrating on core business — tourism facilities and services throughout the Kingdom, and focusing on the development of quality. A critical element of this process is active and regular communication with stakeholders. In addition to the audits and benchmarking discussed in the TOR, the project team recommend at least one best practice demonstration programme in the short term to show how safety practices can make a very positive contribution to tourism.

Acknowledgements

The authors would like to formally acknowledge the leadership and support of HRH Prince Sultan bin Salman bin Abdulaziz (Secretary General, Supreme Commission for Tourism) in the development of the tourism safety and security initiative. The project team are also grateful for the guidance and support provided by Dr Salman bin Abdullrahman Al-Sudairy (Deputy Secretary General, SCT). For their important contributions to the project: Dr Saad N. Al-Hussein, Dr Sami bin Abdulaziz Al-Damigh, Mr Trevor Atherton and Mr Thamer Saeed Al-Ghamdi. Finally, without the support of key stakeholders in other agencies, especially Prince Mohammad bin Naif bin Abdulaziz (Assistant Minister of Interior for Security Affairs) tourism would not be able to contribute to issues of safety and security, in what is still a very new and emerging area of collaborative work.

References

Beirman, D. (2003). *Restoring tourism destinations in crisis: A strategic marketing approach.* Sydney: Allen & Unwin.

Department of Industry Tourism and Resources. (2004). *National tourism incident response plan.* Canberra: Department of Industry Tourism and Resources.

Drabek, TE. (1995). Disaster planning and response by tourist business executives. *Cornell Hotel and Restaurant Administration Quarterly, 36* (June), 86–96.

Emergency Management Australia. (2000). *Emergency risk management applications guide.* Canberra: Emergency Management Australia.

Federation of Tour Operators. (1999). *Health and safety handbook.* Lewes, UK: Federation of Tour Operators.

Federation of Tour Operators. (2003). *Preferred code of practice.* Lewes, UK: Federation of Tour Operators.

Handszuh, H. (1997). *Policing in tourism for visitor and resident protection.* Report from a WTO survey. Madrid: World Tourism Organization.

International Strategy for Disaster Reduction. (2002). *Living with risk. A global review of disaster reduction initiatives.* Geneva: ISDR (CD Rom, preliminary version July).

Janega, J. (2004). Scientists lacked means to warn region of threat. *Courier Mail* (Brisbane, Australia), 29 December, 9.

Mitroff, I.I., & Pearson, C.M. (1993). *Crisis management: a diagnostic guide for improving your organization's crisis preparedness.* San Francisco: Jossey-Bass.

Pacific Asia Travel Association (PATA). (2003). *Crisis. It won't happen to us!* Bangkok: PATA.

Peterson, J.A., & Hronek, B.B. (2003). *Risk management: park, recreation, and leisure services* (4th ed.,). Champaign, IL: Sagamore Publishing.

Prince Naif Academy for Security Sciences. (2002). *Report on tourism security.* Unpublished report to the Supreme Commission for Tourism, Riyadh.

Qusti, R., & Hassan, J. (2004). Terrorists target Riyadh. *Arab News,* 22 April, 1.

Standards Australia and Standards New Zealand. (1999). *Risk management. Australian/New Zealand Standard*: AS/NZS *4360:1999.* Strathfield, New South Wales: Standards Association of Australia.

Supreme Commission for Tourism. (2002a). *National tourism development project in the Kingdom of Saudi Arabia. Phase 1: General strategy (Master Plan).* Riyadh: Supreme Commission for Tourism.

Supreme Commission for Tourism. (2002b). *Sustainable tourism development plan. Phase 2: Action plan 2003–2007.* Riyadh: Supreme Commission for Tourism.

Wilks, J. (2002). *Safety and security in tourism: partnerships and practical guidelines for destinations.* Report presented at the World Tourism Organization Crisis Recovery Meeting, Berlin, 15 March.

Wilks, J. (2003). *Overview, progress and directions report.* Unpublished report to the Supreme Commission for Tourism, Riyadh.

Wilks, J. (2004). *Terms of reference for the preparation of the tourism safety and security plan for the Kingdom of Saudi Arabia. Phase 1: Master plan.* Unpublished report to the Supreme Commission for Tourism, Riyadh.

Wilks, J., Dawes, P., & Williamson, B. (2005). Patrol Smart 7/52: Queensland's integrated surf life saving program. *Australian Journal of Emergency Management,* 20, 38–45, in press.

Wilks, J., & Moore, S. (2004). *Tourism risk management for the Asia Pacific region.* Southport, Australia: CRC for Sustainable Tourism.

Chapter 18

Project Phoenix: A Benchmark for Reputation Management in Travel and Tourism

Michael Yates

Introduction

It struck suddenly. And it struck with devastating consequences. In 2003, Severe Acute Respiratory Syndrome — SARS, as it quickly became known — swept across the globe at frightening speed. Within weeks it spread from southern China, through parts of Asia, to North America and Europe, on a journey that was at first characterised by confusion and denial; subsequently fuelled by fear and sensationalism, finally to be stopped by decisive action and global co-operation.

The death toll, while severe at more than 900 fatalities (WHO, 2004; see also Chapter 4), was not large by comparison with other major disasters. The tsunami, which hit several Indian Ocean countries on Boxing Day 2004, claimed the lives of more than 170,000 people (WHO situational reports issued daily). However, the outbreak of SARS was indisputably the most damaging crisis in the relatively short history of international tourism.

In the crucial first 6 months of 2003, destinations in South East and North East Asia suffered a decline of close to 14 million visitor arrivals. Even after medical authorities had the disease in check, the fear of travel to affected destinations continued unabated, taking a heavy toll on the economies of the region, and particularly on the travel and tourism sector. By the end of 2003, international visitor arrivals to South East and North East Asia had fallen by more than 15 million, stripping US$11 billion from tourism receipts (PATA, 2004).

Some estimates put the global economic impact of SARS as high as US$30 billion (Roach, 2003). Whichever way you look at it, SARS destroyed the lives and livelihoods of millions of people across the world.

In this Chapter, we review the impact of SARS on the travel and tourism industry and how one organisation, the Pacific Asia Travel Association (PATA), responded to the crisis with a programme called Project Phoenix. In many ways, it was a first of its kind, and today stands as a benchmark in reputation management for the travel and tourism industry. We will also look at some of the larger issues which emerged as result of SARS, and some of the lessons learned.

The Outbreak of SARS

The first few years of the new millennium were not kind to tourism. In 2001, an epidemic of Foot and Mouth disease ravaged much of the United Kingdom and Europe. In October 2002, a bomb blast tore through the heart of Bali, Indonesia's famed holiday island. And in March 2003, United States-led forces landed in Iraq, marking the start of a violent conflict which continues to this day. All three events, along with the increasing incidence of terrorist activity, hurt the tourism industry in various parts of the world as people chose not to stray too far from home. But nothing could prepare the industry for the turmoil that would be caused by SARS.

According to the World Health Organization (WHO), the outbreak may have started as early as November 2002 when a case of atypical pneumonia was reported in Foshan City in Guangdong Province in southern China (see the Appendix). However, it was not until February 2003 when the Chinese Ministry of Health advised WHO of an outbreak of acute respiratory syndrome, with five deaths from 300 cases, that the world began to take notice.

Within weeks, similar cases of respiratory disease were being reported in Hong Kong, Hanoi, Singapore, Taipei and Toronto. On 15 March 2003, WHO named the mysterious illness SARS after its symptoms — Severe Acute Respiratory Syndrome — and declared it 'a worldwide health threat'.

The rapid spread of the disease and the lack of knowledge about its origins, its genetic code and its forms of transmission sparked a media frenzy of speculation and misinformation. This included alarmist reports of highly contagious 'super infectors' and even suggestions, although unsubstantiated, that international aircraft could be spreading the virus through their ventilation systems.

Not surprisingly, travel into and within Asia virtually stopped overnight. It was as if the taps were turned off. Corporations banned staff travel. Conventions were cancelled. Leisure travellers stayed at home or went elsewhere. In many cases, airlines, hotels and tourist attractions lost more than 50 per cent of their business within a few days, and were down by as much as 80 per cent within weeks.

The impact was not restricted to those countries afflicted with SARS — it was felt across Asia Pacific, as nervous long haul travellers, particularly from the United Kingdom, Europe and the United States, chose to avoid travel to the whole region. In the April–June quarter of 2003, international visitor arrivals into Asia Pacific declined 34.6 per cent. In the July–September quarter, they fell a further 5.1 per cent (PATA, 2004).

Of course, in those destinations with SARS, the impact was even more dramatic. In Hong Kong, for example, hotel occupancy rates plummeted to just 12 per cent in May 2003, with Revenue per Available Room across the hotel sector falling to under US$10 per night (Deloitte & Touche, 2003). In Taiwan, visitor arrivals for the 3 months of April, May and June were down by more than 70 per cent over 2002 (PATA, 2004). Table 18.1 shows the impact on international visitor arrivals.

The suddenness of the impact was such that many small operators had to close their doors. Larger companies, such as the big hotel chains were able to keep operating, but most were forced to scale back their operations, introducing compulsory unpaid leave, lower wages, and in many cases, laying off staff.

Table 18.1: SARS impact on international visitor arrivals to worst affected destinations (percentage change, year-on-year, from January to July 2003).

Month	China	Taiwan	Hong Kong	Singapore	Vietnam
January	14.5	9.4	31.0	7.6	23.7
February	3.7	11.1	26.2	2.6	10.4
March	−6.5	−8.3	3.9	−14.6	−0.1
April	−30.1	−55.0	−64.8	−67.3	−28.8
May	−31.0	−83.5	−67.9	−70.7	−54.0
June	−18.0	−76.3	−38.2	−47.5	−51.5
July	−8.5	−34.3	−5.6	−20.4	−32.0

Source: PATA (2004), used with permission.

And it was not just traditional tourism operators who were hit hard. So many businesses, and indeed economies throughout Asia Pacific, now rely on tourism. The flow-on effects were felt by restaurants, shopping malls, dry-cleaning operators, photo processors, not to mention the black market or cash economy. It was later established that as many as 3 million frontline tourism-related jobs were lost as a result of SARS (World Travel & Tourism Council, 2003).

And much of this destruction was caused by fear. Fear that was often unwarranted but, in the absence of more definitive information from the likes of WHO, highly understandable. In the heat of the moment, many in the tourism industry turned on the media, blaming global networks, such as CNN, for fuelling a climate of fear by running constant images of Asian people in masks and stories highlighting the spread of disease. Yet, this was really a case of shooting the messenger. The media were only reporting what was known at the time — and that was precious little!

Governments had little idea what they were dealing with, and accurate information was in short supply. In this information vacuum, the media had little choice but to fill in the gaps in what BBC presenter Nik Gowing once described as 'the race for space'. They invited experts to speculate on likely outcomes, to answer the 'what if' questions that lead to great headlines but rarely give a balanced picture of the situation.

In fact, it was not until April 16 that WHO announced a conclusive identification of the causative agent of SARS: an entirely new strain of the corona virus family.

By May 2003, the tourism industry had realised not only the severity of the crisis but also its likely longevity. This was a problem that was going to stick around for months, possibly years, to come. It was time for action.

The Birth of Project Phoenix

Founded in 1951, PATA is the region's leading travel-trade association. A not-for-profit organisation, it provides leadership and advocacy to the collective efforts of nearly 100 government, state and city tourism bodies, more than 55 airlines and cruise lines, and hundreds of travel industry companies throughout Asia Pacific.

PATA defines its mission as enhancing the growth, value and quality of Asia Pacific travel and tourism for the benefit of its membership. So, it was well placed to lead the industry's fight back against SARS.

In May 2003, the International Air Transport Association (IATA), with PATA's support, called a meeting of industry leaders in Singapore to assess the situation. "The atmosphere was highly charged," recounts PATA Director, Communications Ken Scott. "Everyone was hurting and they desperately wanted someone to step up and show some leadership" (Scott, 2005).

PATA was ready to rise to the challenge. President and CEO Peter de Jong had recently reshaped the organisation's strategic agenda with a stronger focus on advocacy, to position PATA as the leading authority on travel and tourism in Asia Pacific. Here was a chance to bring the new direction to life.

Over the next 3 weeks, PATA Vice President, Development, Peter Semone, worked closely with Ian Lancaster and Michael de Kretser of leading regional PR agency, MDK Consultants, to develop the blueprint for the recovery plan.

In June 2003, PATA launched Project Phoenix, a 3-month project to restore consumer and business confidence in travel to and within Asia Pacific. Given the focus on recovery, the image of the Phoenix, rising from the ashes, was a logical one. MDK was hired to manage the project and Hong Kong-based tourism specialist (and author of this chapter) Michael Yates of Taramax Consultants, was appointed Executive Director.

From the outset, Phoenix was essentially a communication programme. The objective was clear — to persuade consumers and travel agents that it was time to put Asia Pacific back on their shopping list of travel destinations.

Because PATA knew that until Asia Pacific's reputation as a warm, welcoming and relatively safe region for travellers was restored, no amount of price discounting would lure scared and skeptical travellers back on to planes.

The first challenge was to collect a fighting fund from PATA members around the region. Initially, the fund raisers were greeted with predictable responses such as: 'We don't have SARS so it's not our problem'. Or they were rebuffed by the more opportunistic operators who were working on the theory that another destination's pain could be their gain.

But the Phoenix team had a strong counter argument. SARS, and the fear of SARS, knew no borders. And it was not long before countries without SARS soon learnt the harsh truth of this reality. When Phoenix launched at the Shangri-La Hotel in Bangkok in early June, occupancy levels had been hovering around 20 per cent for weeks, despite the fact that Thailand had been virtually SARS free. It was the same story across the region.

The outcome of the funding drive was an unprecedented show of support from governments across the region. Virtually every major National Tourism Office came on board. Plus there were contributions from six key industry players. In a matter of weeks, more than US$350,000 had been raised, with many more pledges of in-kind support.

The Phoenix Challenge: Changing Consumer Perceptions

While the level of support was heartening, it still left the Phoenix team with a major marketing challenge: how to overturn consumer perceptions about travel to and within Asia Pacific with a budget that, in global marketing terms, amounted to a jar of peanuts?

The first response was a proactive public relations blitz, which had the advantage of speed, low-cost and high credibility. Through an intensive burst of releases, interviews and backgrounders, PATA managers tackled the SARS myths and misperceptions. They also worked behind the scenes with contacts at CNN, BBC and CNBC to position PATA as *the* authority for comments and reliable statistical information.

Phoenix achieved a good deal of 'free ink', across both TV and press. But it was still struggling to get global reach and impact. More needed to be done. Fortunately for PATA, it was about to receive a major boost from its Premier Partners, CNN International, TIME and Fortune.

Keen to contribute to the recovery process, CNN pro-actively approached PATA with an offer to jointly develop a campaign to help restore confidence in the region, backed by significant chunk of free airtime and advertising space. The generous offer resulted in a powerful campaign widely acclaimed by the travel industry. Called 'Welcome Back', it was a pitch to the hearts and minds of global travelers, not their wallets.

Welcome Back Campaign

The 60-s TV commercial, which was launched on 18 August, tapped into the hearts of travellers everywhere by recalling memories of past travels and the warmth of Asian people met along the way. It reached an estimated 130 million households in Europe and Asia Pacific.

The 2-month campaign included two print advertisements which were rotated in TIME (US and international editions) and Fortune Magazine (Europe and Asia editions). CNN, TIME and Fortune donated airtime worth in excess of US$1.4 million, and Kuala Lumpur-based advertising agency, TBWA donated their time to make the commercial.

Inspired by the success of "Welcome Back", the Phoenix team began to negotiate free or heavily discounted ad space from other global and regional media players, who relied on a healthy tourism sector for much of their ad revenue. The strategy worked brilliantly, with the launch of four other major campaigns, as follows:

BBC World Vignettes

PATA partnered with BBC World to produce a series of eight, 60-s vignettes called Asia Pacific Guides. The Guides showcased the best holiday attractions of Australia, Canada, Hong Kong, India, Macau, Malaysia, Singapore and Taiwan — representing the top supporters of Project Phoenix. Launched on 17 September, the 2-month campaign was broadcast to 74 million households on BBC World's Asia Pacific and Europe feeds.

National Geographic Channel

National Geographic Channel and PATA combined forces to produce an exciting 30-s TV ad to drive consumer traffic to PATA's new consumer web site, TravelWithPATA.com. The US$400,000 campaign launched on 24 September ran through to the end of December. It was seen by an estimated 12 million households on the National Geographic Channel and its new Adventure One (A1) Channel.

SMILES Campaign

PATA produced its own campaign to encourage travellers back to the region, as well as recognising the National Tourist Offices and travel companies which supported Project Phoenix.

The campaign featured:

- A 20-s TV spot which promoted PATA's new web site.
- A consumer print advertisement which welcomed return travellers and gave brand recognition to Phoenix contributors.
- A trade print advertisement focusing on Project Phoenix and thanking the contributors.

Regional trade publications such as TTG Asia, Travel Weekly and Travel Trade Reporter provided free ad space to support the SMILES campaign.

Phoenix Web Campaign

To reach consumers around the world, Project Phoenix needed to take its message online. So a critical element of the project was the creation of a new consumer web site. The Phoenix team worked overtime with web designers, Open World, to create an exciting new site called TravelWithPATA.com.

Built and launched in less than 6 weeks, TravelWithPATA.com went live in mid-August. It offered travel news and features, travel advice and comprehensive guides to 48 destinations in the region, with content provided by Lonely Planet. There were also special travel deals and offers from PATA members, as well as updated weather reports, maps and currency exchange guides.

The web site played an important role in helping to position PATA with global travellers as a source of reliable and accurate information about travel in Asia Pacific, particularly at a time when this was in short supply.

Of course, once Project Phoenix campaigns were underway, individual destinations began their own campaigns to win back tourists. They were generally more tactical in nature, often with special discounts and value-added offers. The value of Phoenix was that it created a more receptive environment for these campaigns in key source markets.

A Key Issue: Disclosure versus Information Control

In September 2003, Singapore's Ministry of Health called a snap press conference to announce that a 27-year-old Singaporean laboratory worker had become the first new SARS case in 5 months. The news sent shudders throughout the Asia Pacific region.

Within hours of the press conference, the Straits Times Index had fallen 2.6 per cent, wiping millions of dollars from the value of listed companies, particularly travel stocks such as Singapore Airlines and Shangri-La Hotels. The anger emanating from boardrooms across corporate Asia was palpable. The laboratory worker had returned positive blood tests, indicating the presence of SARS, but he did not meet WHO criteria for the official confirmation of a new SARS case. Why did the Ministry not wait until x-ray tests — the WHO standard — proved conclusively that the worker had SARS, before going to the media? Surely, it realised the pronouncement — no matter how many qualifying comments accompanied it — would only trigger unwarranted fears of a return of the SARS epidemic and a blood-letting on regional stock markets? The Ministry, for its part, argued there were much bigger issues at stake. Quick action and public awareness were critical factors in preventing the spread of deadly, highly contagious diseases, it argued. As soon as there was sufficient evidence to suggest SARS had reemerged, it was time to go public. Plus, the Ministry said, it was made clear at the conference that this was an isolated case. Quarantining 25 of the worker's colleagues and friends was merely a precautionary measure.

So who was right — the business community or the Government? The answer lies in the resolution of a conflict between notions of public duty and *realpolitik*. In short, it requires a delicate balancing act between (a) the Government's obligation to act quickly and decisively to safeguard public health versus (b) the risk of exacerbating the problem by generating unwarranted widespread concern.

This is not to question the need for government transparency and accountability. China's stubborn refusal to recognise the outbreak of SARS for several months was catastrophic in its consequences. Similarly, Thailand's initial reluctance to acknowledge the outbreak of bird flu — out of concern for its billion dollar poultry export business — was totally counter-productive. Not only did it cost lives, but it also jeopardised the country's improving reputation as a regional leader.

Rather, what this demonstrates is the need to 'manage' the public release of potentially explosive information. To ensure that facts and not conjecture — not even conjecture based on sound scientific hypotheses — are delivered to the public. Contagious disease is a scary topic. By its very nature, it breeds fear which can be deadly for tourism.

A Key Issue: Health and Tourism — New Bedfellows

If SARS was a stark reminder to tourism industry leaders about the importance of the relationship between the health and tourism sectors, then the more recent outbreak of H5N1 avian influenza, better known as bird flu, has driven home the message.

Of course, health and tourism are not strangers. Many who travelled internationally through the 1960s and 1970s would recall, without much fondness, the mandatory immunisations for cholera and typhoid required before travel visas to many destinations could be issued.

In more recent times, the relationship has developed from regulatory to opportunistic. 'Health tourism' has taken off in a huge way, with services ranging from spas, wellness and detox resorts to full-blown surgery at five-star hospitals. It is big business, and correctly managed, can be a win-win for both health and tourism development.

Over the past 2 years, however, the relationship has been tested by crisis and, at times, found wanting. Both sectors simply had not developed the strategic alliances and personal contacts that form the basis of meaningful co-operation.

During SARS, destinations experienced for the first time, the brutal impact of health-based travel advisories. On 2 April, when WHO warned against all but essential travel to Hong Kong and Guangdong, it was the first time in WHO's 55-year history that it had issued such an advisory. And the consequences were immediate, as global travellers were quick to heed the advice.

Throughout April and May, WHO issued further advisories against travel to other destinations, including Beijing, Shanghai, Taipei and Toronto, with similarly immediate impacts on travel flows.

While the travel industry does not challenge WHO's right to issue such advisories, it does seek to be part of the decision-making process. With advisories issued by either WHO or by the Foreign Affairs departments of governments around the world, PATA is leading an industry drive to establish consultative forums, whereby the travel sector can offer constructive input on the scope of the advisory and its likely impact.

PATA's closer relationship with WHO and the health community was particularly evident in the way both organisations co-operated in making public statements to the media on the threats posed by bird flu. "The simple fact is that the risk to travelers (posed by bird flu) is minimal unless they come into direct contact with livestock or eat raw or undercooked poultry," says PATA's Ken Scott (2005), "however this message will always appear more credible coming from a health authority as opposed to a travel authority with vested interests. So every time we make public statements on this issue, we do so in consultation with WHO".

Scott (2005) says PATA is starting to forge links with health authorities, not just in times of crisis, but also to understand the key issues, and to recognise the symbiotic nature of the two sectors.

Measuring Performance: Was Phoenix a Success?

On almost any measure, Project Phoenix achieved a great deal. Let's look first at its primary objective: to restore confidence in travel to the region. The combined impact of the Phoenix campaigns was enormous. In the 6 months after its launch in June 2003, they delivered free airtime worth in excess of US$2.2 million. Campaigns were running continuously from mid-August to end December — reaching 216 million high-end consumer households worldwide.

Did the campaigns succeed in motivating people to travel again? Qualitative feedback indicates they were well received. "Well done, and you HAVE succeeded in making people travel again!" said UK-based publisher Mary Gostelow (2003), President of Gostelow Travel & Hospitality News.

Hong Kong Disneyland's Vice President, Marketing and Sales, Roy Tan Hardy (2003), told PATA that he circulated the Welcome Back TV commercial to his Disneyland colleagues in the US and asked for their candid assessment. "The feedback has been very good, so I thought I'd share this comment from cast member Derric Cheung who wrote ….. 'Roy, this is very well done, it makes me want to pack my suitcase right now'".

Statistical evidence also points to a recovery in tourism arrivals in the second half of 2003, accelerating into 2004. While it is impossible to make direct correlations between the campaign activity and the upturn in tourist traffic without tracking research surveys, there is no doubt that the campaigns contributed to the rebound in business, particularly when viewed in concert with the individual destination campaigns.

Given that Phoenix campaign activity ran from mid-August through to end December 2003, it would be reasonable to expect the impact on travel behaviour to be reflected in the last quarter of 2003 and the first quarter of 2004. So what happened in those two periods? After 6 months of decline, international visitor arrivals into Asia Pacific increased by 2.9 per cent in the last quarter of 2003 and 8.2 per cent in the first quarter of 2004 (Table 18.2).

Among the worst-affected Asian destinations, Taiwan (which was the last destination to be removed from WHO's danger list) and Singapore (which had a second SARS alert in September 2003) were predictably the slowest to recover. However, by March 2003, just 3 months after the final Phoenix campaigns went to air, all but one of the worst-affected destinations were recording positive growth. By April 2003, all were rebounding strongly (Table 18.3).

Table 18.2: International visitor arrivals to the Asia Pacific region(percentage change, quarter-by-quarter, 2002–2004).

| | Year-on-Year % Change | |
Quarter	2003/2002	2004/2003
January–March	3.5	8.2
April–June	−34.6	76.3
July–September	−5.1	21.2
October–December	2.9	11.8
Total	−8.2	24.5

Source: PATA (2004), used with permission

Table 18.3: International visitor arrivals to worst affected Asian destinations (percentage change, year-on-year, from August 2003 to July 2004).

Month	China	Taiwan	Hong Kong	Singapore	Vietnam
August 2003	−0.7	−18.5	9.6	−10.3	−18.8
September	−6.7	−6.4	7.9	−6.8	0.1
October	−1.7	−13.5	7.0	−8.2	13.3
November	−1.6	−5.6	7.3	7.9	24.2
December	1.2	−13.9	7.4	−2.7	26.5
January 2004	−4.7	−10.6	13.1	1.6	17.3
February	2.1	−15.0	3.3	−3.6	−6.2
March	8.9	−7.2	28.6	11.9	3.2
April	69.0	107.0	251.8	220.9	38.7
May	61.4	477.0	296.6	271.4	115.6
June	36.9	353.1	127.0	117.0	122.4
July	23.4	57.9	54.1	48.4	71.8

Source: PATA (2004), used with permission.

According to the Head of PATA's Strategic Intelligence Centre, John Koldowski, much of the rebound, particularly for Hong Kong (see Table 18.4), can be attributed to the flows generated from mainland China, as a combination of pent-up demand and a relaxation of the rules governing cross-border movements into Hong Kong and Macau. "Mainland China has grown to the point where it now accounts for more than 56 per cent of all inbound travel into Hong Kong SAR," observed Koldowski (2005).

As a reputation management programme, Project Phoenix has received wide acclaim from both public- and private-sector leaders. Canadian Tourism Commission President and CEO, Doug Fyfe (2003), summed up the views of many when he said of Project Phoenix, "In all my years associated with the travel industry, I have never seen such professional expertise. Quick, cogent, informative ... this is damn fine. Thanks".

Lessons Learned — Co-ordinated Communications

Certainly, the travel and tourism sector learnt lessons from Project Phoenix. There is now a much better understanding of the different nature of threats to travel and tourism. While global consumers are becoming more inured to security threats, they are still terrified of undiagnosed health threats. One of the biggest lessons learned is the importance of co-ordinated communications. Truth is an early casualty in many crises, and professional reputation management tools are required to dispel myths and misperceptions before they take root in the public consciousness. Ideally, Phoenix would have started earlier. By June, when the project launched, much of the damage had been done, resulting in a focus of recovery rather than prevention, or at least damage control. Ideally, PATA would have built an earlier relationship with key external influencers like WHO. But of course it is easy to be wise in hindsight.

In an effort to be better prepared to deal with future crises, PATA has established a sector-wide consultative group, called the Pacific Asia Coalition for Travel or PACT. Members of PACT include senior management representatives of international airports, airlines, hotels and restaurants, national tourism offices, distribution companies and duty-free operators. In the event of crisis, the group has two core objectives: to ensure accurate information is distributed as quickly and effectively as possible, with PATA acting as 'one

Table 18.4: Hotel room occupancy rates in Hong Kong during 2003.

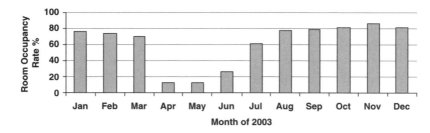

Source: Deloitte and Touche (2003), used with permission.

voice' for the tourism and travel in Asia Pacific; and to share best practices in dealing with the crisis. PATA has also established a database of Tourism Communicators, comprising the marketing communications managers of its various member organisations, thereby ensuring a fast, amplified and consistent flow of messaging.

One of the most valuable outcomes of Phoenix was PATA's increased focus on continuous monitoring and scanning of developments likely to impact tourism flows. "Our heightened vigilance, post-SARS, enabled us to respond rapidly and vigorously to the tsunami crisis," says PATA's Koldowski (2005), "on December 26, within hours of the disaster, PATA was already issuing public statements on the impact of the tsunami and referring people to our website for the latest developments".

In the following weeks, PATA's Strategic Intelligence Centre issued comprehensive twice-daily updates on the tsunami, monitoring the availability of hotel rooms, air services and other vital travel data.

Hopefully, an enduring legacy of Project Phoenix will be recognition of the value of global and regional co-operation, across both the private and public sectors. Phoenix triggered an unprecedented display of regional unity, with highly competitive destinations and brands working together for the common good. Ultimately, this may prove to be the most potent weapon in dealing with the challenges that inevitably lie ahead of us.

References

Deloitte & Touche, L.L.P. (2003). *The hotel benchmark survey.* Available at www.hotelbenchmark.com

Fyfe, D. (2003). Personal communications. September 2003.

Gostelow, M. (2003). Personal communications. September 2003.

Koldowski, J. (2005). Personal interview with John Koldowsik, Head of PATA's Strategic Intelligence Centre. March 2005.

Pacific Asia Travel Association (PATA). (2004). *Annual statistical report 2003.* Available at www.pata.org

Roach, S. (2003). Media comments by chief economist Stephan Roach from Morgan Stanley, April.

Scott, K. (2005). Personal interview with Ken Scott, PATA Director of Communications. March 2005.

Tan Hardy, R. (2003). Personal communications. September 2003.

World Health Organization (WHO). (2004). *Clinical research on treatment of SARS with integrated TCM and western medicine.* Available at www.who.int

World Travel & Tourism Council. (2003). *Special report on SARS.* Available at www.wttc.org

Appendix

SARS: Chronology of a Serial Killer

16 November 2002

First known case of atypical pneumonia occurs in Foshan City, Guangdong Province China but is not identified until much later.

10 February 2003

Chinese Ministry of Health advises WHO of an outbreak of acute respiratory syndrome, with 300 cases and five deaths in Guangdong Province.

21 February

A doctor from Guangdong arrives in Hong Kong to attend a wedding. He checks into the ninth floor of the Metropole Hotel.

22 February

Doctor admitted to intensive care with respiratory failure. He warns hospital staff he had treated patients with atypical pneumonia in Guangdong and fears he has contracted a 'very virulent disease'.

23 February

A female tourist from Toronto checks out of the Metropole Hotel and flies back to her family in Canada.

26 February

A 48-year-old Chinese-American businessman is admitted to hospital in Hanoi, Vietnam, with fever and respiratory symptoms. He had stayed at the Metropole Hotel across the hall from the Guangdong doctor. He is treated by WHO's Dr Carlo Urbani.

1 March

A young Singapore woman is admitted to hospital with respiratory problems after returning from a trip to Hong Kong. She also stayed on the ninth floor of the Metropole Hotel.

4 March

The Guangdong doctor dies of atypical pneumonia.

5 March

The Chinese-American is medivaced to Hong Kong. Seven health care workers, who cared for him in Hanoi, fall ill. The 78-year-old Toronto woman dies. Five members of her family fall ill.

8 March

In Taiwan, a 54-year-old businessman with a travel history to Guangdong is hospitalised with respiratory symptoms.

11 March

Dr Urbani flies to Bangkok to give a presentation on tropical illnesses. He is sick on arrival and immediately hospitalised.

12 March

WHO issues global alert about severe typical pneumonia outbreak.

15 March

SARS is named. WHO names the mysterious illness after its symptoms — severe acute respiratory syndrome — and declares it a 'worldwide health threat'. WHO also issues a rare travel advisory, warning about the dangers of international air travel.

18 March

Cases are now being reported in Canada, Germany, Taiwan, Thailand and the United Kingdom, as well as in Hong Kong, Vietnam and Singapore.

20 March

First cases reported in the US.

27 March

Hong Kong closes schools, with more than 1000 people in quarantine. WHO issues more stringent travel advice, including recommendations for airport screening.

29 March

Dr Urbani dies of SARS in Thailand.

31 March

Health authorities in Hong Kong issue an unprecedented isolation order to prevent further spread of SARS, after it is known that 213 residents of a housing estate have been hospitalised.

2 April

WHO issues a travel advisory against all but essential travel to Hong Kong and Guangdong. It is the first such advisory in WHO's 55-year history.

7 April

Morgan Stanley estimates the global economic impact of SARS at US$30 billion.

8 April

A cumulative total of 2671 cases and 103 deaths are reported from 17 countries.

16 April

WHO announces conclusive identification of the SARS causative agent: an entirely new conavirus.

20 April

The Mayor of Beijing and the Minister of Health, both of whom had downplayed the SARS threat, are sacked. Chinese authorities report more than 2000 cases and 92 deaths. Schools are closed.

23 April

WHO extends it travel advisories to include Beijing, Shanghai and Toronto.

25 April

Outbreaks in Hanoi, Hong Kong, Singapore and Toronto show signs of peaking, following intensive quarantine measures.

8 May

Travel advisory applied to Taiwan, after an outbreak of 100 cases.

22 May

Reported cases of SARS exceeds 8000 worldwide.

18 June

As the outbreak enters its 100th day, the number of new daily cases dwindles to a handful.

5 July 2003

WHO removes the last country with recent transmission — Taiwan — from its list, effectively signalling the end of the outbreak.

Chapter 19

Bali Bombings: A Whole of Government Response[1]

Jeff Roach and Ian Kemish

Introduction

This chapter focuses on the effective whole of government work in extreme circumstances. The Australian Government has considerable experience and a strong record in responding to crises at home and abroad. With the decline in the international security environment following the attacks in the United States on 11 September 2001 and the proliferation of new and frightening security threats including bio-terrorism, crisis management has been elevated as a policy priority for all Western governments.

Crisis management is, of course, well practised and has long been a traditional priority in many fields of public policy, such as civil aviation safety, emergency medical responses and public health. While this chapter focuses on the Australian Government's response to the Bali attacks, it also incorporates a number of lessons learnt in other crisis scenarios, such as natural disasters and exotic animal diseases.

Australia's Emergency Management Arrangements

Under the Australian constitution, each state and territory government retains responsibility for protection of the lives and property of their citizens. Effective disaster prevention, preparedness, response and recovery require the close involvement of police, fire, state emergency service, ambulance, medical services, hospital and other government agencies

---

[1] This chapter was adapted from a paper titled 'Managing Crises and their Consequences' which appeared in Management Advisory Committee, *Connecting Government: Whole of Government Responses to Australia's Priority Challenges* (Australian Public Service Commission, 2004), copyright Commonwealth of Australia, reproduced with permission.

which provide services to the community. Local government and voluntary organisations also play important roles, as both groups have close links with the community.

While no legislation requires the Australian Government to act in emergencies, it has always accepted a responsibility to assist the states and territories where their resources are insufficient or inappropriate for the situation. A number of Australian government disaster response plans are administered by Emergency Management Australia (EMA). The most important for the purposes of this chapter are the Commonwealth Government Disaster Response Plan (COMDISPLAN) for physical assistance to the Australian states and territories, and the Australian Government Overseas Disaster Assistance Plan (AUSASSIST-PLAN) for assistance overseas.

Crisis Response Architecture

In discussing the Australian government's responses to crises, it is useful to note the political context. With agencies taking their cues from ministers, the whole of government response will be conditioned by the strength of political decisiveness and unanimity among ministers. The response to the tragic terrorist attack in Bali on 12 October 2002 underscores this observation. From the outset, the Prime Minister's instructions to senior officials were decisive: the government's response needed to be comprehensive and effective. Issues concerning resources could not be allowed to constrain the policy response — these matters could be addressed later. There was strong bipartisan support for the government's approach.

Reflecting these decisive political instructions, the government established explicit and appropriate chains of command. Given its responsibility for consular services to Australians in distress overseas, the Department of Foreign Affairs and Trade (DFAT) was tasked to coordinate the whole of government response to international aspects of the crisis. Domestically, the Department of Family and Community Services (FaCS) coordinated government policy and delivery of assistance to Australians and their families affected by the crisis. A clear lesson from Bali was the extent to which overseas events can resonate at the local community level, underlining the importance of domestic and state/territory agencies being activated early in response to a major overseas crisis.

The decisive establishment of clear roles and chains of command in this case contrasts with comments by McConnell and Stark (2002) concerning the response by the UK Ministry of Agriculture, Fisheries and Food to the outbreak of foot and mouth disease (FMD) in February 2001. The authors describe the response as "suffering from an institutional malaise and a fragmentary civil service, incapable (at least in the early stages) of providing a 'joined-up' response to match the scale of the crisis"(p. 665).

In the case of Bali, two 'hub and spokes' models were used to coordinate the whole of the government response. DFAT took on the 'hub' role in coordinating the interagency 'spokes' response to the international aspects of the crisis. At the same time, FaCS took on another 'hub' role, coordinating the interagency 'spokes' response to domestic aspects of the recovery. The two clusters of 'hub and spokes' worked alongside each other, attending each other's meetings where necessary, to provide a comprehensive overall response.

The 'hub and spokes' arrangement worked well to draw together key agencies and players to share information and coordinate policy responses. This approach represented the combination of two interdepartmental committees, each chaired by a line agency.

These arrangements provided the context for effective consultation, rapid decision making, close attention to the implementation of decisions and action to address new or unforeseen difficulties. Within each committee, clear directives identified the roles and responsibilities of respective agencies, thereby ensuring that mandated issues were resolved early. Figures 19.1 and 19.2 illustrate these institutional arrangements.

While a 'hub and spokes' structure could be used in a range of crisis scenarios where there is a distinction between international and domestic issues or another clear thematic division, ultimately portfolio departments should ensure that their own crisis plans consider the appropriate linkages and structure for different scenarios relevant to their particular portfolio or industry structure.

A number of observations can be made about this approach. First, within each 'hub and spoke' there was a clear division and respect for the different mandates of respective agencies. Rather than normal bureaucratic rules being abandoned, there was a strong appreciation

Figure 19.1: International aspects: crisis phase — interagency emergency taskforce.

Figure 19.2: Domestic aspects: recovery phase — interagency emergency taskforce.

that the simplest and most direct means of achieving goals was to use the appropriate agency and established channels.

Efforts at short-cutting, even where motivated by a noble desire to expedite an outcome, were ultimately more likely to result in delays and confusion. The use of traditional channels of liaison and coordination means that new relationships do not need to be established in the tumult of a crisis situation. This provides a higher degree of comfort for downstream organisations, such as state authorities, which are involved in delivering a specific response.

Coordination by DFAT for international issues and FaCS for domestic issues reflected the overall responsibilities of the two departments: DFAT has responsibility for consular services overseas, assisting in responding to the deaths of about 600 Australians overseas each year (DFAT, 2003); FaCS supports Australian families in need (see http://www.familyassist.gov.au/).

Both DFAT and FaCS held daily (twice daily in the initial aftermath of the attacks) interagency taskforce meetings, which drew major stakeholders together to share information and coordinate policy responses. Australian Public Service (APS) employees attending these meetings were at a senior level, meaning they had the authority to make on-the-spot decisions on behalf of their agency.

The Bali response brought together a diverse range of agencies, many with little prior experience in working with each other. However, participants worked cohesively and collaboratively throughout the period. They were hindered little by the different departmental cultures and work practices which can be found in the APS.

While it can be argued that organisational culture is the key to the whole of government success (this issue is explored further in "Culture and Capability", in Management Advisory Committee, *Connecting Government: Whole of Government Responses to Australia's Priority Challenges*, 2004), a crisis situation elicits a high level of goodwill which appears to eliminate cultural barriers. One of the key lessons from the Bali attack was the decision to establish an overarching national plan, to be coordinated by EMA, to provide a framework for coordination to:

- clarify the roles of agencies and non-government organisations in crisis responses;
- review links between Australian government and state disaster plans; and
- identify and rectify any gaps in interagency coordination arrangements.

The development of the National Response Plan for Overseas Mass Casualty Events will provide the blueprint for federal and state contingency plans to be examined further and tested against a variety of different scenarios. At the time of publication, the preparation of this plan was well advanced.

While the government's response to Bali was pursued through the parallel processes of the 'hub and spokes' models, there was no competition or mandate clash between the two structures. In the days after the Bali attack, as the evacuation of injured Australians was completed, remains stabilised and positive identification of the deceased began, the transition from crisis phase to recovery phase was well advanced. In fact, it was important that activities associated with the recovery phase were conducted in tandem with activities associated with the crisis response. While there was no clear distinction in the transition from one phase to the next, the emphasis of policy making increasingly shifted from international to domestic aspects.

From Crisis to Recovery

In driving response from crisis to the recovery phase, a high degree of discipline is required to ensure that decision making is followed through by rigorous implementation and follow-up. Coordinated whole of government policy making and implementation is integral in driving towards the recovery phase.

Within the FaCS Bali response taskforce, 15 core issues were addressed in each daily meeting, with recent progress and forward planning reported against each. The core issues were:

- public communication;
- financial support;
- domestic health services;
- disability issues;
- counselling;
- return of effects of deceased victims to next-of-kin;
- community harmony;
- community support;

- rural issues;
- intergovernmental welfare issues;
- role of airlines;
- insurance coverage;
- domestic economic issues;
- international issues; and
- interaction with other disasters.

The daily review of these issues ensured that policy outcomes were closely monitored and driven forward.

Similarly important is the need for crisis managers to rise above the maelstrom of the moment and obtain a more strategic view of the overall policy response. One way to do this is to create a regular opportunity for key decision makers to briefly canvass what might be the policy and media issues of the day. This discipline assists in ensuring that decision making continues to strike a balance between the proactive and the reactive, looking beyond the issues of the moment. In the case of Bali, these approaches meant that within 7 days of the attack the focus of government decision making had moved smoothly from the international to the domestic, from crisis to recovery phase.

Preparing for a Crisis

Effective crisis management is founded on good preparation. This should include: the negotiation of protocols with likely key participants and stakeholders; the maintenance of the crisis infrastructure to ensure that it is ready to use at any time (this includes fundamentals such as after-hours contact lists of key employees from other agencies); and the appropriate training and development to ensure that people can fulfil key roles, whatever the dimensions of the crisis.

Human resource issues also need careful attention — a sustained crisis has the potential to burn out key people. One of the lessons of the Australian Government's FMD simulation, *Exercise Minotaur* (see http://www.affa.gov.au/exerciseminotaur), was the need for agencies to look at human resource capacity in a number of key areas, particularly that of skilled and trained technical employees. Experience indicates that the long-term nature of individual and community recovery will also place significant strain on human resources.

A further recurring issue is the need for a compatible communications system that allows information to be shared quickly between agencies without the need for special handling. The Bali response, for example, showed that two agencies (DFAT and FaCS) that had rarely communicated with each other before found electronic communications difficult.

Review of Crisis Management Systems

It is critical that agencies prepare for a whole of government crisis during normal business operations. As part of this, agencies need to develop — and test — contingency plans that map out how the agency will respond in a range of different scenarios. Such plans require regular review, monitoring and testing to ensure that they can deliver against their stated goal. Desktop and trial exercises are important, both within agencies and across the whole of government.

Furthermore, after a crisis, it is critical that agencies undertake a formal review and, if required, further reform of response plans subsequent to a crisis. This needs to be undertaken on a whole of government basis and it is critical that agencies come together to pool lessons learnt and negotiate reforms to their own departmental processes.

The Australian Government comprehensively tested its response systems in 2002 through *Exercise Minotaur.* The breadth of the simulation was impressive, with the scenario testing diverse issues such as animal health responses, trade advocacy skills and even consular dimensions (see http://www.affa.gov.au/exerciseminotaur). The simulation was conducted over 4 days in September 2002, after 12 months of planning. More than 1000 people from a range of government and industry agencies were formally involved, with the simulation overseen by a panel of evaluators and observers.

Another part of forward planning is the development of financial management protocols to give APS employees the discretion to authorise action. Once a crisis has begun, financial systems must be able to deliver appropriate resources to enable decision makers to quickly meet policy priorities, while also satisfying Australian government financial guidelines.

This lesson is illustrated by the issuing of *ex gratia* payments by the Australian Government that are covered neither by legislation or regulation. Such payments require written authority, normally from the Prime Minister. However, Australian government agencies need to understand how these payments will be handled where a decision and announcement has been made at the ministerial level, but corresponding authorisations are not yet available. While the lag may be only 24 hours, announcements about government assistance will trigger an immediate response from the community. Departmental secretaries may need to develop a consistent approach to flexible bridging arrangements to ensure that financial assistance can be provided quickly in times of crisis.

Review Existing Protocols and Practices

Some private sector corporations have taken testing one step further by using 'internal assassins' — well-versed employees who devise worst-case business disruption crises to test management systems (see Klinger, 2003). Testing such as this on a whole of government basis would mean crisis management responses could be reviewed to ensure that existing protocols and practices keep pace with changes in the threat environment, technology and political imperatives.

Exercise Minotaur enabled a thorough testing of the FMD coordination arrangements. This simulation also highlighted the importance of response protocols that include 'fire drills' to make sure that all systems are working well, including a managed approach to public communication. An approach like this moves beyond frameworks and standards, and puts in place specific action pathways with which all players can become familiar.

The period between crises also provides an opportunity to review possible jurisdictional barriers to an effective crisis management. There are a number of possible sources for such difficulties. The first lies in the balance of powers between the Australian Government and state/territory governments, with divisions of responsibility established by the constitution. Protocols are required to ensure that the whole of government response at the Australian government level is matched by seamless coordination at the state/territory level.

Experience has shown that e-mail should be used with some caution for priority communication during crisis management. Systems need to be robust enough to cope with the increased demands of a crisis and employees need to regularly monitor e-mail to ensure that responses are not delayed.

The potential for information management issues to arise during a crisis also needs to be considered. State and Australian government agencies collect an array of data about individuals. However an agency's obligations under the Privacy Act (see http://www.privacy.gov.au/) will impact on what information can be shared among agencies. The Privacy Act can allow pragmatic decisions in times of national disaster. However, the need for personal data to be protected means it is difficult to collect information from different authorities to support ongoing whole of government work during a recovery period.

Agencies may find it useful to develop a common approach to understanding the way in which the Act applies to their operations in a crisis. Without this common understanding, different interpretations of the Act can lead to inconsistent policy formulation and agency responses during the crisis.

Approaches to whole of government crisis management in other countries can also provide learning opportunities for Australia. The UK Government has established rapid deployment crisis teams which can move within 24 hours to lead the government's response to an overseas crisis (see Response of the Secretary of State for Foreign and Commonwealth Affairs to the Twelfth Report of the Foreign Affairs Committee Session 2001–2002, 2002, p. 4). The exact composition of the teams, possibly drawn from a range of agencies including foreign affairs, law enforcement and aid delivery, would depend on the nature of the crisis, from a natural disaster to a terrorist attack. The capacity of the teams to work together is likely to hinge on joint training opportunities. The pre-crisis development of a solid understanding between team members of each other's responsibilities and portfolio mandate would be vital.

Lessons learnt through crisis management can also be applied to other whole of government work. All agencies address business continuity issues and lessons learnt here can be disseminated throughout the APS using reports such as this one.

Public Communication

Times of crisis provide a litmus test of a government's capacity to work cohesively to convey information, extend medical, financial and counselling support and provide reassurance and leadership to its citizens. Community expectations are influenced by a government's record in responding to previous crises, as well as by media commentary, which closely shadows every government statement and action. The media impact on driving community expectations and turning public opinion cannot be underestimated by crisis managers (Beirman, 2003; Wilks & Moore, 2004).

As the crisis management response unfolds in the context of community expectations, government messages can be roughly divided into two categories:

- Educational messages that seek to reshape community expectations in cases where expectations exceed the power and authority of the government.
- Reassuring messages that confirm that the government response will be generous and equitable.

Getting the balance right in blending these messages requires sophisticated and well-integrated public affairs management. The importance of public affairs management in educating and shaping community expectations was underscored in the response to the Bali bombings. In the aftermath of the attack, there was considerable public anguish about the disaster victim identification process. The Indonesian Government implemented a positive identification process, in line with international norms and protocols. Although undertaken swiftly, the collection of information about victims from Australia meant that the identification process could not be undertaken immediately.

This generated anxiety within Australia. Calls were made for the Australian Government to assume responsibility in Bali, thereby overriding Indonesian sovereign responsibility for its coronial processes. Others suggested that Australia should encourage the Indonesians to set aside international norms, thereby running the risk that a less-rigorous identification process might lead to a serious and tragic error.

Given the intensity of media coverage of the Bali attacks, the educational message was difficult to advance. However, primary agencies, such as the federal and state police services, DFAT and coroners, worked to send a single and simple message: that the positive identification process, which was being properly implemented by the Indonesian Government, was the only appropriate course. Media commentary and community expectations shifted fairly quickly towards a clearer understanding of the issue.

Reassuring messages to the community were delivered swiftly in the Bali example. Given a clear mandate to support Australians affected by the bombing, FaCS established a taskforce that arrived quickly to assist the community on a range of issues: emergency medical treatment, assistance for family members to visit loved ones at interstate hospitals, the establishment of family liaison officers to work one-on-one with those affected and long-term packages of support. Experience has shown that a case management approach can provide effective liaison and support for the affected families. This should be based on clearly defined agency roles and responsibilities and be provided by appropriately trained employees.

Determination of the level of support provided to victims and their families required careful judgement. Issues of precedence were considered as governments frequently offer emergency assistance packages in response to natural and other disasters. There was also a need to be clear about the extent of flexibility around the application of the guidelines which provided assistance. This was important to ensure that the government's approach was not criticised for being either too strict or too lax. Clearly, this balance was struck, as media treatment and the community's response to assistance measures were uniformly positive.

It is important to carefully consider the full range of community needs in the aftermath of a crisis. As well as financial assistance, people affected need information and will naturally turn to media or other sources to meet this need. The Bali experience showed also that people directly affected crave information over emotional support, at first. Over time, as the implications of the crisis become clearer, community need will, however, turn to counselling and social support. Nevertheless, this switch from information to support needs to be judged carefully and timed correctly to ensure that the government's communication efforts are appropriately formulated. In the aftermath of Bali, FaCS established a newsletter for affected families. The newsletter conveyed the government's key messages and ensured that the messages were tuned to the emotional and information needs of families at different times.

A major challenge in informing the community is to make sure every agency is giving out the same message. This is difficult in any whole of government task and more so in the fast-moving environment of crisis response.

While web-based information is an excellent way of providing a suite of information with links to partner agencies and other relevant sites which can be accessed at all hours, some caution is needed as some areas of Australia have difficulty opening and downloading some sites. Caution also needs to be used to ensure that websites are not the only source for information.

In the Bali response, a number of different agencies needed to contact families to provide information on different elements of the government's response. DFAT consulted families about whether their loved ones had told their family that they were safe[2], while police were in touch with families to seek material for the victim identification process, and Centrelink employees provided information about government assistance packages.

While each agency provided contact details about where cross-portfolio questions could be directed, none was initially able to answer queries from a whole of government perspective. However, a common set of questions and answers was quickly developed to meet this need.

One option to ensure that messages are conveyed consistently and to avoid multiple agencies contacting families in times of already high stress is to delegate authority to a single agency to represent the Australian Government. In planning for an approach like this, agencies would benefit from regular contact with each other during normal business operations (e.g. prior to Bali, contact between DFAT and Centrelink occurred only rarely). This would assist people to understand other corporate cultures and the agency's core priorities, roles and responsibilities.

The handling of media briefings in times of crisis is also important. In some cases, a media briefing might be more appropriately handled by departmental employees, given technical or other specific knowledge required on a subject. An example of this was the decision during the Severe Acute Respiratory Syndrome (SARS) outbreak to use the Commonwealth Chief Medical Officer to lead media briefings. Given the technical complexity of many potential crisis triggers (e.g. animal disease) there may be value in establishing a protocol to guide when departmental employees, rather than ministers, should lead public communications.

Work to integrate the whole of government public affairs management has been taken forward by the Attorney General's Department under National Counter-Terrorism Committee

---

[2] Following the attacks, the Department of Foreign Affairs and Trade pursued almost 5000 whereabouts inquiries triggered by families registering concern that their loved ones may have been in Bali at the time of the attack

arrangements. This is aimed at ensuring that if there is a domestic terrorist crisis, careful public affairs management will reduce the scope for both rumour to replace information and for multiple or contradictory statements by different agencies.

These measures rest on five key principles:

(i)   The community has a right to be informed and information should only be withheld if its release would be to the detriment of the national interest, including operational security.
(ii) Public information management and media liaison can play a key role in national security operations, and therefore must be strategic, accurate and undergo all necessary clearances.
(iii) Agencies must not comment on another agency's area of responsibility without first seeking appropriate approval from the agency in question.
(iv) All agencies have a responsibility to ensure that they have a single point of coordination contact, as well as appropriately trained media liaison employees and resources to respond to any national security incident.
(v)   It is the responsibility of all agencies to ensure that they have clear coordination processes within their own agencies, with their ministerial offices and across agencies.

In order to embed these principles in organisational behaviour, training workshops are being run which bring together public affairs employees from various governments. These workshops will not only improve skills but also build links between media staff to ensure that a collaborative approach is taken during a crisis.

Partnering with Non-Government and Private Sector Groups

The community has high expectations about the substance of the Australian Government's actions during a crisis. It can be valuable to use strategic partnerships that agencies have developed in normal day-to-day business operations to assist in this response. In the Bali response, a company with long-standing experience in mass casualty incidents, Kenyons International, was contracted within 24 hours of the attacks to manage the repatriation of all deceased Australians on behalf of the Australian Government. Qantas also agreed to put on additional flights to repatriate the many hundreds of Australians who wished to leave Bali immediately.

From the non-government field, the Red Cross agreed to coordinate all voluntary requests for assistance from the community, drawing on its long record in the field of international humanitarian issues. The Red Cross was also a member of the domestic taskforce and provided important support to individuals such as non-Australian citizens who were affected by the bombing but were unable to access assistance provided by FaCS.

Volunteers too may need to be integrated into the overall crisis response effort. Whether planning for crises at home or overseas, agencies need to include the capacity and desire of Australians on the ground to play a constructive role in the crisis response. Clearly, with the degree of volunteer support unknown until the crisis hits, this role needs to be carefully scoped and defined.

The likelihood of unaffiliated volunteers appearing should also be addressed. If there is no role for volunteers, this willingness to assist could translate into understandable frustration — most likely vocalised — about the Australian Government's handling of the crisis. The Department of Agriculture, Fisheries and Forestry has recognised in developing its FMD plans the need to harness local communities, given their pivotal role in providing additional, appropriately qualified human resources to any FMD emergency.

Ongoing consultation with the community is also important. Once a crisis has begun, it is also important that the affected community is involved in, and has a sense of ownership of, their own recovery. Consultation should also occur before a crisis, as part of an agency's contingency planning arrangements. There are some useful examples of how this consultation can occur. Over recent years, the government and livestock industries have reached a comprehensive agreement on the sharing of costs in dealing with outbreaks of 63 animal diseases (see Department of Agriculture, Fisheries and Forestry, 2004). The agreement was a landmark as it established a positive partnership of responsibility and decision making involving industry.

Lessons from the Bali Bombings Response

In conclusion, the following lessons can be learned from the Bali bombings for a whole of government crisis management response:

- plan early and test the plan;
- establish clear leadership;
- define roles of all players early;
- use formal chains of command; and
- ensure strong public affairs management.

References

Beirman, D. (2003). *Restoring tourism destinations in crisis: A strategic marketing approach.* Sydney: Allen & Unwin.

Department of Agriculture, Fisheries and Forestry. (2004). *What is the industry/government cost-sharing agreement?* http://www.affa.gov.au/content/output.cfm?ObjectID=3AA21CFC-DB3F-44C8-93F2E22329603E29

Department of Foreign Affairs and Trade (DFAT). (2003). *Annual report 2002–2003.* Canberra: DFAT. http://www.dfat.gov.au/dept/annual_reports/02_03/

Klinger, E. (2003). Leadership and terror. Alert: Journal of the Institute of Civil Defence and Disaster Studies, June, 7–8.

Management Advisory Committee. (2004). *Connecting government: Whole of government responses to Australia's priority challenges.* Canberra: Australian Public Service Commission.

McConnell, A., & Stark, A. (2002). Foot and mouth 2001: The politics of crisis management. *Parliamentary Affairs,* 55, 664–681.

Response of the Secretary of State for Foreign and Commonwealth Affairs to the Twelfth Report of the Foreign Affairs Committee Session 2001–2002. (2002). p. 4 at http://www.fco.gov.uk/ Files/ kfile/FACResponse12.pdf

Wilks, J., & Moore, S. (2004). *Risk management for tourism in the Asia Pacific region.* Southport: Cooperative Research Centre for Sustainable Tourism.

Key Websites

Department of Foreign Affairs and Trade (DFAT)
http://www.dfat.gov.au/
Department of Agriculture, Fisheries and Forestry
http://www.affa.gov.au/exerciseminotaur
Department of Family and Community Services (FaCS)
http://www.familyassist.gov.au/
Emergency Management Australia (EMA)
http://www.ema.gov.au/
Commonwealth of Australia Privacy Act
http://www.privacy.gov.au/

AUTHORS' NOTE

Ian Kemish   was head of Consular Branch at the Australian Department of Foreign Affairs and Trade at the time of the Bali attack. He was responsible for the overall management of the Commonwealth's response to the attacks for which he was inaugurated as a Member of the Order of Australia (AM). He is currently the Head of the International Division in the Department of the Prime Minister and Cabinet.

Jeff Roach   was Director of the Consular Information and Crisis Management Section at the DFAT at the time of the Bali bombing. He was responsible for coordinating the activities of Australian Government agencies in response to the attacks, and was awarded an Order of Australia Medal (OAM) for his work. Jeff is currently posted with the Australian Embassy in Paris.

Chapter 20

Shadows across the Sun: Responses to the Public Liability Crisis in Queensland

Nick Parfitt

Introduction

In a book that has its foundation in the dramas of catastrophe, terrorism, risks and dangers, the issue of insurance might appear to be somewhat sedate, something akin to asking First Lady Lincoln what she thought of the play. Yet, insurance provision is the economic corollary and consequence of the topics discussed elsewhere in this book. From mid-2001 onwards the issue of the 'public liability' crisis, in combination with the collapse of Ansett Airlines and the terrorist attacks on Eastern America, clouded the horizons of Queensland's tourism industry.

Although the public liability crisis was global in nature, its impact on tourism in Queensland was always likely to be monitored nervously. Tourism in Queensland includes such major attractions as the Great Barrier Reef, the Gold Coast, Cairns, the Daintree, Fraser Island and the Whitsundays (see www.queenslandholidays.com.au/), and accounts for an estimated AUD$6.3 billion or 6.4% of the State's gross state product. Around AUD$3.5 billion of this is export earnings, making tourism the second largest export earner in the State. It represents over 150,000 jobs or more than 9% of employed Queenslanders, and this rises to 20% of jobs in some regional areas (Department of Tourism, Fair Trading and Wine Industry Development, 2004 www.dtftwid.qld.gov.au/tourism). Tourism is also an important part of Queensland's self-image, based on a favourable climate, considerable natural attractions and a relaxed lifestyle. The whole of the insurance crisis, including the related threats to medical services and to public events, led Queensland Premier Peter Beattie to talk in terms of social rather than merely economic disruption:

> Our problem is we're facing a crisis and unless there are some reforms, the system will collapse and nobody will get anything. We've got doctors who are reluctant to operate, we've got not-for-profit organisations which can't hold fetes, and the whole social fabric in a number of country and provincial cities is starting to be put at risk (Beattie, 2002, p. 1).

Queensland is therefore used here as an example of the impact and manifestations of the public liability crisis, and also to illustrate some of the approaches that have been used in response to the crisis, as well as others that may be developed.

About Public Liability Insurance

Public liability insurance belongs to the class of insurance that includes, in Australia, workers compensation, professional indemnity, medical indemnity, third-party motor vehicle, and products or defects liability. While all these forms of insurance are relevant to different situations and parties, they are characterised by the need for an organisation to protect itself against claims made against it by the public (or by its employees).

While there appears to be consensus on the core function of public liability, there is less consensus on the definition and the legal interpretation of the key concepts of cause, blame and attribution of liability. Furthermore, public liability encapsulates a range of insurance industry products. Some common definitions of public liability insurance are provided below:

> Public liability insurance generally provides cover for insureds in respect of their liability to third parties as a result of an unexpected or unintended occurrence (which in turn results in personal injury or property damage) happening during the period of insurance (AON, 2003, p. 1).

> Public liability insurance is used by owners and operators of commercial and non-commercial activities, including use of property, to protect them against the risk that a member of the public suffers injury or loss that is attributable to these owners and operators (Trowbridge Consulting, 2002, p. 1).

> Public liability insurance provides protection for claims brought by third parties (persons injured or suffering a loss) as a result of some action or inaction by the insured (Liability Insurance Taskforce, 2002, p. 4).

Clearly, definitions of public liability differ according to need and purpose. Nevertheless, common elements remain at the core of the concept; that is, the legal and moral responsibilities towards the public (third parties) carried by tourism operators. The potential financial costs of public liability claims against operators necessitates that this element of risk be transferred to specialised public liability insurers.

What Happened?

A brief chronology of the events covered in this chapter, and other relevant events are listed below. This chronology is not intended to be comprehensive, or even to act as a simple sequence of cause–impact–solution, since the chronology includes a mix of global, national and state events; and events of differing impacts on Queensland's economy, its society and its psyche.

The context of the crisis can be traced back more than 10 years to 1992 when changes in Federal legislation lifted restrictions on legal advertising, introduced contingency fees leading to litigation conducted on 'no win/no fee' basis and ratified the principle of class actions. These legislative moves are considered by some commentators to have opened the gates to a flood of liability claims based on unprecedented legal barracking. Moreover, media coverage through the 1990s highlighted victim claims and payouts at a level previously unseen. The legislative response from a number of State Governments, including Queensland, 10 years later was to reverse the freeing up of the legal industry.

Two more recent and tragic events are imprinted firmly on Queensland tourism history. In November 1998, two American scuba divers — Thomas and Eileen Lonergan — were abandoned at sea at the end of a charter diving trip to the Great Barrier Reef off Port Douglas. The coroner later committed the master of the charter vessel to stand trial for manslaughter, a charge of which he was later acquitted. Both the legal implications for operator responsibility and the subsequent publicity surrounding the case, including a proposed film indirectly based on the case, gained wide publicity. The second incident, 18 months later in June 2000, saw 15 people lose their lives in a deliberately lit fire at the Palace Backpackers in Childers, Queensland. Robert Long was found guilty of murder and arson charges resulting from the fire in March 2002. The government response to the fire incident represents a good example of a strong response. Since evidence indicated defects in fire alarm and emergency exit systems, the Queensland Government embarked on a vigorous and comprehensive program of setting and enforcing fire safety standards in backpacker and boarding hostels. The focus that the Lonergan incident placed on record keeping, Childers placed on infrastructure. While tourism has always engendered some expectation that there will be risks associated with visitors unfamiliar with the climate, the wildlife, the roads or the leisure activity, these two events were sufficiently emphatic to shake that expectation.

Sandwiched between these two events was the merger in December 1999 of the GIO and AMP insurance companies. This had the effect of reducing the number of major insurers offering public liability and this trend continued in March 2001 with the collapse of the HIH/FAI insurance group. September 2001 saw the terrorist attacks on America and the collapse of Ansett Airlines.

The chronology now moved into the response phase. In March 2002, a meeting of State and Federal Ministers was held to discuss and take decisions on the insurance/public liability crisis. An analysis was prepared for the meeting — 'Public Liability Insurance' by Trowbridge Consulting. In the same month, the New South Wales Civil Liability Act came into effect, applying to all proceedings issuing from the courts from this date.

In May 2002, Queensland Premier Peter Beattie proposed in a Ministerial Statement consideration of tort law reform as part of the legislative provisions to address the crisis. This followed the reporting of the Liability Insurance Taskforce. Proposed tort law reforms were introduced under the Personal Injuries Proceedings Act (2002) the following month and passed in November 2002.

In Victoria, Premier Steve Bracks announced a major package of reforms to address problems in public liability. Among these was a grant of $100,000 to adventure tourism operators to assist them prepare risk-management plans and audits. This money was directed to the preparation of the Marsh Report on risk management that produced detailed guidance material for tourism operators (Victorian Tourism Operators Association, 2002).

On a Federal level, the Commonwealth Government established in July 2002 a committee into tort law reform, chaired by the Honourable David Ipp. The committee reported in two stages in September and October 2002. 'The Review of the Law of Negligence' contained over 60 recommendations for tort law reform (Ipp, Cane, Sheldon, & Macintosh, 2002). In April 2003, the Queensland Civil Liability Act was passed, implementing most of the Ipp Committee recommendations on tort reform, in particular, restricting the types of claims that might be made and limiting damage claims.

The Causes of Crisis in Australia

The reasons for the public liability crisis in Australia were underpinned by a number of factors, most being common to other developed economies but some unique to Australia.

It seems, retrospectively, that Australian premiums for public liability were evidently charged at unsustainably low levels for most of the 1990s (see Figure 20.1), causing subsequent declines in profitability to insurance providers as the volume of claims and average claim size increased. Data provided by Trowbridge Consulting for the meeting of ministers on 27 March 2002, are intended as indicative only, however, it suggests:

- An indicative increase in claim size of 12% per annum between 1990 and 2000.
- A doubling of writs lodged in the Sydney District Court, based on preliminary figures from 1000 in 1996 to 2000 in 2001. Other figures from the Insurance Council of Australia

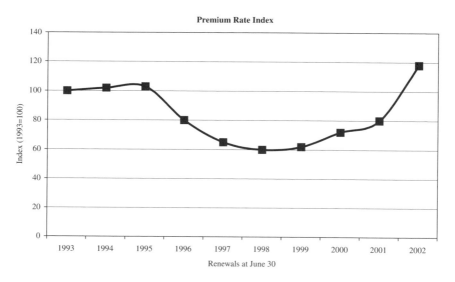

Figure 20.1: Premium rates 1993–2002.
Source: Trowbridge Consulting (2002, p. vii).

indicate that the number of liability claims rose from 55,000 in 1998 to 98,000 in 2001 (and this does not include any figures from HIH, the major insurer in this class of insurance until 2001).

- A premium rate that had fallen to three-quarters of its 1993 level by 1998, and data on indicative insurer profitability, which indicates a loss equivalent to 60% of income from premiums by the same year.

It should be noted that some experts (e.g. Davis, 2003) have provided sound arguments and alternative data to show that premium increases during the 1990s were not directly attributable to an explosion in litigation claims (second dot point above). However, the underpricing of premiums for various reasons may still have created unrealistic expectations across the tourism and other industries of the true long-term price of public liability insurance. While the economics of price correction began to assert themselves through the last year or so of the 1990s, other shocks were to follow in 2001.

The demise of insurers HIH and United Medical Protection in early 2001 effectively removed 50% of the capacity in the local market for small and intermediate risk insurances, while effectively removing one of the key props on which under-pricing had been based:

> Ironically, in many ways, the damage in relation to spiralling premiums relates not so much to HIH's collapse and departure from the market but the extent to which it and those which followed it underpriced their risks for so long. In HIH's case, financial chickens have come home to roost. In the case of others, there is now a determined claw-back to more realistic premium levels (Ashton, 2002, p. 7).

The global effects of terrorist attacks, notably those of 11 September 2001, compounded the ramifications produced by the local insurance market shakeout. The result was a decline in the numbers of major multi-line insurers in Australia offering public liability insurance, from over 20 in the early 1990s to fewer than 10 by 2003.

A common, if somewhat simplistic, statement that also emerges in commentary is that 'Australia is becoming more like America'; that there is a greater resort to litigation in the event of injury or misfortune, and that fuelling or reacting to the 'blame mentality' is lawyers' advertising since the lifting of advertising restrictions on them in 1992. This, in part, is seen to have fuelled the increase in claims and was highlighted by Ministerial comments made during the announcement of the Queensland Government's legislative response:

> It's time to change the culture that is driving people towards a 'sue-for-anything' mentality. We have to balance what is in the public interest in ensuring that injured people can gauge which lawyer to engage and what is against the public interest where unscrupulous lawyers are seeking to create business through urging people to sue … we see no value in the possibility of people being seduced by advertising to pursue frivolous or vexatious claims (Welford, 2002, www. newsinternational. com, archives, p. 1).

The Manifestation of Crisis

A 'crisis' can be defined as "any situation that has the potential to affect long-term confidence in an organisation or a product, or which may interfere with its ability to continue operating normally" (Pacific Asia Travel Association, 2003, p. 2; see also Chapter 1). The weight of evidence submitted to government and industry taskforces in Queensland, both statistical and anecdotal, indicated that the key characteristics of the public liability crisis included:

- The difficulty for some tourism operators to obtain public liability insurance cover.
- The prohibitive costs to purchase public liability insurance for some tourism operators.
- The implications of carrying the higher cost for some tourism businesses.

This reflects a wider, national situation:

> There is a crisis today in public liability insurance. The crisis is that there are too many people seeking insurance who can find it only at very high prices (compared to prices during the last 5 years) or cannot find it at all (Trowbridge Consulting, 2002, p. 1).

According to the Chief Executive of the Queensland Tourism Industry Council, Daniel Gschwind, around 1000 tourism operators in Queensland had already closed their doors as a result of the crisis by May 2002 (Cameron & Odgers, 2002).

The following comments were made by tourism industry operators as part of the consultation exercise, which prompted the QTIC's warning above (Parfitt, 2002, p. 6).

> The cost of our commercial insurance tripled and our excesses increased, i.e., $25,000 excess for a named cyclone. Have also been told by our broker that we may not be able to have our insurance renewed in June 2002. If this occurs we will have to shut the doors, throw 5 people out of work and destroy the longest established restaurant in the area. This restaurant just so happens to be the first tourism development in the area and has never had an insurance claim in 22 years.

> Increases in insurance premiums are just another burden which businesses in this region, which are involved in tourism (nearly everyone) will find difficult to carry. Most businesses are struggling to survive as it is.

> Businesses have no other option than to make the public pay. If small business feel they can't do this then they will go to the wall or take the risk of not having adequate *cover.* This is a very scary situation.

> 50% of small business will vanish if the rising insurance spiral does not stop.

> Change to contractors for cleaning services but not cost effective as they will raise their costs in take into account increase in insurance costs.

Investors want to maximise their return not minimise it. As owners of ****** we're on duty 24/7 but would consider performing cleaning duties ourselves. Then five casual staff would be unemployed. With the increase in super guarantee next financial year, work cover and insurance we will have no option.

The insurance company was not interested in looking at our Standard Operating Procedures or Risk Management Manuals. We thought this might show we were professional/careful operators!

We operate a B&B — two rooms with approx. 100 room nights per year. We have never had a claim or heard of any claim against a B&B anywhere. We have round 87,000 guests each year and we have only had one claim, which we feel is suspicious. We meet all safety requirements and have well-trained staff — we can't understand why our premium has substantially increased. (NB claim only lodged 4 weeks ago — we know nothing about it).

We have not been able to find an insurance company since the news that our insurance company wouldn't insure us. We only have 6 weeks until existing policy expires. Need to find new insurer ASAP. I don't want to go without insurance and we'd have to close if I couldn't find any. We would also suffer great losses. Insurance cost $2015 in 2001 and went to $10,000 in 2002 but they have cancelled my remaining insurance for this year.

Help!!!

Other related industry sectors, accessed through parallel consultative exercises, presented a similar picture:

Our public liability cover has risen over 500% and we are seriously thinking of not only cancelling our event but also closing the association (Liability Insurance Taskforce, 2002, p. i).

The period of consultation to the Queensland Government Liability Insurance Taskforce, which ended with the presentation of their Report in February 2002, saw the submission of information on the impact of the crisis on tourism, sporting and recreational organisations, outdoor recreation and events organisations. A number of consultative surveys were conducted as part of this exercise.

Evidence of sharp insurance premium rises within the tourism sector was provided by the March 2002 Queensland Tourism Industry Council survey (Parfitt, 2002). Results from 269 self-completion surveys from the membership database indicated actual or projected rate of increase of 219% in the public liability premium paid by members (based on those who returned a questionnaire). Figure 20.2 presents the reported premium changes.

The survey also revealed the key projected impacts from increases in public liability premiums to be higher prices passed to consumers (stated by four operators in ten);

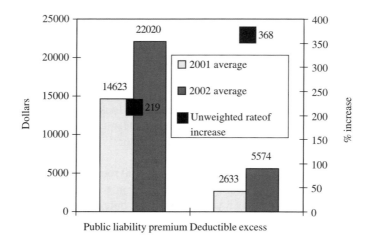

Figure 20.2: Queensland tourism operator reported premium changes.
Source: Parfitt (2002, p. 4).

reduced investment (stated by one operator in six) and reduction in the numbers of casual or part-time staff (stated by one operator in six). Figure 20.3 presents these results.

The QTIC survey needs to be viewed as indicative rather than conclusive as its findings are based on a return rate of less than 10%, one-third the level of what might be expected from a survey of this kind. Anecdotal responses in following up the survey indicate that this low level of response is, in itself, of interest since it may denote:

- Some operators had already given up (as indicated by some earlier comments).
- Some operators had already made their concerns known through other channels.
- They had no comparable data on which to base answers as the survey was conducted before the peak mid-year renewal period.
- That, while the term 'crisis' has been widely used, in reality the situation may affect certain clusters of operators very hard and leave many others relatively unscathed.

Similar pictures were presented by comparable industries in Queensland. The Liability Insurance Taskforce (2002) summarised some of the main industry findings as follows:

- A survey of members of the Queensland Council of Social Services conducted in July 2001 obtained 357 responses. Of these, 47% indicated their premiums would increase at the next time of renewal, at an average rate of increase of 30–40%.
- The peak advisory group, Commerce Queensland conducted a survey in January 2002, which indicated that 47% of respondents suffered a 10–30% increase in public liability premiums.
- A study by Deloitte Touche Tohmatsu on behalf of the Queensland Events Corporation and based on approximately 400 responses indicated that 41.6% of respondents had been faced with premium increases (including public liability) of more than 50% over the previous 3 years; that two-thirds had found it more difficult to obtain cover over the

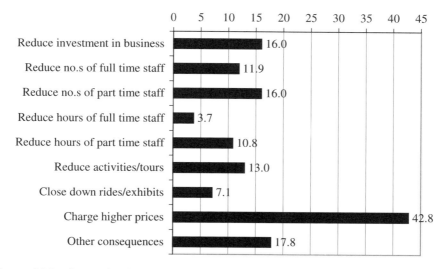

Figure 20.3: Queensland tourism operator reported implications of premium changes.
Source: Parfitt (2002, p. 5)

previous 3 years; and 21% indicated that activities had been cancelled or scaled back due to the cost or lack of availability of necessary insurance cover.

The Response to Crisis

As indicated in the previous section, the response to the crisis can be described broadly from a number of perspectives:

1. Government, which given the structure of Australia's democratic system, can be separated into Federal (national) initiatives, and initiatives particular to the individual States and Territories that comprise Australia.
2. Peak industry bodies both national and State such as the Queensland Tourism Industry Council, Tourism Queensland, the Australian Amusement, Leisure and Recreation Association Inc. and the Australian Hotels Association.
3. The insurance industry.
4. Individual tourism operators.
5. Those providing service and expertise to those operators (universities, consultants).

The Government Response

At the meeting of 15 November 2002, the final reports of the Ipp Committee were considered by the Commonwealth Government and State Government Treasurers. The first thrust of the Queensland Government's response was to introduce a series of legislative responses, as summarised below.

The Personal Injuries Bill 2002

- Limiting economic loss to three times the average weekly earnings.
- Limiting loss of comfort claims to actions following a person's death or where the damages exceed $30,000 before any determination on contributory negligence.
- Capping loss of service claims at three times the average weekly earning.
- Not permitting punitive, exemplary or aggravated damages against an insurer.
- Excluding jury trials.
- Placing an obligation on the claimant to mitigate the loss suffered.
- Restricting the amount of costs lawyers can charge on 'small quantum' matters to discourage them being pursued.

The Queensland Civil Liability Act 2003

- Modifies negligence and causation principles through the re-definition of the content of care and breaches of that care.
- Provides that the fact of risk of harm could have been avoided by doing something in a different way does not in itself prove negligence.
- Provides also that subsequent action taken to prevent a similar occurrence happening in the future is not of itself evidence of negligence or an admission of negligence.
- Subject to some exceptions, provides that there is not a duty to warn of 'obvious risk' and that there is no liability for injury suffered from the materialisation of an inherent risk, or of an 'obvious' risk in the situation of a 'dangerous recreational activity' (of particular concern with overseas tourists, who are clearly not aware of risks that may be obvious to locals — see Wilks & Davis, 2003).
- Replacing joint and several liability by proportionate liability in cases of economic loss or property damage worth more than $500,000.

The Queensland Government has also produced risk management literature and information through its relevant agencies. Examples are:

- 'No More Risky Business' — a guide prepared by the Liquor Licensing Division of the Department of Tourism, Racing and Fair Trading in May 2003 to assist licensees in reviewing their safety and compliance procedures and including self-assessment and remedial systems for all aspects of patron protection. The context of this publication — the increasing number of claims made against hotels by patrons — is described by Surawski and Wilks (2002).
- The publication of 'Safety Information for Scuba Diving and Snorkelling' by Workplace Health and Safety Queensland (2004).
- Sections of the Workplace Health and Safety Queensland web site devoted to risk management (see www.whs.qld.gov.au/publications/index.htm).

As a further initiative, the Queensland Government extended its group insurance arrangements to cover certain community activities — such as Parents and Citizens Associations. This did not impact upon the private tourism sector.

Industry Responses

Industry responses to the crisis have clustered around peak tourism organisations and specialist groups within the industry. Aside from the lobbying of government, and a role in the consultative process, which worked towards legislative change, there is also an educative risk-management-based role. This appears more nascent in Queensland than in New South Wales or Victoria except where Queensland tourism organisations form part of a national structure.

In Victoria, $100,000 was provided by the State Government to the Victorian Tourism Operators Association (now the Tourism Alliance Victoria) to undertake a risk evaluation of three recreational sectors defined historically as higher risk — horse-, rope- and water-based activities (Victorian Tourism Operators Association, 2003). These evaluations established the levels of compliance of operators across the three sectors with risk-management criteria, and established areas of required improvement for each participating organisation. These audits have proven important in obtaining insurance cover in these sectors.

Similarly, there are efforts to accredit operators according to their compliance with risk-management criteria — such as that established by the Victorian Adventure Activity Standards www.orc.org.au.

To these industry-specific approaches can be added a raft of more general publications on risk management, including:

- Emergency Risk Management — Applications Guide: Emergency Management Australia (2000).
- Tourism Risk Management for the Asia Pacific Region: An Authoritative Guide for Managing Crises and Disasters (Wilks & Moore, 2004).

Lessons for the Future

While this chapter has provided a brief, historical overview of the sequence of the public liability crisis in relation to the tourism industry in Queensland, its application is continuing and ongoing. The legislative changes noted above provide a context for the tourism industry to seek solutions, but do not represent the answers by themselves, particularly as the test of those legislative changes will be the interpretation and application in the courts:

> Premiums have risen, claims have fallen and there is greater protection for the leisure industry in relation to defences available to them. However, it would be a foolish operator who seriously considered such a climate provides a relief from risk, and a reduced need for adequate insurance cover. There are significant criminal and civil penalties that would flow from such a position, and the industry would be crippled by government regulatory control in the event that an uninsured operator was unable to pay claims arising from an accident. The industry needs to ensure that it is on top of risk management and effective claims control in line with the assistance provided by the raft of legislative changes (Davidson, 2004, p. 28)

The need for legislative changes to be viewed as the starting rather than the end-point is accentuated by the fact that Federal initiatives (the Ipp Report recommendations, in particular) have been utilised in different ways by the different state legislatures. While the idea of sorting through legislatures for the most amenable may take the concept of the 'ambulance chaser' too far, there have been calls for the standardisation of risk-management policies, procedures and incident protocol on a national level. The Ipp Report recommended that all actions for personal injury be subject to a single legal regime.

One area of common responsibility across different State Governments is the management of national parks. This is very relevant to tourism as parks are a significant site for visitors (see Chapter 13) and appear to have similar liability intent between the different Australian States and Territories, but at the same time differing interpretations and policies. To quote one recent example from a report on tourism and parks (Buckley, Witting, & Guest, 2001, p. 8):

> All Australian park agencies refer to written policies on risk management but there are considerable differences between the types of policies and frameworks referred to by the various park agencies, and the level of detail they contain...

It is clear that the future health of the tourism industry will depend upon its adoption and implementation of risk-management procedures in relation to visitors and guests. This in itself is not a new proposition. It is also clear that the expertise and materials for so doing (some of which have been listed above) are available, but that ensuring that risk management is proactive and effective across an industry as diverse as tourism will require an approach based on:

- Existing skills and capabilities.
- Proper monitoring and information gathering.
- Targeted communication (and persuasion).
- Partnerships and coordination.

One conclusion is that an approach based substantially on existing programs adopted for the protection of employees and staff is the most effective way forward (Wilks & Parfitt, 2004). A culture based on workplace health and safety has already been fostered in most workplaces, and most employers understand their responsibilities to provide a safe workplace (Workplace Health & Safety Queensland, 2000). There are already mechanisms in place for education and enforcement, and the paradigm of reward for proper practices and penalty for improper ones is also established. To function fully, some attitudinal modification is required through partnering in order that employers view the government and insurance providers as helpers rather than just enforcers.

A good example of this process of partnering and targeting is demonstrated by a recent CRC-scoping study in 2004 (Parfitt, Arup, Morgan, & Wilks, 2005). The objective of the study was to identify and assess relevant data and legal frameworks applicable to workplace health and safety for the tourism industry in the states of Queensland and Victoria.

The study had an additional objective to identify current initiatives and issues across tourism industry sectors. The study was conducted in three phases:

Phase One. Identification and review of data sources relevant to tourism industry risk exposure. This information was provided by government agencies and insurance organisations. The data were used to develop a preliminary risk exposure profile for the tourism industry.

Phase Two. Review of the legal framework applicable to tourism industry health and safety. This review included recent initiatives of government in response to rises in public liability premiums.

Phase Three. Tourism industry consultation. Tourism industry stakeholders in Queensland and Victoria were consulted for input to the project and to indicate future direction and coordination for ongoing industry benefit.

One of the streams of inquiry incorporated data provided by Workplace Health and Safety Queensland, including 594 reported incidents involving visitors and staff from the years 1999–2004. Analysis was based on the qualitative reporting of these incidents.

The first application of these data was to indicate tourism sectors at greatest risk of claims (Figure 20.4). The Australian and New Zealand Standard Industrial Classification

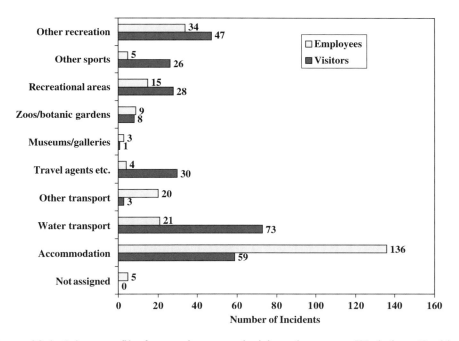

Figure 20.4: Injury profile for employees and visitors by sector. Workplace Health & Safety Queensland; reported incidents 1999–2004; as at August 2004.
Source: Parfitt et al. (2005.)

(ANZSIC) categories with the highest reported numbers of visitor/tourist incidents included water transport, accommodation and other recreational activities. The majority of employee incidents occurred in the accommodation sector, although this is consistent with the high proportion of employees working in this category.

From this general targeting, the further issue of the specific risk situation was examined. Based on the qualitative reporting of incidents, the majority of visitor/tourist incidents took place in scuba diving or snorkelling situations (see also Chapter 14). Employee situations occurred in dedicated work locations (such as plant rooms and warehouses), in work kitchens and accidents with work vehicles (Figure 20.5).

The data also showed the consequences of these incidents. Among visitors and tourists in Queensland, the most common incident results included death, sudden decompression illness ('the bends'), water ingestion and unspecified fall injuries. Among employees, the most common results included lower back injuries, cuts/abrasions, hand injuries and unspecified injury associated with a fall (Figure 20.6).

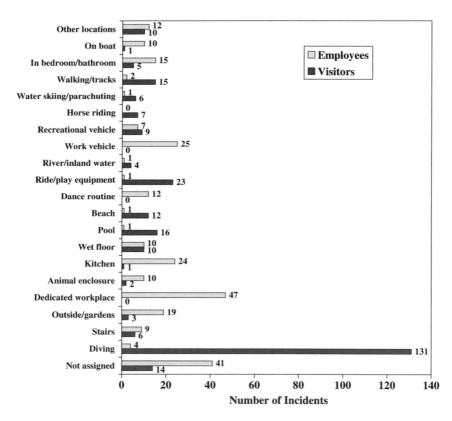

Figure 20.5: Injury profile for employees and visitors by location. Workplace Health & Safety Queensland; reported incidents 1999–2004; as at August 2004.
Source: Parfitt et al. (2005.)

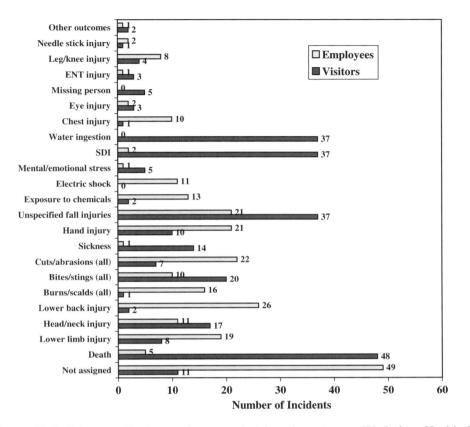

Figure 20.6: Injury profile for employees and visitors by outcome. Workplace Health & Safety Queensland; reported incidents 1999–2004; as at August 2004. *Source*: Parfitt et al. (2005.)

The data presented here are not comprehensive. However, it indicates briefly how an approach based on targeting tourism sectors, focusing on riskier activities within those sectors, and examining the undesirable consequences that may be avoided, might start. It also points to the partnerships that are necessary between government, the insurance industry and tourism operators. And while the profiles of incidents for employees and visitors are different, the discipline required to prevent both is necessarily the same.

One of the features noted in both State and Commonwealth Government consultation processes has been the difficulty of accessing complete and accurate information on the public liability crisis. The Liability Insurance Taskforce (2002) report, for example, cites a range of sources that are anecdotal, if powerful. More specifically, in relation to tourism, only relatively recently have tourism activities been separated out from adjacent ANZSIC categories in workplace health and safety and insurer data. In terms of the collection and analysis of data, there are international benchmarks such as those utilised by Bentley and Page (see Chapter 11). It is clear that priority needs to be given to an agreed and accepted system of evaluation, reporting and monitoring in this area.

Conclusions

This chapter indicates that the only way in which tourism operators can deal with the ongoing crisis in public liability premiums is through a greater sense of mutual obligation among all relevant parties.

For governments, this means striking a legislative balance between the rights of individuals and their legal representatives to pursue rightful claims for damages suffered as a result of injury, and the need to ensure that relevant legal systems do not spiral out of control. In large part, this means moderating public and industry expectations of the system.

For the insurance industry, this means striking their own point of balance between profitability and sustainable pricing, and also the need to recognise efforts by their clients to improve risk management and educate them in that process.

For tourism operators and their representative bodies, it means recognising that care of their visitors and guests is as important as any other activity. Chapter 1 of this book indicated that perceptions of safety now play a prominent role in consumer decision making. This chapter shows that satisfying these expectations is a matter of local just as well as national responsibility.

References

AON Risk Services. (2003). Latest legislative responses to the public liability crisis. *AON Risk & Insurance Review, 3,* 1–4.

Ashton, R. (2002). 2001: A catastrophe odyssey — The effects of HIH and September 11 on insurance litigation. Paper delivered at the Continuing Education Program Insurance Law Update, School of Law, The University of Queensland, Brisbane, 11 April.

Beattie, P. (2002). Cabinet Acts on Medical Indemnity and Public Liability Insurance. Ministerial Press Release, 7 May available at http://statements.cabinet.qld.au.

Buckley, R., Witting, N., & Guest, M. (2001). *Managing people in Australian parks. 3. Risk management and public liability.* Southport: CRC for Sustainable Tourism.

Cameron, M., & Odgers, R. (2002). One in five tourism workers facing axe. Courier Mail (Brisbane), 9 May, accessed from Archives section at www.newsinternational.com.

Davidson, G. (2004). The public liability solution? Australian Leisure Management, January, 26–28.

Davis, R. (2003). The tort reform crisis. *University of New South Wales Law Journal, 25*(3), 865–868.

Department of Tourism, Fair Trading and Wine Industry Development. (2004). Available at www.dtftwid.qld.gov.au/tourism.

Emergency Management Australia. (2000). *Emergency risk management applications guide.* Canberra: EMA.

Ipp, D. A., Cane, P., Sheldon, D., & Macintosh, I. (2002). *Review of the law of negligence.* Report submitted to the Minister for Revenue and Assistant Treasurer. Canberra: Canprint Communications. [Retrieved 14 January 2005 from http://revofneg.treasury.gov.au].

Liability Insurance Taskforce. (2002). Report to the Queensland Government. [Online] Available at www.premiers.qld.gov.au/about/pcd/economic/insurancetaskforce.pdf, accessed January 2005.

Pacific Asia Travel Association (PATA). (2003). *Crisis. It won't happen to us!* Bangkok: PATA.

Parfitt, N. (2002). *The impact of changes in the provision of public liability insurance on the Queensland Tourism Industry.* Southport: CRC for Sustainable Tourism.

Parfitt, N., Arup, C., Morgan, D., & Wilks, J. (2005). *Public liability in the Australian Tourism Industry: Risk exposure profile and legal responsibilities.* Southport: CRC for Sustainable Tourism.

Personal Injuries Proceedings Act (Qld) 2002. Brisbane: Queensland Government Printer.

Surawski, M., & Wilks, J. (2002). Hotel safety in Australia: Current legal issues. *International Travel Law Journal, 3*, 164–179.

Trowbridge Consulting. (2002). *Public Liability Insurance.* Analysis for meeting of Ministers. [Online] Available at www.trowbridge.com.au/dir095/home.nsf, accessed 27 March 2002.

Victorian Tourism Operators Association. (2002). *Risk management guidance material.* Melbourne: VTOA.

Victorian Tourism Operators Association. (2003). *Public liability assessment findings summary.* Confidential Report prepared by Marsh Risk Consulting, 22 March.

Welford, R. (2002). *Cabinet acts on medical indemnity and public liability insurance.* Ministerial media statement from the Queensland Minister for Justice and Attorney General, 7 May.

Wilks, J., & Davis, R. (2003). International tourists and recreational injuries. *Plaintiff, 59*, 8–14.

Wilks, J., & Moore, S. (2004). *Tourism risk management for the Asia Pacific region.* Southport: CRC for Sustainable Tourism.

Wilks, J., & Parfitt, N. (2004). *Seeking solutions for public liability issues in tourism.* Presentation to the CRC/QTIC Public Liability Industry Forum, Brisbane, 29 November.

Workplace Health and Safety Queensland. (2000). *Risk management advisory standard.* Brisbane: Department of Employment, Training and Industrial Relations.

Workplace Health and Safety Queensland. (2004). *Safety information for scuba diving and snorkelling.* Brisbane: Department of Industrial Relations.

Chapter 21

A Travel Industry Perspective on Government Travel Advisories

David Beirman

Introduction

Before 11 September 2001, government travel advisories constituted a background decision-making consideration for most international travellers. Travel industry professionals
in the majority of travel-generating countries had a low awareness of government travel
advisories, which rarely featured as an issue during overseas travel transactions between
travel consultants and their clients. Conversely, foreign ministries that issued travel advisories made perfunctory attempts to disseminate them to the mass media, the travelling
public or travel industry professionals. Notable exceptions to this global trend were Japan
and the USA, where the large outbound tourist markets tended to be far more security and
safety conscious than other countries with large numbers of outbound travellers.

   Government travel advisories are not a recent phenomena. Most Western governments
and Japan have issued travel advisories for their citizens since the advent of mass international tourism in the late 1960s and in some cases, earlier. The term "travel advisory"
requires a basic definition. Although fleshed out in more detail during the course of the
chapter, a government travel advisory constitutes several elements:

1. It is a security and safety assessment issued by the government of a travel-generating
   country to its citizens applying to specific destinations.
2. Advisories incorporate information and advice on legal, cultural, religious and social
   mores, which may apply to the destination and suggest appropriate conduct for travellers to observe in order to optimise personal safety and minimise legal entanglements
   at the destination in question. They incorporate relevant contacts, including the diplomatic legation for travellers in the event of emergencies and outline the services the
   legation can provide while in any given foreign country.
3. In essence, government travel advisories are an extra-territorial security measure
   designed to protect travellers when leaving their country of citizenship.

The 11 September 2001 terrorist attack involving hijacked aircraft which destroyed the World Trade Centre in New York City and damaged the Pentagon in Washington, DC foreshadowed a period of heightened security awareness for the global travel industry. As a consequence, there were demands for a range of government initiated and supported security measures to protect travellers globally. Intensified airport security measures and upgraded international standards of airline security were implemented by IATA — International Air Transport Association (Gaillard, 2002). Governments of travel-generating countries encountered public and media pressure to issue and disseminate travel advisories applying to "risky destinations". The focus of attention were countries deemed affected by the "global war on terrorism" launched by the George W. Bush Administration and widely supported (albeit with varying interpretations) by most of the Western world from September 2001. The exponential growth of the "World Wide Web" in the early years of the 21st century made widespread dissemination of travel advisories an operationally feasible and financially viable exercise for the governments of virtually all travel-generating countries.

The sudden and widespread prominence of government travel advisories since September 2001 had several significant consequences. They included:

1. *Diplomatic Consequences* Many countries cited in travel advisories objected to being identified as risky or unsafe destinations. They were concerned that being subject to a cautionary or negative travel advisory reflected on them as a nation and would prejudice their reputation as a tourism destination and harm their economies. Many developing countries with a high level of economic dependence on tourism viewed negative travel advisories as a form of economic warfare against them. A frequently raised objection related to problems specific to a locality or region magnified as applicable to an entire country. Former Philippines Secretary of Tourism Richard Gordon, angered by cautionary advisories directed at his country because of terrorism in Southern Mindanao, demanded that travel advisories should apply the principle *specificity* to problem area rather than condemn an entire country (Gordon, 2003).

Gordon's view was enthusiastically embraced in South East Asia. Accusations were made by developing countries, especially in Africa, that they were more likely to be subject to negative travel advisories than developed countries. A prime example of the diplomatic dimension of the travel advisory controversy was the response of ASEAN countries following the Bali bombing of 12 October 2002. Several South East Asian nations including Singapore, Malaysia and Thailand in which the Asian Islamic group Jemaal Islamiya was suspected of planning terrorist attacks, were subject to negative travel advisories from the governments of many of their most lucrative source markets, notably Japan, USA, several European countries and Australia. In November 2002, the ASEAN heads of states re-established the ASEAN Tourism Marketing group as a direct response to these advisories and the governments of ASEAN countries undertook a diplomatic campaign against their imposition (ASEAN, 2002).

2. *Market and Media Consequences* The heightened profile of government travel advisories resulted in some significant shifts in demand for tourism destinations based on their depiction and interpretation by the media in travel-generating countries. Post

11 September 2001, negative or cautionary travel advisories were increasingly treated by the media and the market as an indication of an unsafe destination. This trend has often been exacerbated by the mass media, which frequently misinterpreted a cautionary travel advisory as a "government travel ban", contrary to the actual wording or intent of the advisory. Security perceptions were clearly a growing determinant in travel patterns following September 11.

3. *Travel Industry and Travel Insurance Consequences* Travel industry associations and professionals globally felt a sense of alienation from the determination process of government travel advisories. As the visibility of advisories grew, the travel industry was increasingly informed about them but they were rarely, if ever, consulted. Until 2003, the dominant paradigm within most foreign ministries assumed that travel professionals would automatically oppose negative or cautionary travel advisories on the grounds that it would prejudice their interests in selling destinations. However, industry lobbying on a global, regional and national level initiated a dialogue between governments and the travel industry. The World Tourism Organization (WTO), Pacific Asia Travel Association (PATA) and other major travel industry organisations including the British-based global lobby group Tourism Concern (www.tourismconcern.org.uk) sought to convince governments that the tourism industry should be treated as a responsible negotiating partner on the issue of travel advisories.

In June 2003, the world's first formal agreement between a foreign ministry and the travel industry leadership on the issue of travel advisories was signed in Australia between the Department of Foreign Affairs and Trade (DFAT) and the Australian Federation of Travel Agents (on behalf of a consortium of Australian tourism industry associations: see DFAT, 2003). It was a precursor to future agreements. The Australian government sought the support of the industry to disseminate travel advisories, while the industry demanded a consultative role in their formulation. In July 2004, the British travel industry and the Foreign and Commonwealth Office sealed the world's second agreement between a government and a national travel industry (www.fco.gov.uk).

The proliferation of travel advisories since late 2001 led to a re-assessment by travel insurers of their tendency to link insurance cover to the wording of government travel advisories. Post-9/11, major travel insurers tacitly concluded that government travel advisories frequently overstated the level of risk to tourists in certain destinations. Advisories are now one of a number of risk assessment factors insurers take into account. Linkage between travel insurance coverage and government travel advisories is increasingly assessed on a case-by-case basis. The random and unpredictable nature of terrorist attacks against tourists worldwide has also led to a re-assessment of coverage applying to victims of terrorism by travel insurance providers. The "general exemption" which until 2002 used to signify a refusal by insurers to extend cover to travellers who suffered injury, loss or death due to political violence, has undergone extensive review (Beirman, 2003).

This chapter focuses primarily on the changing relationship between the travel industry and governments on the issue of travel advisories. However, this cannot be examined in isolation and the introductory remarks have been designed to provide essential contextual background. The chapter also contains a detailed analysis of the "Charter for Safe Travel" in Australia, which was the world's first agreement between a government foreign ministry and a national travel industry leadership. This case illustrates the dynamics and tensions that have existed between governments and the travel industry globally.

Determination of Government Travel Advisories

Foreign ministries of the majority of travel-generating countries today issue travel advisories on all destinations likely to be visited by citizens of that country. Most government travel advisories aim to inform citizens of relevant legal and social mores which apply to the destination. These may include dress codes, proscribed activities such as the use of narcotics in most countries and alcohol in strictly Muslim nations. Advisories will also outline the extent and limitations on services that the national legation provides in specific countries to citizens, who encounter difficulties. Advisories brief travellers on the destination and highlight issues of cultural, social, religious and political sensitivity, which travellers should observe and respect. Most significantly, a government travel advisory outlines safety, health risks and security advice relevant to each destination. Frequently, there is an assessment of security and crime threats to travellers graded either by the wording of the advisory or a more specific grading system. Advisories recommend a range of actions travellers should take to minimise or avoid threat. Significantly, Western government travel advisories rarely reach the level of a travel ban or prohibition and if so, this is explicitly stated. Grounds for a ban or prohibition include grave security or health threats to nationals, the absence of diplomatic relations, a state of war or conflict between the issuing country and the target destination, or a severe breakdown of law and order due to weak central government and rampant crime.

The determination of travel advisory security assessments by countries as varied as Japan, the USA, UK, Canada, France, Germany, Israel, Australia and New Zealand include a number of common elements. The primary sources which governments have traditionally used in determining the analysis of the content and the wording of each advisory are:

1. The legation of the country in the target destination or its representative legation.
2. The national intelligence services or intelligence assessments from "friendly countries".
3. Expatriate business people working in the target country.
4. Media reports.
5. Traveller feedback from nationals visiting the target country.
6. Analysis of home-based Foreign Ministry officials specialising in targeted destinations.

Governments rarely regarded travel professionals as serious sources of analysis for travel advisories until 2003. Off the record, foreign ministry officials tended to treat travel industry sources as unreliable due to a perception that as a consequence of their vested commercial interest in promoting tourism to destinations in which they operated, they would oppose advisories which undermined or compromised perceptions of those destinations. The counter-argument posed by the travel industry to this attitude was that the reputation of their business to all destinations relied on advisories that accurately reflected the level of tourism safety. Ethical operators share a common commitment with governments to ensure the safety and security of travellers to all destinations they market. Prosaically, dead, injured and endangered tourists are detrimental for any travel-related business. Travel professionals, especially airlines and tour operators conducting frequent business in a given country, argue that they have at least as much, if not more knowledge of the state of tourism safety as any source used by governments, except in the field of sensitive security and military intelligence exclusively available to national governments.

Travel Advisories and Travel Insurance

Until recently, there was a very close correlation between travel insurance risk assessment and government travel advisories. When travel advisories reached a level of warning in which deferral of non-essential travel to a specific destination was advised (or words or a grading to that effect) it was a frequent, although not universal practice, for travel insurance companies to refuse or limit travel insurance coverage applying to affected destinations. September 11 and subsequent events such as the Sari Club bombing in Bali on 12 October 2002 has led to a diminution of this correlation. This trend resulted from the growing proliferation of negative or cautionary travel advisories applied to tourism destinations in which minimal hard evidence existed of perceived threats to tourist safety. There has been a proliferation of "*speculative advisories*" (i.e., warning of a *potential* threat to tourists in a specific country). Additionally, the growth of identifiable terrorism since 2001 has resulted in increased demand from travel consumers, travel retailers and marketers for travel insurers to factor in terrorism as an integral element of the risk travellers face when travelling abroad.

The development of the "risk assessment gap" between travel insurers and government travel advisories in Western countries has aroused minimal comment within the travel industry and in government circles. Yet, it is a potent development in which private industry risk assessors are tacitly questioning the accuracy of travel advisories as reliable assessments of tourist risk (Wilks & Moore, 2004).

Awareness of Travel Advisories

The September 11 attack corresponded with the widespread use of the Internet during the early 21st century. Increased access to global media reporting propelled the profile of government travel advisories from a background issue and minor determinant of travellers' destination decision making to that of a major issue and a significant determinant.

Prior to 9/11, the overall level of awareness of travel advisories amongst travellers and travel professionals was low. With the exception of conflicts such as the 1991 Gulf War and the Balkan conflicts of the 1990s, government travel advisories were rarely reported by the international media and mentioned only *en passant* by commercially published travel guides such as Lonely Planet, Fodors, Frommers and Insight. Travel articles or electronic media travel reports on specific destinations referred to travel advisories but only in instances, where a destination was considered potentially dangerous. Although accessible to travel agents, their awareness of travel advisories tended to be low. Since late 2001, the situation has changed radically and there is a high level of awareness about travel advisories among travellers and travel professionals. The growth of Internet usage in Western countries and its expanding use as an economical information medium and source has enabled governments to use the World Wide Web as an efficient means for mass communication of government travel advisories during a period of heightened security awareness and concern amongst international travellers.

Increased awareness of security and safety as a major consideration in travel decision making in the early years of the 21st century led to a more intense scrutiny of travel advisories' content by the media, the travelling public, travel insurers and the travel industry. The bureaucratic language used by governments in their travel advisories was subject to multiple interpretation and misinterpretation. In government parlance, "deferral of non-essential travel" means that the destination is considered a security risk, but it is left to the traveller to determine whether their need to visit this destination is essential or otherwise. According to Australian DFAT officials, this wording does not constitute a travel ban. However, it is hardly surprising when the media misinterprets "deferral of non-essential travel" as a "travel ban" that a proportion of industry professionals and travellers may reach a similar conclusion. Until the onset of the *risk assessment gap*, travel insurance firms took such wording as a cue to review or (at the most extreme level) exclude insurance coverage to destinations referred to in this manner. The lack of clearly categorised rankings of travel advisories leaves them open to varied interpretation.

The proliferation of cautionary travel advisories since the advent of the "war on terror" has given rise to the suggestion that advisories issued by some Western countries have tended to be over-cautious.

Issues of Inequality

An issue raised by PATA and Tourism Concern was the claim that the travel advisories of Western countries tended to be far more cautionary about travel to developing countries that had experienced terrorist incidents than Western countries. The terrorist attack against the Madrid railway station that killed 200 people in March 2004 did not result in negative travel advisories on travel to Spain nor did the World Trade Centre attack in September 2001 lead to negative travel advisories to defer "non-essential travel" to the United States. Advisories on Spain specified concerns about rail travel and major railway stations. The Basque separatist organisation ETA had indeed conducted several attacks targeting hotels, resulting in deaths and injuries among tourists in Spain between 2000 and 2004. Yet, no Western country issued a travel advisory cautioning travellers to defer non-essential travel to Spain. Conversely, terrorist attacks in Istanbul, Turkey, in late 2003 led to many Western countries issuing strongly cautionary advisories on travel to Turkey.

In 2003, the fear of a possible attack in Kenya, during April led the USA, Australia, Germany and Britain to issue strongly cautionary advisories against travelling to Kenya. Although the German and British advisories were moderated by July 2003, the USA and Australia's strongly cautionary advisories were not relaxed until November 2003, despite the fact that the foreshadowed "imminent" terrorist threat never materialised. The leaders of ASEAN accused Western countries of practising a latter-day form of economic imperialism through alleged discrimination against developing countries via negative travel advisories (ASEAN, 2003; Sundar, 2002).

The WTO, PATA and Tourism Concern are three prominent global travel industry organisations that called upon governments to treat all destinations equally on the matter of travel advisories. Tourism Concern has been an active advocate of this approach since 2003. PATA's Code for Fair Travel Advisories issued in October 2004 was the most recent of these demands (PATA, 2004).

In discussions between the author and foreign ministry officials from several Western countries in 2003 and 2004, there was an admission that differences do exist. The common justification cited was that Western democratic countries tend to have far more reliable and accountable security infrastructures in place than most developing countries. Even in the extreme case of a September 11, the US security apparatus is more responsive to multiple threats than the security services of developing countries. Related issues include proposals by multinational and global tourism industry associations for all countries issuing travel advisories to consider the economic impact on target destinations; that is, equal treatment of all countries and for the determination of travel advisories to be subject to discussion with the target country and "transparent". These demands are fanciful for several key reasons:

1. Government travel advisories by definition reflect the specific security concerns of the issuing country. One of the reasons the United States issues more cautionary travel advisories than New Zealand is that in certain countries, US Citizens are singled out as targets for politically or economically motivated violence whereas New Zealanders rarely attract such attention, partially due to New Zealand lacking similar prominence in world affairs. Travel advisories applying to destinations frequently reflect the state of bilateral relations between the issuing country and the target destination.
2. If governments were to issue travel advisories on the basis of economic impact then no travel advisory would be issued against travel to Iraq or any other developing country in a state of internal or external conflict. From a security standpoint, such an approach would be grossly irresponsible.
3. There are obvious limits to transparency in the formulation of travel advisories. A key determinant involves intelligence assessments. It is simply unrealistic for governments to open their intelligence services to public scrutiny as secrecy and confidentiality are the core elements of modern intelligence gathering.

Many aspects of the PATA, Tourism Concern and WTO proposals are universally relevant, including calls for advisories to be timely and specific to the actual problem area. As a key stakeholder in global tourism business, the travel industry's demand to be involved as part of the consultative process in formulating government travel advisories is legitimate. The agreements between the Australian and British governments and the travel industry associations in both countries represent models which are likely to be replicated elsewhere. However, proposals by some multinational travel industry associations to establish global standards for travel advisories, while laudable in principle, tend to ignore the particular national interests inherent in travel advisories.

The apparent *naiveté* of some of the industry's demands on the issue of government travel advisories has stemmed, to some extent, from the industry's lack of experience in managing an issue that suddenly arose as a priority concern in the early 21st century. There is ample evidence to support the contention of travel insurers and many travel industry associations that government travel advisories should be treated as declarations well short of "holy writ". The post-September 11 era, dominated by growing global security concerns, including well publicised acts of politically motivated violence against tourists and tourism infrastructure, was reflected by a growth in the number of cautionary government travel advisories issued by travel-generating countries. The increased dissemination and heightened profile of travel advisories in consumer travel decision making challenged the travel industry to ensure it has a viable role in the travel advisory decision-making process.

Australia's "Charter for Safe Travel"

As a travel industry participant in the formulation and implementation of the *"Charter for Safe Travel"*, the author writes from the perspective of a participant observer. Necessarily, little exists on public record regarding the process that led to the Charter's signing and implementation. Consequently, only a participant could adequately explain the industry's perspective. No confidences have been divulged in this account and every effort has been made to provide an impartial analysis.

The process leading to an agreement between the Australian DFAT and the Australian travel industry began with the Bali bombing of 12 October 2002. The simultaneous bombings of the Sari Club and Paddy's Bar in Denpassar resulted in the deaths of 200 people from 24 countries including 88 Australians. Chapter 19 has previously detailed Australia's whole of government response to the crisis. However, DFAT still came under intense attack by the Australian media and opposition political figures for an alleged failure to warn Australians in advance of threats made to tourist targets in Bali. Andrew Wilkie, former analyst with the Office of National Assessments (a key intelligence assessment unit reporting to Australia's Prime Minister), who resigned in opposition to Australia's involvement in the 2003 Iraq War, outlined many of these allegations in his book 'Axis of Deceit' (Wilkie, 2004).

The Australian government vehemently denied these allegations and stated that no government could predict the precise nature and timing of any specific terrorist attack (see Kemish, 2004). Without detracting from the importance of this issue, it is not germane to the content of this chapter to debate the accuracy or otherwise of these allegations. However, the bombing brought the American government's "War on Terror" to Australia's doorstep and to Australia's civil and political consciousness. The Bali bombings led to travel advisories emerging as a significant issue of debate in Australia. From DFAT's perspective, there was an imperative to ensure that "accurate travel advisories" would be used as a means to warn Australian travellers of potential threats. Additionally, the Australian government sought to assure the public and the media that it took the issue seriously by disseminating travel advisories to as many Australian travellers as possible. Following the Bali bombings, the Australian government was one of a number of Western governments that issued cautionary travel advisories on Indonesia and several other South East Asian countries, including Singapore, Philippines and Malaysia. The advisories were based on intelligence reports that stated that Al Qai'da and allied Islamist cells, some of which had long been operating in the region, were planning a series of attacks throughout South East Asia.

The sudden release of advisories alarmed and incensed South East Asian governments, which believed their tourism industry specifically, and their economies, were under attack. The revitalization of ASEAN tourism by South East Asian heads of State in early November

2002 was the most significant regional response to negative travel advisories (ASEAN, 2002). The Australian government was singled out for especially bitter criticism by the governments of Indonesia, Singapore, Philippines and Malaysia.

The Australian travel industry leadership expressed concern that the government's travel advisories in South East Asia were an over-reaction to the situation on the ground and some industry leaders suggested that DFAT was over-compensating in response to the political flack it had undergone for its alleged "failure" to warn Australians about the Bali attacks. Specifically, it was alleged that Western government foreign ministries, including DFAT, considered it *politique* to issue cautionary advisories concerning South East Asian destinations, irrespective of justification, accuracy or specificity, as a contingency measure designed to protect the government of the day from local accusations of failure to give due warning (Heard, 2003a,b).

The post-Bali period led to growing demands from Australian travel industry professionals to be consulted in the formulation of Australian government travel advisories. In January 2003, the Association of National Tourist Office Representatives (ANTOR) organised a meeting in which travel industry professionals were invited to meet with DFAT in Sydney to discuss the travel advisories. A senior member of DFAT met with 80 senior travel industry executives, many of whom were openly critical of government travel advisories. The meeting was an important event in exposing the contrasting perspectives of DFAT and the Australian travel industry. Australian Federation of Travel Agents Chief Executive Officer Mike Hatton sought to channel the differences between the industry and DFAT towards a more constructive dialogue. In conjunction with DFAT, Hatton established a working committee to examine areas of co-operation between the industry and DFAT. Hatton enlisted the support of all the major travel industry associations representing wholesalers, business travellers, travel agents, national tourist offices, Qantas (Australia's largest airline) and QBE travel insurance, asking each to send a single representative to participate in a series of discussions with DFAT officials.

In order to re-establish its credibility with the media and the public, and to address the concerns about dissemination of relevant health, safety and security information raised in a number of quarters, DFAT developed a major campaign to inform Australians about travel advisories under the marketing name "Smartraveler". DFAT saw the travel industry as a potentially crucial and supportive ally in disseminating the *Smartraveler* message to the travelling public. Tour operators, national tourist offices and the Eastern Mediterranean Tourism Association took the position that if they were to disseminate travel advisories to their clients and contacts they would expect to be involved in their formulation.

By April 2003, DFAT proposed the *Charter for Safe Travel* in which the travel industry would pledge its support for the dissemination of travel advisories and DFAT would ensure that the industry would be consulted and informed. The *Charter for Safe Travel* was signed by Australian Foreign Minister Alexander Downer and AFTA CEO Mike Hatton (on behalf of the Australian travel industry) in Sydney, Australia, on 11 June 2003 (DFAT, 2003).

Following the signing of the Charter, DFAT held meetings with a consultative committee of travel industry leaders comprised of the same organisations that originally negotiated the Charter. DFAT has also actively engaged with Australian travellers and the travel industry at travel agent seminars, consumer travel shows and via an extensive media campaign to publicise and promote the *Smartraveler* concept, which includes travel advisories and other aspects of government-produced travel advice. The Australian Federation of Travel Agents, in common with most other major tourism industry associations, recruited their affiliated travel agents, tour operators, airlines, hoteliers and travel-marketing authorities to register as signatories to the *Charter for Safe Travel*.

On issues of specificity, accuracy and timing of advisories, there still remain matters of disagreement between the industry and DFAT. The industry's minimal involvement in the process does not mean that it will passively accept all government advisories. One example was Australia's November 2003 advisory to "defer non-essential travel" to Turkey, issued following two serious terrorist attacks in Istanbul. In the short-term, there was little debate about issuing the initial advisory. However, the Australian government extended the advisory for almost 1 year and refused to moderate it until November 2004. In the meantime, when the Turkish government upgraded security shortly after the bombings, almost every Western government relaxed their Turkish advisories within a few months, including Britain whose consulate had been the target of one of the November 2003 terrorist attacks. The Australian government's decision to maintain its "defer non-essential travel" advisory (applying to all of Turkey) was widely viewed by the Australian media, the travel industry and many travellers as paranoid. This was unambiguously demonstrated on 25 April 2004, ANZAC Day (commemorating the first military actions of the Australian and New Zealand Army Corps on 25 April 1915) when between 15,000 and 20,000 Australian travellers attended ANZAC services in Gallipoli, Turkey, addressed by the Australian Defence Minister Senator Robert Hill.

Closer to Australia, significant questions were raised by Australian tour operators concerning the relevance of maintaining a highly cautionary advisory on "all" of Indonesia, including Bali, 2 years after the Bali attack (especially as Australian travellers resumed their place as Bali's largest source market during the 2 years following the October 2002 bombing). However, the bombing of the Australian Embassy in Jakarta in September 2004 temporarily silenced dissent on this issue.

Conclusion

After 11 September 2001, the issue of government travel advisories emerged as a global source of friction between governments and the travel industry. The uncertain security environment for world travel necessitated a fundamental review in tourism risk management strategies. Government travel advisories became an increasingly visible element in tourism-orientated security contingency planning. Governments that issue travel advisories regard them as an expression of their commitment to the security of their citizens, who travel abroad. Political capital can be gained or lost based on the prescience of travel advisories. The status of the tourism industry as a major sector in the economies of many countries, especially in the developing world, has resulted in bilateral differences over travel advisories assuming a diplomatic dimension, especially when travel advisories are deemed as negatively affecting the perception of cited countries that have a high level of dependence on tourism for their economic viability.

The relatively sudden development of government travel advisories as a major issue in global tourism policy caught the travel industry unprepared to effectively respond. Travel industry executives in virtually all travel-generating countries were alienated from the decision-making process. Despite their significant financial stake in outbound tourism and their overwhelming commitment to their ethical responsibilities of ensuring the safety of the travelling public, the industry was barely consulted about government decisions that impacted on their businesses.

During 2002 and 2003 the global travel industry began to pay serious and critical attention to travel advisories. By 2003, global and regional associations including Tourism Concern, PATA and the World Tourism Organization engaged governments of travel-generating countries on the issue.

In 2003, Australia was the first country in the world in which an agreement was negotiated between the DFAT and the national travel industry leadership.

In mid-2004, the British Foreign Office and the British travel industry signed a similar agreement. There remain differences between the industry and governments over the nature of their relationship on the matter of travel advisories. The dialogue that emerged from the rash of travel advisories post-9/11 was predicated on the broad principle of a shared interest between governments and travel industry professionals on travellers' safety. The prevailing view among international travel industry leaders is that consultation and co-operation between them and governments will contribute more to the security of the travelling public than acrimonious debates and that "*travel*" is integral to government travel advisories.

References

ASEAN. (2002). ASEAN tourism agreement, Phnom Phen, 4 November. Available at: www.aseansec.org/13157.htm. Last accessed 17 January, 2005.

ASEAN. (2003). Beijing declaration on revitalising tourism for ASEAN, China, Japan and Korea, Beijing, 9 August. Available at: www.aseansec.org/15024.htm. Last accessed 17 January, 2005.

Beirman, D. (2003). *Restoring tourism destinations in crisis — a strategic marketing approach.* Sydney: Allen & Unwin.

Department of Foreign Affairs and Trade (DFAT). (2003). *Charter for safe travel.* Available at: www.smartraveler.gov.au/industry_charter/index.html. Last accessed 17 January, 2005.

Gaillard, W. (2002). IATA crisis communication responses to 9/11. Paper presented at the IATA (International Air Transport Association) crisis management conference, Hong Kong, 22 April.

Gordon, R. (2003). Revitalizing the tourism industry of the Philippines. Paper presented at the TRICON (Tourism Related Industry Conference), Manila, 2 September.

Heard, M. (2003a). DFAT defends travel advisories. *Travel Daily, 1*(22 January), p. 1 at www.traveldaily.com.au.

Heard, M. (2003b). DFAT accuracy under fire. *Travel Daily, 3*(22 January), p. 1 at www.traveldaily.com.au.

Kemish, I. (2004). South East Asia and Australia: New opportunities and challenges. Paper presented to the Australian Institute of International Affairs, Sydney, 30 November. Available at: www.dfat. gov.au/media/speeches/department/041130_aiia_kemish.html. Last accessed 17 January, 2005.

Pacific Asia Travel Association (PATA). (2004). *Fair code for travel advisories.* Available at: www.pata.org/patasite/index.php?id=872. Last accessed 17 January, 2005.

Sundar, C.S. (2002). The great Western establishment lie. *Kashmir Herald, 2*(2 July), p. 1.

Wilkie, A. (2004). *Axis of deceit.* Melbourne: Schwartz Publishing.

Wilks, J., & Moore, S. (2004). *Tourism risk management for the Asia Pacific region.* Southport, Australia: Cooperative Research Centre for Sustainable Tourism.

CONCLUSIONS

Chapter 22

Continuing Challenges for Tourist Health, Safety and Security

Jeff Wilks

Introduction

All of the challenges confronting the tourism industry cannot be examined in just one text. Indeed, new challenges are constantly emerging as transport and technology make access to remote locations more available and customers seek different and novel experiences. In addition, global events external to tourism continue to shock and disrupt the world's largest industry. However, as a starting point, most of the current health, safety and security issues identified in Chapter 1 will remain in one form or another as continuing challenges in the immediate future, so it is worth taking another look at them from a strategic management perspective.

Enhancing Quality Service

The first challenge is to firmly establish tourist health, safety and security as a critical and legitimate element in the delivery of quality service. In English common law there is an 'implied warranty' in contractual arrangements that the goods provided will be 'fit for the purpose intended' and that services 'will be delivered with due care and attention'. In various jurisdictions these expectations have been written into legislation (e.g., Australia's Trade Practices Act 1974 s.74). This implied warranty represents a long-standing tradition that customers can expect certain standards in their commercial dealings. In the case of vulnerable tourists relying on the goods and services of operators in foreign destinations, or at least in unfamiliar environments, how well this expectation is met will be reflected in both the business success of the individual operator and also the wider destination's reputation and image overall. For example, in the purchase of a boat trip ticket to the reef for a day's scuba diving, there is an implied term or expectation that the tourist will be safely transported to the reef and back again. Failing to ensure the safety of visitors in such situations

Tourism in Turbulent Times
Copyright © 2006 by Elsevier Ltd.
All rights of reproduction in any form reserved.
ISBN: 0-08-044666-3

can have huge ramifications, as in the case of lost scuba divers Thomas and Eileen Lonergan (Nunan, 1998). To its credit, the Queensland government responded to this tragic accident by putting in place some of the world's best scuba diving safety legislation (see Chapter 14).

Including tourist health, safety and security as a foundation of quality service makes good business sense, and responds directly to changing consumer demands. For example, the United Kingdom travel magazine Wanderlust www.wanderlust.co.uk has a category of 'safest country' in its reader awards and for 2003 the popular choice was New Zealand, with the UK Foreign and Commonwealth Office (FCO) taking out the best website category largely on the basis of the safety information and advice it provides for travelers. In what is a very new initiative for government travel advisory services, the FCO www.fco.gov.uk provides actual stories from travelers who have become sick or injured overseas, highlighting the importance of having appropriate travel insurance and the costs that would otherwise have to be met by individuals. Recent industry reports also confirm the continuing importance of safety in travel decision-making (Hall, Timothy, & Duval, 2003). In order to make safety a key part of quality service, the tourism industry needs to employ people whose primary and specialist job is to protect tourism and safeguard visitors. This is not a part-time 'ad hoc' undertaking, but rather a decision based on sound risk-management principles.

Who Should be Responsible?

A second challenge is to determine who should be responsible or at least take the lead role in responsibility for tourist health, safety and security. To a large extent the answer depends on which areas of tourism are involved. Here the WTO framework of potential threats is useful. As discussed in Chapter 1, for issues within tourism-related areas (e.g., fire safety) and with individual travelers (road and water safety) the tourism industry needs to take an active role in risk management and visitor protection. Government assistance by way of legislation is also critical to guide and direct operators in their legal and practical responsibilities. For example, the *European Council Directive on Package Travel, Package Holidays and Package Tours* (see Chapter 8) has introduced clear requirements for operators to inform their customers about health formalities for the journey and the stay, particularly the need for vaccinations and for taking preventive medicine (Vansweevelt, 1999).

In a quite separate area of concern, new Queensland fair trading legislation has been introduced to protect international tourists in their dealings with inbound tour operators and tour guides. The *Tourism Services Act 2003* particularly targets unfair retail arrangements, whereby tour groups are transported only to outlets that have exclusive commercial dealings with the tour operators and wholesalers. Such anti-competitive practices restrict freedom of choice for the visitor and most often vastly inflate the cost of goods purchased. The negative perception that operators are taking advantage of and 'ripping off' unsuspecting visitors can also do considerable damage to a destination's image in international markets (Keech, 2004). Although not examined in detail in this book, visitor safety must also include protection of the psychological and economic integrity of travelers (Wilks, 2002); this includes continuing challenges for the industry in terms of fraud (Khan, 2001).

There are also very practical reasons for the tourism industry taking control of health, safety and security issues affecting its customers. First, the availability of public liability

(Chapter 20) and other commercially necessary insurances (such as professional indemnity, see Cordato, 1999), and their protection should there be a claim, rely on operators dis-
charging their duty of care responsibilities. Sound risk-management practices can provide
a useful defense against civil claims of negligence (Wilks & Davis, 2003a) and even criminal claims of manslaughter should the issue be one of gross negligence (Kan, 2001).
Second, the negative media attention from even a single death or serious injury can ruin a
business, even if legal sanctions are not imposed.

Where events external to tourism are the source of threats, the industry must establish
partnerships with other specialist agencies, and to a large extent rely on the leadership of
national governments. This perspective does not remove personal responsibility from operators or tourists for their actions; indeed, recent tort law reforms are placing greater
emphasis on personal responsibility (Ipp, Cane, Sheldon, & Macintosh, 2002; Wilks &
Davis, 2003b), but rather to acknowledge that national governments have the resources and
authority to protect their tourism product. A continuing challenge for the industry is to
demonstrate to governments that tourism, as a major generator for social and economic
growth, is a valuable sector worth protecting (Wilks & Moore, 2004).

The need to protect the tourism industry and its customers is perhaps most obvious in
relation to external events such as terrorism, crime, infectious disease and natural disasters. These major shocks to tourism have huge economic and social implications for destinations, so there is a clear role for national governments. However, equally important is
the safety net in place for individual travelers in unfamiliar environments, especially those
undertaking unfamiliar activities. As Queensland State Coroner, Michael Barnes noted in
the recent inquest into the death of David John Eason, a British tourist who went missing
on Fraser Island in March 2001 and whose bones and personal property were discovered
2 years later:

> Australia is deriving increasing economic benefits from eco-tourism and is
> advertising our wilderness in the national and international market place as
> suitable for such activities as those engaged in by Mr Eason and the tour
> group he traveled with. It is inevitable that some of the tourists who respond
> to this marketing will become lost and it is incumbent on the Australian
> authorities to respond to these incidents as effectively as possible (Barnes,
> 2004, p. 23).

These expectations for visitor health and safety hold true for other destinations around
the world. Indeed, the importance of a 'safety net', described in various ways, appears to
be a common feature of current thinking. Walker and Page (2003, p. 217), for example,
refer to visitor 'well-being' at the destination, and argue that:

> It is no longer acceptable for tourism managers and the wider tourism
> industry to view the tourist as a passive consumer who is unaffected by the
> use and interface with tourist health and safety-related services.

In relation to responsibilities, Walker and Page (2003, p. 221) agree that the well-being
of the visitor at the destination is, to a large extent, dependent on government policy on

tourism and the value placed on it. There is now considerable evidence that tourists have different risk and injury profiles compared to local residents at a destination (Chapter 5; Wilks, 2004a) and that accommodating visitors within local health and safety services infrastructure is important so as to optimally use community resources. According to Walker and Page (2003, p. 220) this involves three elements: an *acknowledgment* that tourists have distinct needs; an *acceptance* that the community/destination should provide for these needs and an *allocation* mechanism that delivers resources to meet the needs of the visitors.

By way of summary, the responsibility for tourist health, safety and security is a shared one. For external events that impact on tourism, the primary responsibility must lie with national governments, which have the resources and authority to protect tourism interests, infrastructure and the reputation of travel destinations. The responsibility of the tourism industry for external events is to be adequately prepared and willing to work in partnership with other agencies and groups.

In the case of events within or related to tourism, the industry must adopt a more active and equal leadership role, taking control for its operations and the well-being of its customers. However, recognizing that the vast majority of tourism businesses are small- to medium-size enterprises (Wilks & Moore, 2004) there will always be a significant role required of government at all levels to assist tourism safeguard its customers. In practical terms, this assistance will be through developing genuine and effective partnerships.

Developing Partnerships

Chapter 1 recommended that tourism adopt a risk-management approach to protecting its assets, including its customers. The first step in the risk-management approach was described as Establishing the Context, whereby key stakeholders are identified, along with their roles and responsibilities. Through the formation of a National Tourism Safety and Security Committee (Wilks, 2003), tourism can then ensure that policies, plans and partnerships are in place so that destinations are adequately prepared for adverse events. This model has been recommended for governments in several major reports in recent years (World Tourism Organization, WTO, 1997; Wilks, 2002; Wilks & Moore, 2004), but there is little evidence of it being applied in what could be described as best practice. For example, while South Africa has been applauded for adopting a whole-of-government approach to tourist safety and security policies (Wilks, 2003) the continuing high level of crime in the country remains a major deterrent for visitors — see www.smartraveller.gov.au which advises Australians that while the South African Government is actively tackling criminal activity and protection of tourists is a high priority, nevertheless the risk of violent crime (including robbery and armed assault) remains high throughout the country and car-jacking, muggings, theft and pickpocketing are common. Clearly, the implementation of policy and its translation to practice requires further support. Still, most destinations have not reached the first stage of any formal, high-level commitment to tourist health, safety and security, even though this was a recommendation from the World Tourism Organization in 1991 (see Chapter 16). Without this foundation effective partnerships will not develop.

The impediment to this process seems to be a simple fact that it is no one's job to facilitate and link the various stakeholders. Like the security guard analogy in Chapter 1, there needs to be some group whose primary and paid task is to add value by drawing together the expertise of agencies and groups, across government and industry, for the benefit of protecting tourism. Too often, government funds and expertise are directed toward producing quality tourist health and safety resources that are not used by industry because the production formula does not include provision for applied dissemination (see industry review by Surf Life Saving Queensland, 2003).

This is not to say that some excellent partnerships do not exist. In terms of a safety net for tourists, the State of Hawaii is a world leader both in terms of individual programs and by virtue of the high level of coordination across government agencies and with the tourism industry. One example is the Visitor Assistance Program operated by the Department of the Prosecuting Attorney www.honolulu.gov/prosecuting. The program coordinates resources with the tourism industry in order to provide prompt and comprehensive services to visitors who have been traumatized by crime during their stay in Hawaii. Excellent working relations exist between this program, the Honolulu Police Department, the Governor's Office, Hawaii Tourism Authority and several other key tourism industry groups.

A similar program called the Tourist Victim Support Service operates in Ireland www.clubi.ie/tvss/contactus.html. This program is also widely acclaimed and enjoys the support of the Minister for Tourism, Sport and Recreation, the Minister for Justice, Equality and Law Reform, the Garda (police) Commissioner, Bord Failte and many tourism-related industries. Tourist Victim Support is based in Garda Headquarters, Harcourt Square, Dublin, courtesy of the Department of Justice and the Garda Siochana. The success of the service depends on extensive support coming from a cross section of the tourism-related industry by way of direct funding and benefit in kind.

Other successful tourist health, safety and security partnerships that have been identified (Wilks, 2002) include:

- The United States Vessel Sanitation Program, an initiative with the Centers for Disease Control and Prevention (CDC) that assists the cruise ship industry in fulfilling its responsibility for developing and implementing comprehensive sanitation programs in order to minimize the risk for gastrointestinal diseases.
- The Caribbean Tourism, Health, Safety and Resource Conservation Project, which seeks to strengthen the overall quality and competitiveness of the tourism industry in the Caribbean through the establishment and dissemination of quality standards and systems designed to ensure healthy, safe and environmentally conscious products and services.
- The African Medical and Research Foundation, which provides travel health information and offers tourists the opportunity to join the Flying Doctor Society of Africa. Membership to the Society guarantees visitors a free emergency evacuation flight, should it be required.

With perhaps Hawaii as the exception, most successful tourist health, safety and security programs tend to run in isolation. The challenge for the industry, and for national governments given their responsibility for protecting tourism, is to integrate quality programs and partnerships within operational plans. Australia, for example, has a very good National Tourism Incident Response Plan (see Wilks & Moore, 2004), but it is designed to be reactive rather than proactive. Guided by a filter mechanism, which assesses such things as the level of threat to Brand Australia, domestic travel patterns and industry profitability, the plan responds in cooperation with various stakeholders to manage and minimize the impact of a crisis on the tourism industry. In contrast to the main areas suggested in the WTO National Tourism Safety and Security Plan (Chapter 16), the Australian plan is focused on response and recovery, rather than reduction and readiness (Pacific Asia Travel Association, 2003).

Tourism Queensland (2003) has developed an alternative crisis planning approach in partnership with the Queensland Tourism Industry Council. Figure 22.1 presents the model. Here potential shocks to the tourism industry are divided into direct and indirect events with short, medium or long-term consequences for individuals, communities, regions and countries. The model acknowledges that certain shocks may be triggered or magnified by others; for example, increases in public liability insurance as a result of the September 11, 2001 terrorist attacks. However, the common factor in this categorisation is that a potential tourism shock will have either a direct or indirect impact upon the industry (Tourism Queensland, 2003).

The advantage of this approach is that it places more emphasis on indirect shocks that may not be as obvious for their effects on tourism. Examples of indirect shocks include currency fluctuations, exotic animal diseases (such as the outbreak of Foot and Mouth Disease in the United Kingdom during 2001) and economic downturns (such as the Asian financial crisis of 1997). The Tourism Queensland approach distinguishes between Pre-Shock (involving Prevention and Preparation) and Post-Shock (Response and Recovery) phases. In terms of developing partnerships, the Queensland approach highlights the range of stakeholders required to assist the tourism industry in times of crisis.

While the Queensland model provides a more robust approach to prevention and preparedness, the devil remains in the detail. Items like 'promote benefits of preparedness to operators' remain a huge challenge, given the diversity of activities undertaken within the rubric of tourism. However, this is a positive starting point. So, while it is impossible to develop a comprehensive list of all incidents that have the potential to develop into crises, it is possible for business and destination managers to identify areas of risk that are most likely to threaten them.

Identifying Risk

Chapter 1 considered a number of ways to identify current issues in tourist health, safety and security, including: industry sector surveys and reports; government travel advisories; the work of international organizations; and general business environment assessments. Added to this are profiles of tourist incidents generated by insurance companies based on claims (Chapter 20) and profiles of tourist injuries reported to government agencies (e.g., National parks, Chapter 13; Workplace Health and Safety, Chapter 20). Industry and government statistics are extremely valuable when they are available (see Ryan, 1996), so the challenge remains to harness these sources of information for the benefit of protecting tourists.

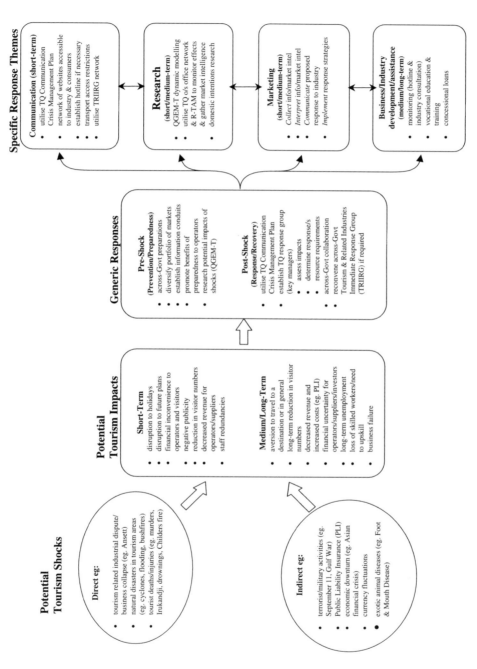

Figure 22.1: Queensland crisis management plan framework.

Another source of knowledge not specifically mentioned in Chapter 1, but obvious throughout this book, is the contribution that can be made by academics to both understanding and responding to visitor safety. As Bentley and Page observe (Chapter 11):

> Without national tourism injury databases or surveillance systems, and/or any one body reliably collating and reporting national or industry injury statistics, the true extent of the tourist injury problem is masked.

Through their cross-national injury studies, Bentley and Page have provided an excellent baseline for understanding visitor risk exposure. However, the challenge remains to expand and integrate this work with the practice of travel medicine (Chapters 2–4) since profiles of visitor deaths show pre-existing illness to be the largest cause of mortality (Chapter 2; Wilks, 2004a). At the level of serious illness and injury requiring admission to hospital, Table 22.1 shows that applied academic research can be very useful to tourism policy and planning personnel by identifying the extent of both common (motor vehicle) and more destination-specific (scuba diving, venomous bites and stings) injury presentations (Wilks & Coory, 2002).

Table 22.1: Type of injury-related incident for overseas visitors admitted to Queensland hospitals, 1996–2000.

Type of injury-related incident	No. (%) overseas visitors
Motor vehicle traffic accident	567 (21.8)
Fall on level ground, slip or stumble	408 (15.7)
Diving accidents	302 (11.6)
Fall from height, fall from one level to another	250 (9.6)
Struck accidentally by object or person	121 (4.7)
Bite from venomous spider, snake, marine animal	99 (3.8)
Fight, rape, assault	94 (3.6)
Accidental laceration	92 (3.5)
Drowning, near drowning	81 (3.1)
Water transport accident	79 (3.0)
Horse riding accident	77 (3.0)
Dog bite and other non-venomous animal bites	65 (2.5)
Other transport accident	44 (1.7)
Overexertion	43 (1.7)
Fire, smoke or heat	37 (1.4)
Suicide and intentional self harm	30 (1.2)
Suffocation, inhalation of food or foreign body	28 (1.1)
Accidental poisoning	28 (1.1)
Other	153 (5.9)
Total	2598 (100.0)

Source: Wilks and Coory (2002). Used with permission from the Journal of Tourism Studies.

Such monitoring over time, as recommended in the Australian and New Zealand Standard for Risk Management (Standards Australia and Standards New Zealand, 1999), can provide valuable feedback on the success (or otherwise) of visitor injury prevention programs (Wilks, Coory, & Pendergast, 2004). To date, academic research on visitor health, safety and security has not been used very effectively by tourism planners and policy-makers. In contrast, outdoor education and recreation research has been well integrated over time into broad leisure programs and policies (for example, Petersen & Hronek, 1997; Priest & Gass, 1997). To some extent, this is again tourism's historical position of not acknowledging or playing down illness or injury events affecting its customers; relying on insurance and leaving the details to other 'specialist' groups such as medical practitioners and the police. This position is now untenable since published academic work can be used in legal proceedings to show that there was public knowledge of risk and as a benchmark for duty of care responses. Developing a closer relationship between tourism academia and the industry it seeks to understand is a very worthwhile challenge that will benefit both groups.

Returning to Partnerships

From the common and continuing safety issues identified by the tourism industry in Chapter 1 (fire, food and water safety; crime and infectious disease), it is clear that partnerships with emergency services, health authorities and the police are critical for tourism to protect its customers. Many of the chapters in this book have directly examined the health and safety partnerships required. Less developed are the relationships between tourism and security services, with the exception of perhaps the police in particular tourist destinations (Handszuh, 1997). The challenge remains for tourism to fully engage and work collaboratively with groups like the consular services, customs and immigration, quarantine, coast guard and border protection. For tourists as a vulnerable group reliant on others in times of need, consular services are a particularly important source of information, support and resources (Murdock, 2004; Wilks, 2004b). However, there should not be an expectation that these critical groups will automatically understand or respond to tourism without appropriate engagement and an educative process. For example, as Muehsam and Tarlow (1995, pp. 9–10) observe in relation to the police:

> Law enforcement agencies have long argued that they treat all individuals alike, yet at the same time they admit that they have discretionary powers when handling any specific situation. Our research indicates that the tourism industry historically has done a poor job in communicating to the police the complexities and motivations of its industry. This lack of communication means that officers often must make decisions while being ignorant of the needs and impact on the local tourism industry. When faced with an unknown circumstance, it is human nature to follow strictly departmental guidelines. As officers more fully understand tourism's intricacies, greater procedural options become available. Cooperative efforts between the tourism industry and law enforcement agencies contribute to protecting a city's economy, and improving its public relations and state or national image.

These observations hold true for all of the key stakeholders that tourism needs to engage for the health, safety and security of visitors. In particular, the value of tourism to each economy must be effectively conveyed to decision-makers and a progressive risk management strategy adopted at the highest levels of government. Perhaps the most effective way of summarizing the continuing challenges for tourism in the area of visitor health, safety and security is to present the nine recommendations made to the 21 Asia Pacific Economic Cooperation (APEC) Tourism Ministers (Table 22.2) based on a thorough review of risk management in the Asia-Pacific region (Wilks & Moore, 2004). The recommendations, if implemented, would establish the foundation of a best practice network for tourist health, safety and security. These are huge challenges, in keeping with the importance of visitor and industry protection.

Risk Management is Not Crisis Management

Since the terrorist attacks of September 11, 2001, there has been enormous interest in the topic of crisis management. Many tourist destinations have now commissioned consultants to produce crisis management manuals and plans for them. The Bali bombings, SARS and the Asian Tsunami have further emphasized crisis work. Even our APEC recommendations were written in terms of crisis management (Wilks & Moore, 2004).

While this overall awareness is a positive move for tourism, unfortunately a crisis focus is one largely of reaction and recovery, rather than prevention in the first place. In order to effectively provide protection to visitors in uncertain and turbulent times, governments need to be proactive. To the best of our knowledge, none of the APEC recommendations have been systematically (tangibly) adopted by the member economies. There have been some excellent examples of partnerships and responses to recent crises (the Chapters on SARS, Bali bombings, Project Phoenix), but it is questionable whether the lessons learned are being effectively shared for ongoing prevention initiatives. In the case of SARS, however, the medical response and lessons learned are clearly being applied. Through the networks and collaborative partnerships developed in response to SARS the health sector is much better prepared now for Avian (Bird Flu) and other potential outbreaks of infectious disease (Mackenzie, Gubler, & Petersen, 2004).

As the first wave of lawsuits are filed against destinations and tourism industry members by tourists involved in the tsunami crisis some hard questions are being raised about adequate preparation and duty of care responsibilities. To protect itself in the future, the tourism industry must establish genuine partnerships across government agencies and internationally with organizations that specialize in health, safety and security. Rather than just rely on the services and goodwill of others (e.g., the police — see Muehsam & Tarlow, 1995), tourism must spend some time and money on growing and maintaining these critical relationships. It is only through a wide and comprehensive safety net that visitors can be assured of protection.

As a final note, at least some tourists will continue to do unexpected things. Tourist operators and governments cannot be expected to prevent all possible mishaps or misadventures. However, they can be expected to provide a quality service that automatically includes visitor health, safety and security.

Table 22.2: Recommendations made to the 21 APEC tourism ministers.

Recommendation 1: Each APEC economy undertakes to develop a whole-of-government approach to supporting and protecting tourism. This would involve a formal agreement at the highest level of government to develop a national crisis management plan for tourism that was adequately resourced and supported by relevant legislative authority. A review of existing legislation may be necessary to ensure that potential risks are adequately covered.

Recommendation 2: Each APEC economy should form a National Tourism Council, comprising key government and external stakeholders, especially peak tourism industry representative bodies. The Council should establish a National Safety and Security Committee; designate roles and responsibilities for members in all areas of risk and crisis management, and integrate these tasks into the national crisis management plan.

Recommendation 3: APEC should establish a dedicated research and monitoring group for the APEC economies, with a brief to collaborate with PATA, WTO, ASEAN and other international groups and agencies to provide up-to-date strategic knowledge and information on risk and threats to tourism in the Asia-Pacific region.

Recommendation 4: APEC develop formal relations with international agencies that provide expert advice and services in areas of natural disaster management, emergency services and health so that tourism gains the benefit of expertise in other specialist areas.

Recommendation 5: APEC should coordinate with PATA, WTO and other potential partners to deliver workshops, training programs and practical support in risk and crisis management for APEC members. This should be a program of incremental steps to ensure all key areas of need are adequately covered.

Recommendation 6: Based on the specific needs of APEC members for training and support in risk and crisis management, operational manuals and other resource material should be developed that build on the material in this report. In particular, a template for small- and medium-sized tourism businesses may be required, that links to the broader government roles and responsibilities described in this report.

Recommendation 7: Each APEC economy establish and work on a partnership with their peak tourism industry body to develop risk-management plans and policies, especially business continuity programs in the event of a crisis.

Recommendation 8: Each APEC economy should have a detailed media strategy in place as part of any crisis management plan. To facilitate this, specialist workshops and media training programs should be provided to key tourism staff in all APEC economies.

Recommendation 9: APEC members should be encouraged to discuss and form a group response to the issue of Travel Advisories, including positive steps to assist each other through safety and security measures.

Source: Wilks and Moore (2004). Used with permission.

References

Barnes, M. (2004). *Findings of the inquest into the death of David John Eason*. Brisbane: Coroners Court.

Cordato, A.J. (1999). *Australian travel and tourism law*. Sydney: Butterworths.

Hall, C.M., Timothy, D.J., & Duval, D.T. (Eds). (2003). *Safety and security in tourism: Relationships, management and marketing*. Binghamton, NY: Haworth Hospitality Press.

Handszuh, H. (1997). *Policing in tourism for visitor and resident protection. Report from a WTO Survey*. Madrid: World Tourism Organization.

Ipp, D. A., Cane, P., Sheldon, D., & Macintosh, I. (2002). *Review of the law of negligence* [Report submitted to the Minister for Revenue and Assistant Treasurer]. Canberra: Canprint Communications. [Retrieved 14 January 2005 from http://revofneg.treasury.gov.au.]

Kan, G. (2001). Danger zone. *Australian Leisure Management*, Issue 24, 32–33.

Keech, M. (2004). Rogue tourism operators in sights. Press release by the Queensland Minister for Tourism, Fair Trading and Wine Industry Development, 11 October.

Khan, M. (2001). Ticket fraud: Being taken for a ride. *Aviation Security International*, 7(2), 16–17.

Mackenzie, J.S., Gubler, D.J., & Petersen, L.R. (2004). Emerging flaviviruses: The spread and resurgence of Japanese encephalitis, West Nile and dengue viruses. *Nature Medicine Supplement*, 10(12), S98–S109.

Muehsam, M.J., & Tarlow, P.E. (1995). Involving the police in tourism. *Tourism Management, 16*(1), 9–14.

Murdock, A. (2004). What happens when things go wrong? *Sun Herald*, 28 November, p. 22.

Nunan, N. (1998). *Inquest into the cause and circumstances surrounding the disappearance of Thomas Joseph Lonergan and Eileen Cassidy Lonergan*. Brisbane: Queensland Coroners Court, No 52 of 1998.

Pacific Asia Travel Association (PATA). (2003). *Crisis. It won't happen to us!* Bangkok: PATA.

Petersen, J.A., & Hronek, B.B. (1997). *Risk management: Park, recreation, and leisure services* (3rd ed.). Champaign, IL: Sagamore Publishing.

Priest, S., & Gass, M.A. (1997). *Effective leadership in adventure programming*. Champaign, IL: Human Kinetics.

Ryan, C. (1996). Linkages between holiday travel risk and insurance claims: Evidence from New Zealand. *Tourism Management*, 17(8), 593–601.

Standards Australia and Standards New Zealand. (1999). *Risk management. Australian/New Zealand Standard: AS/NZS 4360:1999*. Strathfield, NSW: Standards Association of Australia.

Surf Life Saving Queensland. (2003). *Benchmarking best practice beach safety management. Beach safety research*. Brisbane: Author.

Tourism Queensland. (2003). *Tourism crisis management plan*. Brisbane: Tourism Queensland.

Vansweevelt, T. (1999). The EC package travel directive and the health advice of the travel organizer, the travel agent and the physician. *Vaccine* 17, S88–S89.

Walker, L., & Page, S.J. (2003). Risks, rights and responsibilities in tourist well-being: Who should manage visitor well-being at the destination? In: J. Wilks, & S.J. Page (Eds), *Managing tourist health and safety in the new millennium* (pp. 215–235). Oxford: Pergamon.

Wilks, J. (2002). *Safety and security in tourism: Partnerships and practical guidelines for destinations*. Report prepared for the World Tourism Organization. Madrid: WTO.

Wilks, J. (2003). Safety and security for destinations: WTO case studies. In: J. Wilks, & S.J. Page (Eds), *Managing tourist health and safety in the new millennium* (pp.127–139). Oxford: Pergamon.

Wilks, J. (2004a). Injuries and injury prevention. In: J. Keystone, P. Kozarsky, H.D. Nothdurft, D.O. Freedman, & B. Connor (Eds), *Travel medicine* (pp. 453–459). London: Mosby.

Wilks, J. (2004b). Tourism recovery after a crisis. Paper presented at the Asia Pacific Homeland Security Summit and Exposition. Honolulu, HI, 16 November.

Wilks, J., & Coory, M. (2002). Overseas visitor injuries in Queensland hospitals: 1996–2000. *Journal of Tourism Studies*, 13, 2–8.

Wilks, J., Coory, M., & Pendergast, D. (2004). Tourists still getting the bends. *Tourism in Marine Environments*, 1, 61–62.

Wilks, J., & Davis, R. (2003a). Duty of care to resort guest who drowned. *International Travel Law Journal*, 2, 77–79.

Wilks, J., & Davis, R. (2003b). International tourists and recreational injuries. *Plaintiff*, 59, 8–14.

Wilks, J., & Moore, S. (2004). *Tourism risk management for the Asia Pacific region*. Southport, Australia: CRC for Sustainable Tourism.

World Tourism Organization. (1991). *Recommended measures for yourism safety*. Madrid: WTO.

World Tourism Organization. (1997). *Tourist safety and security: Practical measures for destinations* (2nd ed.). Madrid: World Tourism Organization.

Author Index

Subject Index